DOROTHY PICKLES

The Government and Politics of France

VOLUME II

Politics

METHUEN & CO LTD
LONDON

First published 1973 by
Methuen & Co Ltd
11 New Fetter Lane, London EC4
© *1973 Dorothy Pickles*
Printed in Great Britain by
Butler & Tanner Ltd, Frome and London

SBN 416 75540 2 hardback
SBN 416 75550 x paperback

distributed in the USA by
HARPER & ROW PUBLISHERS, INC.
BARNES & NOBLE IMPORT DIVISION

Contents

The Nature of French Politics
*Political incoherence – The importance of history – Intellectualism,
legalism and symbols – Theories and interests – Politics and scandals –
The Republican tradition*

The Nature and Content of Politics
under the Fifth Republic
Traditional factors and innovations – The pattern of events

*Legitimacy – Decolonization and Algeria – The aftermath of the
Algerian war – The foundations of future Gaullist internal policies –
Parliamentary opinion and priorities – The confrontation between
President and Parliament – The Gaullist opportunity*

*The political atmosphere of the second Parliament – The problem of
special courts and the* Conseil d'Etat *– Economic and social problems
– Positive economic policies (i) The Plan – Positive economic policies*

v

Preface

In this second volume the presentation is partly chronological, but it must be emphasized that it is in no way intended to be a historical study. Indeed, to a political scientist, a chronological approach is *in se* less attractive than one based on considerations of different political issues – for instance, the evolution of the relations between State and citizen; Gaullist ideas and policies; the relation between parties of the Left; economic and social problems and achievements. But each approach has its own disadvantages, and so the best solution seemed to be to combine them in the way explained in the first chapter. Without some chronological sign-posting, it is difficult to convey any overall picture of the evolution of the régime. Some issues are fully comprehensible only if seen against the particular background of the time. The 1970 *loi anti-casseurs*, for instance, is not just one aspect of the relations between citizen and State, but mainly a direct consequence of the 1968 May events. The 1971 'Debré law' was passed in a political atmosphere largely explicable by the fact that over ten years had elapsed since the passage of its predecessor in 1959. On the other hand, the atmosphere in which the 1959 law had been passed is comprehensible only in the light of long-standing left-wing attitudes to relations between Church and State in the field of eduction, going back beyond the present century. The fate of the Gaullist policy of participation depends less on the course of events than on certain permanent political attitudes shared by Right and Left.

What this volume seeks to do is to describe and comment on the main political issues which have been, and in some cases still are, at the centre of party and parliamentary controversy. French politics, however, as well as being highly articulate, sophisticated, complicated and divisive, are also intellectually insular – in the sense that politicians and journalists regularly take for granted backgrounds and contexts that are less familiar to foreign than to their own citizens. For that reason, a certain amount of factual background material or bibliographical reference to available additional information has been included in the notes. These, as in the previous volume, constitute a separate section at the end of the volume, with indications of the pages of the text to which they refer. However irritating this system may be to serious students, it does at least have the advantage that those readers who are not interested in sources or in more detailed digressions on specific points can easily ignore the notes.

No study of a régime in which, for over ten years, General de Gaulle was regarded both by himself and by his supporters in Governments and Parliaments as the sole source of policy can afford to leave out of account his frequent statements of what he himself believed, or professed to believe. Nor is it possible to follow his advice and ignore the off-the-cuff remarks and re- ported conversations that he himself described as of no signifi- cance, for they were sometimes taken seriously by others, and were sometimes deliberately used by him for political ends. Quotations from the first three volumes of the Memoirs and from press conferences and television interviews are given in English (author's translation), with references to the French text. Those from the two final volumes of the Memoirs are given in the English translation by Terence Kilmartin, with references to both English and French texts.

In discussing the politics of the Fifth Republic, I have tried to steer a cautious course between a partisan over-involvement and the kind of over-remoteness that is sometimes taken for objectivity. No attempt has been made to hide the inevitable personal convictions built up during a lifetime's interest in French politics, but where personal opinions are expressed, I have tended where possible to quote evidence of support for them from French sources that I have come to rely on as being significant, balanced and accurate. Among these is *Le Monde*, to which, in common with all serious students of French politics, I owe a great debt not only for its extensive coverage of political news, and especially of the declarations of political leaders and the activities of political parties, but much more for its frequent articles by specialists in various fields, and most of all for the unique forum that it regularly provides for a continuous stream of high-level political debate between academics (some of the most eminent of whom are also actively politically committed), political leaders, politicians of all parties, publicists and journalists. It is a debate in which it is impossible to draw the line between academic analysis and the best political journalism – and how good that is in France!

In such a controversial field as this, I should expect to meet with criticism and disagreement, as anyone who deals with current politics must. But I should hope to have succeeded at least in avoiding important factual errors. To the extent that I may be found not to have done so, I offer my apologies.

Dorothy Pickles
June 1973

Abbreviations

CD	Centre démocrate
CDP	Centre Démocratie et Progrès
CERES	Centre d'Etudes, de Recherches et d'Education socialistes
CFDT	Confédération française démocratique du Travail
CGT	Confédération générale du Travail
CGT–FO	Confédération générale du Travail – Force ouvrière
CID	Comité d'Information et de Défense
CIR	Convention des Institutions républicaines
CNPF	Conseil national du Patronat français
CODER	Commission de Développement économique régional
EDC	European Defence Community
EEC	European Economic Community
FEN (i)	Fédération de l'Education nationale
FEN (ii)	Fédération des Etudiants nationalistes
FGDS	Fédération de la Gauche démocrate et socialiste
FLN	Front de Libération nationale
FNSEA	Fédération nationale des Syndicats d'Exploitants agricoles
GD	Gauche démocrate
GPRA	Gouvernement provisoire de la République algérienne
IFOP	Institut français d'Opinion publique
INSEE	Institut national de la Statistique et des Etudes économiques
MRP	Mouvement républicain populaire
NATO	North Atlantic Treaty Organization
OAS	Organisation de l'Armée secrète

OECD	Organisation européenne de Coopération et de Développement
ORTF	Office de Radiodiffusion – Télévision française
OURS	Office universitaire de Recherche socialiste
PCF	Parti communiste français
PDM	Progrès et Démocratie moderne
PS	Parti socialiste
PSU	Parti socialiste unifié
RI	Républicains indépendants
RPF	Rassemblement du Peuple français
SMAG	Salaire minimum agricole garanti
SMIC	Salaire minimum interprofessional de Croissance
SMIG	Salaire minimum interprofessional garanti
SNE-Sup	Syndicat national de l'Enseignement supérieur
SOFRES	Société française d'Enquêtes par Sondages
TVA	Taxe à la valeur ajoutée (*v.* VAT)
UCRG	Union des Clubs pour le Renouveau de la Gauche
UDR	Union des Démocrates pour la République
UER	Unité d'Enseignement et de Recherche
UGCS	Union des Groupes et Clubs socialistes
UGSD	Union de la Gauche socialiste et démocrate
UNATI	Union nationale des Travailleurs indépendants
UNEF	Union nationale des Etudiants de France
UNEF–Renouveau	Union nationale des Etudiants de France – Renouveau
UNR	Union pour la nouvelle République
URP	Union des Républicains pour le Progrès
VAT	Value-added Tax
WEU	Western European Union

PART I
Internal Politics

CHAPTER I

Gaullism in the Pattern of French Politics

The Nature of French Politics

POLITICAL INCOHERENCE

Perhaps the simplest description of French politics is that it is a series of passionate controversies, carried on by politicians from generation to generation, in a political atmosphere that is normally one of general apathy and sectional partisanship, but that occasionally flares up into near or actual revolution. The most important and lasting subjects of controversy have been the problems of the régime, the Church and the electoral system. Republic or monarchy? Strong or weak Governments? A Parliament that reflects the strength of divisions at the cost of governmental deadlock, or that provides a majority of sorts at the cost of a greater or lesser degree of disproportion between the numbers of votes and the numbers of seats obtained by different parties? A Parliament that represents primarily the interests of local areas – *départements*, constituencies and regional economic interests – or that provides for a confrontation between a certain number of political philosophies, whether based on notions of class or nation, or on Socialist or capitalist principles regarding the organization of society? These have been questions perpetually posed and never definitely answered during the century and three-quarters following the French Revolution.

Our political system [wrote Charles Morazé in 1956] is a waterfall. Its fall is broken by level stretches, to which it clings with some success in periods of relative technical progress. But as soon as it encounters any real difficulties, there is a brusque fall to a new level.[1]

He went on to give a lightning survey of the 'brusque falls', or changes of régime, that France has known since the replacement in 1791 of absolute monarchy by a form of parliamentary government. These were the 'proletarian dictatorship' of the Convention, a kind of parliamentary Republicanism, the 'Monarchic absolutism' of Napoleon, a parliamentary followed by an absolutist Monarchy, revolution followed by a few months of Republicanism, Imperialism and, after defeat in the war of 1870, parliamentary Republicanism. All these régimes left their mark, and almost all have provided material for the permanent debate on political institutions that still lies at the heart of French politics.

The fact that the régime of Republican parliamentary government has not been seriously challenged since 1875 has not brought the kind of consensus that has up to now been taken for granted in the United States and the United Kingdom (excluding Northern Ireland). For the controversies within the Republican framework have been hardly less divisive than those between Republicans and supporters of rival forms of government. A little before the end of the century there was Boulangism. The 'Republic of Teachers'[2] was responsible for the mixture of Radical politics, educational reformism and anti-clerical sectarianism that still characterized left-wing parties in the Fourth Republic, and whose influence was still strong enough in the 1960s to envenom some of the quarrels of the Fifth. There were Monarchist as well as Fascist paramilitary groups in the 1930s, sporadic and weaker nationalist and anti-Republican movements in the 1950s. And the quarrels within the Republican and parliamentary parties during the Fourth Republic, many of which were on constitutional and electoral issues,[3] led Charles Morazé to claim that

> What happens in our parliamentary assemblies justifies the conclusion that they do not exist in order to govern France, but in order to teach contenders for power how to administer under the pressure of events.[4]

Among the results, as he points out, was a high degree of 'political incoherence' – the kind of incoherence that explained how a Parliament that produced the Popular Front could bring to power a Marshal of France who was shortly to assume monarchical powers, and how a Government headed by General de Gaulle could appoint the first Communists to hold governmental office. It must be remembered, however, that the 'pressure of events' in both these cases was that of the second world war. Nevertheless, it is true that one of the characteristics of French politics, even in times of relative peace and calm, has been a degree of incoherence, directly caused by unstable parliamentary majorities, themselves the result of fundamental and permanent divisions, among which those concerned with institutions and elections have played an important part.[5] A more convincing explanation of the Fourth Republic's 'political incoherence' was given by Alfred Grosser, who attributed it to the fact that, at a time when two conflicts dominated the Western world – that between old and new nationalisms and that between Communism and anti-Communism – France was the only country to be torn apart by both.

> This double cleavage [he says] made freedom for overseas peoples obtainable only with a majority including Communists, while the defence of the freedoms threatened by Communism was possible only with a majority that refused freedom to Asia and Africa. Italy without colonies and Britain without a Communist electorate were more favourably situated.[6]

This was surely the dilemma to which General de Gaulle was referring in more ambiguous and lofty phraseology when – for once giving credit to the men of the Fourth Republic as being 'neither incapable nor ignoble', but 'worthy, honest and patriotic' – he attributed their failure to a party system that was the expression of 'a profoundly divided people living in a terribly dangerous universe'.[7]

THE IMPORTANCE OF HISTORY

It will be for future historians, able to see the Third and Fourth Republics in better perspective, to judge the extent to which their 'political incoherence' was the cause or the consequence of circumstances. Political scientists must first note the facts, together with the theories about them held by French politicians and political observers who had to contend with them. Among these facts, at least four have certainly helped to increase the political divisions and incoherence of the French system. The first is the length of French historical memories, which has meant that politicians and political parties have been perpetually haunted by the ghosts of past quarrels and past dangers. Fears of personal rule are intensified by memories of Louis XIV, Napoleon, Napoleon III, Boulanger and Pétain. Disagreements on institutions revive memories of divisions regarding the nature and importance of the Revolutionary tradition, the rights of property in a democratic Republic, the place of religious education in a State-controlled educational system, and each of these becomes a principle for which battle has perpetually to be done afresh. In foreign policy, although the problem of Germany has dominated all other problems since 1870, disagreements with Great Britain still recall past Franco-British conflicts, rancours and misunderstandings, and arouse old suspicions that have never been finally eradicated.

The example of Franco-British relations is particularly illustrative of this tendency to add the fuel provided by memories of old quarrels to the flames of current ones.[8] But long memories have divided political parties no less than nations. Issues of more than half a century ago live on, though sometimes as little more than time-honoured rituals. The annual Socialist pilgrimage to the *Mur des Fédérés*, in memory of the martyrs of the *Commune*, has today much the same significance as references by Labour party orators to Keir Hardie and the Tolpuddle martyrs. It has taken a very long time for anti-clerical prejudices, inherited from the French Revolution and strengthened by the separation of Church and

State at the beginning of the twentieth century, to weaken sufficiently for Christian Democrat parties to be regarded by the orthodox Left as being authentically Left. The candidate who complained, following his defeat by a right-wing candidate, that his constituents 'would unhesitatingly have trusted me where public interests in this world were concerned, if only we could have agreed about the next',[9] was merely commenting on one side of a perpetual argument, the other side of which had led Robespierre to declare that 'wherever an aristocrat priest makes a proselyte he turns him into an enemy of the Revolution; for his ignorant victims forget that, whilst appearing to defend his religious opinions he is really preaching despotism and counter-revolution'.[10]

INTELLECTUALISM, LEGALISM AND SYMBOLS

Another characteristic of French political life is its combination of intellectualism and legalism. Highly theoretical and ideological political goals are sometimes apparently divorced from any plans for attaining them and at other times are allied to highly complex and precise juridical procedures. These procedures can become highly unrealistic, since the desired juridical commitments will, in practice, have to be amended, modified, reinterpreted, or frankly evaded in order to enable them to work at all.

To aim impossibly high and end by achieving little and sometimes virtually nothing has been regarded as preferable to experiment, pragmatism and compromise, in part because the fiduciary element that is so strong in British politics is comprehensibly absent from French politics, with their violent swings from one régime to another, and their recurrent questioning of existing institutions. But there is more to it than the need to make it more difficult for opponents to challenge an accepted constitution or institution by tying it up in red tape – though that can be a natural reaction in a country frequently subjected to violent change. There is a general assumption in French politics that such precise and legalistic commitments can provide positive aid to supporters as well as positive discouragement to opponents. The very existence of the commitments will, it is felt, encourage adherence to them, so that signatories, like those committed to Rousseau's *contrat social*, will be 'forced to be free'. In practice, of course, things do not work out like that, and French political history has provided more demonstrations of the ingenuity of French citizens in escaping from legalistic restrictions of their own devising than of their assiduity in respecting them.

If legalism is sometimes used as an effective political instrument to gain specific immediate objectives,[11] French intellectualism sometimes leads to an excessive concentration on goals, which prevents effective steps to deal with urgent immediate objectives. The first years of the Fifth Republic saw prolonged conversations between the Socialist and Communist parties with the ostensible aim of working out an agreed programme for a Government of the Left. What really happened was a series of hair-splitting discussions on different interpretations of Marxist doctrine, totally unrelated to any conceivable five-year governmental programme. The result was that both parties were compelled to face the electors, in 1962, 1967 and 1968, as a loose electoral alliance which committed neither side to any governmental policy at all.[12]

Intellectualism is closely related to another characteristic of French politics, which is the importance of certain issues that have become symbols. These exist mainly on the Left and often have historical as well as political importance. The most striking is the clerical issue. This has already been mentioned in the context of the importance of history in French politics. But anti-clericalism is also an issue that is of tremendous symbolic importance. It would be impossible to understand why, under the Fourth Republic, two modest measures such as the Poinso–Chapuis decree and the Barangé law should have created such a furore, unless their symbolic significance is taken into account. The first, in 1948, was an authorization to 'family associations' to receive subsidies to be distributed among families needing help in the education of their children. It was objected to by anti-clericals on the ground that it constituted an indirect method of providing State aid to Catholic schools, and so infringed the principle of State neutrality in education. The second, in 1951, provided for a small subsidy to Catholic schools, used mainly to supplement the inadequate salaries of Catholic teachers. The result was the break-up of a Socialist–MRP alliance in the 'Third Force', which had enabled the two parties to work together in Governments from 1944 onwards – an estrangement that lasted until 1956. Yet the State system alone was quite inadequate to meet the educational needs of all French children.

Another symbol which was responsible for disturbances in the educational world during the Fifth Republic was that of 'non-selection' in universities. The principle of 'equality' proclaimed in the Declaration of the Rights of Man has traditionally been interpreted by important sections of opinion on the Left to mean the unrestricted right of individual students, once admitted to universities, to study the subjects of their choice, irrespective of their own qualifications, the availability of facilities and teachers, and statistical evidence that the consequences of such freedom would be a 50 per cent chance of failure in the end-of-year examination.[13]

On the Left, Marxism has become a symbolic political battleground. For orthodox Communists, it is an operative doctrine, but at the same time a permanent source of conflict, both with other left-wing organizations that adopt differing interpretations of Marxist thought, and with dissident elements within the Communist party itself. For Socialists, it provides a philosophical framework that can vary from acceptance of the basic principles of Marxism (but rejection of Communist methods of applying them) to a theoretical attachment to Marxist explanations of society that demands merely verbal recognition in policy statements or theoretical political writings, and can otherwise be ignored. For many intellectuals, both inside and outside the Communist party, it has become primarily an intellectual exercise, often merely a form of political escapism, entirely divorced from practical politics. One of the reasons for the persistence of anti-clericalism is the inevitable clash between two equally powerful doctrines, Catholicism and Marxism. The Church quarrel, said André

Siegfried, is complex, 'because it is complicated by doctrine and this is serious in a country in which those actually concerned with politics are doctrinaires'.[14]

There are at least two characteristics of French politics that might be regarded as logically inconsistent with the highly intellectual attitudes so far mentioned, but that are taken for granted by Frenchmen of all political parties, irrespective of their ideological differences. The first is the importance of sectional interests, not merely in the relations between parliamentary representatives and their constituents, but also in those between Governments and Parliament. All Governments, parliamentary representatives, local councils and Mayors are expected to provide clear evidence that they are serving the economic interests and remedying the specific grievances of the more vociferous sectors in the country, the constituency, the *département* and the *commune*. This aspect of politics has already been mentioned in the previous volume dealing with institutions.[15] What has not been discussed is the political problem of why this should be so in a country in which the ideological and intellectual approaches to politics are so much more important than they are in Anglo-Saxon and Scandinavian democracies.

It may be, as Charles Morazé claims, that the attraction of ideas and of theories has become a kind of exercise that France is addicted to, partly because she is historically conditioned to regard herself as excelling in this field. During the century and a half when absolute monarchy survived in France and had disappeared in England, a predisposition to legalism going back to Roman times was encouraged by the proliferation of judges, lawyers and notaries, whereas opportunities for practical experience of politics were denied to these classes as well as to intellectuals. The result, according to this theory, was the development of a highly developed intellectual and legal expertise that has been a source of both satisfaction and prestige to France – 'religion, constitution, the code, systems, anti-clericalism and techniques. France holds the world record for theories.'[16] On the other hand, he argues that her comparative lack of confidence and achievement in economic and commercial fields created an inferiority complex that has been expressed in a permanent tendency to turn to the State as soon as difficulties are encountered.

> In times of crisis, the French entrepreneur does not criticize himself: on the contrary he is indignant, angry and accusatory. He accuses the State, the workers, foreigners. And public opinion is often on his side. In England, the cyclic depressions of 1828–1830, 1847–1848 brought bankruptcies accepted with resignation. In France they brought revolutions that brought to power those that the depression threatened with failure, namely, the *petit bourgeois*, the craftsman (the Poujadist), not to mention the small farmer crippled by mortgages on his uneconomic farm.[17]

The theory is attractive and is developed at some length, with examples.[18] But it is possible to suggest other explanations of the facts quoted, and also of more recent facts illustrating the same tendencies. In reality, through all periods of history – Republican no less than Monarchical – the State has been a dominant, bureaucratic and centralizing machine. To realize the invulnerability of this citadel, it is enough merely to recall the various attempts that have been made to introduce a certain degree of regionalism, all of which have failed to dislodge the State from its traditional position as the centre and head of 'France one and indivisible'. The most recent proposals, introduced in 1964, were immediately watered down, and were further watered down by a new Bill in 1969, under pressure from 'Jacobin' elements in the Gaullist party (ably led by M. Michel Debré), although they had not by then even come fully into operation. The 1968 reform of the highly centralized State university system, which introduced some degree of independence of the Ministry in Paris, was also seen in 1973 not to have significantly loosened the State's grip.[19] It may be, therefore, that the rôle of the State is not only consequential, but also causative, and that its stranglehold, under all régimes, has effectively inhibited individual, local and regional political initiatives, to the point of creating and maintaining a permanent tendency to over-reliance on it in all fields and by all political parties.

Whatever the cause, however, the process has continued under the Gaullist régime. The State has been expected by farmers – and indeed, by all parties in France, for the farmers' vote is important to all of them – to use the institutions of the Common Market in order to protect French agriculture from the economic consequences of its own over-production and under-rationalization, and to protect French industry from the consequences of its own inadequate competitiveness, largely caused by a long history of protectionism. Small tradesmen have brought pressure to bear on Governments, by violence if necessary, to protect their own uneconomic businesses and to relieve them from some of the burden of taxation that they are ill-equipped to bear.[20] The Gaullist State, no less than its predecessors, has been obliged for political reasons to satisfy some of these requests, however much Gaullist theory and economic desiderata might require it to resist them.

Interests, then, are no less an integral part of the French political context than theories and symbols. This fact is sometimes denied, because the two are often incompatible bedfellows. 'Politics', wrote Albert Thibaudet, 'is autonomous, not an extension or an addition to economics. No party will get anywhere by inscribing "Interests" on its banner.'[21] There is some truth in this second sentence. But it does not follow that political parties expect the noble political sentiments and theories that they do inscribe on their banners or include in the official political declarations published by parliamentary groups in the *Journal Officiel* to be translated into practical policies in the near future. 'Our politics', wrote André Siegfried, 'are discussions of principles.' But he was careful to add that when these are put into practice 'if at all, it is in an atmosphere of virtual indifference'.

To vote, in an atmosphere of excitement, for a Boulevard du Maréchal Foch, an Anatole France Square or a Ferrer

Street is an affirmation of a certain conception of life, politics and man . . . after which everybody goes off peaceably to the café and, except for a few blue plaques on walls, nothing has changed.[22]

In other words, theories, ideas, principles and symbols are often kept in separate compartments from interests.

The most striking case [says Charles Morazé] is that of the Socialists. For half a century they preached anti-capitalism. The 1930 crisis brought them to power in 1936, with the support of the Left. Their assiduous adherence to monetary and 'liberal' economic orthodoxy made the British Labour party appear staggeringly adventurous ten years later.[23]

This dichotomy of theory and practice should, nevertheless, not be over-emphasized. To some degree, it is a characteristic of democratic politics everywhere. It is more evident in France than in other European democracies for two principal reasons. First, the long tradition of unstable coalition Governments has meant that the compromises that, in more stable systems, and especially in two-party systems, can be made *within parties*, and so at pre-electoral level, have so often had to be made in France (when they have been possible at all) *within Governments*, which has meant that, whether Socialist or not, Governments have rarely had the necessary margin of freedom of action to undertake adventurous policies. And second, doctrinal quarrels, which affect primarily the Left, are less important and far less divisive in the more pragmatic politics of the Anglo-Saxon and Scandinavian countries.

POLITICS AND SCANDALS

The combination of interests and political divisiveness helps, perhaps, to explain the fourth striking characteristic of French politics, which is the frequency and the impact of political scandals. All countries, of course, have such scandals from time to time, but in France, they seem to be a regularly recurrent feature of political life – with the result that at least one distinguished British political scientist has concluded that 'France is the classic land of political scandal'.[24] They have also had important political repercussions. Moreover, they follow a recognized and consistent pattern. For a period of some months they dominate the headlines. Prominent personalities, usually including political personalities, become involved, and there are hints that others may be. As the weeks drag on, the *affaire* becomes more and more complex and confusing, and the original issue tends to become submerged in side issues or, at times, to be lost sight of altogether. Then, with surprising suddenness sometimes, the whole business drops out of the headlines, without leaving any conviction that justice has been done or the truth made clear. The following description of this process during the course of the Dreyfus affair is equally illustrative (*mutatis mutandis*) of the course of many others, including contemporary ones.

> By whatever end one takes an incident one is faced by mystery. There are leakages of information; there are striking alliances and friendships; obvious questions are not asked; curious coincidences pass unnoticed; there is an unexpected carelessness about detail within the military administration; there is a lack of commonsense on a number of important issues; while the cynical expect experts to disagree, the extent of disagreement among handwriting experts is disconcerting; and the ability of the entire cast to tell lies must also be noted as unexpectedly impressive.[25]

Over half a century after the Dreyfus affair, the following description was given of a scandal of the Fifth Republic, the disappearance and presumed murder of the Moroccan left-wing leader, Ben Barka, in 1965:

> . . . every day, accounts in the press and gossip mentioned police officers who contradicted themselves, civil servants hiding behind superiors, strong-arm men quoting names with impunity, a former Gaullist Deputy penalised by his colleagues following public accusations of lying. All this took place in a noisy babel of secret agents, sordid or terrible

stories, calumnies, dubious revelations and even more dubious *démentis.*

This affair stinks. Ministers are visibly embarrassed. . . . It is obvious that errors have been made, that instructions have not been carried out, that men have failed in their duty, that there have been some shady conspiracies, and that political expediency has been the rule.[26]

The Ben Barka *affaire* had begun in November 1965. Three months later, so much political damage had been done, especially by the involvement of members of the Moroccan Government, that General de Gaulle felt obliged to refer to it in his press conference of 21 February 1966. He promised to see that justice was done, to overhaul the organization of the police, and, at the same time, tried to minimize the importance of the affair as far as the régime was concerned, by describing the French side of it as 'commonplace and unimportant' (*vulgaire et subalterne*), and as exaggerated by the press and opposition elements for political reasons.[27] Even presidential concern, however, did not lead to the successful unravelling of the affair. Some eighteen months later, some of the men charged had at least been given prison sentences. But the comment made in 1967 in the *Année politique* seems likely to remain applicable: 'Oblivion, powerlessness and silence surround an event that in no way redounds to the glory of humanity.'[28]

These classic scenarios have regularly served as an invaluable aid to the achievement of at least one political objective. Whether a particular *affaire* begins as a financial scandal – as it often does – or whether it is political from the start, there are always those who seek to politicize it, to use it as a political weapon in order to discredit right-wing or left-wing politicians, the Government, or the 'Establishment' – civil servants, the police, the army or the legal system. They succeed to the extent that the invariable outcome is a vaguely unpleasant after-taste of suspicion that 'the powers that be' or financiers or politicians have been in some ways incompetent, corrupt or dishonest, and that some things have been hushed up by people who should know better and that the truth will never be

known. By this time, everybody is so heartily sick of the unending succession of headlines announcing fresh sensations,
complications and mystifications that the disappearance of the
whole thing from the daily newspapers is greeted with general
relief.

In his detailed study of such scandals in post-war France,
Philip Williams attributes their prevalence to the clash between
'an over-centralised, over-bureaucratic administration' and
what has been called by General de Gaulle (and not only by
him) 'the most fickle and unmanageable people on earth'.[29]
They are regarded as expressing 'the indignation and suspicion
with which the ordinary citizen regards rulers who seem
remote and inaccessible'. This is undoubtedly an important
contributory factor, as is the permanent mistrust of 'the other
side' caused by the 'deep divisions in the country, which help
to encourage the scapegoat-hunting mentality of the public'.[30]
But there are at least two other characteristics of the national
political temperament that play a part in explaining the atmosphere that these scandals engender – a peculiar mixture of
credulity and virulence, which builds up in the course of the
long series of detailed press reports. In a country made up of over
37,000 small villages, in which peasant farmers and small tradesmen play an important political rôle, and in which local politics,
whether conservative or revolutionary, have strong traditional roots, suspicion, rumour and gossip are bound to exist
in politics no less than in everyday life. And they are encouraged by the relative licence allowed to the press in the
matter of personal and political attacks. The French citizen has
an almost pathological tendency to suspect that he is being
duped, together with an astonishing capacity for credulity,
both in financial matters (hence the number of financial
scandals) and in politics. The late Paris correspondent of *The
Guardian*, Darsie Gillie, once remarked, apropos of the electoral
success of Poujadism, that in no other country would it be
possible for so many intelligent people to believe so many silly
things. The second characteristic is that, in a country in which
interest groups – and especially those of the small man – are
making perpetual demands on the State, suspicion of it can

more easily be aroused by its apparent involvement than by its remoteness, if it is being suggested that that involvement is on behalf of *other* claimants.

It is in this climate that scandals, and especially those alleging financial irregularities or advantage and involving politicians, find a receptive audience. It is all the more receptive because many of the critics, whether of individuals or of the Government, are not above seeking for themselves concessions and advantages that they condemn when received by others, including opportunities for tax avoidance or evasion. It would be impossible to transpose to the British political context the reactions in 1972 to revelations in a weekly newspaper of the details of an apparently surprisingly modest income-tax demand received by the then Prime Minister, M. Chaban-Delmas. Not only did he himself feel obliged to put forward on the radio a detailed defence of his own position (which by general admission and on the specific assurance of the Minister of Finance was in perfect accordance with the law), but he also felt it necessary to furnish copious details regarding the sources of his income and the value of his property – details that only the income-tax authorities had the right to demand.[31]

It is not being suggested that British politics does not have its own quota of scandals, including financial irregularities. But it would be highly unlikely for a British Minister in a similar situation to feel obliged to respond in this way. For one thing, of course, the British press is less free to indulge in personal hints and innuendos, and so a politician feeling himself attacked would be more likely to take the matter to the courts. But the main difference is that the political repercussions would be different. In France, where the built-in conviction of so many citizens is that the slightest whiff of smoke is a pointer to the indubitable existence of a large fire, it is possible for such an incident to affect a politician's prestige to an almost unbelievable extent. For some time after the revelations relating to M. Chaban-Delmas there were hints in the press, and in some political speeches, that the Prime Minister might have to be dropped from office as a possible political liability.[32] And when he finally did resign the following July, it was difficult not to conclude that this ridiculous affair had had something to do with it. But if involvement in scandals or mild smear campaigns, even incidentally or innocently, can sometimes affect a politician's career (particularly if there are other more solid reasons for his unpopularity) and can occasionally have tragic consequences,[33] the involvement, or suspected involvement, can surprisingly often be lived down or forgotten – perhaps because scandals are so frequent in French political life.

On the other hand, in cases where certain emotions are aroused, such as some of those discussed earlier in this chapter, political memories can be very long indeed. Collaboration with the German occupation authorities is something that the French find it hard to forgive, even after thirty years. There was, for instance, far more indignation at the news that, in 1971, the President had granted a pardon to the former head of the pro-German militia in Lyons (who was still subject to certain civil disabilities) than there was to the pardons granted to members of the OAS in 1968, only six or seven years after the events for which they had been convicted.[34] It is difficult to resist the conclusion that there is in the minds of the French public an instinctive classification of the degree of heinousness or venality of the particular offence, comparable with the instinctive recognition of the political mentality of Left and Right, or with the Englishman's instinctive recognition (according to one French writer who knew England well) of British class distinctions.[35] In other words, the political scandal is in some way that is very difficult to analyse a vehicle for the expression of political and sometimes petty grass-roots reactions. Sometimes, however, and *par excellence* in the Dreyfus case, it expresses deep-rooted national prejudices.

THE REPUBLICAN TRADITION

Perhaps the most powerful single idea in French politics – and certainly the most difficult to define or describe – is the idea of the Republic. It is neither a doctrine nor an intellectual conception, but rather a complex of beliefs and emotions concerning the kind of relationship that ought to exist between State and citizen, Government and Parliament, and Parliament and people. These have been built up over the years, mainly on the basis of experience, and the language in which they are expressed has acquired a certain number of symbolic undertones, transforming words or phrases into a kind of political shorthand that serves to sum up political conflicts, past victories and future hopes.

Some of these beliefs or feelings are shared by a majority of Frenchmen. On others, there are wide differences of opinion. For instance, the French Revolution stands for quite different things in the hierarchies of emotions and loyalties of the Left and those of the Right. A phrase such as 'France one and indivisible' means for some elements on the Left a Jacobinism that demands uniformity and centralization and that, therefore, regards as inadmissible any breach of the traditional rule of religious neutrality in the State system of education. But there is room in some left-wing parties for more tolerant attitudes in education, and also for the admission (at least in principle) of some regionalism in local administration. Under the Gaullist régime, the strongest support for a development of regionalism that would give real powers to local-government authorities has come from a section of the Radical party, which is by tradition both Jacobin and unchallengeably Republican, while the main opposition to such a conception of regionalism has come from Gaullist 'Jacobins', such as M. Debré, who fear that any significant devolution of State power to regions would threaten the unity of the State. The Centre and most opinion on the orthodox Right do not regard European supranationalism as inconsistent with the idea of 'France one and indivisible', whereas the Communist party is very firmly of the opposite opinion.

For the Left in general, words and phrases such as 'equality', 'the sovereignty of the people', 'the sacred right of insurrection', 'equal and secret ballots', 'a secular, democratic and social Republic' represent Republican convictions that have been defended repeatedly by left-wing parties in constitutional debates, and as far as possible expressed in Republican constitutions. Their exact flavour can be appreciated only in the light of their significance in past politics. According to a recent piece of linguistic research, General de Gaulle's ten favourite nouns were, in that order, '*la France, le pays, la République, l'Etat, le monde, le peuple, la nation, le progrès, la paix, l'avenir*'.[36] They constitute in themselves an impressionistic summary of his political objectives. Their juxtaposition is impeccably Republican in tone. But both in his speeches and in his Memoirs his emphasis on French military glory, the need for political unity, for political leadership, and for direct links between leader and people . . . would lead nine Frenchmen out of ten to regard him as a man of the Right. M. Guy Mollet, the secretary-general of the Socialist party, could nevertheless justify his support for General de Gaulle in 1958 on the ground that, though not 'by upbringing and tradition' a Republican, he had become one and remained one.[37]

What, then, does the idea of the Republic stand for in French politics? It is much more than the choice of a Republican as opposed to a Monarchic system. It is important to both Left and Right, though the latter does not share the former's attachment to the Revolutionary tradition or regard it in the same way as part of the Republican tradition.[38] The area of common ground between Republicans of different political persuasions that could be said to constitute a common Republican tradition includes at least four generally held political beliefs. The first is the belief in the supreme authority of universal suffrage, as expressed normally in parliamentary elections and at times through the referendum. General de Gaulle made what the Left regarded as excessive use of the referendum, and had insufficient respect for Parliament, but it must be remembered that, except for his final referendum, he resorted to this method of universal suffrage in quite exceptional circumstances. It is by no means certain that his successor, having resorted to the referendum once, with somewhat disappointing results, will want to repeat the experiment. But there would be general support for a referendum on issues such as constitutional amendment, or ratification of Parliament's acceptance of a new Constitution.

The second belief is in the essential principle of parliamentary government, the responsibility of the Government to the legislature, which in France means *de facto* to the National Assembly. Here again, there is a difference of emphasis between Left and Right, the former being traditionally readier to admit the predominance of legislative over executive authority. The third is the belief in certain fundamental liberties of the citizen, summed up in the 1789 Declaration of the Rights of Man and the Citizen and expanded by later statements in the Preambles of Constitutions.

Among these rights, that of political equality occupies a special place and could, in itself, be held to constitute a fourth belief.[39] In politics it stands for more than the 'equality before the law of all citizens without distinction of origin, race or religion' and the 'respect for all beliefs' proclaimed in article 2 of the 1958 Constitution. It means a positive recognition of the equal dignity of all citizens, which is interpreted to imply not merely their *right* to fulfil the obligations of citizenship, but the *duty* of the State to give them equal opportunities to do this, in the form of a comprehensive State education, available to all and used by all on the basis of merit as judged by the State. The requisite qualifications for employment in the liberal professions and in the State service, and in many of the higher posts in industry too, are State diplomas, following training in a number of State-controlled colleges for higher education. This conception of Republican equality does not imply, nor does it produce, a classless society. It does imply the existence in the public services of an intellectual élite – an administrative, professional and largely managerial or technocratic 'meritocracy' that has been a specific result of educational policies developed since the Radical party first campaigned for '*l'école unique*' some time after the separation of Church and State in 1905. It constitutes a quite special 'old boys' network' that, until the spread of fashionable sociological theories on '*participation*', '*cogestion*', '*confrontation*' or '*concertation*', satisfied the majority in all parties, and of which they were uniformly proud.

The Nature and Content of Politics under the Fifth Republic

TRADITIONAL FACTORS AND INNOVATIONS

Although the circumstances differed in significant respects from those that existed under the Fourth Republic, the preoccupations and priorities of Governments and parties during the first fourteen years of the Fifth Republic remained those of Republican government, as they have been briefly summarized in the preceding pages. The recurrent arguments about the régime were, in the main, restricted to the opposition parties, which spent the first two to three years of the 1960s discussing the need to replace the Constitution at the earliest opportunity and devoted the following years, after they had come to accept its general principles and provisions, to discussing how to use it and which specific articles would nevertheless have to be amended. The régime was, moreover, directly threatened twice by insurrections in Algeria led by supporters of a French Algeria, and twice potentially – by the activities of the OAS and by the brief so-called 'students' and workers' revolution' of May 1968.

There was, however, little general interest in electoral machinery, in contrast to the repeated parliamentary controversies on that issue during the 1950s – though the Communists remained firmly committed to support for proportional representation. On the other hand, electoral tactics were a constant preoccupation, for during the period covered by this book, there were six referenda, five parliamentary elections, and three presidential elections. There was, therefore, hardly a year which was not either an electoral or a pre-electoral period.

One important change in French political life during the later years of the 1960s was the challenge to the Communist party in particular, and to a lesser degree to the orthodox Left in general, presented by the numerous extremist 'Leftist' groups, some of which were active in the 1968 events. Dissident Communist groups were, of course, nothing new, but they had hitherto constituted a divisive irritation rather than a challenge. The new activist, often pro-Chinese, revolutionary groups and commandos regarded the Communists, no less than the Socialists, as being part of the 'bourgeois' establishment and no longer authentic revolutionaries. Anarchistic and violent groups created difficulties within a number of trade-union movements, and especially in teachers' and students' organizations. The Communists were, therefore, faced with a new problem. Their hitherto comfortable position on the left of the Left was now challenged by groups outside the party, and especially by some elements in the trade-union movement.

The special attraction of leftist groups for students, and even for some school-children, made them a recurrent threat to law and order, especially in Paris, which by the end of the decade had a student population of well over half a million, and still growing. Although housed in thirteen universities (where Paris had formerly had only one) students found accommodation, staff and equipment still inadequate. Universities were, therefore, peculiarly vulnerable to disruption by active, political minorities. Several suffered repeated destructive attacks and some schools as well as universities had to be closed for shorter or longer periods.

As far as sectional influences on French political life were concerned, the Fifth Republic differed far less from the Fourth than unconditional Gaullists would care to admit. During the first half of the 1960s there was serious farming unrest, and during the latter half similar agitation among organizations of small tradesmen, both movements being characterized by a certain amount of violence. And the consequences of the inflationary spiral were seen in endemic strikes, mainly small and of short duration, but symptomatic of discontent and of fear of the effects on employment of the modernization of industry and agriculture. The 1968 student revolt would have been far less important if it had not been used by trade-union movements in order to strengthen their own bargaining position on wage demands.

Nor was the Fifth Republic immune from the normal quota

of political scandals, from the mysterious affair of the alleged attack on the left-wing political leader,M. François Mitterrand, in 1959, the disappearance and presumed murder of the Moroccan revolutionary leader, Ben Barka, in 1965, and the Markovicz murder in 1969, to the classic politico-economic scandal of 1970–72, involving alleged fraud by property companies, in which several Gaullist Deputies were said to be implicated.

Though these did detract somewhat from General de Gaulle's desired image of the Fifth Republic as a régime un-sullied by the weaknesses and venalities of the past (just as the Fourth Republic's founders had imagined it as *pur et dur*, in contrast to the Third), there were, nevertheless, important differences between the politics of the two régimes. Some old problems disappeared – that of colonization, for instance, that of budgetary and economic instability (for a number of years), that of governmental instability at least for fourteen years. The focus of politics ceased to be Parliament, with its never-ending dramatic debates entailing the resignation of Prime Ministers and the presentation of their successors for parliamentary approval. Debates existed, of course, but they were comparatively few and undramatic. The fireworks and the drama came from presidential press conferences (seventeen during General de Gaulle's presidency), the tireless presidential tours of the French provinces, journeys abroad and receptions of foreign statesmen and heads of State in Paris. The press (with the exception of one or two Gaullist papers) expressed frequent criticism of the President's words and actions—the tone varying from moderation to systematic opposition. The State radio and television services were recurrently under attack by opposition parties and press as being biased in favour of the Government (a complaint which had traditionally been made by oppositions under other régimes).

THE PATTERN OF EVENTS

The first fourteen years of the Fifth Republic can be looked at chronologically to the extent that they fall into four quite distinct periods, differing in length and importance, but each with its own special characteristics and dominating problems. Their atmosphere alternates between crisis and a calm that tends to become boredom. The first period, from 1958 to 1962, was dominated throughout by the problem of Algeria and characterized by the danger of a repetition of the kind of insurrection that had led to the fall of the Fourth Republic. It was followed, from 1963 to 1967, by a period of calm, in which internal politics, except for questions of electoral tactics, did not arouse much general interest, though a great deal of useful legislative and governmental work was in fact done. It was a period in which the President's interest was concentrated on the achievement of certain of his foreign-policy objectives. And on these, there was not only less opposition to him than there was on internal matters, but also a Republican tradition which, except in periods of special problems or crises, regards foreign policy as being primarily the concern of the executive. In foreign policy, though not in internal affairs, there was some justification for General de Gaulle's reported assertion that everyone in France was or would become Gaullist!

The period from April 1967 to April 1969, when General de Gaulle resigned and retired from political life, was, on the contrary, one of intense internal political activity and of relatively little activity in the external field. It was dominated by social and economic problems and, in particular, by the clash between Gaullist and traditional approaches to these. Though a short period, it was one of the most dramatic in French political history, for it included the quite unprecedented phenomenon of a Paris student revolt that developed into a movement in which small, disorganized and anarchic student and trade-union groups seemed for a few days likely to constitute a real threat to the State. These weeks were followed by a series of problems, created or exacerbated by the events. Internal policy was dominated from then on by four issues. The first was that of social and industrial relations, and especially the Gaullist application of the principle of 'participation' of workers in industry. The second was the highly controversial proposal to reform the French university system, including its partial liberation from the centralizing stranglehold of the Ministry in Paris, a reform which aroused a great deal of political feeling and the kind of traditional responses called forth by measures such as the Debré Bill of 1959. The third was the proposal for regionalization or partial regionalization, under the plan introduced in 1964. And the fourth was General de Gaulle's proposal to change the composition and functions of the Senate in a way that amounted to a *de facto* amendment of the Constitution – the proposal on which he was defeated and that led to his resignation.

The fourth period, beginning with the election of M. Georges Pompidou to the presidency was, at least during the first three years, characterized by a second transformation from storm to calm. But this time the defusing process was in the hands of a new and as yet unknown President, whose immediate impact falsified a number of predictions. General de Gaulle's disappearance from the political scene did not bring the chaos that he himself had predicted, but a calm that had degenerated within two years into what was described as 'moroseness' in Parliament and indifference in the country. The change from Gaullism to '*Pompidolisme*' did not at once galvanize the opposition parties into political dynamism and produce the long-sought unity, but led to an apparently deeper retreat into in-turned in-fighting. In the field of foreign policy, it did (though only with some delay) lead to French agreement to British membership of the European Community. But it did not make the future of the Common Market any easier to predict, nor did it bring about any apparent fundamental change in France's attitude either to America or to NATO. And what ought logically to have been the collapse of the politically successful slogan of 'entente and co-operation' with the Eastern bloc, following the Soviet invasion of Czechoslovakia, did not occur.

What France was not doing and not thinking was easier to recognize than what she was thinking and where she wanted to go, which is why a summary of the political content of this period must conclude with a question mark. There was one difference, however, between internal and external policy that has led to a difference in the treatment of these in the following pages. Whereas in internal policy, the four periods were to some extent self-contained, there were no discernible breaks of continuity in the field of foreign affairs. Indeed, to any regular reader of General de Gaulle's pronouncements who pays attention to what he actually said, instead of looking for what it was hoped that he would say, the main characteristic of the foreign policy of the Fifth Republic was its consistency and its steady evolution along what appears as an undeviating course. Or perhaps more exactly, its course seemed to be as undeviating as any policy in the modern world and in a democratic State can be, when conducted by a highly pragmatic leader, confronted with many political difficulties. The chapters on foreign policy are, therefore, treated according to subject matter instead of chronologically. The division of subject matter is of necessity somewhat arbitrary since, as General de Gaulle was fond of saying, '*tout se tient*'. But there are guiding threads that may perhaps be regarded as giving each chapter its own distinctive unity.

It is paradoxical that the most striking characteristic of a régime that by 1972 had lasted longer than its predecessor and in conditions of unprecedented stability in both the internal and external fields, should be that, to all but Gaullist observers, it still appeared essentially ephemeral. At each turning point, its future looked uncertain. Pierre Viansson-Ponté's conclusion was that 1972 was 'the end of a transition, the moment when the past is already dead, yet the future is still unborn'.[40] The trouble about the French political past, however, is that it so often turns out to be far from dead, which makes prediction of its future a more than usually hazardous undertaking.

CHAPTER II

Preparation

The four years following the collapse of the Fourth Republic
in May 1958 were essentially years of preparation for a political
rôle that General de Gaulle regarded as going far beyond the
premiership of the Government of Public Safety that military
and civilian insurgents had called for. For him, the Algerian
problem was merely an obstacle that was preventing France
from occupying her rightful place in the world of the twentieth
century. And he regarded himself as better equipped than the
previous six Prime Ministers of the Fourth Republic had been
both to understand what that place was and to make it possible
for France to occupy it.

He was faced initially with two immediate and two longer-
term problems, all of which had necessarily to be taken into
account at the same time. He had first of all to provide himself
with the tools for the job. That entailed ensuring that the
method of his accession to power would not deprive him of
the necessary moral and political authority to obtain from
Parliament and people consent, first, to the replacement of
what he had always regarded as a deplorable and unworkable
Constitution, and, second, to his own occupancy of the key
office in a new constitutional system. If it had not been for the
breakdown of authority in Paris and the threat of civil war, it
would have been impossible in 1958 for him to obtain the
consent of the National Assembly, which, at that time, included
only a handful of Gaullists, and at most a hundred or so likely
sympathizers.[1] Even as it was, complicated negotiations were
required.

Legal power was in Paris. Real power was in Algeria. Moral
power was his, but he had still to take over the first two. A

28

little luck and a great deal of skill enabled him to do this in eighteen days.[2]

His second immediate task was not only to convince the majority of French citizens in 1958 that he would eventually be able to find a way out of the Algerian imbroglio, but also to persuade them to accept his methods during what must inevitably be a long and difficult interim period of trial and probably of error. If he succeeded, he must be sure that he could retain power in order to go on to pursue his real objectives. For, as had always seemed probable, and as the final volume of the Memoirs now confirms, he had realized from the outset that the first consequence of peace in Algeria would be that he himself would become expendable. His compatriots were, he said, relying on him 'to relieve them of the millstone of Algeria, and calculating that as soon as this had been done, I should be obliged to depart, whether I wanted to or not'.[3] His two longer-term tasks were, first, to use the intervening period in order to create political conditions in France that would ensure that this did not happen, and second, to lay as many foundations as possible for the positive policies that could be put into application only when the war was over. The years 1958–62 were thus years of liquidation of obstacles and of preparation for a Fifth Republic whose aims and methods were to be very different from those of the Fourth.

LEGITIMACY

The story of General de Gaulle's accession to power has often been told – by journalists, politicians, biographers and political scientists.[4] What, in retrospect, appears far more important than the clandestine activities of the various 'plotters' generally reported to have been involved, whether these were three or thirteen,[5] are the methods by which the situation was transformed, within a week, from one of insurrection in Algeria, an insurgent occupation of Corsica, and a threatened occupation of France, to an orderly change of Government in Paris. On 1 June, a majority of Deputies 'invested' General de Gaulle as the twenty-first Prime Minister of the Fourth Republic. The 329 who voted for him,[6] and the 23 Ministers who formed his Government, represented political opinions ranging from conservative to Socialist. Indeed, he himself is reported to have remarked somewhat acidly at his first Cabinet meeting that everybody seemed to be present except Maurice Thorez and Ferhat Abbas.[7] The following day, a majority of the Assembly accorded him special powers to govern for six months by decree and to draw up a new Constitution, to be presented for the approval of the electorate in a referendum. The Bill laid down four specified Republican principles that the Constitution must respect – universal suffrage, the responsibility of the Government to Parliament, the separation of the legislature and the executive, and the independence of the judiciary – together with provisions 'to organize the relations between the Republic and the associated peoples'. General de Gaulle also undertook verbally to maintain the distinction between the offices of President and Prime Minister, a distinction reaffirmed by him later.[8]

These decisions would certainly not have been possible even a few days earlier. And though he had reason to regard them as highly satisfactory, they were not achieved by his efforts alone. The President of the Republic (René Coty, conservative), his predecessor (Vincent Auriol, Socialist), the Presidents of the two parliamentary assemblies (one Radical and one Socialist), together with a number of prominent politicians, including two former Prime Ministers (Antoine Pinay, conservative, and Guy Mollet, Socialist) and Maurice Deixonne (a Socialist Deputy noted for his fervent anti-clericalism) had all sought to advise General de Gaulle on the methods by which he could legitimately return to power or sought reassurances from him as to what his policies would be if he did return. M. Guy Mollet had raised three specific questions on which the Socialist party in particular was anxious to obtain answers from General de Gaulle. Did he recognize the existing French Government as the only legitimate authority? Did he dissociate himself from those who were setting up committees of public safety in Algiers? And, if asked to form a Government, would he appear before the National Assembly and withdraw if it refused to accept his programme?[9]

The questions were really different facets of a single question, which was a request for assurances from General de Gaulle that he would not accept power as the nominee of revolutionaries, but only in accordance with the regular parliamentary procedures provided for by the existing Constitution. He had not answered these questions specifically or directly, but had provided *de facto* assurances on two of them in his press conference on 19 May, in which he had stated that he would accept power only if it were delegated to him by the Republic. He had added, however, that it might be necessary to modify the regular procedures of investiture in view of the special circumstances, though he had not suggested how this might be done. In reality the procedures were modified in only two significant ways,[10] and the investiture itself, together with the decisions taken by the National Assembly, provided a sufficiently satisfactory answer to M. Mollet's questions for him to feel able to accept office in the Government formed by General de Gaulle and to state later that he had never regretted doing so.[11]

It is easy to understand why General de Gaulle should not have wanted to give the required assurance on the second of the three points – his willingness to disavow the illegal Committees of Public Safety. The reasons he gave in his press conference were that to do so would only widen the existing differences between France and the French Algerians, and so make the task of restoring national unity more difficult, and that he could not reasonably be asked to condemn army officers to whom the French Government itself had delegated and was continuing to delegate legal authority in Algeria.[12] The plain truth was that, if he had disavowed the illegal organizations at that time, he would probably never have been able to return to power at all. For the nature of the insurrection was such that it presented any would-be head of Government with an initial and insoluble problem. It was a heterogeneous movement, including French Algerians and army officers, whose main purpose was to keep Algeria within the French

Republic, and Gaullists, whose main purpose was to change the political system in France, but who also believed that Algeria must remain French. Their only point of agreement was the need to retain the status quo in Algeria, and so to defeat the nationalist rebel movement. They disagreed in their attitude to General de Gaulle, who had never had any following in Algeria, and whose views on Algeria had not been expressed. The support for General de Gaulle's return among non-Gaullists in France, however – and in particular, that of politicians such as MM. Mollet and Defferre, who represented the majority of Socialist Deputies – was based almost wholly on the belief that he would *not* carry out the policy in Algeria desired either by the insurgents, by the majority of the Gaullists or by right-wing and some Radical politicians in France. Socialist votes in the National Assembly were necessary in order to ensure his legitimate return to power. The army's loyalty was necessary if he were to remain in power. Silence or ambiguity regarding the General's hopes or plans for Algeria were, therefore, politically essential until his hold on power was secure.

There was no possible doubt regarding his success in achieving his first aim of a legal and constitutional return to power. He obtained the consent of the majority in the National Assembly to his premiership and over three-quarters of the votes in the constitutional referendum. The general election gave the Gaullists 199 seats in the National Assembly – a result not attained by a single party since the Radical heyday at the beginning of the century. And of the 81,284 members of the presidential electoral college, 78·5 per cent voted for General de Gaulle as the first President of the Fifth Republic.[13]

> It was not without profound significance [wrote André Siegfried] that the Fifth Republic should thus appear as the legal continuation of the Fourth. In June, France had escaped the worst, that is, a civil war.[14]

Could it be said, however, that formal 'legitimacy' had been obtained only as a result of his own political ambiguity and of illegal political pressures from Algiers amounting to a threat of civil war? He himself categorically denied ever having been associated with any 'plots',[15] and neither at the time nor later was any published evidence produced to disprove his statements. It cannot be denied, however, that some of the 'plotters' were, both then and later, loyal and respected members of the Gaullist party. Whether or not this fact could be regarded as detracting from the moral authority that he sought is a question that must be decided in the light of the circumstances, as well as in the light of his conceptions of political leadership and of his own 'legitimacy'.[16]

The basic fact that must not be lost sight of is that the situation in France in May 1958 was already one in which the normal political machinery was not functioning as it should when it was called on to deal with the Algerian situation. On 13 May, when the insurgents were launching their attack on the *Gouvernement-général* in Algiers, a new French Government was on the verge of taking office after a month's interregnum, during which two would-be Prime Ministers had tried and failed to form a Government, and two candidates suggested by the President had refused even to try. There was, therefore, at this crucial moment *no* Government in France with the authority needed to take the vital decisions that the situation required. The outgoing Prime Minister, though entitled to deal with current business, regarded himself as no longer having the authority to commit France to actions whose consequences the incoming Government would have to answer for, while the incoming Prime Minister had not completed his investiture speech in the National Assembly, and so was not yet technically speaking in office. Neither Government could estimate the extent of support for the insurrection in France. The man who on 15 May became Minister of the Interior, M. Jules Moch (a man who, in the same office in 1948, had shown himself to be a Minister of both courage and authority), confirmed subsequently that the Government had not been able to rely on the loyalty of a number of army commanders, of some officials and of some elements in the police.[17]

The activities of prominent politicians, already referred to, were, in these circumstances, an expression, not only of the need to obtain assurances regarding General de Gaulle's intention to respect Republican and democratic principles, but also of a last despairing hope that he would be able to return to power before it was too late for the situation to be saved, even by him. Inevitably, however, reports of visits to Colombey-les-deux-Eglises, of conversations between General de Gaulle and the Prime Minister, and of an interview between him and the Presidents of the two parliamentary assemblies added to the general impression that Government and Parliament alike were confused, helpless and at the mercy of events. Even the most vigorous defenders of the view that the Republic must defend itself were by no means sure that it would in fact do so. The strike called on 27 May, and the 'mass demonstration' called the following day as evidence of support for the Republic were disappointing to those who hoped to avoid the return of General de Gaulle. The Minister of the Interior (whose estimates were likely to be more accurate than those of the press) recorded that although, on 28 May, there were 98 demonstrations in 48 *départements*, as well as the 'mass demonstration' in Paris, the results were 'frankly mediocre'.

> In Paris [he wrote], estimates varied between 50,000 (which was that of the *Préfecture de police*) and 'more than half a million' according to American journalists. The most probable estimate, including meetings held in the *départements*, is that the numbers did not amount to 1 per cent of the adult population of the country.[18]

Nor were other Ministers any more confident of their own ability to control the situation. The Minister of Foreign Affairs, M. René Pleven, solemnly warned members of the *Conseil de Cabinet* on 27 May that, notwithstanding their majority in the National Assembly (represented by an investiture vote for the new Prime Minister, M. Pflimlin, of 408 to 106), some Ministers were in fact helpless. The Ministers for Algeria and the Sahara were not obeyed and could not visit these territories. The Minister of the Armed Forces was obeyed neither by the army in Algeria, the forces in Corsica, nor the air force. He himself was not sure that, as Foreign Minister, he could guarantee that any undertaking he might give would be kept. The Minister of the Interior was unable to restore order in Corsica. The Minister of Information had only partial control over the press and the radio. The Minister for Overseas Territories could not prevent the creation of a Committee of Public Safety in Dakar. In these circumstances, said M. Pleven, 'We ought to ask ourselves seriously whether we are more than shadows, phantoms, and whether we are capable of governing.'[19]

More and more, then, events in France were leading politicians as well as the public to the conclusion that General de Gaulle offered the only remaining hope of saving France from civil war. It is nevertheless true that events in Algiers, and especially the manipulation by various plotters of both the insurgents and the Algiers crowds, exercised a powerful pressure that intensified these fears in France. General de Gaulle's own tactics are therefore relevant to any attempt to assess the legitimacy of his return to power. They were characterized by a mixture of caution, subtlety, astuteness and ambiguity, and involved some breath-taking gambles in the matter of timing. But three political facts need to be emphasized. First, he made no public statement at all until 15 May, by which time it was clear that the new Government was not in control of the situation and that the call for his own return to power by the insurgents in Algiers was increasingly insistent. This first statement was merely a brief declaration of his readiness to 'assume the powers of the Republic'. Second, in his press conference four days later, he stated that he hoped to be 'useful, if the people so wish it, as during the last great national crisis, at the head of the Government of the French Republic'. And the third declaration, on 27 May, that he had 'set in motion the procedure necessary for the establishment of a Republican Government capable of ensuring the unity and independence of the country', though admittedly premature, did, in fact, *follow* a number of interviews, and exchanges of letters, of which the main purpose was demonstrably to make possible the adoption of such procedures.[20]

There remains the question as to why he made this last statement at the precise time and in the precise terms that he did. It certainly took a number of politicians by surprise and created some dismay on the Left. But it was generally assumed that the Algerian insurgents had been planning to follow up their Corsican coup by an imminent landing in France, and that the two concluding paragraphs of this declaration, with their call for the maintenance of order and explicitly for disciplined obedience by the armed forces, effectively nipped this plan in the bud. This was certainly the opinion held by both M. Guy Mollet and M. Jules Moch, neither of whom was prepared to support the return of General de Gaulle to power, except in accordance with the normal constitutional and legal procedures.[21]

Did General de Gaulle, either then or later, in effect condone illegal actions encouraged by and sometimes shared in by his supporters? It has already been suggested that he could not, for practical reasons, openly condemn either the Corsican coup or the formation of the Algiers Committees of Public Safety before his accession to power. If he had done so, he would have condemned himself to failure and France to civil war. That he did condemn them in private was, however, revealed in the reports made to the Socialist party executive by both M. Guy Mollet and the former President of the Republic, M. Vincent Auriol, following their conversations with him on 28 and 30 May respectively.[22]

That he did not condemn them publicly later was in accordance with his views of leadership and of the need to maintain national unity. He combined long-term consistency with a short-term pragmatism that included deviousness, secrecy and ruthlessness. He was prepared to use men, movements and circumstance for his own purposes, but never to allow others to use him for theirs. He condemned Communism, but was prepared to work with Communists (during and after the war) for as long as it suited his purposes to do so. He condemned politicians of the Fourth Republic, yet included the most prominent of them in his 1958 Government, because they were useful to him. As soon as he was strong enough to get rid of the illegal Committees of Public Safety without risking another insurrection, he did so. He used the loyalty of army officers to himself, taking the risk of having to face later the inevitable sense of betrayal that numbers of them were bound to feel when the time came for him to be able to talk unambiguously about his plans for Algeria. Until that time came, he used his Prime Minister, M. Michel Debré, a fanatical supporter of both himself and of the policy of keeping Algeria French. M. Debré was then confronted with the brutal alternative of making a political *volte face* and applying a policy in which he did not believe, or of ceasing to serve the President in whom he did believe.[23]

General de Gaulle did not, however, indulge in words or in gestures for their own sakes, but only if they appeared to him to serve some useful political purpose. He had the greatest contempt for politicians, particularly those on the Left, whose words so often seemed to him to be meaningless gestures. As he said in a speech made only a few days after his return to France in 1944, 'the noblest principles in the world are useless without action'.[24] On the same principle, where 'action' demanded that the political past be ignored, he was prepared to eat his own words, as he did, regarding the eventual political necessity of negotiating with the Algerian nationalist leaders, whom he had for so long referred to as merely one element in Algeria (*l'organisation extérieure de la rébellion*), and therefore not necessarily representative of the nation. It was, however, very unwise of any opponent to conclude that, where no such compelling political motive existed, the General would ever be ready to 'forgive and forget'. On the personal plane, his memory was implacable.

The specific actions that he expected from his own words – or from his own silences – were not always clearly apparent to others (and perhaps not always to him) and the result was that he often created resentment when individuals or groups felt that they had been 'used' by him. His single-mindedness some-times looked – and, indeed, sometimes was – unscrupulous. Which is perhaps why the editor of *Le Monde*, who regarded General de Gaulle's diplomacy as made up of 'nicely calculated proportions of conciliation and blackmail, providing a subtle mixture of light and shade', concluded: 'There is a lack of balance that impairs its fundamental legitimacy.'[25]

For General de Gaulle, however, the judges of his legitimacy were himself and the nation. His own interpretation was mystical rather than political, and has already been mentioned in Chapter V of the previous volume, in relation to his conception of his own leadership. But he always accepted the political verdict of the nation. In the 1940s, he had sought its approval at the earliest opportunity, which was in 1945, and in his first speech to the Council of the Resistance, only three days after his return to France following the liberation of Paris, he had spelled out precisely how he had understood his obligations to the nation, or in other words, what were, for him, the practical conditions of legitimacy.

> The Government [he then said] is that of the Republic, not only because, until such time as French democracy can take over, its policy is in accordance with the wishes and interests of the nation, but also because it is applying and will continue to apply the laws, just laws, Republican laws. . . . As long as these remain unmodified by the sovereign people, it is the strict duty of an executive, be it only provisional, to apply them (as it has done without hesitation or weakening for over four years) in the spirit and in the letter, to the men and the territories recovered from the enemy and from Vichy. No doubt, circumstances sometimes obliged it to take measures not included in our codes. . . . It will be for the future elected representatives of the country to decide whether or not to retain them as laws. If these principles were not to be adhered to, the result would be arbitrary government and chaos, and that the nation does not want. . . .[26]

Between 1958 and 1962, there were criticisms of General de Gaulle's interpretation of these conditions. For some of his actions would be regarded as unjustified if judged by the standards that normally prevail in a democratic system such as that of the United States or Britain. But two things must be remembered. The first is that, even in normal conditions, French politics belong to a Hobbesian rather than to a Lockeian world. The depth and persistence of divisions between political parties, and consequently within Governments as well as between Governments and opposition parties, make politics much more a war of all against all than it is in the more relaxed and fiduciary Anglo-Saxon political climate. In France, any Government's hold on power is precarious – or potentially precarious – and so all Governments use what means they have at their disposal to strengthen their position, while all oppositions automatically protest against measures that they would themselves adopt if in power. Government abuse of its control of radio and television services is the most obvious and striking example of this permanent war.

The second fact to be remembered is that the condition of General de Gaulle's accession to power, both in 1944 and in 1958, was the existence of a highly abnormal situation, combining acute national danger, greatly intensified political divisions, and overwhelmingly difficult political problems. Critics of his methods must at least concede that between 1958 and 1962, three insurrections and a terrorist threat did not prevent him from applying faithfully his own criteria of legitimacy. He consulted the nation twice in 1958, once in 1961, and three times in 1962. He was entitled to claim that its repeated verdict 'legitimized' his leadership.[27]

DECOLONIZATION AND ALGERIA

Though Algeria was never, constitutionally speaking, a colony, its relation to France was, in General de Gaulle's mind, essentially part of the general problem of decolonization. This was not made clear at the time, because no party in France was prepared to accept for Algeria the policy that he was able to carry out peacefully between 1958 and 1960 in twelve of the eighteen former colonies, renamed by the Fourth Republic 'Overseas Territories'. He explains in *Mémoires d'Espoir* that he intended from the first to decolonize them. The strength of nationalism in developing territories had, he thought, made the disappearance of Empire inevitable. France's situation as he had seen it in 1958, therefore, was that, 'however regrettable it might be, the maintenance of our dominion over countries no longer prepared to consent to it was becoming a hazard. We have nothing to gain and everything to lose by it.'[28]

Self-determination should, however, in his view, be accompanied wherever possible by mutually acceptable arrangements for the continued association of former overseas possessions with France – for the sake of the territories themselves as well as for that of France. In spite of their different problems, he did not envisage much difficulty regarding France's relations with the two North African protectorates, already independent, or with the African territories south of the Sahara, including the two mandated territories of Togo and the Cameroons.[29] By and large, his assessment proved to be correct, though there were long periods of tension between France and both Morocco and Tunisia. The offer of membership of the Community – a half-way house to independence – was accepted in 1958 by Madagascar and eleven of the twelve African territories.[30] Only Guinea opted for immediate, complete independence and, by voting 'No' in the constitutional referendum, immediately severed all links with France.[31] The rest drew up and adopted their own constitutions, but, almost immediately, decided to take advantage of the opportunity provided in the French Constitution to become entirely independent.

By June 1961, all had become members of the United Nations. They signed 'co-operation agreements' enabling them to receive economic, financial, technical and educational aid from France, and a Convention of Association, which provided for preferences in the markets of the countries of the European Community as well as for aid from the Six.[32] Most of them agreed to co-operation in the field of defence, and, in general, political links between France and all of them (except Guinea) remained friendly. Since all of them were French-speaking and trained in French administrative ways, French cultural as well as economic influence remained strong. Generous arrangements were made for the supply of French teachers, and for scholarships in French universities and other establishments where African administrators and technicians could be trained.

Though the economic advantages of trade with these

countries were far from negligible, they were partially offset by the cost of aid, whether financial or in the form of personnel. For France also needed more teachers, technicians and industrial investment. The main advantage of continued association lay undoubtedly in the field of foreign policy. The position of Algeria was quite different. Relatively few French citizens were permanent residents of the former overseas territories. But more than a million Algerian residents were French citizens who were anxious to remain within the Republic. Some of the educated Moslems shared their views. The country was militarily and politically, as well as economically, important to France. And its administration as well as its economy were dependent on the European population. Nevertheless – and again, if the account given in *Mémoires d'Espoir* is to be believed – General de Gaulle was already convinced in 1958 that the time was long past for integration to be possible, that it had become 'no more than an ingenious and empty formula',[33] and that for Algeria 'there was no longer any alternative to self-determination'. To prolong the status quo would, he thought, mean

> submerging France, politically, financially, and militarily, in a bottomless morass, at the precise moment when she needed to have her hands free to accomplish the evolution that the times demanded. For the army, it would mean a blind alley of useless and endless colonial repression, whereas that country's future depended on its advancement to the rank of a great power.[34]

In case it should be thought that General de Gaulle's intentions in 1958, as recorded towards the end of his life, might perhaps owe something to hindsight, it is perhaps worth noting that he made very similar remarks in his private conversations with both M. Guy Mollet and M. Vincent Auriol in May 1958. Ex-President Auriol reported him as saying:

> For me 'integration' simply means equality between Moslems and Frenchmen. I shall hold elections in order to produce negotiators. But that will not be the last word. I am in favour

of a federal system – of African and Algerian federations, which will be a part of a confederation including France and that will be a confederation of associated peoples.[35]

What his remarks did make clear was that the decolonization of Algeria was, in his view, necessary in order to carry out his plans for France. It was, in other words, a political and not a moral problem, as was also the decolonization of 'black Africa'. And he certainly intended that decolonization should be, if possible, achieved in conditions that would allow France to retain both political influence and economic advantage. As he put it to ex-President Auriol, where Algeria was concerned the choice was between losing Algeria and saving it through federation, that is, saving it for a rôle that would be of advantage to France. Since, however, Algeria constituted a special case, independence, if that was Algeria's choice (and he believed that it would be), should be subject to certain conditions. In the first of his two final volumes of *Mémoires*, *Le Renouveau*, he states that, in 1958, he envisaged three conditions. First, independence must be *granted by* France, not *imposed on* her by military action or by international pressures.[36] Second, it should be achieved by consent, and should also include provisions for Franco-Algerian association and co-operation. And third, independence could be achieved only by methods characterized by caution and gradualness, which meant that an essentially pragmatic attitude was called for. The conditions were 'too diverse, too complex, too unstable' for him to be able to lay down precisely in advance 'the details, phases and pace of a solution'.[37]

Caution and gradualness were, indeed, imposed on him for the next four years. Every development in the struggle merely hardened the positions of both sides. The result was a series of complicated advances, followed by setbacks, retreats and crises, in the course of which the Algerian problem went through four distinct stages.[38] The first lasted up to 16 September 1959 and was essentially tentative and preparatory. It included at least one overture by General de Gaulle that he could never for an instant have seriously expected to be successful – the offer of the '*paix des braves*'.[39] But two important steps were taken. The first was the restoration of civilian rule in Algeria, and of the authority of the State over the French army. A considerable army purge was undertaken and officers were transferred from Algeria to France. Local elections were held in Algeria in the spring of 1959 – the first since 1956 – in order to gain Moslem confidence and to provide for Moslem majorities on a number of local councils, thus enabling them to gain experience of local administration.[40] The second was the application in October 1958 of what was called the 'Constantine plan', providing for a five-year programme of economic and social development intended to do something to raise the miserable standard of living of the Algerian Moslems, and also to provide for the training of Moslem administrators through the reservation of a certain proportion of educational and administrative posts exclusively for them. Part of the value of these measures lay in the fact that they involved no commitment to any specific future status of Algeria and would be equally necessary in any eventuality. It was, therefore, possible for some progress to be made without the sacrifice of support for General de Gaulle of either settlers or the army, both still fanatically determined to keep Algeria French.

The second stage began with the President's declaration of 16 September 1959, openly recognizing for the first time the right of Algeria to self-determination. Its importance was mainly psychological, since he did not believe that any referendum on this issue could be held for a long time. He mentioned, as an outside limit, four years after the effective restoration of peace. The President clearly hoped to retain the support of advocates of *Algérie française* by offering the Algerians three options: what he called 'secession, which some believe to be independence' – a choice that would involve the immediate withdrawal of French aid and would, he believed, be disastrous for Algeria; '*francisation*', or integration, which would offer Algerians French citizenship on the basis of complete equality; and 'the government of Algeria by the Algerians, with the help of France, by means of close links in the fields of economics, education, defence and foreign relations'. This third choice was presented as being the solution clearly favoured by the President himself.[41] He believed that, if it was also the choice of the Algerians, then the form of government would have to be federal, in view of Algeria's diverse communities.

The response in Algeria was the 'revolt of the barricades' the following January by activists and a certain number of army officers. The President's immediate reactions provided an impressive demonstration of what he had been able to do to restore authority to the State and to create confidence among the public. He delivered a broadcast to the nation, reshuffled the Government (eliminating one of the most influential supporters of *Algérie française*, M. Jacques Soustelle), banned seditious organizations, obtained a large parliamentary majority for a Bill according him special powers, and carried out a new series of army postings and an administrative reorganization, replacing officers by civil authorities. He received loyal support in France from Parliament, trade unions and local representatives, and the bulk of the army in Algeria remained – even if only reluctantly – loyal to his orders. Whether or not the General ever did say (as was reported) that the insurgents had found themselves this time 'in the wrong Republic', the facts themselves proved that this was so.

Shortly after this apparent setback[42] a further step forward was taken. Following secret talks between the President and some rebel leaders, the first official negotiations between the French Government and the 'provisional Government' of the nationalist movement, the *Gouvernement provisoire de la République algérienne* (GPRA), were held at Melun at the end of June 1960. They broke down almost immediately because it was still impossible to find any significant area of common ground, but they did, nevertheless, achieve something. At least one obstacle that had hitherto helped to prevent negotiations had been overcome, *de facto* if not *de jure*. The French no longer refused to recognize the nationalist *Front de Libération nationale* (FLN) as an organ competent to negotiate. As the second round of negotiations was to show, however, nearly a year later, there was still no agreement on exactly *what* the FLN could be regarded as being competent to negotiate.[43]

The response by the French electorate to the referendum of January 1961, which provided for the setting up of provisional governmental organs in Algeria in preparation for the eventual referendum on self-determination, made it clear that the President's policy was irreversible. French supporters of *Algérie française*, however, were far from beaten. Their response was another insurrection in Algeria – the 'revolt of the Generals' of April 1961 – led by four retired Generals, two of whom had been Chiefs of Staff in Algeria. Though the revolt itself collapsed in four days, it divided the army and led to the declaration of a period of emergency in France, during which, for five months, General de Gaulle assumed the special powers provided for under article 16 of the Constitution. It led also to the arrest and subsequent trial of a number of the officers involved, and to further measures to restore discipline and loyalty in the army. The second round of negotiations with the FLN nevertheless opened in May 1961, only to break down in July, because the basic difficulty could still not be overcome. The French still regarded the FLN as competent merely to negotiate a cease-fire, since only the consent of the Algerian people could give them the authority to represent Algeria. The FLN, on the other hand, would not agree to a cease-fire without guarantees regarding the conduct of the subsequent referendum on self-determination. Some advance was made, however. The issue of the Saharan *départements*, which the FLN insisted on regarding as part of Algeria, was settled shortly afterwards by General de Gaulle himself who, in his press conference of September 1961, specifically recognized Algerian sovereignty over these regions.

The months following this second breakdown of talks constituted a third period, which was one of apparent deadlock and confusion. General de Gaulle appeared by now to be losing patience and was more and more frequently referring to the possibility of what he called a *'regroupement'* (he did not specifically refer to it as partition) which would provide for the continued residence in Algeria of those French citizens who wished to remain. Such a *de facto* partition was, of course, the last thing that the nationalists wanted.[44] There was, however, by this time growing evidence of support in France for a negotiated peace and for an Algerian Algeria. There were strikes, demonstrations and declarations – by political parties, trade unions, religious bodies.[45] The best-known of these declarations, the 'Manifesto of the 121', by a number of left-wing writers, academics and civil servants, even went so far as to accompany its support for Algerian nationalism with openly expressed approval of those national-servicemen who decided to resolve their problems of conscience by 'refusing to take up arms against the Algerian people', a statement that could not be regarded as anything but seditious, and shocked a great many Frenchmen of the Left as well as of the Right.[46] There had also been growing evidence of Moslem support for the FLN since General de Gaulle's visit to Algeria in December 1960, when Moslems had demonstrated in the streets, for the first time with FLN banners and shouts of '*Algérie algérienne*'.[47]

Three developments in particular were now influencing public opinion. The first was the series of trials by military courts in Paris between 1960 and January 1962. They involved FLN supporters of the 'Jeanson network' in September 1960, the leaders of the 'barricades revolt' between November 1960 and March 1961, two of the 'four Generals' in May 1961, a number of other officers who had taken part in the revolt between June and September, and, in January 1962, that of the Abbé Davezies, accused of helping the FLN.[48] These provided propaganda material for both sides, and so helped to build up the tension and anxiety. The second development was the impact of revelations of the use of torture by French army and police interrogators. There had been incontrovertible evidence of the use of torture by Moslems and also of the mutilation of French soldiers by them. Nationalist Algerians were also carrying out a campaign of indiscriminate bomb attacks directed against the civilian population. Nevertheless, the discovery that torture was being systematically used by French army and police interrogators came as a shock to many French people, and the discovery of the facts by young national-servicemen in Algeria created a serious moral problem for many of them.[49]

It was the third development, however, that more than anything else made possible the opening of the fourth stage, which led to the final successful negotiations of a cease-fire and the independence of Algeria. From the middle of 1961 onwards, first in Algeria and then in France, white settler activists had formed a terrorist association known as '*l'Organisation de l'Armée secrète*' (OAS). By the end of 1961, this organization constituted an even greater danger to the Algerian nationalists than to France, and the withdrawal of French troops would have been a catastrophe for them. But the growing number of 'plastic-bomb' attacks in France was also adding to the war weariness.[50]

The combination of all these factors led to preparatory talks culminating in a third round of official negotiations in March 1962, at Evian, as a result of which a cease-fire agreement was signed on 18 March, on the basis of a Franco-Algerian agreement on the conditions in which the subsequent referendum on self-determination was to be held. This overcame previous French objections by providing for *de jure* French sovereignty to be retained during the transitional period, while Algerian fears were allayed by the provision that *de facto* responsibility for much of the administration was to be exercised by an Algerian provisional executive, including Europeans, Moslem representatives of the FLN, and 'neutral' Moslems. A second compromise was the agreement in principle on Franco-Algerian relations in what it was assumed would be an independent Algeria, a complicated and detailed agreement that was to come into force only when the referendum and elections had duly taken place. The long-promised referendum, held the following 1 July in Algeria, provided a 91 per cent vote in favour of independence in co-operation with France, on the terms provided for in these agreements.

THE AFTERMATH OF THE ALGERIAN WAR

It was obvious that such a war must leave a great many problems, the solution of which would require time, effort and money, and that might also be politically explosive. The problem of the OAS proved less difficult than might have been expected. Its 'scorched-earth' policy in Algeria had perhaps been the deciding factor in bringing the FLN finally to the conference table. Its sporadic, indiscriminate violence in France, together with its systematic attacks on the homes of prominent politicians and journalists, and its attempts to assassinate General de Gaulle, ceased within a very short time of the cease-fire and, from 1963 onwards, the movement seemed to have virtually disappeared. There remained, nevertheless, large numbers of Frenchmen who were serving sentences in France for offences committed in connection with the war, and there were some leading personalities who had still to be caught and tried (or re-tried, if they had been tried *in absentia*).

The trials, and especially those of Generals Jouhaud and Salan (April and May 1962, respectively) and (in 1963) of the authors of the OAS attempt at Le Petit-Clamart to assassinate the President in 1962, helped to keep alive memories of past divisions and the sense of betrayal in some sections of the army. But army reorganization speedily restored unity and, as time went on, the President's periodical use of his right of pardon freed, or reduced the sentences of, considerable numbers of the prisoners. According to an official statement made in 1966, 3200 people had been tried for subversive activities by one or other of the special courts and, of these, 1769 had been sentenced to periods of imprisonment, 294 had been tried *in absentia*, and 13 condemned to death. But by then, 430 had already had their sentences remitted under an amnesty law of 23 December 1964 and, following the re-election of General de Gaulle for a second septennate at the end of 1965, the eighth list of presidential pardons brought the total of prisoners released to well over 800. By 23 April 1966, there were only 85 still in prison, of whom 21 were serving life sentences. These were OAS activists, including Generals Jouhaud and Salan, the 'Colonels' who had played a leading rôle in the 1961 revolt, together with 73 convicted of assassination or attempted assassination, some of them involved in attempts to assassinate the President. In 1968, six years after the end of the war, all remaining prisoners were freed. None – not even the most serious offenders – had served more than eight years and, of the 13 condemned to death, only 4 had finally been executed.[51]

The most immediately obvious problem – the influx of hundreds of thousands of European Algerians – did not create the political difficulties that some had feared. M. Guy Mollet, for instance, had feared what he called 'the Algerianization of France', that is the perpetuation of political divisions regarding *Algérie française*, owing to the presence of the *rapatriés*, especially since they were for the most part being 'repatriated' to a country that they did not know, and in which they had to build up a new life for themselves in very difficult circumstances. In fact, not only did this political danger not materialize, but the Algerians were absorbed into the economic system with surprising ease and rapidity. They formed a considerable element in Maître Tixier-Vignancour's small right-wing party, but this itself was uninfluential. They did, however, have long-term and very difficult economic problems that continued well into the 1970s. These were bound to have political repercussions and though they did not lead to the formation of separate political parties, they did lead to the formation of a number of associations that acted as pressure groups for their specific interests.[52] And, since most of the Algerians had settled in *départements* in the South of France, they played a not uninfluential rôle in local politics in these regions. In 1972, it was stated that there were 2500 *maires* who were *pieds noirs* (people of European descent, born in and formerly or still living in Algeria). This may seem an unimpressive figure, when it is remembered that there are between 37 and 38 thousand *maires* in France, most of them in tiny villages. But in the context of the local politics of *départements* in which there are large concentrations of Algerians it is not unimportant. In the Var, for instance, there were, in 1972, 2347 *maires*, of whom 115 were *pieds noirs*, and, in local elections, the lists in these regions of the South and South-East normally included at least one *pied noir*.[53]

What it amounted to was that former Algerians could constitute centres of potential political discontent. They had grievances about housing, employment and, above all, about compensation for houses, farms or businesses abandoned in Algeria. Their claims were inevitably dealt with only partially and very slowly, for one thing because of the numbers involved, and for another because the problem was a continuing one. The numbers arriving in France dwindled rapidly after 1962, but even in 1972, they were still arriving at the rate of 5000 or more a year. Over a half came from Algeria. The rest came from Morocco and had similar problems.[54] At the then existing rate of progress, it was likely to be from ten to fourteen years before all the claims could be dealt with. Many *rapatriés* were, therefore, in financial difficulties, having resorted to loans that they were unable to repay – loans incurred sometimes to buy farms, businesses or vineyards, most of which were in precisely those areas of 'static' France that were being overtaken by the consequences of economic modernization and the technological revolution. They thus helped to swell the numbers of resentful survivors of the nineteenth century, represented by the more militant of the organizations of small tradesmen and crafts-men, some of which were creating political problems in the early 1970s as well as in the early 1960s. In the circumstances, it was surprising how few political complications they caused, just as it was surprising, in spite of the ups and downs of Franco-Algerian relations, how small were the repercussions of Algerian independence in French politics.

There were, nevertheless, two problems arising directly or indirectly from the Algerian war that affected French politics. The first was the controversy that followed the ruling by the *Conseil d'Etat* that the special court (the *Cour militaire de Justice*) set up to try leaders of the OAS was illegal. This caused the first important political battle in the new Parliament.[55] The second was the challenge to General de Gaulle himself, which he had anticipated would come as soon as France was no longer threatened by external war or internal disruption. By the autumn of 1962, it was safe to defeat the Government. The National Assembly promptly did so on 5 October, on a motion of censure condemning the decision, announced by the President on 20 September, to seek to amend by referendum the articles of the Constitution governing the election of the

President of the Republic. The constitutional implications of the controversy that arose over this issue have already been discussed in the previous volume.[56] The political battle of the referendum and the general election – for General de Gaulle promptly dissolved the National Assembly following the vote of censure – had, as has already been said, been expected by him.

The settlement of the Algerian problem had of course immensely increased his prestige. It is true that there was a debit side. He had not obtained the conditions that he himself had postulated in 1958 (according to his account in the fourth volume of the Memoirs). Algeria was not a federation; it was not going to be possible for the French population to remain an integral and important element in the new Republic of Algeria; there was not even any real conviction in informed political circles that the Evian Agreements would last for very long. This scepticism proved justified, for its provisions were, within a very short time, either abandoned unilaterally by the Algerians or re-negotiated on terms more acceptable to them. But on the credit side there were, nevertheless, some powerful items, and they did not fail to strengthen General de Gaulle's position in the electoral confrontation. Although it had taken him four years to end the war, he had succeeded at the end of that time in bringing peace, whereas his predecessors had failed. And he had done it without allowing the régime to succumb a second time in the face of insurrection. He had got the best settlement possible in the circumstances. He had got rid of this problem that for so long had politically 'blocked all roads'. He had completed France's decolonization. Moreover, the atmosphere, after nearly eight years of an increasingly painful war, had changed a great deal. War-weariness and the effects of the OAS attacks in France had increased the public's evident desire to see at all costs a return to peace and normality. And since, at that stage, it was by no means certain that the OAS was not going to continue its attacks, this uncertainty in itself was a powerful influence making General de Gaulle appear in 1962 far less expendable than the opposition parties had hoped.

He had also taken deliberate steps to ensure that the battle that he had foreseen should be fought on terrain chosen by him, and in conditions favourable to him. He had spent the war years in laying as many foundations as he could for the policies that he intended to carry out once his hands were free, and so he already had a substantial record to present to the electors and had won substantial parliamentary victories over his opponents. And the issues on which he had chosen to fight, that of the election of the President by universal suffrage, and that of his right to seek the approval of universal suffrage for the change, were popular ones that he could and did exploit to the full.

THE FOUNDATIONS OF FUTURE GAULLIST INTERNAL POLICIES

In General de Gaulle's view, the first condition of France's recovery of status as a great power was her capacity to become politically, economically and militarily strong. Gaullist leadership and the new Constitution were seen by him as the necessary instruments of stability. In reality, what more than anything else had given him the power to act during the first years of the régime was the support of the public, and the acquiescence of the opposition parties, based on the belief that he alone could extricate France from the Algerian war. This *de facto* support of the nation had enabled him to embark on a number of measures which made it clear that he intended the Fifth Republic to be a permanent and a reforming régime.

During the eight-month period of provisional government alone some 300 or more decrees were made, and these were complemented and completed by further measures during the years 1959–62. These reforms and plans for future reforms fall into four main categories. There were first those concerned with improving the working of the administrative and judicial systems. Plans were made, for instance, for the creation of a new regional administration of 'greater Paris', called the 'Paris district', and for the creation of 'urban districts' in the suburbs of large towns. These were to be followed in 1964 by a plan to divide France into economic regions, each with its own regional advisory bodies. In the field of local government, the traditional system of list-voting with two ballots, which had existed under the Fourth Republic only in villages with populations of under 9000, was extended in 1959 to all towns with populations of up to 120,000.[57] Ordinances were promulgated providing for long overdue reforms in the local tax system, though this still remained a problem in the second decade of the Fifth Republic, and seemed likely to continue to be one for many years. The status of civil servants as laid down in a law of 1946 was amended, and a charter for the State radio and television services announced – though this was not actually voted until 1964 and the subject of the administration of the radio and television services was to remain one of the thornier problems of both the 1960s and the 1970s. A large-scale reorganization of the law courts was carried out in order to take account of changes in the distribution of population and to eliminate some of the smaller and less efficient courts. The procedure of administrative courts was amended in order to improve the working of the system and to reduce delays.

The second category consisted of grandiose plans in the fields of defence policy. An ordinance of 7 January 1959 provided the framework for a wholesale reorganization of the defence system and the modernization of the army, though this could not be effectively carried out until the large number of soldiers serving in Algeria had returned. The *loi-programme* of 1960, providing for the creation of an independent nuclear striking-force, was also to be a very long-term undertaking.[58]

The third category consisted of a number of long-term social and economic reforms, including a comprehensive re-thinking of the educational system, with the aim of modernizing teaching methods, improving methods of selection at the ages of eleven or thirteen, changing the conditions of the *baccalauréat* examination and eventually of raising the school leaving-age to sixteen (though this did not in fact happen until 1967). Laws were passed both in 1960 and in 1961 to speed up modernization in agriculture. Measures that had a specifically Gaullist flavour included provisions, in 1959, for a small amount of profit-sharing in industry, the first step in the application of the

Gaullist principle of '*l'association capital-travail*', put forward as
early as 1950 by the then Gaullist movement, the *Rassemblement du Peuple français* (RPF). This was to be followed up in
1967 by a much more ambitious scheme for what was to be one
of the most important elements in General de Gaulle's own
plans for the Fifth Republic – the policy of 'participation'
between management and workers. In the same field, that of
social policy, a law was passed in 1959 to provide for systematic State aid to Catholic schools. [59]

The fourth category consisted of immediate measures to
convince the world of France's intention to set her own
economic house in order, measures which would, at the same
time, help French producers and exporters to withstand the
first impact of the more competitive conditions that application
of the Rome Treaty would involve from 1959 onwards. The
'austerity' programme announced at the end of 1958 included
a 17 per cent devaluation of the franc, and the introduction
from 1960 onwards of a new franc (worth 100 old francs),
together with reductions in expenditure, increases in investment and in a number of taxes and prices. [60] Unpopular as these
measures were, they did succeed in achieving these objectives.
The 'austerity' budget was followed by some years of expansion
during which inflationary price rises were contained, though
not eliminated. In 1960, for the first time for twenty-five years,
the budget was voted before the end of the year. The hitherto
steadily increasing deficit was reduced and, by 1961, France
had a favourable balance of payments. The fourth National
Plan then being drawn up was counting on a 24 per cent
increase of production by 1965 and an average rise of 20 per
cent in the standard of living. Not all of its targets were
achieved, but, even by 1962, there was no doubt that France's
economic situation was much healthier than it had been in
1958 and 1959, and General de Gaulle did not fail to emphasize
this fact in his press conferences and annual New Year messages. There had been no large-scale labour disputes. Measures
had been taken to enable the lower-paid workers to keep pace
with the rise in the cost of living. France's prosperity, said
General de Gaulle in his New Year message for 1963, had

reached 'a level that we have never known at any previous time, and social progress that is without precedent'.[61]

General de Gaulle's speeches and messages during these years revealed very clearly the high priority that he attached to economic health. Their tone and content, indeed, makes of them a series of progress reports, from the sombre reminders of December 1958 of the need for austerity and effort, in view of a situation that was both precarious and dangerous, to the cautious confidence of June 1960 and the confident optimism of October and December 1961. '*Rénovation nationale*', France's 'vast enterprise of national renewal', became a constant theme,[62] enabling him to contrast the confusion and uncertainty of the past régime with present prosperity and 'unshakeable confidence'. In December 1962, he pointed out that:

> In 1959, 1960, 1961, no month passed in which France's receipts from abroad did not exceed her payments. The harsh measures taken under the great monetary, financial and economic operation did a great deal to bring this reversal of the situation. But these measures were successful only because the majority of the French people accepted and approved of them.[63]

PARLIAMENTARY OPINION AND PRIORITIES

To judge by reports of parliamentary debates, the majority of the Deputies were singularly uninterested in this mass of reforming legislation. Apart from the subject of Algeria, which naturally remained priority number one, their main preoccupations were the restrictions imposed on them by the new Constitution and the new Standing Orders. The only topics that aroused real political passion were old and familiar subjects of parliamentary controversy. They were the long-standing issue of ex-servicemen's pensions, the privileges of home distillers, the perennial grievances of small farmers, and the traditional battle regarding the issue of State neutrality in religious education and its relation to the status of Catholic schools.

In his first message to Parliament as President, on 15 January

1959, General de Gaulle had expressed his conviction that, under the new régime, Parliament would, as he put it, 'associate itself with the national interest, refusing to yield to sectional appeals'.[64] By the following November, he had discovered that this conviction had been decidedly over-optimistic. For instance, he had hoped, he said, in his press conference of that month, that ex-servicemen would understand that the Government's decision to reduce their pensions was in the national interest. In any case, what had been done would not be changed. 'Where the national interest is concerned', he said, 'the State stands firm (*le pouvoir ne recule pas*).'[65]

In reality, it did not stand firm, though it was, as usual, the Prime Minister who had the unenviable job of eating the President's words. The issue revealed typical parliamentary reactions. The amounts involved, though adding up to a significant total, were negligible as far as the losses to individual recipients were concerned. But this was an old battleground between Government and Parliament, going back for years,[66] and Deputies refused to forgo this opportunity of showing their constituents that their interests were being defended by their parliamentary representatives. The result was that this item of the budget was almost the only one that met with real hostility, and that finally led the Prime Minister to declare the vote of the budget a question of confidence. Deputies retaliated by tabling their first motion of censure of the régime. Though this was of course lost, the Deputies really won, in that the Prime Minister finally conceded a partial restoration of the cut in 1960, with a promise of full restoration the following year, if circumstances permitted.

The question of the home distillers (*les bouilleurs de cru*) was also one that stimulated facile demagoguery, and was a problem that Governments had wrestled with unsuccessfully for over a decade. By 1960, the number of these home distillers – who enjoyed the privilege of distilling a small quantity of tax-free spirits, ostensibly for their personal use, but in practice often for selling on the black market – had risen to over three million. All attempts to get rid of or reduce the privilege, which deprived the revenue of considerable sums, met with

parliamentary opposition, in which Communists were as solidly
lined up in defence of the interests of this section of their
constituents as were conservatives. In 1954, M. Pierre Mendès
France had tried during his premiership to reduce the numbers
of those enjoying the privilege.[67] The Mendès France decrees,
however, were never applied. In 1958, a paper directed by
M. Michel Debré had castigated politicians of the Fourth
Republic for their cowardice in failing to deal with this problem. A year later, M. Debré discovered for himself that the
difficulties were greater than he had thought. He first tried to
get a Bill voted restricting the privilege to existing distillers,
and then to obtain special powers for the Government to deal
with the matter by decree, if his request to apply the Mendès
France decrees was refused. He ultimately obtained these
powers at the end of 1960. But Deputies and Senators did not
give up so easily. They then tried to prevent the vote of the
ratifying Bill which was needed to transform the ordinances
into laws. The struggle continued for years and it was only in
1965 that Deputies finally gave way.[68]

The two most explosive issues, however, were those concerning small farmers and the relations between State and
Catholic schools. The 'Debré law' of December 1959 sought
to replace the arrangements made under the Barangé law of
1951 by a permanent contractual relationship between Catholic
schools and the State. Looked at from the point of view of
British citizens, who have long taken for granted the need for
co-operation between State and Catholic schools, the terms of
the Bill were innocuous enough. They have to be seen, however, in the context of French doctrinal quarrels on the anti-
clerical issue over more than a century. During the war, by
granting subsidies to Catholic schools, the Vichy Government
had made what anti-clericals regarded as the first infringement
of the 1905 principle of State neutrality in the matter of
religious education. The measure had been promptly repealed
by the post-war National Assembly. In 1951, however, the old
battle had flared up again over the Barangé law, supported by
Gaullists and the predominantly Catholic MRP, under which
a small subsidy was granted to Catholic schools (mainly to

improve the very low salaries of teachers in these schools). Opponents had insisted on similar payments to State schools, which of course amounted to much larger sums.[69]

That law had at least left the principle of separation of Church and State intact. The 1959 law went much farther. It offered Catholic schools four options. The first was to remain completely separate from the State system, in which case the small subsidy payable under the Barangé law would continue. The second was to become completely integrated in the State system (which was what anti-clericals wanted). This would have entailed the loss of the privilege of providing religious instruction as part of the regular curriculum. The third was a contractual relationship under which, in return for increased aid, they accepted State control of teaching standards and qualifications (*le contrat simple*). The fourth was a more comprehensive contractual relationship in which, in return for the State's assumption of complete financial responsibility, the teaching standards and curricula of Catholic schools would have to conform entirely to those of the State schools (*le contrat d'association*). To the anti-clerical Left, naturally, only the first and second of these options were acceptable.

There was strong opposition to the Bill, but much more in the country than in Parliament, where Gaullists and conservatives (who supported it) were in the great majority. The actual vote, therefore, was quite unrepresentative of the intensity of feeling aroused by the measure.[70] Before the Government succeeded in getting it voted, it had entailed the expulsion of a former Socialist Deputy from the party merely for agreeing to chair an impartial Commission of Enquiry,[71] as well as the resignation of half the members of the Higher Education Council – which deprived it of the quorum necessary to consider the Bill – and even the resignation of the Minister of Education (also a Socialist). The powerful *Comité national d'Action laïque* had organized a 'national protest day', following the opening of the debate in the National Assembly on 22 December. It seemed as if the hopes expressed by the Prime Minister in the debate in the Senate, that the measure would herald peace between Catholics and anti-clericals,[72] were less likely to be realized than were the fears expressed by M. Guy Mollet in the National Assembly that it would 'revive old oppositions' and lead to the restoration by a future majority in the Assembly of total separation between Church and State.[73]

For a time, there were repeated calls on the Left for the repeal of the Act, but the protests gradually died down and there were even hopes that, by the time it came to reconsidering it at the end of the prescribed nine years, its prolongation might no longer arouse opposition. This proved to be an over-optimistic view. The anti-clerical issue was not destined to disappear quite so easily.

The problem of farming interests was equally traditional and long-standing, but proved to be more complicated in several ways. First, it cut across the Right–Left division, which (excluding the MRP) roughly coincided with that between clericals and anti-clericals. And second, the issue raised constitutional problems regarding Parliament's right to meet in special session, and so became part of the 1961 constitutional battle between Government and Parliament, in which the opposition was by no means restricted to the Left.[74] The situation of agriculture was, moreover, in the short term, and even the medium term, impossible to deal with. The process of economic modernization was transforming France into a country divided in two – on the one hand, the static, backward areas of small, uneconomic farms and poor wine growers in the South and South-West, and on the other, the go-ahead industrial regions round Paris and in the North-East, and the prosperous large-scale farming of the Beauce. For political reasons, it was impossible to eliminate the uneconomic concerns as fast as was desirable on economic grounds. Most of the farmers and small tradesmen who were becoming redundant or were due to become redundant were unwilling or too old to be trained for alternative occupations, and these were, in any case, few and getting fewer in what were areas of declining economic activity. Farmers also claimed that the Government had sacrificed their interests in order to keep down industrial prices.[75]

The traditional reaction of farmers was to put pressure on their Deputies and to follow this up with direct pressure in the form of demonstrations, riots and sometimes violence. In 1960, there were numerous and widespread demonstrations (some of them involving violence) in the areas most affected – Brittany, the Centre and South-West. The largest of the farmers' organizations, the *Fédération nationale des Syndicats d'Exploitants agricoles* (FNSEA), was demanding higher farm prices, at least a partial restoration of the 'indexation' (the tying of farm prices to a retail-price index) that had been introduced in 1957 and suppressed in 1958, professional training and health insurance. The Government's response, the *loi d'orientation agricole*, did take account of these demands. But it was a highly controversial Bill, passed only on its fourth vote in the National Assembly at the very end of the session (25 July), and then only in 'outline' form, requiring numerous implementing decrees. Though it did partially restore the 'indexation' that the farmers wanted – that is the establishment of a fixed relationship between farm prices and the cost of living – it was not popular with all farmers. It was a long-term measure, and the decrees were issued with such delay that by the following summer little progress had been made. Some farmers did not want the extensive State intervention that it involved. Most of them were more interested in short-term returns than in long-term planning. They wanted higher prices and more aid in disposing of current crops, including improved transport and storage facilities, especially in Brittany.

The result was renewed agitation in 1961, of a more serious kind. Its immediate cause was irritation at the Government's failure to issue the necessary decrees to apply the provisions of the 1960 Act, exacerbated by the problems created for farmers by some of the consequences of the Government's encouragement of expansion of production. 1961 saw a glut of a number of products and a consequent fall in their prices. The character of the agitation differed from that of the previous years in several ways. It was more widespread and prolonged. It was more violent, involving barricades across roads, sabotage of railway lines and in some areas of ballot-boxes, and even the occupation of the *Sous-Préfecture* of Morlaix by angry farmers. There were also attempts by the Communist party to politicize it.

The Government response was to hold a series of 'round-table' discussions with representatives of the farming associations, in order, in the first instance, to restore calm. There were debates in the National Assembly, and the Government announced its intention to take rapid action to issue the delayed decrees. But this was not enough. The farmers' reaction was that '15 days agitation have produced more results than 15 years of discussion. . . . Bad temper, when accompanied by bad eggs, has become a paying method.'[76] 'Round-table' meetings continued through July, and there were repeated governmental warnings that the problem of agriculture could be solved only by the farming community itself, not by appeals for disorder or for public subsidies, and also that the Government would not yield to violence.[77] In fact, it did, because it had no other option. In his study of the French agricultural problem, Gordon Wright concludes that the demonstrations of 1961 constituted 'the first peasant revolt since the sixteenth century that forced the Government to retreat on a fundamental issue'.[78] It was not to be the last. And the methods of giving way were to be similar. A number of immediate concessions were offered, including the promise of special measures to help Brittany and to deal with the problems of surpluses. New measures were to be taken to improve markets, investment and social benefits for farmers.[79] They were admittedly palliatives, as they were bound to be, for as the new Minister of Agriculture, M. Edgard Pisani, bluntly stated, 'no solution to agricultural problems could be found within French frontiers'.[80]

For some farmers, however, the opening of frontiers to the countries of the Common Market appeared as a threat of competition at home, rather than an opportunity to compete elsewhere. But the Government was by now looking to the Common Market to provide a solution to the more acute immediate problem arising from France's too large, too backward, and too firmly established peasant farming community. The achievement of a Common Market agricultural policy was destined to be a long and hard struggle. In the meantime, there was no alternative but to continue with palliative measures. 1962 saw a fresh series of demonstrations (mainly in the North-West and the South-West), and the vote of a 'complementary law'. This was intended to speed up structural reforms, and to encourage old peasants to leave the land and surplus young ones to train for alternative jobs. It also provided for the regrouping in larger, modernized and more productive units of the still too large number of small farmers who were clearly destined to remain for some time.[81]

Though farming problems occupied a large amount of parliamentary and Government time between 1960 and 1962 – and their entanglement with constitutional controversies between President and Parliament of course gave them additional importance – it would be a mistake to assume that there were no industrial problems. In his broadcast at the end of 1961, the President appeared to be endeavouring to create that impression, for he commented on the comparative social peace enjoyed under the Fifth Republic, noting that 'whereas, under the previous régime, nine million French workers lost on average seven million days per year in strikes, under the existing régime the loss was only a million days'.[82] He attributed this happy state of affairs partly to the benefits of economic expansion and partly to the French worker's realization of the uselessness of strikes in a situation in which workers and their organizations were playing an increasing rôle in the economic activities of the nation.

The picture was over-optimistic, as 1963 was to demonstrate. But it was true that what strikes there were – and a great many were reported in the press – were for the most part in the public sector, especially in transport, and that nearly all were of very short duration, some merely token stoppages of an hour or two or of twenty-four hours at most – a series of 'down-tools' demonstrations (*débrayages*), lightning strikes (*grèves surprises*) and rolling strikes (*grèves tournantes*). Moreover, many of them were local disputes, sometimes involving only a single factory, and this was especially the case in the smaller number of strikes in the private sector. They were expressions of discontent rather than of deep-seated grievances.[83]

The public sector did have a grievance, and one that was to

continue to threaten social peace from time to time. It was that, like the farmers, workers in State-run concerns felt that they were paying an undue share of the cost of the Government's efforts to avoid runaway inflation. There was truth in the allegation. The Government could appeal to private employers to keep wage increases within certain norms, but could not give them direct orders. There was, therefore, a permanent tendency for wages and salaries in the public sector to lag behind those in the private sector, which explained why the succession of strikes continued to be among transport workers, gas and electricity workers, dustmen, civil servants, and even (occasionally) the State-owned Renault concern.[84]

THE CONFRONTATION BETWEEN PRESIDENT AND PARLIAMENT

The balance-sheet of the régime, presented as part of the campaign preceding the constitutional referendum announced by the President in a televised broadcast on 20 September 1962 – and also forming the leitmotif of the Government appeal in the subsequent general election – made two things abundantly clear. The first was that the dominant interests of Parliament and public during the previous four years had been political rather than economic. They were the Algerian problem, the construction of Europe (including the pros and cons of a European rather than a national nuclear deterrent, and the pros and cons of British membership of the Common Market), the relations between President and Parliament and between Government and Parliament. Apart from the traditional sectional controversies already discussed, of which the agricultural problem was the most permanent and the most important, economic problems had been mainly related to the wage-lag in the public sector. The absence of similar agitation elsewhere was due to the fact that the severe austerity measures of December 1958, together with devaluation, the progress of modernization through the agreed methods worked out in successive national plans, and the efforts of industrialists themselves to prepare for competition in the Common Market, had combined to produce a general atmosphere of economic prosperity. There was also the fact that political stability had helped to maintain confidence in the franc. The Prime Minister's programme, outlined in his declaration following the Gaullist victory in the 1962 general election, was peculiarly revealing on this point. It was characterized by the 'low key' in which economic tasks were couched. They included expansion, better markets, more investment, the encouragement of decentralization and town planning, the provision of aid for the old and the low-income groups, the maintenance of full employment (a reference to the fears caused by the influx of over 700,000 refugees from Algeria), and the transformation of the relations between State, employers and workers through 'association'. It was hardly an inspiring package.[85]

Another impression that emerged from the broadcasts of the President was his realization that one of his chief assets in the confrontation was precisely that he could claim the credit for having brought about this recognized state of economic prosperity. In the televised broadcast of 7 November, ten days before the first ballot, having recalled how he had saved the nation from disaster, first in 1940 and then in 1958, he asked rhetorically what, in 1962, could be seen to have happened. His answer was:

> A nation in a period of full expansion, with full coffers, with a franc stronger than it has ever been; decolonization completed, the Algerian tragedy ended; an army in which discipline has been restored; French prestige higher than it has ever been – in a word, all immediate danger is over and France's situation at home and abroad is secure, which is why all yesterday's parties turned against de Gaulle.[86]

If his share in this achievement was his greatest asset, then his second most important asset was certainly the impotence of what he called 'yesterday's parties'. If nothing has been said so far in this chapter about the contribution of non-Government parties it is because there is nothing to say. M. Guy Mollet's description of their position was that

80 per cent of the French were for de Gaulle and 85 per cent against, or, in other words, 15 per cent were unconditionally for him, 20 per cent unconditionally against, and 65 per cent divided among themselves.

He had added that

> these 65 per cent support the General's Algerian policy and will do so as long as insane criminals of the OAS continue their misdeeds, but on other matters they are discontented for many reasons: peasants, civil servants, old people for economic reasons; democrats because he does not respect the Constitution.[87]

In practice, this meant that, on everything except Algeria, their attitude, and especially towards the President, was critical, but negatively so. As has already been pointed out in the previous volume, their attitudes to each other prevented the achievement even of common electoral tactics in order to attain the only objective on which they were agreed, namely the need to end Gaullist rule as soon as the Algerian problem was out of the way. Nothing resembling a common positive programme was ever in sight, and so, in 1962, the opposition, or rather the oppositions, had no credibility as a possible alternative Government.

Another of the President's assets was that, having foreseen accurately that opposition parties would try to get rid of him once he had dealt with the Algerian problem, he had made better preparation than they had to meet the challenge when it came. He could not only base his campaign on his record of positive achievements, but he could also choose the specific ground on which to fight. He chose the issue of presidential election by universal suffrage, on which he would have been admirably placed to out-general a far more competent opposition than he actually had to face. It was a constitutional amendment accepted by a significant section of the Centre and Left.[88] It could be presented to a number of those who did not want to return to the governmental instability of the Fourth Republic as a device for ensuring governmental stability, particularly as the first Parliament of the Fifth Republic had lived longer than any previous one in living memory. To ask the public to approve of a constitutional amendment by referendum (instead of appealing to Parliament under article 89)[89] was politically astute, because the method could be presented as demonstrably democratic. The complex arguments of the opposition to the effect that it was demonstrably unconstitutional carried far less weight from a propaganda point of view than the simple political assertion that the French citizen – 'the man who takes the *Métro*' – was as capable as any politician of deciding how he wanted to be governed.

> The Bill submitted to you [said General de Gaulle on 4 October] proposes that the President of the Republic, your President, shall be elected by you. Nothing is more democratic, and I add that nothing is more French, for it is clear, simple and straightforward.[90]

Yet another presidential asset was the fact that, as in previous referenda, General de Gaulle made it plain that, if defeated, he would resign. In the absence of any likely successor, at a time when the activities of the OAS and their threats to law and order were too recent to have been forgotten, and when the Cuba crisis was a present danger, this threat was, perhaps, for many, a decisive enough reason for voting Yes.[91]

THE GAULLIST OPPORTUNITY

The result of the referendum – 62·25 per cent of the votes for the Bill – was no more than a modest success, compared with the 79·25 per cent who had approved the 1958 Constitution. But it was enough. The announcement of the President's decision to hold the referendum had led to the tabling of a motion of censure in the National Assembly and, in the vote of 5 October, following the debate on it, the Government had been defeated for the first time, and for what, at least during the following ten years, proved to be the only time. The referendum was, therefore, followed exactly three weeks later by the first ballot of the first election to be held in normal peacetime conditions since that of 1951.

The result was an indisputable Gaullist victory. With nearly six million votes at the first ballot (31·9 per cent) and over six million at the second, the Gaullists emerged as by far the largest party. The Communists, with 21·84 per cent, fell to only just over four million, their lowest figure since the war, but remained well ahead of the rest. Nevertheless, the situation by no means approached that predicted in October 1947 by André Malraux: 'Tomorrow there will be, in France, the Communists, ourselves and nothing.' On the contrary, there were over two and a quarter million Socialist votes at the first ballot (12·6 per cent) and the combined conservative vote, though it fell by about a million and a half, still amounted to nearly two and a half million (13·36 per cent). The Christian Democrat MRP, with just over one and a half million, occupied only fourth place (8·92 per cent). These votes were, of course, by no means accurately reflected in the distribution of seats, owing to the disproportions introduced by the second ballot. Only 96 candidates had been elected at the first, and so 369 contests took place the following Sunday (25 November). The Gaullists gained altogether 64 seats, while conservatives and MRP together lost over 100. Gaullists alone were within some 15 of an overall majority in the National Assembly.

What the election made clear was the extent of what it was becoming fashionable to describe as '*dépolitisation*': 31·25 per cent did not vote at the first ballot, a figure for abstentions that had not been reached since 1946.[92] Moreover, the preference of a number of Centre party electors for Gaullist candidates at the second ballot indicated their desire for a quiet life and political stability. Better the Gaullists they now knew than the unknown quantity represented by divided opposition parties.

There was no doubt that the election was a defeat for the parties of the non-Communist opposition.[93] They had hurriedly formed before the referendum a loose coalition of Conservatives, MRP, Radicals, and Socialists, described as the '*Cartel des Non*', a not wholly accurate description in that its members did not in all cases hold together even enough to say No. M. Guy Mollet's advice, given frequently during the campaign, was to vote at the second ballot for anybody likely to defeat the UNR. MRP and conservative electors fairly frequently ignored this advice, where acceptance would have involved voting for Socialist candidates associated with the Communist party. The alliance of these two left-wing parties succeeded, however, in doubling their combined strength in the National Assembly. The 10 Communists increased to 41 and the 41 Socialists to 65. But they constituted no serious threat to the Gaullists either with or without the votes of the 100 or so Radicals, MRP and other non-Gaullist Deputies. Of the eight leaders of the Cartel, only two survived, MM. Mollet and Maurice Faure. M. Mollet and M. Moch were elected only at the second ballot, and then thanks to Communist support.

The 233 members (including affiliates) of the Gaullist parliamentary group were ensured a comfortable majority by an alliance, which lasted throughout the Parliament, with the 32 conservative *Républicains indépendants*, led by M. Giscard d'Estaing. Though unquestionably a junior partner, and very nearly powerless in the National Assembly, this party could not be dismissed as no longer counting in politics. Maurice Duverger's obituary for it – his prediction in the press of the disappearance of what M. Mollet had once called 'the most stupid Right in the world' – proved to be premature,[94] as local and senatorial elections were shortly to demonstrate. Conservatism does not die so easily in the French countryside. But it was for a time in a kind of parliamentary limbo.

For Gaullists, the victory was seen as an opportunity – an opportunity for the party to put down local roots, to strengthen its organization so that it no longer depended entirely for its cohesion on its loyalty to one man, who could not be expected to remain indefinitely at the head of the State. For General de Gaulle himself it was seen as an opportunity to provide France with the external and internal policies that he wanted, free from the obstacles that had been imposed by the Algerian problem and from other obstacles that would have been imposed if the election had been won by 'yesterday's parties'.

CHAPTER III

Consolidation

THE POLITICAL ATMOSPHERE OF THE SECOND PARLIAMENT

The first turning point of the régime ushered in a period of over four years, during which the prevailing characteristic was normality. In his New Year messages for both 1963 and the following year, General de Gaulle emphasized the fact that France was now at peace. 'Between 1 January and 31 December,' he said on 31 December 1963, 'we have not had to fire a single shot, which is something that has not happened for a quarter of a century.'[1] And looking back in *l'Effort* to the beginning of the new Parliament, he describes himself as having led the country through rough seas, but as then able, for the first time, to envisage the possibility of calmer weather ahead.[2]

These hopes were, generally speaking, realized, though the first months were certainly far from calm in Parliament, and March saw the longest and most serious strike that had occurred since the beginning of the régime. But, except for the accounts of trials of OAS leaders, the OAS was beginning to be forgotten and the quarrels about the Constitution had abated, for the nation had clearly approved of the President's view of how he should be elected and also, implicitly – at least in the Gaullist view – of his conception of the nature of his office. The Cuba crisis was over. And in the National Assembly, Gaullists and their conservative allies had two-thirds of the seats. Those *Républicains indépendants* who were not in the Government coalition had disappeared as a separate parliamentary group. The MRP, though constituting the majority of the heterogeneous group called the *Centre démocratique*, numbered only 40 – a sad decline from the 150 or more MRP Deputies during the early post-war years. By the end of the Parliament, they had disappeared as an organized movement. The Radicals constituted the majority (26) of the *Rassemblement démocratique*, numbering 35. The opposition was unable to endanger the life of the Government, and could hardly even harass or embarrass it. In foreign affairs, on which the President's attention was mainly focused, there was some restiveness on the majority side among the *Républicains indépendants*, but this was counterbalanced by the surprising degree of sympathy on the Left for some of the President's foreign-policy objectives.

The result was that, after the first six months or so, normality was fast degenerating into boredom, at least where internal affairs were concerned. The previous four years had seen only one change of Prime Minister, but four motions of censure initiated by Deputies, five tabled in response to Government demands for confidence on a Bill, and three votes of confidence on its programme or on a declaration of general policy. The second Parliament ran its full term – in itself an unprecedented occurrence – with no change of Prime Minister, only one vote of confidence on a declaration of general policy (in December 1962) and only two motions of censure (in 1964 and 1966), one mainly on the perennial problem of agriculture and the other on France's decision to withdraw from NATO. Even debates on the budget could no longer be counted on to arouse the customary parliamentary combativeness,[3] for one thing because, with the increase in *lois-programme*, more and more of it was made up of expenditure already agreed to in principle and, for another, because the Constitution and the Standing Orders ruled out so many of the traditional demagogic amendments dear to opposition parties.

If the National Assembly was bored, the Senate was ignored. The result of its president's active hostility to the President of the Republic – which had included an accusation, as regards the 1962 referendum, of unconstitutionality amounting to a political crime deserving of impeachment (*la forfaiture*)[4] – was that the Government sent the Senate to Coventry for the whole of the Parliament. It refused to be represented in debates in the Senate, except by junior Ministers, and, according to press reports, the president of the Senate was no longer *persona grata* at Elysée receptions.[5] It was not, indeed, until 1968, when the Senate elected a new president, that normal relations between the two Houses were restored.

A situation in which the parliamentary opposition is unable to harass the Government, though familiar to British MPs, was a relatively new situation for French Deputies. In Britain, such a situation is in general considered desirable, since it gives the Government a chance to demonstrate to the electorate the extent to which it intends to honour its electoral promises. It certainly does not detract from the interest of debates, since British Governments do not expect to be defeated on the floor of the House. During the first two years of the 1963–7 French Parliament, however, Deputies did not seem very interested in politics. Their main concern was the general problem of inflation and the state of the economy, and few specific issues really aroused parliamentary combativeness. One, the Government's reaction to the *Conseil d'Etat's* annulment of the ordinance creating the *Cour militaire de Justice*, did not interest the country in general as much as it did members of Parliament. The miners' strike in 1963, the problems of agricultural prices, especially the price of milk, and the problem of the administration of the State radio and television services, did arouse general interest. But from about the end of 1964 onwards, political parties were increasingly obsessed with the problems of electoral tactics, first in the local elections of 1965, then in the presidential election at the end of the year, and from then until the end of the parliamentary term in 1967, with tactics and strategies for the election in March of that year.

THE PROBLEM OF SPECIAL COURTS AND THE *CONSEIL D'ETAT*

The issues raised by the conflict concerning special courts were complicated, and involved a series of political actions and reactions. The conflict really began in 1962, when the *Haut Tribunal militaire*, set up in 1961 under the President's emergency powers under article 16, gave contradictory verdicts in the trials of two of the four Generals involved in the 1961 insurrection in Algeria. General Jouhaud, who had attracted some public sympathy because he was himself a *pied-noir*, was condemned to death, while General Salan, whose trial was about a month later, was spared the death penalty on the ground of extenuating circumstances. It was by no means clear to anybody outside the court what extenuating circumstances could apply to him that did not also apply to General Jouhaud. Indeed, General Salan was generally regarded as having been the real leader of the insurrection. General de Gaulle's response was to abolish the court within forty-eight hours. It was replaced by the *Cour militaire de Justice*, set up by ordinance on 1 June 1962, under the special powers accorded to the President by the law of 13 April 1962, voted by referendum. Just before the October referendum, the *Conseil d'Etat* annulled the ordinance as illegal, on the ground that its failure to provide for any appeal from its verdicts was 'contrary to the general principles of penal law'.[6] The President had already been exasperated by the Council's opinion that the referendum ought not to be used to revise the Constitution – an opinion, given (as required) in private, as part of the Council's general duty to advise the Government on legislation, but which had become generally known. The Government, however, was under no obligation to take any notice of the advice, and did not do so. The ruling on the *Cour militaire de Justice* incensed the President so much that, according to the account he gives in the Memoirs, he threatened to treat it as 'null and void'.[7]

In reality, his response was more complicated. The decision of the *Conseil d'Etat* was formally respected in that the *Cour militaire* was replaced by a permanent *Cour de Sûreté de l'Etat*, whose function was to try a certain number of offences against the State committed by civilians as well as by soldiers. The important points about this court were, first, that it was created by a law and, as such, could not be challenged in the *Conseil d'Etat*, and second, that it did provide for appeals. But the law that created it also contained a provision prolonging the life of the *Cour militaire de Justice*, and since this was done by law, it meant that what the *Conseil d'Etat* had declared illegal had been legalized, though only for the interim period until the new court began to function.

The result of the Government's action was the creation of a number of political problems. The first concerned the provisions of the new law relating to legal procedure and the protection of the rights of defendants. The parliamentary debates on the Bill revealed that the opposition parties disliked the provisions regarding the constitution of the new court. They would have preferred it to be composed of members of Parliament, as was the former High Court of the Fourth Republic, on the ground that crimes against the State ought to be tried by politicians and not by judges appointed by the executive.[8] Opposition parties also objected to the provisions in the Bill authorizing the holding of suspects for up to fifteen days without their being charged. M. Debré, they said, had considered in 1960 that a period of four days was adequate.[9]

The main political problem, however, was the prolongation of the life of the *Cour militaire*, which enabled the Government to bring before it nine of the OAS defendants charged with attempted assassination of the President. The defence hoped, by the use of various devices, to delay the proceedings until 25 February, when the new court – which would provide an appeal procedure – was to be constituted.[10] But these efforts were defeated by the introduction of a separate Government Bill to prolong the life of the *Cour militaire* until it had completed the cases before it. In the National Assembly, M. François Mitterrand – who, oddly in the circumstances, had been made *rapporteur* of the Parliamentary Commission on the Bill – objected on behalf of the opposition parties to the intervention of either executive or legislature in an affair that was actually *sub judice*, as well as to the absence of an appeal procedure in the case of the men being tried by the *Cour militaire*. He then promptly resigned from the Commission. A Centre Deputy, M. Paul Coste-Floret, tried to amend the Bill in order to provide for an appeal. The debate in the National Assembly degenerated into a general attack, in which the content of the law, the responsibilities of the President and the shortcomings of the régime were confusedly associated. It inevitably ended, therefore, with a final vote in favour of the Government's measures.[11] The practical result was that, when the self-confessed leader of the assassination attempt, Lieutenant-Colonel Jean-Marie Bastien-Thiry, was condemned to death by the court (along with two of his associates), he was not reprieved (though his associates were), but was shot, without appeal, on 11 March, the day before the new court tried its first case.

This controversy not only constituted a far from peaceful début for the new Parliament, but also left many Deputies with the feeling that justice was not being seen to be done. M. Mitterrand was expressing a general criticism by the opposition parties, and also echoing criticisms made earlier by liberal lawyers,[12] when he said in the debate in the National Assembly in January:

> *Le pouvoir a obtenu tout ce qu'il désirait. Il a sa Constitution, son gouvernement, sa majorité, son référendum, sa télévision, sa force de frappe. Il s'apprête à avoir son Sénat. Il a son Europe. Peut-être voudrait-il maintenant sa justice.*[13]

Some of the uneasiness created by these events can be explained as being part of the psychological aftermath of the Algerian war. The trial of Lieutenant-Colonel Bastien-Thiry itself, for instance, had turned into an argument for and against *Algérie française*. There was, in any case, never any doubt as to his guilt, and he was certainly regarded as deserving the death sentence. The objections to the procedure were matters of general principle and not, as in the case of General Jouhaud, of personal sympathy. The President's reactions were explicable, however, in terms of the irritation of a soldier who was certainly no jurist, and to whom the *Conseil d'Etat* had appeared to be both partisan and obstructive. He was reported as having insisted on the death penalty for Bastien-Thiry in order 'to make an example', a decision that was comprehensible in the light of the activities of the OAS (which made yet another attempt on his life in February 1963).[14]

In his Memoirs, the President explains why he had regarded the *Conseil d'Etat*'s conduct as obstructive and partisan, and had, therefore, decided that it ought to be reformed. He had had four main grounds of complaint. The first two were comprehensible, and to some extent justified. In the matter of the referendum, he thought, as has been said, that the Council was exceeding its powers in considering the constitutionality of the Bill, instead of restricting its advice to questions of legality or advisability. He had also objected to the leakage of its opinion, which ought not to have been made public.[15] On both these points, he was, in strict theory, in the right, though it should be said that the Council had often previously expressed its opinion on questions of constitutionality (and was, indeed, under the Constitution of the Fifth Republic, expressly entrusted with decisions of constitutionality in certain circumstances). Nor was it by any means uncommon for its views to become known, as were at times the Constitutional Council's opinions, also in theory expressed privately.

He was on more shaky ground on the third point – in objecting to the Council's ruling with regard to the legality of the *Cour militaire de Justice*. It was perfectly true, as he maintained, that, in times of war and special danger, special courts existed to act rapidly. It was true that the *Haut Tribunal militaire*, which was such a court, had had no procedure providing for appeal either.[16] But he apparently failed to take account of the fact that the *Haut Tribunal* was outside the jurisdiction of the *Conseil d'Etat*, because it had been set up by a *décision* under article 16 and so had the status of law, whereas the *Cour militaire* was set up under a law conferring special powers. These are legislative powers granted to the executive normally only for a specific period or for specific purposes laid down in the enabling Act. Unless ordinances made with the authority of special powers are ratified by Parliament (thus acquiring the full status of law), they are regarded, when the specified period is over or the conditions in which they are granted cease to exist, as executive acts, and, as such, come within the jurisdiction of the *Conseil d'Etat* like other executive acts.[17] In the case of the Act under which the *Cour militaire* was set up, no time limit was mentioned and the conditions laid down were somewhat vaguely formulated. The *Conseil* had held, however, that it had jurisdiction, and that, in its view, the conditions no longer justified the use of special powers depriving citizens of normal legal and constitutional rights. These rights, described as being required by 'the general principles of law', included the right of appeal.[18]

In the view of those who opposed the President – and they included a number of liberal-minded lawyers as well as politicians – the *Conseil*'s ruling, though admittedly an interpretation of the terms of the Act, based on principles evolved as part of its case law and not stated in any law or constitutional enactment, was, nevertheless, the view of the supreme administrative court, whose function was to guarantee respect by the executive for the fundamental rights of citizens. The President, however, was looking at the problem as a statesman and a soldier, whose first duty was to maintain the authority of the State. He had been faced with two insurrections within a period of fifteen months, and could not be certain at that time that the second had yet been brought finally under control. Nor, indeed, was the electorate certain that he had yet entirely succeeded, as the results of the election had clearly revealed. This fourth objection was, therefore, essentially a conflict between the claims of normal law and those of politics in a national emergency.

Looked at as a political problem, the conflict of views and priorities was almost a classic example of what the General himself had sometimes complained of, namely, the Right's inability to understand the people and the Left's inability to understand the State. Just as he failed throughout his political life to appreciate the importance of political parties in Republican politics, so he also failed to realize the depth of Republican feelings about the need (except in moments of grave crisis) to prevent executive interference with the judiciary. When, in *l'Effort*, he belittled the authority of the *Conseil d'Etat* as 'a body made up of officials holding office by Government decree and not by election',[19] and dismissed its insistence on the right of appeal to the *Cour de Cassation* on the ground that the powers that it regarded as illegal had been granted to him by 'the sovereign people',[20] he was belittling what, to the majority of Frenchmen, was the chief virtue of the *Conseil d'Etat*, namely, its *de facto* rigorous independence of the Government.

The Government decided, as a result of these two conflicts, to set up a committee to consider the need to reform the *Conseil d'Etat*. In the circumstances, this step was generally regarded as heralding a further conflict, and possibly also measures to make the *Conseil* more dependent on the State. In the event, this did not happen. When the reforms were made, following the report of the committee in May 1963, they proved to be essentially moderate and concerned with the improvement of the internal organization and working of its administrative and judicial sections.[21]

ECONOMIC AND SOCIAL PROBLEMS

The controversy over the *Cour de Sûreté de l'Etat* died down very quickly, partly because it had an element of unreality about it, partly because the focus of political interest shifted almost immediately to the social and economic fields, and remained there until, with the approach of the presidential election, and then the general election, interest became centred almost exclusively on electoral tactics. The optimism engendered by official statements at the opening of the second Parliament received a considerable shock when a miners' strike that began on 1 March 1963 as a 48-hour strike spread rapidly to involve almost all coal mines and, later in the month, workers in iron mines and the State-run railways and electricity industry as well. The movement was primarily an expression of discontent regarding the persistent and widening gap between levels of wages in the private and public sectors of the economy.

The situation in the mines, where a wage settlement had seemed about to be reached, was exacerbated by Government reactions that created a degree of tension not seen since the miners' strike of 1948. It was clearly a political error, as was, indeed, later admitted by the Prime Minister,[22] to use the Government's legal power to requisition miners. For this was immediately interpreted by opponents as a denial of the constitutional right to strike. It was also a tactical error, since it was impossible to enforce the order in face of the refusal of miners to obey it. By 6 March, almost all coalfields were immobilized and there were token strikes in sympathy with the miners by gas and electricity workers and by Paris transport workers.

In his television broadcast on 8 March, the Prime Minister made a further tactical error by insisting on a return to work before any opening of negotiations. The response was a 'symbolic' march on Paris by miners on 13 March. The Council of Ministers then announced the setting up of a committee under the chairmanship of the Commissioner for the National Plan, M. Pierre Massé, to report on wages in the private and public sectors.[23] What the miners were interested in was not reports, but immediate decisions. M. Massé's *comité des sages* reported very promptly on 23 March that, between 1958 and 1963, the gap between wages in the nationalized and private sectors had actually increased by 8 per cent where the miners were concerned, by 4 per cent to 5 per cent in the case of railway workers and by 3·1 per cent to 3·6 per cent in that of electricity workers. By this time, however, the strike had already caused considerable dislocation and the miners themselves were beginning to tire of it, and so, after complicated and difficult negotiations, a settlement was finally reached at the beginning of April. The Government was obliged to pay more than it had hoped and was now faced with increased pressures from other nationalized industries. The miners agreed, however, to payments spread over about a year, on promise of a general review the following September.

As was to be expected, therefore, the autumn saw a revival of strikes in the public sector in support of wage demands. The Government set up two committees – the Toutée Committee to study ways of improving the procedures of wage negotiations in the public sector in general, and a conference under the chairmanship of M. Massé, including representatives of

Government, employers and trade unions, to look into the possibilities of an incomes policy.

Another consequence of the miners' strike and of the numerous strikes in the early months of 1963 was the vote on 24 July of a Bill to regulate the right to strike in the public services. This was not intended to curb the constitutional right to strike, but to limit the kind of strike that had become the rule in the public services, and especially in transport – token 'lightning' and 'rolling' strikes, short enough to avoid depriving workers of their wages, but creating an amount of dislocation, and consequently of public irritation, out of all proportion to their importance. To quote only one example, between January and June 1963, such strikes had brought the Paris transport system to a halt, for shorter or longer periods, on 54 days.

The need for measures to regulate the exercise of the right to strike had been under discussion since 1946, for the Constitution of that year had, in its Preamble, proclaimed the right to strike 'within the framework of the laws regulating it', and the 1958 Constitution had accepted this formula. Though laws had been voted to regulate the right to strike of specific categories of the civil service, no general legislation existed, with the result that there was considerable uncertainty regarding the limits within which strikes were or were not legal. The 1963 Act did not completely clear up the difficulties, since it dealt only with strikes in the public sector, but it was, after all, in this sector that most of the strikes had so far occurred, and in which specific categories of employees were subject to restrictions on their right to strike.[24] The law provided for an obligatory notice of five days before a strike in the public sector, prohibited 'lightning' and 'rolling' strikes, and made strikes lasting for periods of over two hours incur the loss of a whole day's pay. It did not make negotiation compulsory.

The Bill had a stormy passage in the National Assembly and was defeated in the Senate. Trade unions objected to it and the main confederations, the Communist-dominated CGT and the CFDT, called a short protest strike on 17 July. But the unions were in a weak position vis-à-vis the public, which had been irritated by the numerous irresponsible transport strikes.[25] The Government itself was also in a somewhat weak position vis-à-vis the workers, following the miners' strike, which had not only demonstrated the powerlessness of regulations in face of determined solidarity by large numbers of trade unionists, but had also revealed widespread public sympathy with the miners. There was, consequently, no desire on either side for a general confrontation.

In any case, by then, troubles in the public sector were only one of a series of graver economic problems. All was not well in the private sector either. French retail prices had risen during the previous four years twice as fast as British and German prices and three times as fast as those of Belgium. The advantage of the 1958 devaluation had disappeared and new brakes were needed. France's growth rate was slower than that of her European partners and her industrial investment, already inadequate, was increasing at a slower rate than theirs. The pockets of unemployment that were to be a continuing problem were beginning to appear.[26] Following a visit to France in June 1963, a group of British investment managers had reported that, in spite of the tremendous achievements of French planning, 'grave financial, economic and social problems' faced the country, owing to 'the revival of inflationary pressures, the poor organization of the capital market, the steep rise in public expenditure, and the great backlog in housing'.[27]

The immediate problem was still in the public sector. The tranquil peace and progress predicted by General de Gaulle had not occurred. Instead, in the first six months of 1963 alone, five million days' work had been lost through strikes, most of which had been in the public sector. The Government, therefore, took a number of steps to remedy what the Minister of Finance called the 'psychological deterioration' caused by fears of runaway inflation. By July 1963, for instance, retail prices, already more than 5 per cent above those of the previous July, had shown the largest annual increase since the 1958 devaluation.[28] The measures taken included some increases in wages and family allowances for the lower paid, a lowering of customs duties on some industrial goods, together with credit controls, some increases in taxation, and some limited price increases – especially in food and tobacco.

The most important measures, introduced on 12 September 1963 and applied in stages over the following months, were those of the 'stabilization plan', whose effects lasted up to 1965. It was said to have been drawn up by senior officials in response to a specific demand by General de Gaulle, who wanted it within a fortnight, because he was tired of seeing prices perpetually going up. 'Rain or shine', he was reported to have said, 'hot weather or cold, good harvests or bad, prices always go up.'[29] The plan was intended to check the rate of price increases without checking expansion too much. But since there was no agreement among experts as to the real causes of the persistent inflation, there was no real certainty as to how it could be cured. The OECD believed that the disease was cost inflation, though it conceded that there were also important psychological elements. Too long familiarity with inflation had bred in the French public, not the fear of it that had haunted the Germans since 1921–3, but inertia and acceptance. Living with inflation meant that retailers automatically charged higher prices and customers automatically paid them, secure in the knowledge that they could maintain their standard of living by automatically demanding higher earnings.[30] The Government shared the OECD's belief in the need for a psychological shock, but regarded the essential cause of the inflation as being increased consumption, and produced some impressive figures in support of that view. Internal spending had certainly been increasing fast. There was more hire purchase,[31] there were many more supermarkets, the influx of Algerians had greatly increased consumer demand, as had increases in wages and social-security payments.[32] Government spending was higher, owing to subsidies to nationalized industries and farmers, to the development of roads, schools and housing, and to the increasing cost of the nuclear programme.

The stabilization plan was consequently directed mainly toward cutting expenditure. In spite of the publicity surrounding the announcements of the first measures – with the intention of producing the required psychological shock – these were in themselves both modest and conventional and were criticized as being 'much ado about nothing', or alternatively as being an 'ado' concerned more with politics than with economics. 'What it is all really about', wrote one commentator, 'is not the profound transformation of the economy, but de Gaulle's position in France and his policies in the world.'[33] They included some classic budgetary economies, the imposition of a number of fixed prices (some being reduced, and some import duties on highly priced goods being temporarily reduced), the taxation of capital gains from the sale of building land (which had been called for for some years), larger down payments on the hire purchase of television sets and cars, and the issue of a new State loan (which had, in fact, already been authorized by Parliament when the plan was announced). It was essentially a price freeze and a credit squeeze and it encountered the classic French criticism of palliatives, that of being 'a cautery on a wooden leg'.

In the OECD view, what had been needed was a pay pause in order to cut the costs that were reducing the competitiveness of France's best sellers in the export market – cars, lorries, machine tools and steel. On the other hand, it was estimated in some circles in France that if nothing were done before the autumn to raise some wages in the public sector, there might well, by then, be a gap of up to 6 per cent between the levels of wages in the private and in the public sectors.[34] The Government was obviously in difficulties over the wage situation, anxious above all not to spark off more strikes on behalf of wage claims, yet unable to obtain from French workers any more support for M. Massé's proposals for an incomes policy than was forthcoming a little later from British workers for the British Labour Government's attempts to introduce an incomes policy.

The reports of both the Toutée Commission and the Massé Conference were cautious.[35] The former limited itself in the main to suggestions for improving negotiating machinery, especially through established methods of wage-fixing. These were to be discussed by management and workers within individual firms and then submitted for the views of a sub-committee of the National Plan to ensure their conformity with its objectives. Its most positive proposal was for con-tractual agreements (*contrats de progrès*), under which workers would undertake not to strike for the duration of the contract, except in cases of extreme gravity, when all possibilities of conciliation had been exhausted. M. Massé's report stressed the voluntary and long-term character of an incomes policy. He had denied from the start any intention of proposing a detailed plan for the permanent regulation of wages and the ironing out of wage disparities, emphasizing his aim to make possible 'a freely agreed incomes policy'.

The reactions of the trade unions were predictable. They objected to the Toutée plan's proposal for the intervention of a sub-committee of the Plan in wage negotiations, and to the inclusion in the proposed *contrats de progrès* of any limitation of the right to strike. They were suspicious of M. Massé's pro-posals, on the ground that they involved too much co-opera-tion with Government organs and were likely to prove in practice a device for blocking wages. The CGT, for instance, regarded an incomes policy as being 'a threat to the rights and liberties of the workers', while the Socialistic confederation, *Force ouvrière* (FO), reaffirmed its attachment to 'the freedom of collective negotiations and agreements in all sectors'.[36]

In spite of the criticisms and setbacks, both 1964 and 1965 saw some improvement in the economic situation. By August 1964, however, wages in the private sector were creeping up again and increases were estimated to amount to between 7 per cent and 8 per cent for the whole year. The gap between the public and private sectors was actually increasing. By the end of the year, the Government was facing two additional prob-lems. The first was renewed agricultural discontent. A bumper harvest in 1963 had led to the by now familiar riots, especially in Brittany and the Rhône valley and among the wine growers of the South. A milk surplus the following year led to a pro-longed dispute over milk prices and a stoppage of milk deliveries from farms in mid-September that lasted for a month. The Government's slowness in implementing the long-term measures providing for farm modernization was also still an irritant. Agriculture was, therefore, the subject of the first motion of censure tabled by Deputies in the new Parliament.[37] The Government was, as usual, obliged to concede higher prices than were justifiable on economic grounds, with the result that its own plans for rationalization and modernization were held back and its economic position as an agricultural exporter weakened.[38]

The second problem was the rise in unemployment and the consequent increase in trade-union pressure for reduced hours of work. The car industry was already complaining of short time, owing to the falling-off of demand.[39] At the end of 1963, the Minister of Finance had stated optimistically that inflation was on the wane and the economy on the move, and had predicted that the following year would be one of 'expansion without inflation'.[40] The initial increase in production had been due, in fact, more to good harvests and to expansion in the building trade than to the provisions of the stabilization plan. The plan had succeeded to the extent of cutting the rise in the cost of living by half and bringing French prices below the level of German, British, Italian and Dutch prices. But this achievement seemed bound to be temporary, since it had been brought about almost wholly by Government price-fixing and restrictive measures, and it could be assumed that, once these restrictions were lifted, the upward movement would be resumed.

The signs of a new spiral were, in fact, provided by announcements at the beginning of 1965 of increased prices in the public sector – 5 per cent on railway fares, 20 per cent on postage, 8 per cent on telephone rates, together with increases in the cost of industrial electricity – all of which were bound to increase industrial costs. It was clear by the end of 1964 that the stabilization plan had failed to touch the deep-seated economic problems. While there was a permanent shortage of skilled labour, employers could not afford to lose labour to their competitors and so conceded wage demands, thus perpetuating the discontent caused by the wage-gap between the public and private sectors. Chronic under-investment meant that the growing number of young people due to come on to the labour market in the following years would not be absorbed.

Though the Minister of Finance remained obstinately optimistic, affirming in March 1965 that the likelihood of a recession could now be categorically rejected, his view was shared neither by press commentators nor by numbers of professional economists and prominent politicians.[41] The Government's policy was nevertheless merely to prolong the stabilization plan by a fresh series of price blockings and selective price rises in the public services in order to restrict spending.

POSITIVE ECONOMIC POLICIES (i) THE PLAN

There were more optimistic forecasts, based on longer-term Government policies, and especially on the provisions of the Fifth Plan (for the years 1966 to 1970), which, by 1964, was in active preparation. To estimate how much importance to give to these, it is necessary to take into account the real significance of the Plan in French economic life, what it seeks to do, what it does do, and what it can and cannot do. It goes back to 1946, when its creator, Jean Monnet, regarded France as facing the stark choice between modernization and decadence, and it provided a framework within which the painful but imperative process of transition to a twentieth-century economy could be combined with essential post-war reconstruction. It has been described as

> at one and the same time a vast study and a series of future options, an analysis of a known situation and a formulation of actions recommended in order to move from one stage to another; '. . . a kind of charter between the private and public sectors, and within the latter, between the Government organs themselves.[42]

It is thus both a pioneering and a subordinate organization. It is subordinate because it works within the existing framework of Government economic policy and the general provisions for its application, beginning with the budget. It is pioneering in that, within that framework, it seeks to find the most practical and efficient methods of co-ordinating and harmonizing the actions of different sectors of the economy and of building up permanent procedures by which co-operation and efficiency can be maximized. It can work equally well under a progressive or a conservative régime. It is an instrument at the service of the State, which seeks to influence, to mould conditions to its purposes, but not to dictate. It also seeks to adapt its own action to the realities imposed by conditions, whether political or economic. It is in some senses a negative organization. As Stephen Cohen points out in his study of the place of the Plan in the French system,

> The Planning Commission by itself exercises no direct powers over the economy. None of the targets and programmes of the Plan is enforceable by law. Business (including the nationalised industries) is under no legal obligation to follow any of the Plan's programmes. Nor does the Planning Commission have any direct authority within the state bureaucracy over the administration of the whole range of state economic activities. The coercive implementation methods of planning are all under the control of the various ministries (mostly the Ministry of Finance).[43]

French planning machinery, then, is neither 'capitalist' nor 'Socialist', but an instrument of the Government, whatever its political complexion may be. It is thus, comprehensibly, accepted by all parties in France, and (with some exceptions) by trade unions, which have come to accept the advantages of working with it. The nature of the Plan has, however, changed a good deal over the years. The first two Plans (1947–52 and 1952–7) were essentially short-term and limited in their approach. The first concentrated on the reconstruction and modernization of France's six basic industries, the second on economic modernization in more general terms, including the beginning of the long task of modernizing French agriculture. The third (1958–61) was concerned mainly with problems of the balance of payments and the need to increase productivity in order to enable France to stand up to competition in the Common Market. All these had specific targets. It was only with the fourth (1962–5) that there was any real attempt to look at the economic system as a whole and to try to forecast its evolution.

The extent to which the Plans have influenced the course of economic development can, therefore, be exaggerated. A number of factors helped to make them useful in the special circumstances of the early post-war years. Their provision for regular co-operation between civil servants, industrial executives, employers, and trade-union representatives strengthened the Government's authority in the considerable nationalized sector and its influence in the private sector. The latter relied heavily on the Government for subsidies, investment and the forecasting for which firms themselves lacked the resources, and so co-operation with the organizations of the Plan helped to reduce economic uncertainty. This co-operation was assisted by a number of other factors. High civil servants and business executives in France have far more in common than they normally have in Britain. Education gives them similar intellectual backgrounds and they often have closer social interrelations. There is throughout the economic system much more reliance and dependence on the State than there normally is in Anglo-Saxon countries. French employers have been more conservative and less ready to accept the organized contacts that have for a long time existed in Britain between management and trade unions. Trade unions have welcomed such contacts less than British trade unions, partly for political and doctrinal reasons, partly because they have been weaker and more divided than British unions, and so both sides have been readier to accept contacts within organizations in which the State played an essential and dominating rôle.

It was within this framework that, under the Gaullist régime, the fourth and fifth Plans broke new ground, by focusing on the economic system as a whole and seeking to obtain planned growth and long-term stability of the economy. To obtain even partial success was a difficult process, in which the Ministry of Finance inevitably played a dominating rôle, for it required judicious combinations of sticks and carrots. Even with the help of these, the Government found it difficult to bring influence to bear effectively on France's far too numerous small farmers, retailers and manufacturers, who were able to resist successfully many drastic changes that were economically imperative, but politically vote-losing. The political difficulties of parliamentary control were obvious in these circumstances. The earlier Plans had not been submitted to Parliament at all. The fourth and fifth Plans were submitted to Parliament but, since virtually no control was exercised over them, the only result was the generation of parliamentary discontent.

The main priorities of the fourth Plan were growth (a target figure of 24 per cent in four years, estimated to provide a 23 per cent increase in consumption), full employment, involving the creation of some quarter of a million new jobs per year, a favourable balance of payments and an increase in the standard of living of the lower-paid sections of the community, especially in the rural areas and the industrially backward regions. As has been said, not all of these targets were reached and the considerable progress that was made was accompanied by distortions – too much consumer spending, lagging investment, a continued upward movement of prices, and difficulties about the balance of payments.

The fifth Plan (1966–70), which was in preparation from 1964 onwards, presented a number of innovations, some of which were intended to prevent such distortions, as well as to meet criticisms of previous achievements. It was for five instead of four years. In response to the demands on the Left for 'democratization', it was submitted to Parliament and voted on in general outline (*les grandes options*) before being drafted in detail.[44] It took account, too, of the new decrees on regionalism which, after five years of discussion and consultation, began to be applied from 1964 onwards.[45] The 21 economic regions were, therefore, consulted before the Plan was drawn up. It attempted to look ahead and to forestall future difficulties in an increasingly complex economic situation. It was hoped that it could do this by devising a series of indications of approaching trouble – warning signals (*des clignotants*) –

based on such factors as the evolution of prices, production, investment and unemployment. Such indicative information was to be published regularly. It was also hoped to devise methods of looking farther ahead than the period of application of the existing Plan and, on the basis of sophisticated mathematical and statistical data, to try to estimate how influence could be brought to bear on discoverable future trends.

These were admittedly experimental and ambitious objectives – perhaps too ambitious given existing French techniques. The main concerns within the period of application of the Plan remained, however, foreign trade, internal efficiency and a growth target that would make expansion possible without threatening stability. More emphasis was placed on the need to increase the self-financing of industry, and to use public investment in order to catch up the by now only too apparent backlog in the social field – the inadequacies of roads, housing, hospitals, universities and schools. It was clear that the objectives would be difficult to attain and that the trade unions would continue to oppose anything that looked like an incomes policy. They were interested in immediate benefits rather than in future prosperity and were, therefore, in favour, not of holding back consumption, but of increasing it by tying the minimum wage level to the cost of living and reducing unemployment by earlier retirement and shorter working hours, all of which were bound to have inflationary effects. They did not believe in M. Massé's *clignotants*, nor in his suggestions for establishing broadly agreed categories or 'norms' of 'appropriate' wage levels and calling attention to cases where such norms were being seriously infringed. Such procedures were, in their view, merely camouflage for a policy of keeping wages down. Of the Plan's social options, only one was acceptable to them, namely, the generalization of the four-week paid holiday (introduced in the State-run Renault concern at the end of 1962).

The Plan, therefore, came in for criticism both in the Economic and Social Council and in parliamentary debates. The impossibility of preventing the politicization of the debate (particularly in a pre-election year) was revealed by the tone of opposition speeches in the National Assembly, and especially by that of the main Socialist spokesman, M. Gaston Defferre, who was then trying to become the presidential candidate of a united Left. He criticized the Government's economic policy, expressed fears of American economic colonization, complained of inadequate housing, schools and hospitals, of increased prices in the public services, and condemned excessive expenditure on defence. 'Houses, schools and hospitals in Moscow', he said, 'have little to fear from our striking force. Its first victims are the houses, schools and hospitals of our French towns.'[46] The opposition parties tried to obtain an amendment obliging the Government to increase the guaranteed minimum wage and to undertake to provide over half a million houses in 1970. The Senate rejected the Plan outright. The result was merely that, thanks to the 'package-deal' procedure, the National Assembly voted the Government's version of the Plan (overriding the Senate) and it was applied exactly as it would have been without a debate. So much for 'democratization' in practice.[47]

POSITIVE ECONOMIC POLICIES (ii) REGIONALISM

Something that could more justifiably be regarded as economic democratization was hoped for, and not only by opposition parties, from the regionalization plan introduced in 1964, and regarded by the Government as an integral part of Gaullist planning. The idea itself was far from new. Indeed, administrative reform involving a greater or lesser degree of decentralization had been a panacea put forward by most political parties under the Third and Fourth Republics.[48] What had been lacking was not believers in the need for reform, but unity among the reformers on how far to go and on what was to happen to the key figure in French local government, the Government-appointed Prefect. Was what was needed '*déconcentration*' – that is a slight loosening of the tentacular grip of Paris – or decentralization, that is, something nearer to either real local government or regional devolution? Was the Prefect to disappear, to be demoted, or to continue to be the key figure in a regionalized France? On this point at least, there has been *de facto* unanimity, in the sense that whatever policies parties may have advocated in opposition, no party in power has ever been prepared to relinquish any of the political power that it derives from the Ministry of the Interior's control of local authorities through the Prefect.

The result was that all earlier attempts at regionalism had ended in failure. The Vichy Government had created regions and the early post-war Governments of liberated France had appointed regional Commissioners. There had been suggestions that the President of the General Council of the *département* might eventually displace the Prefect. But by 1948, the only remaining element of regionalism was the *Igame* (*Inspecteur général de l'Administration en Mission extraordinaire*). The nine *Igames*, or super-Prefects, were not, however, in any sense regional Prefects. Their job was mainly to organize co-operation between *départements* in order to deal with certain emergencies, and to co-ordinate police and defence forces within the region.[49] By the end of the Fourth Republic, there were still nearly 38,000 *communes* (about as many as those of the other five members of the European Community put together), of which over 16,000 had under 300 inhabitants.[50] The *département*, whose boundaries still reflected the 1790 requirement that they should not be more than a day's journey on horseback from the chief town, remained intact. The Prefect remained the pivot of French administration. If nineteenth-century French administration suffered from apoplexy at the centre and anaemia at the extremities, the centralized France of the mid-twentieth century suffered rather from paralysis of the extremities, while the centre was threatened less by apoplexy than by strangulation in an incoherent network of regions, all of which remained under the firm control of Paris. In his *Droit administratif*, Marcel Waline gives the following picture of it in 1959:

. . . metropolitan France is divided into 17 police regions. . . . 16 *Académies*, nine military regions, four air regions, 23 headquarters of Legions of the *Gendarmerie* and nine CRS areas (decree of 26 March 1948), 10 radio areas, 18 postal regions, 18 postal-cheque centres, 16 regional social-insurance areas, 14 divisions of Inspectors of Labour, 34 of Inspectors of roads and bridges, 14 mineralogical divisions, 11 agricultural regions, 17 divisions of inspectors dealing with frauds, 41 areas for water and forest conservation, 71 for rural civil engineering, 16 health areas, 10 regional areas for inspection of weights and measures, another 10 for supervision of trade marks, 21 economic regions, etc. . . . .

These, and many others, for the list was stated to be incomplete, constituted, he says:

all kinds of different divisions, overlapping and cutting across each other in the most irrational way.[51]

It was the 21 economic regions with which M. Waline concludes his list that were to form the basis for the Gaullist regional reform. The régime had important assets that helped to make its own attempts at regionalism – at least initially – more successful than earlier attempts. Governments were stable, the challenge of the European Community created pressures in favour of economic efficiency, and public opinion was favourable to the idea of economic regions. The difficulties that arose were, nevertheless, those that had always existed, namely that the Government did not want to go far enough to satisfy those who really believed in regionalism, and that there were divisions in political parties and the country regarding what ought to be the institutions and functions of regional organizations. The idea of regions in which a number of *départements* would be grouped for the purpose of furthering economic development was a long-standing Gaullist plan, and preparations for the reform had begun as far back as 1959.[52] Gaullist regionalism aimed at greater administrative efficiency and simplicity as well as at economic expansion, and to begin with, at a reduction of the numerous chaotic existing administrative regions, with their increasing numbers of complicated and overlapping areas.[53] It was also essential in order to prevent the growing tendency of France to become divided into areas of economic expansion on the one hand (Paris, Lorraine, Rhône-Alpes, Provence, Haute-Normandie), and on the other, declining areas (Brittany, Limousin, Aquitaine, Midi-Pyrénées, Loire), in which, according to an INSEE report of 1958, income *per capita* was only half of that in the Paris region. Under the Gaullist regional plan, therefore, regional economic development was henceforth to be carried out within the framework of the National Plan, investment being allocated with a view to meeting the special needs of different regions.

The regional institutions set up between 1964 and 1968 in the twenty economic regions of France (the twenty-first, Paris, has a somewhat different system)[54] included a regional Prefect, himself a Prefect of one of the constituent *départements* of the region, and two organs to assist him, in addition to a personal 'brains trust' of economic advisers. The first, the Regional Administrative Conference, included Prefects within the region and the *trésoriers payeurs-généraux* representing the Ministry of Finance. The second, which aroused more interest and also more controversy, was the Regional Economic Development Commission (*Commission de développement économique régionale*, or CODER) which was predominantly a representative body. As part of the Government's avowed intention to bring citizens and administration into closer contact, and so to avoid bureaucracy or technocracy, a quarter of its members were elected representatives of local authorities, chosen by the General Councils of the *départements*, a half were chosen by social and occupational bodies within the region, including employers' and trade-union organizations, and the remaining quarter were appointed by the Prime Minister, after consultation, to represent special interests, such as town planning, family associations, and so on.[55] It was emphasized from the first that these two organs would both be advisory, that they would be concerned with economic matters only, and were not intended to be, or lead to, the creation of new local government areas. The Government's aim was to keep politics out of them, but predictably it failed to do this.

Summarized very briefly, the new structure had three main

aims. The first was to co-ordinate administration on the level of the *département* and restore the authority of the Prefect by making him the focal point – the centre through which all communications between local representatives of Ministries passed, and to whom all officials in the *département* were responsible. It was thus hoped to put an end to the frequent bypassing of the Prefect by decisions reached between Ministers in Paris and their representatives in the provinces.[56] The second was to make the regional Prefect the co-ordinator and initiator of policy for the group of *départements* making up the region. His function, with the help of his expert advisers, was to follow through the regional application of the current National Plan, and especially to establish priorities for public investment within the region. The third was to increase contacts between administrators and administered through regular consultation of the CODER on the regional aspects of the Plan.

These reforms were intended by the Government to lead both to better organization and greater efficiency and to the acquisition by the region of some limited responsibilities in fields hitherto controlled directly by Paris, responsibilities which, it was hoped, would help to overcome local inertia, apathy and the irritation caused by administrative red tape and delays, and by the constant need to refer even very minor matters to Paris for decision.[57] They met with criticisms on both administrative and political grounds. Since it took some years to set up the new regional organizations, the political criticisms – and it is, of course, with these that this book is primarily concerned[58] – became really important only in 1968 and 1969, when the Government undertook a prolonged consultation of opinion in the *départements*, prior to the submission to a referendum of a slightly amended version of the 1964 decrees. They are therefore discussed in the following chapter. But it was already clear during the first years, both that the CODERs themselves were not content with their purely advisory functions and that their desire for elected regional assemblies was shared by considerable sections of public opinion, mainly on the Left.[59] In the Senate debate on the reforms in June 1964, fears were already being expressed that the Government would not merely refuse to make concessions on these points, but, by increasing the powers of the Prefect, would actually reduce the importance of the General Councils.[60] In 1965, for instance, it was necessary for General de Gaulle, during his provincial tours, to reassure local representatives that the *département* would not be abolished or its boundaries altered.

There were also criticisms by the CODERs of the conditions in which they were called on to work. They had no real secretariat and no budget of their own. They could not, therefore, study their dossiers seriously. The Prefect, who had his own team of official and expert advisers, did not necessarily feel in need of their advice and it was all too often ignored. There were, too, mainly in progressive circles and especially among some of the political Clubs, more fundamental grounds for dissatisfaction. Critics wanted regionalism to be something more than what one of the Clubs described as 'merely *déconcentration*', no more than a delegation of Government powers to the Prefect.[61] The Club Jean Moulin, for instance, regarded decentralization – that is, real decentralization – as a cure for something more than inefficient and bureaucratic administration. Its members hoped that it would

> reawaken initiatives, free energies, and so transform a passive France, discontented with herself and with others, perpetually waiting for decisions (generally objectionable) from an anonymous central authority, into a dynamic France made up of *communes* and regions running their own affairs and at last daring to act for themselves.[62]

For anything like this to happen, much more radical changes in the structure of local government would have been needed. The Club Jean Moulin was not alone in pointing out the inadequacies of the existing plan, in particular the refusal to touch the traditional boundaries, not merely of *départements*, but also of *communes*. Its members believed that the reform was bound to go the way of earlier ones, unless it involved a reduction of the number of *communes* from the existing 37,000–

38,000 to something like 2000, and a reduction of the number of regions to eight or ten, with boundaries that would have some economic justification instead of being merely an arbitrary juxtaposition of a variable number of *départements*, often incapable of forming real economic units.[63]

Criticisms by the orthodox parties were less ambitious, partly because they were well aware of the strength of the political opposition that any such radical proposals for reform of local boundaries would encounter. Neither the Government nor the main opposition parties would have contemplated any real regional autonomy, and the Government had certainly no intention of granting more than a token financial autonomy – described by some critics as 'pocket money'.[64] The main criticisms were, therefore, directed to the composition and functions of the CODER and to the desirability of some degree of directly elected representation, which it was clear from the first that the Government would be unwilling to agree to.[65] Prefects and local representatives of Ministries were cool about the whole reform and, in consequence, passively sabotaged it. It was difficult not to feel that it would eventually go the way of earlier regional reforms, particularly in the light of views expressed by Gaullist Ministers during the presidency of M. Pompidou.

POSITIVE ECONOMIC POLICIES (iii) PARTICIPATION

There were some faint evocations of the idea of 'participation' in the often reiterated governmental idea that regionalization could bring administration and citizens into closer contact, but it was difficult to regard these as more than vague and pious hopes. The Gaullist conception of participation had always been concerned mainly with industrial relations. It was in this field that the first Gaullist plans in the late 1940s and early 1950s for what the Gaullist movement then called *l'association capital-travail* were put forward,[66] and it was in this field that the idea was revived, first in 1959 and then from 1966 onwards, when it gave rise to far more acrimonious discussion than did the regionalist policies. For whereas the idea of regionalism was generally popular, that of economic participation was not. Moreover, Gaullists themselves were not agreed in the 1960s and 1970s on how the idea ought to be put into practice.

General de Gaulle sometimes seemed to imply that participation was a Gaullist invention, whereas, in reality, it goes back to the nineteenth century, and Bills providing for some workers' participation had actually been introduced and discussed before the first world war.[67] The first Gaullist plan (in 1950) was, of course, never applied and the ordinance of 7 January 1959 was no more than a modest pioneer scheme for voluntary agreements within firms to distribute a certain number of shares to the workers. Even so it met with a chorus of objections from trade unions, who saw the whole idea as an attempt by managements to deprive the workers of wage increases that they were entitled to, or else as a means of 'weakening the impact of the class war'.[68] It met with timid approval from some employers who hoped that it might indeed have this effect.[69]

Supervision of the working of the agreements under the 1959 Plan was entrusted to Works Committees where these existed or to special committees, and the managements were required to communicate to the committee documents specified in the agreement as being necessary. Personnel were to receive this information with a view to 'favouring the development of a climate of association within the firm'.[70] The scheme proved to be not very much of an ado about nearly nothing, for the number of workers involved and the extent of their participation were both negligible.

As revived in 1966 and 1967, participation was intended to be more ambitious. It was introduced in principle indirectly, by the addition of an amendment to the budget proposals for 1965, henceforth known as the *amendement Vallon*, but which became article 33 of the finance law of 12 July 1965. It provided for a compulsory scheme of participation, and for the tabling of a Bill by the Government by May 1966. Its terms were, however, extremely vague,[71] and so the Government appointed a Commission (the Mathey Commission) to make proposals for applying the provisions of the amendment. The Mathey Commission, however, reported that neither the time nor the method proposed was satisfactory in the existing circumstances. Employers were opposed to such a measure on the grounds that it would compromise economic growth and that it would be inequitable, since it would provide only a relatively small proportion of workers with any significant benefits and so would create interminable industrial disputes. The trade unions remained opposed on the ground (additional to their general opposition on principle) that it would involve an incomes policy, and this they also objected to. The only type of participation likely to encounter any sympathy in trade-union circles was one that could lead to ultimate control of firms by the workers. There followed, therefore, up to and beyond the 1967 election, a prolonged controversy on the subject, before any legislation was introduced, not only on these grounds, but also between more conservative and more progressive wings of the Gaullist party itself, that is, between those who favoured the Mathey approach, and prominent left-wing Gaullists such as MM. René Capitant and Louis Vallon, whose views were associated with what was called the 'Pan-Capitalism' of M. Marcel Loichot.[72]

THE POLITICAL CLIMATE, ELECTORALISM
AND ELECTIONS

This first full parliamentary term for thirty years, during which the Gaullists were unimpeded by any predominating and divisive issue such as that of Algeria, and during which the governmental team remained virtually unchanged except for a relatively minor reshuffle following the presidential election, was characterized by a degree of political apathy and economic *immobilisme* worthy of the Fourth Republic. This was partly because Governments were beginning to discover, as previous ones under other régimes had done, how difficult it is to make radical changes in established French political and economic habits, in the absence of some compelling stimulus such as war, threatened revolution, or serious social or economic discontent. But, in spite of the recession and the introduction of the stabilization plan, these were, on the whole, years of relative economic prosperity, in which it was possible for one sectional interest after another to negotiate advantages for itself. Agricultural prices, wage demands, regional unemployment, the state of the social-security services, economic advantages for France, and especially for French farmers, in the Common Market – these were problems dealt with or evaded by means of familiar pressures on Deputies and Ministers, by employers, trade unions, professional interests, as well as by Mayors and by constituency and national parties. It was a period in which the major political interests were in the field of foreign affairs and it was primarily on these that political parties concentrated their activities, though these, too, took second place to the overriding interest, which was in electoral and pre-electoral tactics.

They were, nevertheless, years of increasingly rapid changes in social and economic life, changes that were bound sooner or later to influence both the political and the economic climate. The number of farmers dwindled steadily – too fast to please farming interests and those of small-town tradesmen, and too slowly to satisfy the requirements of economic modernization. Some regions became more highly populated, creating problems of urbanization, while declining areas continued to present problems of employment and of alternative forms of economic development. The economic system adapted itself as best it could to the rapidly growing numbers of tower blocks in suburban areas, of supermarkets, drug stores and industrial mergers. The social system suffered from increasing inadequacies in the fields of housing, school and university building and staffing, hospitals and other social services, the provision of telephones and of the roads, on which every year more and more French families travelled for an annual holiday, by then generally lasting a month.[73]

General de Gaulle recognized the need to deal with this social backlog. In the period immediately preceding the presidential electoral campaign, he prophesied that the following five years would see increasing numbers of motorways . . . the development of the telephone system . . . *collèges*, *lycées* and institutes in which technology would be on the same footing as conventional subjects . . . wider opportunities for young people and adults to learn a trade, change it, acquire more qualifications . . . greater mobility of workers, both between regions and between occupations, and more opportunities for redundant farmers in industry and in service occupations. What is now being done in the fields of housing, hospitals and sport will be actively continued.[74]

Since he also recognized that France's inadequate resources would continue to impose priority for economic over social requirements, it was not clear how far these promises could be carried out in the near future without jeopardizing the economic revolution that was in his view essential for France's future rôle in the world. But he was obviously not at that time anticipating that social discontents would so soon play a major part in threatening the political as well as the economic achievements of the régime.

Nor, indeed, was there any general anticipation of trouble ahead. Up to the election in March 1967, prices continued to be kept down to a level lower than that of all the other Common Market countries except Italy. Investment was increasing, though not fast enough, and wage increases were slowing down. The stabilization plan was, in effect, being continued by M. Debré (who replaced M. Giscard d'Estaing in the reshuffle at the beginning of 1966). His plan for *contrats de programme* was a plan for a 'contractual stability', which would justify limited price increases only in so far as certain economic conditions were satisfied. M. Debré also continued attempts to hold prices down in the public sector.[75] The relative position of farmers' incomes was somewhat improved and the purchasing power of the lower-paid workers brought more nearly into line with increases in the cost of living. There were certainly some warning signs of trouble ahead – a rise in unemployment and imports, and over-dependence of the export trade on a few industries (in particular, cars and heavy machinery) and on the West European market, the low rate of industrial concentration, of building (France's rate was the lowest in Western Europe except for Italy), and of agricultural modernization. But these were not disquieting enough to prevent French parties from concentrating their attention on their favourite political activity, the discussion of electoral tactics.

The second Gaullist Parliament afforded them ample opportunity to do so. The introduction of presidential election by universal suffrage meant that there would be two national election campaigns between 1963 and March 1967. There were, in addition, three sets of local elections, two of which, the cantonal elections in March 1964 and the senatorial elections in September 1965, aroused, as usual, little political interest and resulted in no politically significant changes. Their only political importance was the revelation of the continued failure of the Gaullist party to make any real headway in its attempts to permeate local politics.[76]

The municipal elections, held in March 1965, were regarded, however, and not only by the Gaullists, as politically important indications determining tactics in the forthcoming presidential election. Having somewhat belatedly discovered the importance of local politics, the Government had introduced a new electoral law, applicable in 1965 in Paris and the 158 towns with populations of over 30,000, which, it was hoped, would help to polarize the electorate round the UNR on the one hand, and the Socialist and Communist parties on the other, and so persuade Centre parties and some conservatives to vote with the Gaullists. Thanks to the strength of traditional local loyalties this did not happen, the Socialists, for instance, forming politically heterogeneous alliances in different regions.[77] The result was that, out of a total of 5524 seats in municipalities in which the new law applied, the UNR won only 684, a net gain of only 21. Out of over 450,000 seats in the country as a whole, the UNR won under 40,000. Of the 158 towns with populations of over 30,000 (excluding Paris) only 25 had a Gaullist majority (an increase of one) and in Paris, where all parliamentary seats had gone to the Gaullists in 1962, they failed to obtain a majority in the Municipal Council. If this election had been intended, as the Minister of the Interior, M. Roger Frey, had said, 'as a first stage, the beginning of the "hour of truth" that will come at the end of the year with the presidential elections, and later with the general election',[78] then these results could only be regarded as disappointing.

The local elections monopolized the political stage during the month of March 1965. But preparations for the presidential election had begun long before that, and political interest on the Left was focused almost wholly on electoral tactics from the end of 1963 onwards. Presidential 'electoralism' fell into four distinct periods – leaving out of account the campaign in certain left-wing papers during the autumn of 1963 in favour of a mysterious candidate called 'Monsieur X'.[79] The first lasted throughout 1964 and up to April of the following year, during which time a great deal of publicity in the press was given to the attempts of the President of the Socialist parliamentary group, M. Gaston Defferre (who turned out to be 'Monsieur X'), to become the accepted candidate of a united Left. The second saw the failure of his attempt, between April and June 1965, to obtain agreement between the proposed partners on the actual setting up of a federation of parties of the Left. The third was the formation by M. Mitterrand of a smaller federation, excluding Centre parties, together with the announcement of two more presidential candidates – M. Lecanuet, President of the *Centre démocrate*, and a right-wing former Minister, M. Paul Antier, representing the *Mouvement démocrate et paysan* and supported by M. Pierre Poujade. Two other contenders had declared themselves candidates earlier, though neither was taken very seriously. The first, Maître Tixier-Vignancour, who announced his candidature in April 1964, represented the extreme Right, and especially the interests of Algerian *rapatriés*. The second, a conservative Senator, M. Pierre Marcilhacy, had been nominated by a small centre-right movement in April 1965, but had made it clear that he represented no political party. The fourth period began on 4 November with the announcement by General de Gaulle that he intended to stand.

The campaign opened officially on 19 November, and at the last minute yet another candidate appeared on the scene, M. Marcel Barbu, an individualist describing himself as 'the candidate of all under-dogs'. Since M. Antier had by then withdrawn, the first ballot included three serious candidates, who, in spite of the refusal by all of them to regard themselves as speaking for any specific party, represented respectively the Gaullists and the pro-Governmental *Républicains indépendants*, the Left, including the Communists, and the Centre and Centre-Right. Nobody expected the other three to poll more than a handful of votes, and they in fact polled only 8·2 per cent between them, 5·3 per cent being cast for M. Tixier-Vignancour.

Both the abortive Defferre federation and the Federation of the Democratic and Socialist Left have already been mentioned briefly in the previous volume in the context of the attitudes and policies of parties of the Left. Looked at in the broader context of French politics, M. Defferre's campaign is important, in the first place because the initiative came from him, and not from the Socialist party, and was supported by a certain number of political Clubs, some trade unionists and also some prominent academics.[80] Their hope was to produce a candidate who would have a wider and a more modern appeal than one put forward merely as the nominee of the Socialist party. They wanted a candidate prepared to accept the presidential provisions of the 1958 Constitution (on which the Socialist party had still not officially made up its mind), and one who, though he would obviously have to count on the support of Communist voters, would not be a prisoner of Communist party policies or tactics. M. Defferre's initial statements satisfied both these requirements.

> I will not [he said] engage in discussions with the Communist party. I will not negotiate with it. I will not accept a common programme.[81]

And on the rôle of the President he said:

> The President must be the guarantor of the application of a policy outlined by him and on which the majority have

elected him. . . . The Prime Minister must govern under the supervision of the President of the Republic, but in conformity with the choice of the electors.[82]

This was all very well, but it was obvious that he would have to answer some very pertinent questions before he could hope to be accepted by his party as their candidate too. Would the Socialist party agree with these tactics? Would it regard M. Defferre as a suitable candidate in himself? And would it be possible on the basis of such tactics to rally both Communist and Centre votes, for both were necessary if he were to have any hope of defeating General de Gaulle?

The Socialist party was itself divided on these points, though anxious to reach a decision that would commit the party to united action.[83] But M. Defferre got off to a promising start, for one thing because, in spite of the hesitations within his party, he had confronted it with a *fait accompli*. He also had the support of the very powerful Socialist federation of his own *département* as well as that of a number of organizations representing what were called *'les forces vives'*, which the Socialist party had proclaimed itself anxious to attract in order to revivify and rejuvenate its ageing cadres. M. Defferre was, therefore, in a strong position. The special Congress called to consider his candidature on 2–3 February 1964, after a heated and prolonged discussion, endorsed the candidature on the basis of seven political priorities, or *options*, which were merely restatements of ritual Socialist declarations that either ignored or evaded the issues on which conflict between the hoped-for allies was bound to arise.[84]

During the following months, the obstacles came thick and fast. Two factors in particular eventually defeated him. First, his own personality created a certain number of doubts inside as well as outside his own party. He was not an inspired speaker. He had neither the intellectual agility of a Mitterrand nor the political astuteness of a Mollet. He got rapidly out of his depth when trying to explain what was implied by his conception of presidentialism.[85] He was too Atlanticist and 'European' both for the left wing of his own party and for the

Communists. Yet, in a sense, he was also too Gaullist for them, partly because he wanted the President to play a more active rôle than some were at that time prepared for, and partly because he was critical of certain rigidities of left-wing attitudes and structures. Left-wing Gaullists had, indeed, approved of his attacks on 'the sclerotic machinery of the old parties'.[86] Yet it was precisely on these parties, including mainly his own, that he was counting for the necessary votes to enable him to defeat de Gaulle! His entente with Radicals and MRP in the Marseilles municipal elections left him open to the accusation of 'Centrism'. He was too anti-clerical for the MRP, but not sufficiently so to satisfy his own party.

The other factor contributing to his defeat was the failure both of the Socialist party itself and of its potential partners in the proposed federation to realize that, for any significant degree of unity on the Left to be possible, a certain amount of give and take was needed. By the beginning of 1965, there was no sign that any party was prepared to make the essential concessions, and the campaign seemed to be petering out. It was revived, however, following the municipal elections, when M. Defferre's movement, *Horizon 80*, presented a specific proposal for the immediate formation of a federation of the Socialist party, political Clubs, the Radical party and the MRP. Put forward on 8 May, the suggestion was approved within a month, at least to the extent that immediate negotiations were agreed to.[87] Less than a fortnight later, the plan was dead.

This brief and decisive second stage of 'electoralism' provides a classic example of the obstacles to unity on the French Left that have prevented it from ever achieving any genuine understanding or coalition. From the Popular Front of 1936 up to and not excluding the so-called 'common programme' in June 1972 of the Socialist and Communist parties, every agreement, whatever the verbal acrobatics employed to disguise the fact, has been, at best, a short-term electoral bargain, accepted because it was regarded as bringing immediate advantage to the signatories.

The Socialist party leaders were from the start profoundly divided about the Defferre campaign. Three of the four main groups within it never really believed in either the possibility or the desirability of co-operation with Centre parties, which was the basis of M. Defferre's plan. The strongest group, led by M. Guy Mollet, wanted to concentrate on building up the Socialist party, on the basis of fidelity to traditional principles and formulae as decided by Socialist Congresses. M. Defferre's ultimate goal of 'fusion' in some larger unit was, therefore, anathema to this group, for whom the Left meant primarily the Socialist party, together with any junior partners whom it might accept on its own conditions and mainly for electoral purposes. For M. Mollet and his supporters, any 'dialogue' ought to begin within the 'Socialist family', as did the various *colloques* held between December 1963 and June 1964.[88] M. Mollet himself refused on more than one occasion to contemplate 'our dilution in some nebulous, supposedly democratic body'.[89] M. Jules Moch posed as a condition on which no compromise was possible the acceptance of the Socialist party's conceptions of Socialism and anti-clericalism.[90] Others, including leaders of the powerful Nord federation, simply wanted to leave the Socialist party as it was, concentrating on efforts to strengthen the party's own cohesion.

The second group was made up of those on the left of the party, or outside it in the dissident Socialist PSU, who accepted the need for something that could be called negotiation but wanted the dialogue to be with the Communist party, not parties to the right of the Socialists. The third group, on the other hand, represented by some members on the right of the party, including MM. Max Lejeune, André Chandernagor and Francis Leenhardt, did not want a *rapprochement* with the Communist party. The fourth group, consisting of M. Defferre and his supporters, including MM. Georges Brutelle, Albert Gazier, Christian Pineau and Gérard Jaquet, really wanted the impossible. They wanted to make the Socialist party – or the 'Socialist family' – the centre of a *rassemblement*, including MRP and Radical parties, which would be strong enough to obtain from the Communist party terms of co-operation that would eliminate the danger of Communist domination of the coalition.[91]

Whether negotiations were within the 'Socialist family' or not, the difficulty was that they were never likely to succeed if Socialist conditions were so rigid as to be obviously unacceptable to their would-be partners. Nor were the Socialists alone in their egocentricity. The PSU, for instance, never in practice found it possible to reach agreement within itself, let alone with any other party, except on short-term electoral policies.[92] Socialists on the one hand, and members of the MRP and Radical parties on the other, both assumed that their own indispensability to the formation of a non-Communist Left implied the acceptance by the other side of certain conditions on which they would not compromise. The result was that approval in principle of M. Defferre's proposal for a federation was accompanied in each case by implicit or explicit conditions that in practice nullified it. For instance, at its Congress in May 1965, the MRP voted a general-policy resolution extending a tepid welcome to the idea of the federation, on condition that it should exclude the Communist party, which had already threatened to present its own presidential candidate if there were to be no common programme of the Left.[93] Such a programme, even if it had been possible to achieve it at that time, would have been incompatible with the MRP's conditions. M. Defferre himself was finally obliged to recognize that Socialist conditions too made the prospect of achieving any federation remote. The hypothesis of a narrow federation, from PSU to Radicals, that Guy Mollet envisaged in his speech of 4 April was, he said, 'an intellectual abstraction corresponding to no reality'. The PSU would not join a federation without the Communist party and the Radicals would not join one without the MRP. 'There will, therefore,' concluded M. Defferre, 'be no federation at all.'[94]

A fortnight later, his prophecy was fulfilled. The conversations between the seventeen representatives of the parties concerned rapidly reached deadlock, because

for Guy Mollet a reformer meant a 'Socialist' and an 'anti-clerical', whilst for M. Fontanet it meant 'a modern Socialist', that is to say 'a liberal Socialist'. They reached deadlock on anti-clericalism, on the title of the federation, on electoral alliances – namely, on whether there should be acceptance with or without reservations or formal and definitive refusal of any agreement with the Communists.[95]

If the Defferre proposal could justifiably be described as

a queer mixture of Gaullism without de Gaulle, Mendésisme without Mendès France and a Popular Front without contacts with the Communists,[96]

then the *Fédération de la Gauche démocrate et socialiste* (FGDS), proposed by M. François Mitterrand and supported by the majority of the Socialist party with almost indecent haste following the withdrawal of M. Defferre's candidature, was not a potentially governmental mixture at all. M. Mitterrand resolved the political dilemma that had defeated M. Defferre by falling back on a purely electoral, left-wing line-up. The result was the mathematical certainty that, short of a miracle, the new Federation would not be able to defeat de Gaulle. For to the extent that it attracted Communist votes it would alienate those on the right of the Socialist party. Indeed, the Centre's reaction to the formation of the FGDS and the announcement by M. Mitterrand on 9 September of his candidature was the announcement of a month later by M. Lecanuet that he would stand as the 'democratic, social and European' candidate. The following comment on these manœuvres by a disillusioned left-wing journalist, M. Jean Cau, writing on the eve of the first ballot, probably summed up the views of many hesitant left-wing voters:

If we are waiting, not for Godot, but either for a Left that has cleansed its stables or for new hopes, then alas! it is de Gaulle, de Gaulle in spite of everything. . . . For the past seven years the Left has suffered from a grave malady that it has neither wanted nor been able to cure.[97]

In fact, the 'options' of the Charter of the new Federation, agreed on 10 September 1965 and accepted on 30 October by a Socialist National Council, were verbally almost indistinguishable from those of M. Defferre.[98] The five '*grandes orientations*' of M. Lecanuet predictably emphasized the Centre's social and European priorities.[99] It roused little interest and was, in any case, overshadowed by the expected announcement by General de Gaulle on 4 November of his own candidature. All candidates were now lined up for the fourth phase, the campaign proper, which was characterized by left-wing imprecision, exchanges of economic statistics and, somewhat surprisingly – though General de Gaulle had clearly been counting on this – by the popularity of the appeal of both Gaullist and anti-Gaullist brands of Europeanism.[100]

The first ballot produced two surprises. It did not give General de Gaulle the expected overall majority, but only 43·71 per cent of the votes, with the result that he was obliged to face a second ballot. Though M. Mitterrand received as large a vote as he could reasonably have expected (32·23 per cent), M. Lecanuet polled over 15 per cent of the votes, which was considerably more than any but the most optimistic of his supporters had been counting on. The second ballot, a fortnight later, was therefore a duel between the President and M. Mitterrand.[101] It gave General de Gaulle 55 per cent of the vote, a result achieved in part by the transference to him of votes given in the first ballot to M. Lecanuet,[102] but also in part by the General's change of tactics. He had made only two brief television appearances before the first ballot, in which his lofty remoteness and his familiar predictions of catastrophe if he were to be defeated had appeared to irritate more listeners than they had convinced. Now, he descended into the political arena, using all his undoubted talent for the apparently off-the-cuff, but in reality carefully prepared, television interview, and, abandoning the lofty tone, spoke informally, simply, even familiarly.

How far the results at the first ballot had reflected the decision of some voters to show him that he could neglect the elector only at his peril is a question that can be debated indefinitely. How many of those who voted for him at the second did so because, for them, as for Jean Cau, the choice was '*De Gaulle, Hélas!*' is similarly a matter for speculation.

The 'freak' candidate, M. Barbu, had recommended a vote for
M. Mitterrand because he preferred 'the confusion of the
parties to the order of General de Gaulle',[103] but whatever
their reasons, 54·5 per cent of the electors preferred the latter.
Though not 'a famous victory', this was enough to ensure the
President a second septennate.

Inevitably, however, the fact that 45·49 per cent had preferred M. Mitterrand made this presidential election a run-up
for the general election.

> As for the candidate of the opposition parties [wrote
> M. Jacques Fauvet], he must know that the votes that went
> to him represent neither a majority nor a policy. This should
> persuade him to become the kind of candidate that he was at
> the start, namely, the candidate of the Left. . . . The régime
> would not survive the election of a majority hostile to the
> head of the State. This election will thus be the 'third
> ballot'.[104]

In reality, this widely shared opinion was based on a false
premise, because it was an extrapolation from the presidential
to the general election. (A similar failure to understand the
difference between the two types of election was to mislead
the General and his advisers in 1969.) In 1965, it led to a prolonged post mortem in press, periodicals and parties,[105] and
to preparations for the 1967 elections characterized by unrealistic euphoria on both sides. The Gaullists were the victors
in the presidential election, as they had been in the past two
general elections, and expected to win the parliamentary
election. The opposition parties saw a vote of 45·49 per cent
in the presidential election as only a step away from victory in
the forthcoming parliamentary election. But in a general
election, policies were what mattered, not 'options' and
'orientations', and the strength of constituency and local
interests often called for different attitudes and emphases. The
issues, too, differed greatly. There was, in general, less interest
in the general election, and what there was was concentrated
on economic and social problems – telephones were more
important than NATO.[106] There was not the bi-polarization

of a contest centred on two personalities. Electors were Giscardiens, Faurists, Molletists, Mitterrandists, Defferrists, Lecanuetists, as well as being PSU, Communists, Socialists, Gaullists, left-wing Gaullists, Radicals and Centrists.

Party declarations were characterized by a great deal of vague verbiage, including, on the Gaullist side, a proliferation of phrases about security, independence, stability and progress, together with a noticeable absence of specific commitments. On the Left, tactical manœuvres imposed a similar vagueness, because there was no real agreement on policy but only on the need to combine in order to defeat the Gaullists. The Federation did, it is true, have what was described as a policy, but it contained so many irreconcilable disagreements that it would have been extremely difficult to apply it if the Left had succeeded in winning the election.[107] The campaign was also characterized by a change in election techniques since the previous election, four and a half years earlier. In 1967, not only did opinion polls play a much more important rôle, but so also did American-style methods, with 'hostesses' at giant meetings, sales of badges and scarves, propaganda by telephone and so on. There was a conscious effort to 'sell the candidate'.[108]

The strength of the Gaullists lay in their leadership, their cohesion and their organization. Not for them the complicated controversies regarding second-ballot tactics that dominated the pre-electoral opposition negotiations. A single candidate in each constituency was imposed. The *Républicains indépendants* were allotted 83 candidates, of whom some 50 at most could hope to be elected.[109] The weaknesses of the Left, apart from the absence of any real agreed policy, were first, that their electoral agreement concerned only the second ballot, thus leaving Communists, PSU and Federation as opponents at the first ballot, and second, that there was no electoral agreement at all with the *Centre démocrate*.

The results were an unpleasant surprise for both sides. Gaullists and *Indépendants* had a majority of only one in the new National Assembly – a loss of 40 seats – though they had, in fact, increased their vote.[110] This meant that M. Pompidou was faced with an immediate problem. He must avoid a confidence vote for the first month, when Deputies appointed to Government office, though eligible to sit in the National Assembly, would not be allowed to vote. The Federation and the Communists had doubled their strength in the National Assembly. But together they still had only 193 of the 487 Deputies, and could not count on the support of the 40 or so members of the Centre group.[111]

Perhaps because Gaullists had become accustomed to victory and power, there seemed at first to be little realization on the Government side of the effects that these results might have on the political climate. General de Gaulle was reported to have said in January 1966 that the only important problem was the preparation of the 1972 presidential election.[112] His New Year message for 1967 was extremely optimistic and that for the following year predicted that France would continue to set an example of efficiency in the conduct of its affairs.

> In the political field [he said], our institutions will be applied. It is, therefore, unlikely that we shall be paralysed by the kind of crisis from which we have suffered so much in the past.[113]

He could hardly have been more profoundly mistaken.

CHAPTER IV

Challenge

THE NATURE OF THE CHALLENGE

The third Parliament of the régime presented a striking contrast to the previous one. It was very short-lived, whereas the 1963–7 Parliament had established a record for longevity. It was full of drama and surprises, instead of being dull and predictable. Political interest was concentrated on internal instead of on foreign affairs. And M. Pompidou's sixth year as Prime Minister concluded with a major challenge to the political stability that General de Gaulle was never tired of claiming as the Fifth Republic's greatest achievement, a challenge that the Prime Minister more than anyone else was responsible for meeting successfully, only to find that his success was rewarded by his banishment to the back benches.

It has been suggested by one of France's foremost political commentators that the 1965 election marked the beginning of what was to be a steady decline in the President's authority from its peak point in January 1964, when he had claimed to possess 'the indivisible authority of the State'. Whereas during the previous five years everything had gone well for him, there were to be, between 1964 and 1969,

> more failures than victories, and more mistakes than during the previous five years. For the fact that there had to be a second ballot in 1965 was a defeat. The election of 1967 was a setback for Gaullism. The events of May and June 1968 seriously undermined the authority of the State, and 1969 finally sounded the knell of his hold over the country.[1]

The thesis can no doubt be defended with the aid of hindsight, but few would have predicted in 1967 the sequence of events that actually occurred. And even as it was, none of General de Gaulle's mistakes, except the last, appeared to leave the impression that he could not easily recover the lost ground. The 1965 presidential election was undoubtedly a disappointment to him. But the referendum of 1962 had also been a disappointment, and he had almost immediately recovered confidence and authority and won an impressive electoral victory.

The 1967 election's near stalemate was certainly profoundly disappointing to him and to the Gaullist party. But he and the party had apparently every opportunity to regain what they had lost. The ease with which the President had withdrawn France from NATO in 1966 had not indicated any weakening of his hold on power, as a result of the presidential election. The aggressiveness of his foreign policy after the 1967 election was undiminished, and he incurred criticism and some unpopularity owing to his attitude to the six-days' Arab–Israeli war, to his comments on French-Canadian objectives and, in some circles (though by no means generally), owing to his rejection of Great Britain's second applicatoin to join the European Community. But he withstood successfully, first the challenge presented by the almost non-existent parliamentary majority, and, after some hesitation, the far more serious challenge of the events of May 1968, going on to win the most spectacular electoral victory of the century.

In the referendum of April 1969, General de Gaulle himself deliberately and unnecessarily invited the challenge which defeated him. A number of explanations of his action have been put forward, but the most that can be said for any of them is that they are arguable hypotheses. It is a no less arguable hypothesis that, if he had not chosen to invite defeat on an unpopular issue, the relative unimportance of which is indicated by the fact that his successor ignored it for more than four years, he might well have remained securely in office until his death in 1970 – or even longer perhaps, for experience shows that power preserves. As it was, by disappearing from the political scene literally overnight, he presented the Gaullist party and the new President with a challenge, for he catapulted France without warning into a post-Gaullist era that had been

the subject of much speculation, but for which he had made no
discernible preparation.

THE SOCIAL AND ECONOMIC WAR OF ATTRITION

Although the composition of the National Assembly after the
1967 elections indicated the likelihood of more hard-fought
parliamentary battles, there was at first singularly little to fight
about. No burning issues had been bequeathed to the third
Parliament by its predecessor which, during the last parliamentary session, had been involved in the passage of a highly
technical and not very contentious Bill intended to deal with
the problem of land speculation. A study of 'the pill' was in
progress, perhaps to be followed by proposals for the reform
of France's anti-contraceptive law, which would at most produce some skirmishes. The forthcoming parliamentary programme was mainly concerned with economic and social
questions – unemployment, the situation of the nationalized
industries, the reform of local-government finance – none of
which was either new or particularly inflammatory.

Three subjects proved, however, to be highly controversial,
though of more interest to Parliament and parties than to the
general public. Of these, two – the reorganization of the social-
security system and the introduction of a measure of workers'
profit-sharing in industry – dominated the parliamentary stage
during most of 1967. The third – the Government proposal to
permit a certain amount of brand advertising on the State radio
and television services – was certainly controversial, though
the main quarrel was on the procedures adopted by the Government rather than on the merits or demerits of the proposal
itself.

Procedural problems also dominated much of the discussion
regarding the Government's economic and social measures.
The parliamentary situation was such that, even if, as soon
seemed to be evident, the Centre parties were prepared to
save the Government from the risk of defeat created by their
bare majority,[2] any Bill was likely to encounter time-
wasting obstruction owing to the pressures from interests and

constituencies that would be bound to be exerted on Deputies. The Government, therefore, proposed to carry out its economic and social programme by ordinance, under the special powers that, by virtue of article 38 of the Constitution, could be accorded to the Government for specified purposes and a limited period. This procedure was also, in the Government's view, better suited than the normal legislative procedure to the nature of the measures, which were mainly administrative and technical.[3] This was not enough, however, to persuade Deputies to give up without a struggle the power to harass the Government.

The parliamentary struggle over the proposal is important, not because there was ever any serious danger of a Government defeat,[4] but because it revealed the extent to which Deputies resented the continuing demotion of Parliament under the Gaullist régime. It revealed too that, in spite of their technicality, two at least of the proposed measures aroused political attitudes, anxieties and prejudices that were not unrelated to the underlying causes of the 1968 events, and Deputies felt strongly that they ought to be debated by Parliament. The Government was obliged, therefore, to defeat three motions of censure in order to obtain the required special powers, and a fourth one in October 1967 on its refusal to submit a Bill for the ratification of the ordinances.[5]

The most impressive opposition to the Government came from outside Parliament, with the first really political general strike of the régime. Four of the six main trade-union confederations agreed in opposing the Government's request for special powers, and decided on a one-day general strike on 17 May.[6] Not for a quarter of a century had a general stoppage been called on specifically and exclusively political grounds, and to express trade-union opposition to the use by the Government of a perfectly legal and constitutional parliamentary procedure. It was, moreover, as M. Pompidou pointed out, a perfectly normal procedure that had already been used seven times since the beginning of the régime.

The special powers finally granted to the Government lasted until 31 October. Until then, the Government was authorized to make ordinances on four problems: employment, profit-sharing in industry, reform of the social-security system, and measures to help the economy. A Bill to ratify the ordinances was to be tabled before 31 December, which meant that the Government could be reasonably sure of surviving until the opening of the April session of 1968.[7] Though not debatable in Parliament, the content of the ordinances came in for a good deal of criticism by parties and in the press, and especially the provisions for profit-sharing provided for by three ordinances of 17 August.[8] To begin with, they applied only to firms employing a hundred or more workers, which meant that, at most, slightly under five million workers would be affected by the scheme – that is, about two-fifths of the workers employed in industry and trade. Then the fact that the amounts to be distributed were to be calculated on the basis of the net profits of the firm, and after deduction not only of tax but also of the first 5 per cent of net profits, meant that many workers would not in practice be affected, either because the firm declared no profits (which some 70,000 or more firms in France normally did), or because they declared a figure below 5 per cent. It was also pointed out that there would be great discrepancies between the amounts received by workers in different firms, according to whether they were labour-intensive or capital-intensive.[9] The method of calculation was so complicated that it was likely to create difficulties for accountants and suspicions among workers.[10] For instance, since it was based on declared profits, workers would be likely to want to prove that the firm was making more profit than it was declaring.

Another series of criticisms concerned the method of distribution of workers' shares. There was a choice between three options – the issue to workers of shares in the firm; the opening of a current account in the worker's name; or the investment of shares in another firm. In all cases the amounts were to be blocked for a period of five years at least. There were a number of complications here, too, of which perhaps the most important was that, under the second option (which, failing agreement, was to be obligatory and was likely in any case to be preferred by both employers and workers), the interest on the sums – regarded by workers as deferred wages – was not to be liable to tax. Critics pointed out that these provisions resulted in the cost of the scheme falling on the State. 'The main beneficiary', wrote a prominent supporter of participation, 'is the firm. The wage-earner is a modest beneficiary. Only the State stands to lose. . . . This is not what the Vallon amendment intended.'[11]

This was certainly the view of left-wing Gaullists who had approved of the Vallon amendment. They wanted a system that could develop into something nearer to co-ownership. In the words of René Capitant, the author of the most complete and original scheme, 'all concerns that today belong exclusively to shareholders would become the joint property of shareholders on the one hand and a workers' co-operative on the other.'[12] His plan was for a tripartite organization of firms, in which the two organizations, representing respectively capital and the body of workers, would together form a third body responsible for management. After deduction of profits due to shareholders, remaining profits would be divided equally between the two, the workers' share being in the form of dividend-bearing 'labour shares' (*actions du travail*). Workers would have a right, however, gradually to become individual shareholders. Other plans, put forward by Marcel Loichot and by Pierre Lebrun, a former co-secretary-general of the CGT, who had joined the left-wing Gaullist *Groupe des 29*, were on similar lines.[13] These left-wing Gaullist plans were not in themselves politically important, because they represented only the views of small and divided groups without any real influence on the Gaullist party or on Government policies. But the publicity given to them in the press during 1967 was important, because the wrangle over the content of the ordinances was really only a front for a much more profound dispute about the whole idea of participation.

This was a dispute that divided orthodox and left-wing Gaullists, while it united the orthodox Left and Right. And both sides were uncertain where General de Gaulle really stood – whether his conception of participation was that expressed in the ordinances, whether he really intended eventually to go farther and introduce something nearer the views of the left-wing Gaullists, or whether his very vaguely-worded references to it were intended to be diversely interpreted, and so to help to create an image of Gaullism as a progressive rather than a conservative movement, without any precise commitment to actual policies.

Whatever General de Gaulle really believed, the fact remained that the 1967 ordinances on profit-sharing were the first instalment of a policy to which, verbally at least, he was determined to adhere, in spite of the evidence that it was unacceptable to both employers and trade unions and seemed highly unlikely ever to become a recipe for getting rid of what he called the sterile confrontation between Right and Left. For his reaction to the May events the following year was first to propose *more* participation,[14] and then to put M. Edgar Faure in charge of a highly controversial Bill to extend participation to university administration. The result was that, when the time came to ratify the ordinance the following year, the whole argument was gone over again, and in the infinitely more difficult circumstances created by the students' revolution.

Up to the summer of 1968, however, participation was restricted to the industrial field provided for by the ordinances. The measures did not go far enough for left-wing Gaullists, but they went too far for the employers, while for the trade unions they went in the wrong direction altogether. The CGT castigated them as bogus – '*une diversion mystificatrice*', mere slogans used to camouflage a policy in the interests of capitalism,[15] and intended to bolster up the existing structure of society, which, to the Left, constituted the essential obstacle to any real improvement in industrial relations. The Right, and especially employers' organizations, feared them for precisely the opposite reason. They were seen as the thin end of a wedge that *would* undermine the structure of society, and, in particular, the unified management by directors or owners of firms. This they saw as the essential condition of the efficient functioning of industry.[16]

The remaining ordinances aroused far less interest and passion. They were not new adventures, but were concerned with reforms and developments of existing institutions. More-over, they were highly technical and dealt with concrete problems and immediate preoccupations, of which the most politically important were those of unemployment and social security. By April 1967, official estimates put the unemployment figure at about 300,000, which probably meant the existence in reality of nearer half a million wholly unemployed or working short time. Many miners, for instance, were working only a four-day week or less. Increasing numbers of young people leaving school or university were unable to find jobs. The economic situation was disquieting and neither the state of production nor the increasing deficits in the nationalized industries justified hopes of immediate improvement.[17]

The deficit in the social-security funds was peculiarly alarming. In spite of large subsidies, it was estimated as likely to reach 4000 million francs by 1968.[18] France's total expenditure on social security was the highest in the world in relation to national production. The system was obviously in need of drastic reorganization. Contributions had to be increased, expenditure reduced and management made more efficient. The reforms proposed were announced in four ordinances of 21 August. They provided for separate administration of health, family allowances and old-age pensions. Hitherto, the family-allowance fund, which had a large balance, had been regularly raided in order to reduce the deficit on the health services. Annual contributions to the health service and to old-age pensions (the family-allowance system was financed wholly by the employers) were increased, those of employers remaining, however, almost twice the amount of insured persons' contributions. The percentage of medical charges refunded to patients was reduced, and some services were cut down, including spa treatments, which were said to have become in some cases unofficial paid holidays. Some social charges hitherto paid for by the social-security fund were transferred to the State.

These changes were naturally very unpopular, and it is easy to understand why the Government should have wanted to remove them from the atmosphere of parliamentary debates, where pressure on Deputies from interests and constituents would certainly have created delays, and might, indeed, have involved defeat of a Bill. Trade-union opposition was especially vocal, though the difficulty that unions experienced in getting support for strike action in favour of the repeal of the ordinances showed that the issue was politically less inflammatory than that of participation.[19]

The measures to help unemployment and to stimulate the flagging economy were really only additions to existing ones, and were criticized as being unlikely to do very much to improve the situation. Improvements in information relating to unemployment, better statistical equipment, the creation of a national employment agency, the extension of facilities for vocational training, encouragement of labour mobility, together with the creation of a State system of unemployment allowances (instead of local allowances) aiming at increasing assistance to 80 per cent of the average wage during the first three months – these were all necessary, useful and in the main overdue reforms. The CGT, however, had produced its own unemployment plan before the publication of the ordinance, and this made it clear that the measures did not go far enough to satisfy the Left. The CGT plan claimed, for instance, the right of redundant workers to a classification giving them the right to jobs of equivalent status, a reduction of weekly working hours to forty, and training in the firms' time for equivalent employment.[20]

The economic ordinances consisted of three series of measures intended to stimulate the economy, provide incentives to industrialists, encourage farmers to retire earlier in areas where there were too many farms, and to make others economically viable by merging them with food industries.[21] These were admittedly piecemeal and palliative measures that did not deal with the main difficulty, which was that what was economically necessary was not politically acceptable. And with a parliamentary majority of one, democratic politicians could ignore such considerations only at their peril.

In fact, unemployment and short time continued, with a consequent increase in social unrest. In January 1968, discussions on unemployment were held both in the nationalized industries and between delegations from the main trade unions and employers' organizations. Meetings, processions and even riots expressed fears of unemployment.[22] Nor was the situation likely to improve in view of the persistent stagnation of the economy. Production was below the targets of the fifth Plan; prices were continuing to rise; public building programmes were lagging, and there was a corresponding fall in private building. The Government's response was a further series of measures to encourage industry in depressed areas, to provide more housing and to help the nationalized industries, together with some tax reliefs and increases in family allowances and old-age pensions, which, it was hoped, would help to stimulate internal demand without increasing inflationary pressures. Even Gaullists were not very optimistic regarding future prospects. The fundamental problems were stated frankly by M. Albin Chalandon, a Gaullist Deputy:

> We have enjoyed the roses of the Common Market before feeling the thorns. Thanks to a successful and perhaps too drastic devaluation, our industries have lived for years in a state of euphoria, without carrying out the structural reforms that would enable us to stand up to future competition. It was only in 1966 – mainly owing to the actions of M. Debré – that we realized the facts and that the pace of modernization was stepped up. The ground to be made up is enormous, and the changes still needed are immense.[23]

The Government appeared to be pinning its hopes on German recovery from recession, but by February 1968 this was already a fact, and there was no indication that it would have the hoped-for effect on France. The needed shot in the arm came, in fact, from the as yet unsuspected events of May and June, which imposed economic policies to meet far graver immediate threats.

THE POLITICAL CLIMATE

Once the battle of the ordinances was over, the predominant interest of parties during this Parliament was not parliamentary but party business – family affairs. Both majority and minority parties had their internal problems, and both were conscious of the need for preparations for an election that might come soon. The Gaullist party was concerned with holding its own members as well as the Governmental alliance together, and with the need to strengthen party organization. The left-wing Gaullists had tried at the beginning of the Parliament to form separate groups. There had been differences between left-wing Gaullists and the party concerning the ordinance on participation. The frictions were such that some left-wing Gaullists refused to attend the 1967 party conference at Lille, which was to decide on a reorganization of the party, obviously intended by M. Pompidou and his supporters to prepare for a post-Gaullist era that must come relatively soon. Some left-wing Gaullists believed that there ought not to be a Gaullist party at all, that Gaullism was de Gaulle and that it was for him to decide what ought to be done when he was no longer there.[24] M. Pompidou clearly agreed with Maurice Duverger that it was not possible to 'institutionalize General de Gaulle'.[25] It was time therefore, for the movement to become more like an ordinary party if it was to survive without de Gaulle.

The Giscardian allies were also restive, though they showed little sign of intending to assert themselves very forcibly. M. Giscard d'Estaing, who was not in the Government from 1966 to 1968, made a mildly critical statement to the press in August 1967, regretting the Government's use of special powers and its refusal of 'consultations and debate', and dissociating himself from General de Gaulle's Middle Eastern policy and expressions of sympathy for French-Canadian separatism. But this hardly merited the description of 'another declaration of *oui, mais*', and in any case he was immediately disavowed by the three members of his party who were Ministers. Nor was there any suggestion on his part that the party should abandon the coalition.[26]

The Centre was in what might be described as a *non, mais* situation. It too regarded itself as being in a period of structural change. The problem of the relations between M. Lecanuet's *Centre démocrate* and the parliamentary group, *Progrès et Démocratie moderne*, led by M. Jacques Duhamel, was mainly responsible for the formation in July 1967 of a *Comité d'Etude centriste*, aiming at avoiding divisions among Centrists. By then, the MRP had disappeared as a separate organization and a number of its members had joined the movement *Objectif 72*, led by Robert Buron, which was in spirit nearer to the Federation than to the *Centre démocrate*.[27] 'Structural change' could perhaps be regarded as a euphemism for what looked more and more like the road to disintegration.

The Left was engaged in complex discussions both on fusion between the Socialist party and the *Convention des Institutions républicaines* (CIR), led by M. Mitterrand, and on the perennial question of relations between the Socialist and Communist parties. At the beginning of 1968, the two parties had agreed to try to obtain a special session of the National Assembly in order to discuss the ratification of the ordinances and the questions arising from the British request to join the Common Market. They had not obtained the requisite number of votes, however, and almost immediately were publicly airing their differences on the latter question. The Federation itself had, by the beginning of 1968, already lost whatever cohesion it had had. M. Guy Mollet, still at the head of the only left-wing party except the Communists with a strong and disciplined machine, was at heart opposed to the idea of fusion, but unable to control the pro-fusion sections of the party, led by M. Gaston Defferre, who wanted 'partial fusion now'. M. Mollet's aim, therefore, was to persuade the Socialist party that it was dangerous to go too far too fast, and to obtain support for a formula that would appear to favour the idea of fusion without actually committing the party to putting it into practice at any precise date. This he achieved at the Socialist special conference held on 28 January 1968.[28] In default of a common programme, which proved to be unobtainable at that stage, the Federation and the Communist party agreed in February 1968 to a 'joint declaration', consisting of a common 'platform' of some 7000–8000 words, which was intended to appear as a step nearer to a common programme. It was in reality a statement of divergencies buried in a mass of verbiage and slogans, of which Maurice Duverger wrote: 'Some see it as a glass that is half empty, others as one that is half full.'[29]

The Radical party was, of course, opposed to a common programme with the Communists and also opposed to fusion with the Socialist party and the CIR, but was afraid that the only alternative might involve its own disappearance. For most of the party's Deputies owed their election to the votes of other parties in the Federation, or to Communist votes. The party Congress in December 1967, therefore, produced a statement approving fusion in principle, but with obvious reservations on the part of members of the section of the party led by MM. Félix Gaillard and Maurice Faure. The president of the Senate, M. Monnerville, announced hopefully at the conclusion of the Radical party Congress that the party was 'in process of reconciling Jaurès and Clemenceau',[30] though he might usefully have reflected perhaps that both these men had been dead for a long time, and that the idea of fusion appeared likely to join them in limbo in the near future, as in fact it did. Nor was there much more optimism in any party regarding the chances of achieving a Socialist–Communist joint programme, as even those who supported the idea were openly admitting.[31]

This was the climate in which the 'students' and workers' revolution' erupted in May. It was a climate that could be summed up as one of increasing economic and social unrest, accompanied by the increasing remoteness of political parties from the realities of the situation. The Gaullist party and its allies on the one hand and the parties of the Left on the other were all immersed in party manœuvres concerned to prevent splinter tendencies and dissensions. On the Government side there were

> strict Gaullists with their toes on the Elysée dotted line, Debrétists, Pompidolists, Giscardians of the *oui, mais* and *oui, si* brands . . . those who want a party of *cadres*. . . .[32]

On the opposition side, there were those who wanted, and those who wanted to avoid Socialist fusion in a single party, those who wanted Socialist–Communist partnership and those who did not. The picture was one of

> political parties all, without exception, subdivided into

tendencies or clans, and tearing each other to pieces as they did in the worst days of the previous Republic.[33]

Parliament was equally unprepared for what was to come. In the 'House without windows', Deputies had their backs turned to the outside world and were busily engaged on a long and complicated wrangle on the Government's proposal to introduce brand-advertising on the State radio and television services. In April 1968 they were contemplating a no more serious challenge to the Government than another censure motion.[34]

THE INCREDIBLE 'REVOLUTION' (i) THE FACTS

The events of May 1968 constitute a unique phenomenon in French political history. They were highly complicated and confused, and the bare facts ought, therefore, to be summarized, in so far as that is possible, before the question of what it all meant is discussed. The whole affair resembled a conductorless, chaotic, and discordant symphony in three movements. The first, and longest, lasted from 2 to 18 May. At first, only students were involved. Workers' participation (the 'second subject') really came in only from about the middle of the month, and the two sides remained distinct throughout, although less distinct than union leaders wished them to be. There was also an important background of university unrest and of student conflicts with the authorities, going back to the autumn of 1967. But the events themselves really began with the decision on 2 May by the Dean of Nanterre to close the Faculty, following a series of provocative incidents, mainly inspired by the small band of anarchist students calling themselves *le Mouvement du 22 mars*, an organization founded by a sociology student, Daniel Cohn-Bendit.

The following day, after a protest meeting at the Sorbonne against the disciplining of M. Cohn-Bendit and a handful of his supporters, he and a number of students were arrested. The authorities had decided to call in the police, owing to threats of clashes with right-wing extremists, a decision regarded by students – and, indeed, almost all left-wing opinion – as an unacceptable infringement of the tradition of Sorbonne extra-territoriality.[35] There was, consequently, a serious clash between police and students outside the building. Cobble-stones were thrown and the police used tear gas and truncheons. The Sorbonne was closed. On the following two days, students appeared before the court, and four were sent to prison. This, together with student resentment of police behaviour, brought more support for the revolutionaries from junior staff as well as students. A strike called on 6 May in support of the release of the imprisoned students led to clashes with the riot police and to the spread of sympathetic strikes in universities outside Paris and in some Paris *lycées*. By this time, Nanterre, the Sorbonne and the Censier annex to the Sorbonne had all been closed, and some 49,000 students were, therefore, unoccupied and free to demonstrate in the streets.

The night of 10 May (*la nuit des barricades*) saw the most violent clashes so far. The Minister had refused to negotiate and this time the riot police went in in force. The Prime Minister, M. Pompidou, who returned from a visit to Afghanistan on 11 May, immediately decided to make the three main concessions that the students had demanded as conditions for negotiation – the reopening of the Sorbonne, the withdrawal of police from it, and the freeing of the imprisoned students. But it was by then too late. The Centre Censier was occupied on 11 May, and when the Sorbonne opened on 13 May, the students occupied it too. On 14 May, Nanterre and Grenoble declared themselves independent universities. Other universities were demanding self-government, and almost all universities as well as a number of *lycées* were by then occupied.

Efforts were being made by students to associate 'the workers' with the movement. The Sorbonne was thrown open to 'workers' (undefined). But there had still been no systematic support from the trade-union movements for the student revolutionaries. Both CGT and Communist party leaders had, indeed, attacked them. The Communist majority on the Nanterre Municipal Council had issued a statement accusing the '*groupuscules*' – described as anarchists, Trotskyites, Maoists, etc. – of 'serving the purposes of the Government, by preventing the normal working of the university'.[36] The acting Communist leader, M. Georges Marchais, had called M. Cohn-Bendit and his supporters 'bogus revolutionaries who ought to be unmasked'.[37] The first systematic contacts between the student unions and the CGT and CFDT had originally resulted, on 10 May, in a joint decision to hold a demonstration on 14 May in favour of *both* an amnesty for the imprisoned students *and* trade-union and political liberties. After the 'night of the barricades', however, this became the general strike of 13 May, in which all three main confederations took part. But the trade-union leaders still tried, though unsuccessfully, to keep the student and trade-union elements of the procession apart.

This date, nevertheless, marked a turning point. The demonstration was followed by an official CGT statement of working-class solidarity with the students. The following day, the first factory occupation took place – at the Sud Aviation plant near Nantes. It was followed by the rapid spread of factory occupations throughout the country. These did not have official CGT support, however, and CGT leaders continued to warn trade unionists against 'Leftists'.[38] CFDT leaders were more sympathetic to spontaneous strikes, regarding them as indicative of growing support for 'workers' power'.

The second phase of the 'revolution' – the slow movement of this chaotic symphony – lasted from 18 May, when General de Gaulle returned from a four-day visit to Rumania, to 27 May. It was characterized by belated Government efforts to contain the movement, and by a continued policy of playing things very cool. By now, unofficial staff–student committees in many schools and universities were busily drawing up new constitutions providing for their joint responsibility in running the university or school, and some actually began to apply these provisional constitutions. Examinations – and in particular the all-important *baccalauréat* – had been postponed. Some of the new 'constitutions' had, indeed, abolished examinations. In Paris, the Odéon had been occupied, and the staffs of the State radio and television services had taken over control of their own programmes. Both in Paris and the provinces, the workers in all the nationalized industries were on strike, and so railways, the underground, postal, gas, and electricity services were all partially or wholly paralysed. It was estimated that, in all, between nine and ten million workers were idle.

Political parties had not, as yet, adopted any official position, except for the PSU, which was openly on the side of the revolutionaries. But on 20 May, the President of the Federation of the Democratic and Socialist left, M. François Mitterrand, called for elections, the Communists called for a joint pro-gramme with the Federation, and M. Pierre Mendès France called on the Government to resign.[39] The CGT was still expressing opposition to the students' claims, rejecting them as 'empty ideas on workers' control, the reform of society and other inventions',[40] and pressing for specific measures – in-creases in wages, reductions of hours, guaranteed employment and improved conditions for trade-union activities in factories.

By then the whole affair seemed to have reached a curious stalemate. Neither side seemed to know what to do next. Between the 'night of the barricades' and 23 May, the violent clashes between police and students had ceased. The public was beginning to be more concerned about the effects of the strikes than about the students. On 22 May the Government adopted a Bill to amnesty imprisoned students – a belated and useless gesture, emphasizing the gulf between 'occupied streets, occupied universities, occupied factories and a preoccupied Government'.[41] The National Assembly spent 21 and 22 May debating a motion of censure that failed to interest anyone. 'None of the speeches', wrote a well-known commentator, 'reflected even remotely the reality of a country paralysed by strikes and in which authority, law and the structure of society were all under challenge.'[42] On 24 May, the President broke his silence by a short broadcast declaration promising a referendum on participation. Comprehensibly, this fell very flat, since, in the circumstances, no such referendum could have been held. The night before his broadcast and that following it saw a revival of street violence. On 27 May, after two days of negotiation, the Government and the main trade-union confederations reached agreements on wages and other demands (the Grenelle agreements), only to have them immediately rejected by the rank and file.

Though it was not apparent at the time, Monday 27 May proved to be a turning point. First, on 28 May, following a mass meeting the previous evening at the Charléty Stadium, at which the audience was adjured by one impassioned revolutionary speaker to make the revolution quickly, M. Mitterrand proposed at a press conference that, in the event of the resignation of General de Gaulle and of the Prime Minister, there should be a provisional Government of ten, and announced that he himself would then be a candidate for the presidency. At a press conference the following day, M. Mendès France, who had been mentioned by M. Mitterrand as his first choice as Prime Minister of such a provisional Government, stated that he would not refuse governmental responsibilities entrusted to him by a united Left.[43] This surprising and controversial development focused attention on the political problem of the future of the régime. There followed two days in which political uncertainties were increased. The first was a day of irrelevancies. The Minister of Education's resignation was finally accepted. The date of the proposed referendum (which certainly could not be held) was given as 16 June, and the *Conseil d'Etat* stated that such a referendum would be unconstitutional.[44] The second was a day of anxiety, during which General de Gaulle's intentions (and even his whereabouts) remained a mystery, and rumours of his impending resignation began to circulate.[45] The day of decision came on 30 May. General de Gaulle made a brief, incisive and authoritative declaration, dissolving the National Assembly and announcing a general election forthwith. The referendum was adjourned *sine die*.

The announcement was immediately followed by a massive demonstration of support for him, in which thousands marched from the Place de la Concorde to the Arc de Triomphe. Though M. Mitterrand had himself called for an election, his reaction to the declaration was extremely hostile, and he even went so far as to describe it as 'the voice of dictatorship . . .

a call to civil war'.[46] It was, in fact, a call to normality, and the response was immediate. The Government was reshuffled, Ministers mainly concerned with the events being replaced. Negotiations between Government and trade unions were resumed and successfully concluded early in June. The French public left Paris and other towns in their thousands for the Whitsun weekend, after which strikers returned to work steadily during the following week. On 16 June, the last student bastion, the Sorbonne, was peacefully evacuated. The revolution was over.

THE INCREDIBLE 'REVOLUTION' (ii) QUERIES AND THEORIES

The French always magnify their revolutions in retrospect into great festivals, during which they experience all that they are normally deprived of, and so they have the feeling that they are achieving their aspirations, even if only in a waking dream.

RAYMOND ARON, in *La Révolution introuvable*;
réflexions sur la révolution de mai

With the 22 March, the Soviets in the original and integral sense came to France.... The 22 March imitates all past revolutions, the Spanish war, the cultural revolution, 17 October, the Paris Commune, but with the aim of living and . bringing to life the socialism of councils ... these Soviets of a quite new kind, the 'committees of students and workers'.

EDGAR MORIN in 'Conflit de générations et lutte de classes', *Le Monde*, 6 June 1968

The events left a host of unanswered questions in the minds of people outside as well as inside France, uncertainties that the publication of some hundred books and innumerable articles over the following months did not dissipate. They confronted the Government with social and economic problems that took months to resolve, and of which some were not resolved. And

they provided academics, politicians, and above all sociologists with material for unending post mortems, theories,
arguments and controversies on what actually happened, what
it had all meant and what it ought to have meant.[47] Some of
the questions call for an attempt at an answer in the political
context of this book. Why was the student movement able to
take hold so fast and go so far? Why did the Government and
General de Gaulle remain inactive for so long? How did the
left-wing political parties come to take it so seriously? And
why did the disturbance die down so quickly?

An answer to the second question would seem to supply
part of the answer to the first. Even a few weeks after the
events, many observers who had seemed to take the movement
seriously at the time could no longer do so in the light of the
massive vote in the general election for General de Gaulle and
for law and order. On the face of it, therefore, it looked as if
stronger action by the Government could have prevented the
movement from ever getting out of hand. In reality, however,
the facts are less simple. The reactions of the public, for
instance, changed perceptibly, so that what was possible in
the later stages might not have been possible earlier. One thing
can be said with some degree of certainty. Only in Paris, with
its romantic revolutionary myths of barricades and torn-up
cobble-stones, and with its traditional tolerance for students'
political games, especially in cases of conflict with the police,
could a collection of small, quarrelling, Maoist, Trotskyite and
anarchist groups have hoped to escalate a university sit-in into
a nation-wide threat (or apparent threat) to the State. And even
in Paris it would not have lasted more than a token day or two,
if it had not been for the existence of a quite exceptional conjunction of circumstances.

Two characteristics of the 'revolution' call for some comment, even if no credible explanation of them springs readily
to mind. The first was the rapid contagion of the movement.
This cannot be wholly explained away by the influence of
radio and television, important as that was. It was a contagion
that affected not merely students, but also sections of the
community normally credited with a greater degree of level-

headedness – a sudden delirium followed by a no less sudden oblivion.

> One after the other [wrote Pierre Viansson-Ponté] writers occupied the Hôtel de Massa, the headquarters of the *Société des Gens de Lettres*; *cadres* invaded the offices of the CNPF; young architects and young doctors occupied the offices of their associations; film technicians 'contested' the festival at Cannes and brought it to a halt. . . . All France exploded and challenged professional structures.

The second characteristic was the extent to which the 'revolution' engendered an inexhaustible flow of words, few if any of which left any discernible trace. At the Sorbonne (to quote Pierre Viansson-Ponté again):

> Sexuality, publicity, culture, society, art, ideologies, revolution – everything is questioned. People insult each other, get caught up and carried away in eternal blethering. Entry and speech are both free. . . .

The interminable debates in the Odéon, which had become a meeting-place for 'students and workers' – 'a permanent headquarters of creative revolution' – were described as:

> Verbal delirium, a perpetual flow of words, of which all that survived was the fact that it happened . . . a deluge of ideas, a tornado of words. . . . Demagogy, dreams, mad ideas, powerful ideas, new ideas – all drowned in an ocean of verbosity. . . .[48]

Among the theories produced in explanation of this phenomenon, about half-a-dozen deserve some attention from politicians and political scientists, irrespective of the extent to which they carried conviction either then or later. The leading student revolutionaries and a number of academic supporters saw the revolution essentially as a revolt of youth against age and against a social system of which they proclaimed themselves victims. Many of them were sociologists. It was at Nanterre that the movement was launched. Nanterre housed the sociology department, and there were far too many students of sociology who were destined to find far too few jobs at the end of their studies. They saw, or professed to see, 'society trembling and the Establishment on the verge of collapse'. For them, the student revolution was, at the very least, 'a dress rehearsal', 'a pre-revolutionary situation'. It was a rediscovery of 'the essence of Revolution'. 'The *enragés* of 1968 set out to destroy civilization and prevent the victory of technocracy.'[49]

What these revolutionaries sought to put in the place of technocracy and civilization was never made clear, either in the unending debates in the occupied Sorbonne or in subsequent analyses. According to Daniel Cohn-Bendit, there *was* no constructive side (in the accepted sense of that word) to the revolution. In an interview with Jean-Paul Sartre in the midst of the events, he stated categorically that his aim was a series of revolutionary outbursts – 'a succession of breaks in the cohesion of the system' (*des mouvements de rupture dans la cohésion du système*)[50] – which he thought would fail, but that would destroy 'bourgeois' law and order in the process. Indeed, for him, the first priority was action, and only in the course of action would it become clear what its purpose was. Action itself was constructive, if it was directed towards the destruction of bourgeois society. He and his supporters put the theory into practice, by reducing parts of Nanterre University to a shambles, and making work impossible for its 11,000 students. 'We do not pretend to represent the majority', he is reported as saying. 'But our ten *enragés* at Nanterre have now become 1200.'[51] One of the theorists of the 'revolution' wrote that

It was Daniel Cohn-Bendit who best understood that the only way to break through the doctrinal and organizational divisions was to fuse all radical groups in direct action with immediate aims. Being contagious, action would mobilize growing numbers of students and the tendency of the *groupuscules* to put theory first and to act according to pre-established patterns would be kept in check by mass participation and direct democracy in action committees, specialized working groups. . . . The practice of direct democracy and action would produce a new type of self-organized vanguard, abolishing all authority and responsibility, abolishing the division into 'leaders' and 'led', submitting the theorists to the criticism and control of the rank and file.[52]

For other academic supporters, however, the 'revolution' was a purely utopian adventure. For Edgar Morin,

> Those who believe that its mission was to trigger a workers' revolution and those who feel that it should have restricted itself to university reform have misunderstood its rôle. Precisely because it was utopian rather than constructive it was able to envisage a future which embraced the whole of society.[53]

Offered the choice between, on the one hand, 'constructive destruction' and *'contestation'** carried out on the off-chance that the reasons for them might emerge at some later date, and, on the other hand, a utopian fantasy that, in Edgar Morin's phrase, subsumed 'all the revolutions ever dreamed of, in a "quasi- or peri-revolution" – a "detonator" that would accelerate reform as well as the movement to contest the very basis of society',[54] it is hardly surprising that there were those at the other extreme who dismissed the whole affair as *'révolutionnarisme'*, 'a bogus revolution – play acting, which parodies memories of older tragedies, no longer repeatable or playable'.[55] Supporters of this point of view emphasized that, if the student revolution was a demonstration against the 'consumer society', its main inspiration came from the products of it, for most of the students involved belonged to the middle or upper classes.[56] In the words of a commentator looking back on the revolution two years later,

> In a world where insurrection stops for the weekend, who would not share M. Waldeck Rochet's fear of this generation which is not revolutionary, but 'Swedish' – ready for

---

* There is no satisfactory English rendering of the student revolutionary concept of *'contestation'*. It is 'disputation' that, in practice, implies the right of students to challenge academic authority by breaking up lectures (and even the university) and to challenge political opponents without tolerance and with no holds barred, as upholders of 'bourgeois' society.

any kind of fancy-dress that will provide a rôle for it to play. The crisis of 1968 revealed not so much '*contestation*' as a new kind of practitioner of it, both volatile and hypo-critical. . . . The children of May resembled the world they attacked too much to imperil it.[57]

Some of the manifestations of revolutionary enthusiasm were certainly more easily explicable on this thesis than on any other, for instance, what was often called its '*aspect folklorique*'. There was, wrote John Gretton, a sympathetic academic eye-witness,

something more than a little bourgeois about this aspect of the student revolt (French students are essentially a bour-geois phenomenon). From being an austere temple of learn-ing (it was built at the end of the nineteenth century as a temple *to* French culture) the Sorbonne became a sort of gigantic theatre, a kind of 'Round House', where total free-dom was allowed to everybody to live as they pleased and to express themselves in their own way, where the quadrangle resembled a garden fête . . . this kind of total rejection of normal social values is only possible for those who start off with a secure base in the society that they reject. The 'beat' or 'hippy' movements of the last two decades have recruited their followers almost exclusively among the middle classes.[58]

The attempt to associate 'the workers' (never defined) with this aspect of the revolution was regarded even by some sym-pathetic academics as not merely bourgeois, but also either spurious or wildly romantic.

To believe in the possibility of using an available and dis-organized working class in order to bring about a funda-mental socialist revolution by means of spontaneous action committees [wrote Professor Maurice Duverger] is to in-dulge in a frightening utopianism. The mass of the workers is not ready for any such thing, and the nation – which is predominantly conservative – would not support it. The nature of an industrial society rules out such methods.[59]

Academic observers emphasized not only the essentially

unrealistic nature of '*ouvriérisme*',* but also the essentially non-educative nature of interminable 'teach-ins' – or rather talk-ins –in the occupied university. These were attended by ever-changing, haphazard audiences, spontaneously discussing heterogeneous subjects ranging from 'revolutionary warfare to the social function of orgies in the late Roman empire'. And the committees they set up began, of course,

> with sociology and went on to literature and sex . . . thousands of discussions which expressed and celebrated the vision of a university utopia where true knowledge, stripped of its 'class' content, could be interchanged freely.[60]

This was only one side of the picture. If what it describes was harmless, it was all the same unlikely to add to the sum of human knowledge. But there was another side. An example of it is provided by the factual account of what was actually involved in the application of the decision, announced in *Le Monde* on 5 June, to occupy the British Institute in Paris, rebaptize it *Institut britannique populaire* and invite 'workers' to join in organizing it as a 'critical university'. On 15 June, the Director of the Institute, Mr Francis Scarfe, wrote, in a letter to *The Times* (19 June 1968):

> The British Institute in Paris was thus occupied at 4 p.m. on June 4 by an anonymous group of students and non-students of various nationalities, including British, French, American, German, Dutch, Spanish, South American and Cuban. Since then it has proved almost impossible to negotiate with them as they are not students of this institute and the occupying body is constantly changing.
> . . . As a group they have turned the institute into a doss-house for all comers, have fouled the premises, broken locks, destroyed doors and furniture, and written slogans all over the inside walls. They have hoisted black and red flags outside. They have prevented the institute from carrying out its legitimate functions. Apart from some £2000–£3000

* '*Ouvriérisme*' is an emotive term, meaning the attribution to a notional entity called 'the workers' of special virtues and special claims to leadership.

damage which they have now done, their occupation has already caused a loss of income of about £10,000 to the institute, which has very limited resources, as well as imperilled its future. . . . Meanwhile the livelihood of 92 employees and their dependents is at stake, as well as the studies of about 6000 students. . . .

Whatever grievances the students had against French universities, they could have had none against this British institution. Clearly, in the revolutionary-student hierarchy, some 'workers and students' were regarded as being definitely less equal than others!

If there were 'hippy', 'beat', and 'squatter' elements among the revolutionaries, the revolution itself was a kind of *Fronde*, in that it had no coherent objectives. This led some observers to conclude that the escalation of the movement was purely fortuitous. It has been suggested that the various revolutionary theories were not a cause, but a consequence, being thought up *en cours de route*, or even after the event.[61] For instance, Jacques Sauvageot of the students' union (UNEF), Alain Geismar of the teachers' union (SNE-Sup), and Daniel Cohn-Bendit emerged as leading personalities in quite haphazard ways. They were not in any way representative of their respective organizations, and Daniel Cohn-Bendit himself rejected the whole concept of leadership. He did not play an active rôle after the first week or so, and he was actually out of the country for much of the time. The participating movements disagreed on both tactics and aims. Individuals and movements quite extraneous to either the student or the trade-union world joined in both occupations and demonstrations.

Though a number of participants interviewed appeared to have had only the vaguest ideas of what they hoped to achieve, many spoke of the need for reforms in the educational system, and a great many of the student and *lycée* action committees did actively concern themselves with trying to work out provisional plans for reform. For some of these would-be reformers, the spontaneity and licence of the revolutionaries were seen as reactions against the excessive formalism and rigidity of both

school and university curricula and methods, and the main aim
of the movement was reform of the educational system. Some
of the plans that they produced were demagogic and unrealistic, but others were well thought-out and intelligent documents, produced by joint staff and student or staff and pupil
committees. This aspect of the revolution was recognized as
having made a positive, if only very limited, contribution to
the actual reform of university education carried out later in
the year.[62]

None of these theories necessarily excludes any other, since
the 'revolution' was essentially pluralistic and unorganized.
There were also circumstances which exercised an indisputable
influence over the development of the movement, but whose
importance it is impossible to estimate with any degree of
accuracy. Among these must be included the effects of radio
and television reporting. It enabled organizations and areas to
feel themselves part of a larger movement, directly encouraged
imitative adventures, and so contributed to the speed with
which strikes and occupations spread throughout the country.
The influence of transistors had been much commented on
during the 'revolt of the Generals'. Then, it was a factor that
certainly strengthened the President's hand. In 1968, it equally
certainly assisted the students.[63]

Another factor of importance was the already existing
acceptance by much of public opinion of a degree of violence
in pressing political demands. General de Gaulle at first attributed the student revolt to 'the immense political, economic
and social transformation' that France was going through, and
therefore urged the need to adapt institutions to meet these
new stresses, especially through participation. A week later, he
had decided that it was due to 'intimidation, brain-washing
and tyranny, carried out by groups which for a long time have
been organized by a totalitarian party'.[64] M. Pompidou also
emphasized the importance of changing structures, recalling
events in the fifteenth century, 'that despairing period when
the structures of the Middle Ages were collapsing and when
students of the Sorbonne were also in revolt'.[65] The students
could quote precedents much nearer at hand – farmers' riots,

the violence of small tradesmen's associations, and the concessions that followed the violence. M. Pompidou's own
immediate announcement, on his return to Paris from Afghanistan, of concessions to student demands did not pass un-
noticed. There had been ample evidence during the ten years of
the Fifth Republic that violence paid. Why should it not pay
for students and trade unions?

> The revolt of youth [wrote a commentator] certainly went
> too far; but who would have listened to them without
> barricades, without burnt-out cars, without police bâtons?[66]

Algerians, farmers, and small tradesmen had also concluded
that violence was the only way of forcing the Government to
pay attention to them. The Grenelle agreement and the
Government's speedy introduction of the university-reform
Bill immediately after the election could reasonably be seen as
further confirmation of the accuracy of this view.

Nevertheless, although the revolt can be regarded as a
'happening' to which all these factors contributed something,
and which evolved in a haphazard way in response to circumstances, without either coherent objectives or even an agreed
strategy, it could reasonably be argued that it would not have
become the unique phenomenon that it was without the conjunction of a number of political circumstances, none of which
was in itself determinant. Two of these circumstances created a
potentially revolutionary situation. They were, first, the existence of long-standing political, economic and social grievances,
in this case caused primarily by the discontent of two specific
sections of the community that seemed to have been left
behind in the upheavals of the economic and technological
revolution. The too numerous – sometimes intellectually inadequate – pupils and students and the underpaid workers in
nationalized industries and in under-modernized industries
provided two large and permanently dissatisfied classes of the
community, both of which had repeatedly proclaimed their
grievances during the previous years.

The second circumstance was the underlying fear that the
political system itself might be vulnerable. This was never far

below the surface. The fact that Gaullist leaders (and General de Gaulle in particular) so often claimed that the Fifth Republic had eliminated this constitutional vulnerability and established stable political institutions was in itself an indication of the extent to which both politicians and public needed to be reassured on this point and yet, despite reassurances, remained unsure. The frequent predictions of 'a crisis of the régime', when General de Gaulle ceased to be head of the State, frequent disagreements regarding interpretations of the Constitution, the growth of violence among certain sectional interests, the spread of extremist groups (some of them violent) on both Right and Left – all these helped to strengthen both memories of the ease with which in the past political crises had escalated into constitutional crises, and also fears that this might happen again.

To transform what was no more than a potentially dangerous situation into revolutionary action that threatened immediate danger, two additional conditions were required – the spark to ignite the conflagration and the high winds to spread it. The spark was provided by the Sorbonne incident, when what began as merely another in a long series of university incidents suddenly flared into a political challenge, thanks to the accidental conjunction of vacillations on the part of the authorities, traditional resentment of police action against students (both magnified by tactical errors), public apathy, and the presence on the spot of the potential mass support of some forty to fifty thousand involuntarily idle and resentful students.[67]

The high wind, which enabled a confrontation between students and the authorities to develop rapidly into a nation-wide political crisis, was the fact that the situation was capable of being exploited by at least four separate sections of the community. The factory workers used it in order to press their claims for better wages and conditions. Some teachers and students used it to publicize long-standing complaints about educational conditions, while revolutionary student minorities used it to preach 'instant' revolution. Left-wing politicians used it to try to recover the political appeal that had eluded them for ten years. And finally, when the spread of wild-cat strikes became serious, the most powerful trade-union movement, the Communist-dominated CGT, was presented with the alternatives of coming in and trying to dominate the movement, or of being itself undermined by undisciplined groups of the ranks and file that it had been trying to control since 1966. All these elements were seeking to manipulate the 'revolution' to serve their own ends, but none of them in reality wanted a successful revolution, as was made clear by the speed with which normality was restored, once the trade unions, whose organizing ability was essential to the maintenance of the revolutionary movement's momentum, had reason to believe that their major demands could be met without its continuance.

Why and how did the Government allow the situation to get out of hand? Allowance must be made for the extent to which Governments in all developed countries have appeared powerless in face of the relatively new problem of direct and violent action by small 'commandos', whether in universities or in industry. In France, there were also a number of specific contributory factors. For one thing, the explosion was entirely unexpected. On 2 May, nobody foresaw its rapid escalation into a national threat. The Prime Minister was absent from 2 to 11 May in Afghanistan, and the three Ministers most vitally concerned (Education, the Interior and Justice) were all relative newcomers to their jobs.[68] In addition, the Minister of Education had inherited from his predecessor the peculiarly delicate problem of a half-completed and highly unpopular reform of the school system. He was young and ambitious and so had not dared to do anything. Nor did he dare to take initiatives in May 1968. The situation of the university authorities was rendered more difficult by the nature of the French educational system, which was so highly centralized that almost all decisions of any importance had to be referred to Paris. Once the students had decided to defy the university authorities, they were, in reality, challenging the State, and what was needed was decisive action from the top. Not only was this not forthcoming from M. Pompidou until too late, but three days after he returned, General de Gaulle himself left on a visit to Rumania, just at the crucial moment when the industrial strike movement was beginning.

The first weaknesses, then, were uncertainties as to where authority really lay and failure to realize soon enough the potential seriousness of the situation. The domination of President and Prime Minister in the French quasi-presidential system inevitably tends to increase the danger of a vacuum of authority at the ministerial level. The result in this case was 'a classic example of how not to manage a crisis, of dithering, crossed lines of authority, flight from responsibility and of too little too late'.[69]

The third question is: Why did the Left, and especially such experienced political leaders as MM. Mitterrand and Mendès France, make the political mistake, at the end of May, of appearing to present themselves as leaders of an alternative Government that would have been brought to power by insurrection and processions in the streets? This question is answerable only in the context of the traditional myths of the Left, and of its political frustration during the past ten years. M. Mendès France had always opposed the régime and had predicted, with what many even on the Left regarded as excessive confidence, that it would not outlive de Gaulle. He also believed that the change would come, 'not from a man, a group of men, parties' but from 'the voice of the people'.[70] It was perhaps comprehensible, therefore, that he should eventually persuade himself that the May marches and mass meetings represented that voice.

M. Mitterrand was in a somewhat different position. As head of the left-wing Federation's 'shadow Cabinet' (*le contre-gouvernement*) and the former left-wing presidential candidate, he was the obvious candidate for power, if General de Gaulle were either to resign or to be beaten in the proposed referendum. His mistake was, first, to misread the state of public opinion, and second, to couch his statements in terms that could be used as more effective propaganda by his opponents than by his friends. The Left's over-estimate of the political importance of the movement has to be seen, too, against the background of the difficulties of a situation of apparently permanent opposition. The non-Communist Left had spent the past ten years in an effort to do several impossible things at once – to increase its own cohesion, and especially that of the Socialist party; to improve its image in the country, in which the Socialist party's appeal to the electorate had been steadily declining; to obtain a working electoral agreement with the Communist party in order to maximize its parliamentary representation, but without appearing to be dependent on the Communists; and finally, to present to the electorate an agreed statement (failing agreement on a joint programme) that could reasonably be expected to appeal to the electorate as the basis for an alternative Government.

Since these objectives were incompatible, if not unobtainable, the prospects of success, after ten years, still seemed remote. It was comprehensible that some Socialists should, if only for a brief period, allow themselves to be carried away to the extent of becoming the victims of their own myths. Like the revolutionary students, some saw themselves as re-living the revolutions of 1789, 1830, 1848, 1871 and, perhaps, especially 1936, when a general strike had been the prelude to a Popular Front Government.[71] In reality, of course, though the 1936 strike has become part of Socialist revolutionary mythology, there was no resemblance between it and 1968. In 1936, the strike had been called *after* a Socialist electoral *victory*, and so had helped to strengthen the hand of the incoming Socialist Prime Minister, who had a majority for an agreed left-wing programme. The participants in the 1968 events had no common policy.[72] By the end of May, they had also lost the support of the public, and were on the eve of an electoral *defeat*.

These facts in themselves help to provide an answer to the fourth question: Why did the revolution collapse so quickly? The short and simple answer is that it did so when trade-union elements that gave the movement its strength were convinced that they could attain their objectives (namely an improvement on the Grenelle agreements) by normal bargaining procedures. At that point, trade-union leaders could afford to get back to the job of restoring normal trade-union discipline. The announcement of an impending general election brought the left-wing political parties back to political reality with a bang – to the world of electoral tactics, in which they had to appeal to an electorate that they had been ignoring, and that was heartily sick of the effects of the strikes. And trivial though it may seem, it was nevertheless a fact in May 1968, as in May 1958, that even a national crisis was not enough to prevent thousands of French families from streaming away from Paris for the Whitsun weekend holiday. This, too, helped to recreate an atmosphere of normality.[73] When they returned, they were faced with other normal requirements – the need to fight an election and to think about overdue school and university examinations.

CHAPTER V

The Aftermath

ECONOMIC AND SOCIAL PROBLEMS

Whatever the difficulties of discerning the causes of the May events, their political and economic consequences made themselves very quickly felt. The election resulted in an overwhelming Gaullist victory. The Government could count on an unprecedentedly large parliamentary majority for the next five years. Almost three out of four Deputies in the new Assembly belonged to one or other of the two Government parties, and the Gaullist party had an overall majority, even without the support of its allies – a unique feat for a single French party in the twentieth century. On the opposition side the number of Deputies had fallen by over a half. Seats held by the Federation had been reduced from 121 to 57 and those held by the Communist party from 73 to 34. M. Mitterrand's *Convention des Institutions républicaines* had been reduced from 16 to one, and he himself, as the sole survivor, now joined the Deputies belonging to no group. By the autumn, the Federation had quietly disappeared. The Radicals decided, however, to remain 'affiliated' to the Socialist parliamentary group 'for administrative reasons', that is in order to enjoy the advantages of an organized parliamentary group, without the political obligation of supporting its policies.[1]

Politically, the Government had never been in a stronger position. The parliamentary opposition parties were politically as well as numerically impotent, for their attention was almost wholly concentrated on internal and inter-party quarrels. Socialists and Communists could no longer agree even on electoral tactics, and neither in the referendum of 1969 nor in the subsequent presidential election was there anything that looked remotely like a united front of the Left. The Socialist party was moreover engaged, following the disappearance of the Federation, in working out its own reorganization.

On the Government side, there were changes, in themselves surprising, but not bringing any break in the solid phalanx of Gaullist supporters. The traditional, and usually formal, resignation of a Government following a general election led, to general surprise, to a change of Prime Minister. How much M. Pompidou himself was taken by surprise, and how much foundation there was for the rumours of friction and disagreement between himself and the President regarding tactics during the May events were questions to which no public answers were provided.[2] Nor was any politically credible reason given for his departure from office at a moment when he was regarded by most people as the principal architect of the Gaullist victory. The President's letter to him, accepting his resignation, merely contained an ambiguous phrase, recalling that contained in the letter accepting M. Debré's resignation six years earlier. It referred to some possible 'future mission' or responsibility that might be 'entrusted to him by the nation',[3] a phrase that naturally stimulated speculation about the President's intentions regarding succession to the presidency. The President, however, provided no elucidation, and M. Pompidou retired to the back benches, a position from which he was to be influential in the Gaullist party, and also very soon to take political initiatives that would have been impossible if he had remained Prime Minister. He was replaced by M. Couve de Murville, who had been barely two months in the post of Minister of Finance since the previous Government reshuffle.

Its position of unprecedented political strength did not mean that the Government had no problems. The economic and financial situation following the disturbances of May and June was serious. The Government was faced with the immediate problem of preventing the troubles from flaring up again before it had had the chance to restore confidence in the franc and get production moving again. This was no easy task. On the one hand, the wage increases granted under pressure from

the trade unions were bound to increase the dangers of inflation, unless the cost could be rapidly absorbed by increased
productivity and the restoration of economic stability. On the
other hand, it was going to be necessary to placate the students
by greatly increased expenditure on buildings and staff, and
this was not the moment for increased education estimates on
top of the increased wages bill. Yet to risk discontent in either
sector was to risk fresh disturbances and calls for solidarity
between workers and students. And these would immediately
place fresh strains on the franc.

The first priorities were to get the workers back to work, to
deal with the financial crisis, and to give the students some
immediate satisfaction, since expansions of buildings and staff
were bound to take time. The last objective was achieved by
the announcement on 14 July of the forthcoming introduction
of a Bill for the comprehensive reform of university education.
The responsibility of piloting it through Parliament was entrusted to M. Edgar Faure, who had exchanged the hot seat
of the Ministry of Agriculture for the far hotter seat of the
Ministry of Education. The Government then took steps to
halt the outflow of capital by imposing exchange control and
increasing Bank rate. Production was encouraged by direct
aid to smaller firms (in which the higher wages were likely to
create difficulties) and to exporters, along with restrictions on
imports, in the hope of keeping price increases down to about
3 per cent during the following months. To meet the cost of
the new measures, taxation was increased and military expenditure cut back by the slowing down of the nuclear programme.
Prevention of a sizeable budgetary and trade deficit was still
impossible, but it was hoped that the generally healthy state
of the French economy and of the reserves would enable the
country to support these measures until production could pick
up. In a speech to the National Assembly on 17 July, M. Couve
de Murville expressed confidence in France's recovery within a
period of eighteen months.

By the following November, however, fresh measures had
to be taken to meet a renewed flight from the franc, largely
caused by speculation regarding the possible revaluation of the

mark, but aggravated by the premature removal in September of the exchange controls imposed in July. Bank rate was further increased and international aid called in to bolster up the franc. There were further tax increases and reductions in Government expenditure. In view of General de Gaulle's refusal to devalue the franc,[4] the only alternative was an unpopular austerity programme, in order to reduce as much as possible a budget deficit, by then estimated to be in the region of eleven thousand million francs.

The Government could at least hope for reasonably good industrial relations. The Grenelle agreements of 27 May had already provided for immediate wage increases of 7 per cent (to be increased to 10 per cent in October), a reduction in some working hours from 1970 onwards, a reduction in the proportion of health charges borne by insured persons, and agreement on the part of the employers to study both the possibilities of better vocational training and the trade-union claim to the right to pursue certain activities on the firm's premises. In addition, the national minimum hourly wage (*le salaire minimum interprofessionel garanti*, or SMIG) was increased to three francs per hour, estimated to be equivalent to an increase of about 30 per cent in the wages of the lowest-paid workers. Renewed discussions at the beginning of June resulted in some further concessions to workers' demands, of which the most important was the lifting of the agricultural minimum wage (SMAG) to the SMIG level, thus increasing the farm workers' minimum by about 56 per cent.[5] It was generally estimated that the wage increases amounted overall to an increase of between 10 and 15 per cent during 1968, that is, almost double the rate that had been expected before the May events.

In fact, France recovered superficially from the effects of the events with surprising rapidity. They had involved a loss of working hours equivalent to 3 per cent of the gross national product, together with a great deal of material damage, but productivity increased at the rate of 4·5 per cent per annum.[6] The weak spot remained the danger of price rises, but these remained at around 3 per cent until the beginning of 1969, and so the increase in purchasing power obtained as a result of the Grenelle agreements remained sizeable. There was no significant industrial discontent until the promised review of wages in March (the Tilsitt 'rendezvous'), when the Government was obliged to refuse to accord more than an increase of 2 per cent, to be followed by a further 2 per cent in the autumn. This led to a 24-hour general strike on 11 March, which, however, was not followed by any general worsening in industrial relations.[7] The trade-union movements had their own problems and were not anxious for any fresh confrontation with the Government. Relations between the CGT and the CFDT were strained as a result of the sympathy shown by the latter for the revolutionaries, and the CGT was preoccupied by the need to deal with the dissident elements in its own ranks.[8]

The last few months of General de Gaulle's presidency, therefore, saw no more than local industrial disputes, mainly in the public sector. The social climate was also improved by the signing in February of the promised agreement on security of employment.[9] From the beginning of 1969 onwards, the ordinance on profit sharing began to be applied. It cannot be said, however, that this either helped or hindered industrial relations, for progress was very slow, and, at the end of six months, only 262 agreements had been signed, affecting in all under a quarter of a million workers.[10] There were, moreover, still disquieting elements in both the social and the economic fields. There was growing public irritation at the persistence of leftist agitation in universities and in some *lycées*, in which work was intermittently disrupted.[11] A number of extremist organizations had been dissolved in June 1968,[12] and in the autumn, the right-wing extremist organization, *Occident*,[13] was also dissolved. But it was impossible to prevent some of the movements from being re-formed under different names. The Government's amnesty Bill and the President's 14 July amnesty decrees had, however, placated some right-wing opinion, since they resulted in the freeing of all remaining prisoners convicted of offences during the Algerian war, including members of the OAS.[14] In the economic field, the trade balance remained unfavourable and export prospects were not good, partly owing to the effects of increased costs on French industrial competitiveness. Between July 1968 and June 1969, French currency reserves fell by almost half. Employment, however, improved somewhat, though the figures remained high enough to constitute a problem.

The main focus of interest during these months was, however, not economic but political. The autumn of 1968 saw the debates inside and outside Parliament on the university-reform Bill, and from then on the headlines were dominated by the discussion, followed by the referendum campaign, on regionalization and the proposed reform of the Senate. The 1968 National Assembly was not one in which a sympathetic welcome was to be expected for a Bill whose aim was, in General de Gaulle's words, to 'organize participation where it does not exist and to develop it where it does', and to do so in conditions which would recognize 'the autonomy of universities in teaching, research, administration and financial matters'.[15]

The merits and demerits of the measure would not *in se* be relevant to the subject of this book, if it were not for the fact that Republican politics has traditionally been so bound up with educational principles and controversies that it is always very difficult to separate educational from political preoccupations, and this Bill had more political implications than most. The 1789 Revolutionaries had proclaimed the obligation of the State to provide education for all its citizens.[16] The nineteenth and part of the twentieth centuries had seen long battles to eradicate or reduce the influence of the Catholic Church on education. Radical and Socialist policies in the 1930s had favoured the principle of *l'école unique* – a French form of the comprehensive principle which sought to break down the social divisions between primary and secondary schools by the introduction of a common syllabus up to the end of the first four years of secondary education. The 1940s and the 1960s had seen efforts to raise the school-leaving age and renewed efforts to introduce a common syllabus up to the age of about 15 (*le tronc commun*), including the postponement of the teaching of Latin, in order to equalize the chances of children in *lycées* (which taught Latin from the age of 11) and those in other secondary schools.[17]

The 1968 revolutionaries wanted to go much farther much faster. But whatever the support of 'progressive' parties for educational reforms, and even for the principles of university autonomy and student participation, no party, either on the Right or on the Left, was prepared in practice to relinquish State control. Just as Napoleon had regarded the educational system as an instrument of the Napoleonic State, so Republican Governments – and especially on the Left – regarded it as an instrument of the Republican State, and especially as a defence against any attempt to undermine the secular character of Republican education. There were, in addition, essentially political characteristics of the system to which the Left as a whole remained fanatically attached, irrespective of their educational effects. These included, for instance, the principle of 'non-selection', which made the possession of the *baccalauréat* a universally acceptable entrance qualification, not merely to universities, but also to whatever Faculty the student might choose, irrespective of his previous preparation in particular subjects, and of the degree of overcrowding in the Faculty in question. This was regarded as a sacrosanct symbol of equality and of the Revolutionary heritage, and the same parents and students who demonstrated against overcrowding and under-staffing also demonstrated with even more fervour against any suggestion for dealing with the problem by the only method that could have provided some immediate relief, namely, the general application of principles of 'selection'.[18]

It was inevitable, therefore, that the university-reform Bill would be politically controversial. The circumstances in which it was voted added to its political character. It was *une œuvre de circonstance* – a response to the revolutionary-student challenge, and one that involved proposals to turn upside down, within a period of months, a system that had been firmly established for more than a century without undergoing any serious modification. Except to a handful of reformers and revolutionaries, this system was an object of national pride, and any attempt to loosen at a stroke the bonds of the most centralized administrative system imaginable was bound to encounter opposition, and not only from the Left. Moreover, since the new system was put forward as a panacea for the ills of May, it was, in its way, as doctrinaire as the one it was to supersede, yet without the latter's most solid advantages, which were its familiarity and its uniformity. The new system was strange, multiform, full of ambiguities and unknowns, incapable of functioning with any degree of efficiency without infinitely more time and goodwill than would be forthcoming on the part of teachers, taught and civil servants, and without infinitely more immediate expenditure on personnel, equipment and buildings than the Government could possibly afford in the circumstances. It was bound, therefore, to be in practice, at least in the short run, a device 'to replace disorderly organization by organized disorder'.[19]

That the Bill was voted in the National Assembly by 441 votes to none and in the Senate by 260 to none in no way indicates the kind of political consensus that such unprecedented votes might seem to imply. The apparent consensus was the result of a general realization that General de Gaulle, whose continued presence at the head of the State had just been approved by a massive majority, was behind M. Faure and intended Parliament to vote the Bill, which it did in record time. Drafted in six weeks, it was voted at the end of the following six weeks. Approved by the Council of Ministers on 19 September, it was debated in the two parliamentary assemblies between 3 and 10 October (that is, at the beginning of the autumn session) and promulgated on 12 November.

The main grievances of the vast 'silent majority' of students and parents were, in fact, educational, not political. They were the shortage of teachers, the inadequacy of buildings, the irrelevance of some university courses to requirements for future employment, the remoteness of senior university staff from the students, and the administrative restrictions applied to students in residence on university campuses or in *cités universitaires*.[20] Only the last of these was capable of a speedy remedy. The main grievances of the small but vocal minority of students (supported by a number of teachers – mainly juniors) were three. Two were essentially political – the problem of 'selection', and the right of students to carry on political activities, including political propaganda meetings, on university premises. The third was a politico-administrative-cum-educational objection to the whole way in which the universities were run. They wanted administrative and financial autonomy, involving what was usually described by the vague term of 'self-management' (*autogestion* or *cogestion*), a change of teaching methods that would permit what were called '*contestation*' and '*confrontation*' (a permanent challenge to everything), as well as changes both in curricula and in the examination system and in some cases the abolition of examinations.[21]

On the principle of selection, the Government was obviously beaten from the start. In 1964, the Minister of Education, M. Fouchet, who undertook a comprehensive reform of the school system, had been obliged to provide assurances that he would maintain the right of university entry to those duly qualified, 'without limitation or planning'. M. Faure was obliged to give similar assurances, though the figures quoted by responsible university authorities provided overwhelming evidence in support of selection. By 1968, the number of students had risen to over half a million. About 95 per cent of those who passed the *baccalauréat* entered universities. This was the highest proportion in Europe. About 50 per cent of these were regularly eliminated by the first-year examinations. One Dean of a Faculty stated that selection would reduce the intake by about 35 per cent.[22] University teachers and others[23] pointed out how bad the system of non-selection was:

It means [said the Dean of the Arts Faculty of Toulouse], the overburdening of the 'first cycle' of higher education by a large number of students who are not up to standard, and the provision of a large number of teachers for them. We *are* operating a system of selection, since 50 per cent of students never reach the 'second cycle'.[24]

The previous Minister of Education had put it more brutally: 'It is', he had said, 'as if we organized a system of shipwreck in order to pick out the best swimmers'.[25]

In spite of these facts, and of the Government's previous announcement that selection would be introduced in 1969, the the Bill made no mention of it, because the Minister had already sold the pass, before the Bill was drafted: 'Selection', he had said in July, 'is in no way absurd; yet this system has not been adopted.' He had gone on to give highly unconvincing reasons for this decision. His real reason was that he hoped to find a way round the problem that would produce the same result without arousing emotive opposition. Better streaming in the higher forms of secondary schools and adequate provision of alternatives to university education, especially in technical institutes, would provide a sounder basis of pre-selection at school level. He admitted, however, that at the moment these alternatives did not exist in sufficient numbers. More important still, they did not have the same prestige in the minds of the public.[26]

The second political grievance – the student demand for recognition of the right to carry on political activities on university premises – revealed even more than the first a division between conservatives and moderates on the one hand and the Left on the other. In theory, political discussions could be held hitherto only if they formed a normal part of the curriculum, though, in practice, there was a general toleration of the posting of notices and the holding of political meetings. M. Faure's Bill allowed debates on political and economic questions, on condition that they did not disrupt university life or disturb order.[27] This condition was in itself a controversial issue, for the May events had made it only too clear that university authorities did not possess the authority or the power to enforce such a provision.[28] Those who were in sympathy with the principle of permitting political activities argued (with truth) that information on political and economic subjects could help to prevent indoctrination. Opponents argued (with equal truth) that political freedom too often meant in practice the freedom of a small minority to prevent free discussion, and so increased the dangers of indoctrination. For instance, the Dean of the Faculty of Arts of Nanterre, M. Pierre Grappin, who had resigned in September 1968 after four years during which he had encouraged free discussion, commented in his letter of resignation on the impossible conditions created by the aggressive intolerance of a small minority.[29]

On the question of the reorganization of the university system, the Government steered a cautious course between concessions and precautions, with the aim of preventing any irrevocable weakening of the State's fundamental responsibility for education. The Bill voted on 11 November 1968 was essentially an 'outline-law', which made it possible for the Government to make concessions of principle on current, emotive issues, and to reserve the possibility of practical limitations on certain powers in subsequent decrees, when it could reasonably be hoped that some of the heat would have gone out of the controversy. Universities were defined as bodies enjoying 'financial autonomy'. They were no longer to be composed of the traditional Faculties, but of a variable number of smaller units, or departments (*unités d'enseignement et de recherche*, or UER), and were to be 'multi-disciplinary', that is, to include as far as possible UER in arts, science and technical subjects, even if they remained predominantly concerned with only one subject – as, for instance, was the University of Paris VI, which was predominantly concerned with the natural sciences. The number of universities was also to be greatly increased, with the aim of keeping the numbers in each of them down to about 15,000. This meant the transformation of the university of Paris into seven universities within Paris, together with two experimental ones, and four in the suburbs. Universities were also to be administratively autonomous, in that both the university itself and its UER were to be run by elected councils, presided over by a president, not appointed by Paris but elected by the council. The councils were to be expressions of the principle of participation, comprising teachers, researchers, students and administrative personnel. Students and teachers were to have equal representation.[30]

When it came to defining exactly how these governing bodies were to be chosen and what they were to do, it became immediately obvious that, though the reforms constituted something of an educational revolution, the Bill's provisions would fall very far short indeed of the political revolution desired by the supporters of the May revolution. For the election of the full quota of student representatives, a poll of at least 60 per cent was required. A smaller poll would bring a proportional diminution in the number of students elected. This requirement successfully avoided the danger of student representatives who would be the nominees of only a small minority. Though the new universities could supplement formal examinations with systems of 'continuous assessment' or group work, examinations conferring national diplomas would continue to be organized and controlled by the Ministry of Education. And though each university would decide its own expenditure and could use funds in addition to those provided by the State, it would depend on Government grants, and would be obliged to submit its accounts for the approval of the Ministry of Finance, while the administration would continue to be inspected by officials of the Ministry of Education.[31]

Parliamentary debates on the Bill revealed fears on the part of some members of the UDR that M. Faure had gone too far to meet the students. On the other hand, some reformists felt that the provisions of the Bill did not significantly weaken the centralized control of Paris. Indeed, one of the senior Paris professors remarked that if so many university teachers appeared to accept with equanimity the idea of joint management, including staff–student parity in the councils, this was quite simply because they had never had any real powers, beyond the settlement of routine day-to-day matters, and so had no feeling of giving anything up.[32] Some expressed a positive desire for the retention of central control.[33] As for the staff and students who had led or supported the May revolution, the Bill did not begin to meet their demands. Professor Ricœur of the University of Nanterre had understood 'autonomy' to mean 'real financial independence', 'the right to control the budget'.[34] The students who drew up the 'Charter of Nanterre' in June 1968 had not only rejected any kind of selection, but had also demanded total independence of universities from the State, their control by 'general assemblies' and their transformation into openly political organizations committed to 'the struggle of the workers against capitalist society'.[35] In the words of one of the prominent revolutionary theorists:

> Refusing *sélection* and the technological university, thus led straight to the demand for collective self-management, self-government and self-administration in all fields of social activity (in the factories, the workshops, the schools, the boroughs, or municipalities). By refusing the logic that underlay *sélection* the students had to refuse also the docile, subordinate, profit-motivated and class-privileged position which capitalist society was offering to the 'good', 'capable', and 'successful' students. 'We don't want to have anything to do with this society; we don't want to work for it, to be used by it, to serve it in any way', the *enragés* kept saying. And several hundreds of them indeed interrupted or gave up their studies to work in factories and to try and win the working class for revolution.[36]

Fortunately for the hundreds of thousands of students who were not interested in this revolution, the experiments of these 'hundreds' were no more encouraging than were their experiments in holding summer schools for 'students and workers'. Two of these summer schools were held in the summer of 1968 – at Montpellier and Grenoble – and both were abysmal failures.[37] Much less was heard subsequently about people's universities. It is a delusion commoner in France than elsewhere – perhaps because of the greater importance of the rôle played by middle-class intellectuals in left-wing politics – that 'the workers' are longing for endless academic and theoretical debates on subjects about which they know little, and burning to sit on committees running factories. French left-wing movements obtained some salutary direct information on these points in 1968, so that the May revolution served at least one useful purpose.

It was not to be expected that revolutionary agitation would die down immediately. In spite of the accumulating evidence of the growing loss of public sympathy for extremist students, the autumn session saw a number of sporadic disturbances in some *lycées*, as well as in universities. Most of the student unions boycotted elections for the provisional bodies on which students were to be represented, and the intermittent agitation reached a point at which, in December 1968, the Sorbonne and a Paris *lycée* were temporarily closed and both M. Faure and the Prime Minister issued statements that further university disorder would not be tolerated.[38] The Prime Minister predicted, however, that these incidents were merely the end of a past crisis and not the beginning of a new one.[39] And so it proved. Although examinations had been held belatedly, a high proportion of the students had sat for them. According to an opinion poll published in November 1968, 56 per cent of students consulted thought that the main reason for the May upheavals had been student anxieties about jobs; 35 per cent thought that they were due to university failure to modernize curricula, methods and equipment; 31 per cent simply wanted to pass their exams; only 12 per cent wanted to transform society.[40]

DOUBLE OR QUITS?

1969 was a year of political as well as educational transition. But while it was bound to take some years to get over the teething troubles of the new educational system and make possible objective assessments of its achievements and short-comings, the political experiment conducted by General de Gaulle in April 1969 had immediate, conclusive, and spectacular results.

Since the two reforms submitted to the electorate in the referendum of 27 April 1969 were defeated, it is not necessary to describe in detail the very complex Bill of 68 articles, which involved the amendment of eighteen articles of the Constitution and the repeal of four others. Very briefly summarized, it provided for the creation of regional Councils, which were, in effect, merely the existing CODERs, together with fundamental changes in the composition and functions of the Senate. Though the Senate was to be consulted on all legislation, it was to be henceforth an advisory body only, and as such, would lose its right to initiate and vote Bills, and to participate in constitutional revision, along with a number of other functions hitherto performed by it in its capacity of a parliamentary assembly. It was to be composed of 323 members, of whom 177 only would be elected as before on a territorial basis. The remaining 146 would be representatives chosen by socio-economic interests. The Economic and Social Council, which had formerly included such representatives, would cease to exist. As a consequence of the Senate's demotion, the Prime Minister instead of the President of the Senate would henceforth be the acting President of the Republic in case of a presidential vacancy.

The criticisms that the measure aroused are important, not only because they were the direct cause of the Presidents' resignation, but also because they formed part of an episode that left a number of unanswered questions. There were the questions as to why the President had considered the measure necessary in the first place, and why he had persisted in holding the referendum in face of the obvious and widespread hostility to it. The decision to hold the referendum was announced by M. Couve de Murville in his declaration of general policy on 17 July 1968, and General de Gaulle, in his press conference of 9 September, spoke at some length of the unsuitability of the Senate to modern economic and social conditions and of the decision to fuse the Economic and Social Council with it, as 'an essential element of the participation that we wish to provide for'. The text of the Bill was not published, however, until the following April, about three weeks before the referendum. By that time, prolonged consultations of regional prefects, local-government representatives, and interest groups had taken place through the winter, and there had been a debate in December in both the National Assembly and the Senate, together with a great deal of speculation and criticism in the press. These facts no doubt helped to explain the relative apathy with which the general public greeted the publication of the terms of the Bill and the opening of the referendum campaign. The Senate, of course, constituted a notable exception, since, in the opinion of almost all the Senators, what was being proposed was not the 'transformation' of the Senate but its abolition. In the words of its new President, M. Alain Poher, in his speech to the Senate on 4 April 1969, it was not in reality the Economic and Social Council that was to disappear, but the Senate.[41]

Almost all the comment was hostile to the reform from the start, and even some Gaullist party members were uneasy about it. Criticisms before and after the publication of the definitive text were much the same, all the arguments being gone over again. They fell into three categories. First, there were general objections to the procedure of the referendum and to the linking of the two reforms in a single question to be answered by the electorate. The *Conseil d'Etat*, whose *avis* given on 17 March was leaked to the press, regarded the use of the referendum in the circumstances as an unconstitutional procedure, and objected to some of the proposals for the 'transformation' of the Senate.[42] Second, there were specific objections both to the proposed composition and to the functions of the Senate. They included general constitutional arguments in favour of a bicameral system, political arguments regarding the utility of the Senate in the legislative process,[43] objections to the 'corporatist' character of its proposed composition, and suggestions that the measures dealt with in the referendum should have been, not merely discussed, but also voted by Parliament.[44] Third, there were objections to the timidity of the regionalist proposals.

In principle, public opinion was favourable to regionalism and to the retention of the Senate in its traditional form. But the Bill was unsatisfactory to regionalists, who considered it did not go far enough. Of those consulted, 67 per cent had been in favour of regional representation by election, yet the nominated socio-economic members were retained. Nor did the Bill provide for the transference of any real powers to the regions. The fact was that any degree of regional autonomy was feared by the UDR as a first step on the road to a 'regional Parliament', or at least as threatening to weaken the authority of the State.[45]

Some of the criticism was of the President rather than of the Bill. His argument that the two measures 'formed a whole'[46] was not convincing, but his long-standing hostility to the Senate was only too evident, and so there were those who felt that the real reason for the reform was to get rid of an organization that was a thorn in his flesh, and that the two measures were tied together only because this was the only way of getting public opinion to swallow the disappearance of the traditional Senate. The tone of the President's remarks sometimes appeared to support this view.

> It is no longer the function of the Senate [he said on 9 September 1968] to play its former rôle – that of counterbalancing the Chamber of Deputies – for, since 1958, the head of the State himself is responsible for preventing excesses and keeping a balance, and has the means to do so. It is easy to understand why their hybrid situation should give Senators the impression that they are being prevented from exercising what appear to them to be their powers. This would account for the *malaise* and even bitterness that leads many of them to oppose, and to do so all the more persistently because their opposition is ineffective.

Others, without necessarily feeling that the President was activated by animosity towards the Senate, still felt that the use of the 'package deal' was dishonest. And the President's familiar threat to resign if defeated was particularly resented in the absence of the kind of crisis in which it had been used before. It was resented too, because, as the Minister responsible for drafting the Bill had admitted, it was 'a political matter, not a fundamental requirement of the régime'.[47]

By the eve of the poll, all the meetings held by the UDR had not succeeded in weakening the hostility to the Bill of all parties except the UDR (the *Républicains indépendants* had decided to allow their members to vote as they pleased). Opinion polls showed an increase of estimated 'No' votes to

53 per cent, as against 45 per cent of 'Yes'. The results showed these estimates to be very nearly accurate. 53·17 per cent voted 'No', as against 46·82 per cent voting 'Yes'. Three million more people voted against the measure than had voted in favour of that submitted to them in the referendum of 1962. And whereas in 1962, only four *départements* had had a 'No' vote exceeding 55 per cent, in 1969 36 *départements* did so. Even in Paris, 28 of whose 31 Deputies were Gaullists, a majority voted 'No'.[48] The President promptly resigned on 28 April and made no further political statements.

Why he had chosen to court political death in this fashion is something that will probably never be known. At least three possible reasons have been put forward. One is, as already suggested, his dislike of the Senate and the realization that it would be constitutionally and politically difficult to get rid of it either by the regular methods of constitutional amendment or by an organic law, both of which required the agreement of the two parliamentary assemblies. This could have been one element in a more general framework of ideas. He had intended from the first (as he explained in *l'Effort*) to introduce presidential election by universal suffrage[49] as soon as he felt himself in a strong enough position to do so. He may have felt the same about his reform of the Senate, for the idea had been put forward by him as far back as the Bayeux speech of 1946, when he had spoken of the desirability of 'a second Chamber composed in the main of representatives elected by municipal councillors . . .' and which would also include 'representatives of economic organizations, families, intellectuals, in order to allow the nation's important activities to make their voice heard within the State'.[50] As an old man, he may well have felt in 1969 that this might be his last chance to complete the institutions he had suggested at Bayeux.

A second suggestion is that he had been so badly shaken by the events of 1968 that he doubted his ability to restore his authority, and so deliberately invited defeat on an issue which was relatively unimportant, and on which he could, if defeated, resign honourably and without any loss of face. This is essentially the thesis put forward by the editor of *Le Monde*, writing

under the name of Sirius, who described his action as 'a
theatrical exit, a kind of political suicide by Russian roulette'.[51]

A third suggestion, which is perhaps no more than a variant
of this, is that, though shaken by the 1968 events, he did not
despair of recovering his authority, but, on the contrary, still
regarded the theme of participation as having a sufficiently
positive appeal to give him, with the help of the threatened
resignation, the success in this referendum that he had had in
the previous three, as well as in the 1958 constitutional referendum. In other words, this was not Russian roulette, but
double or quits. If he lost, then resignation was an honourable
exit. If he won, he could confidently expect to have the necessary authority to complete his septennate. It is perhaps ironic
that, if this was indeed his aim, then one little phrase in a
broadcast shortly before the poll probably contributed to his
defeat. His statement that, if he won, he would be greatly
encouraged in his intention to fulfil his mission to the end
(*accomplir ma mission jusqu'à son terme*)[52] was interpreted in some
quarters as meaning that he would, in any case, step down in
1972, which led to the conclusion that it might be as well for
the change to come in 1969, when France was enjoying
political calm.

'ADIEU DE GAULLE?'

Whatever the factors responsible for General de Gaulle's defeat
and resignation in 1969, the event and the subsequent presidential election placed the new President in the difficult situation of succeeding a man who had become a legend, and of
inheriting a system of government devised in important parts
by his predecessor for his own use. General de Gaulle saw
himself as a statesman, not a politician, but he was not a man
for all seasons. His leadership depended essentially on the
existence, the memory or the fear of a national crisis dangerous enough to persuade his compatriots to grant him special
personal authority.

The General [wrote Douglas Johnson in 1965] has two
fundamental and contradictory beliefs. That France is

united, that there is a fundamental unity; that France is diverse and multiple, with many spiritual families. . . . The contradiction is resolved in great moments of crisis and drama. . . . It reappears when the tension slackens. . . . It is necessary, therefore, to maintain the tension and the drama.[53]

The May events had not constituted the kind of crisis that called for a de Gaulle, and, if the accounts of his conversations with André Malraux are to be believed, he himself had recognized that he had not been able to deal with it.[54] Certainly much of public opinion had accorded M. Pompidou the credit for the three decisive acts that had made it possible to end the disorder – the wages agreements, the preparation of the massive Gaullist demonstration in support of the President, and the organization of the successful Gaullist election campaign. Similarly, whether or not the President's decision to hold the 1969 referendum had been dictated by a kind of political death wish, both the decision itself and the choice of issues had revealed a lack of the political flair that he had shown in previous referenda. He himself was reported to have attributed his defeat to opposition to his policy of participation,[55] and not to opposition on the questions of regionalism and reform of the Senate, a conclusion difficult to accept. But it is unwise to attach much importance to reported remarks of General de Gaulle, when made in private conversations, and possibly half in joke or in pique.[56] What is significant about both the events of May 1968 and those of April 1969 is that they involved normal political issues that divide parties and people, whereas General de Gaulle was at his best in really dangerous national situations, such as insurrection or war, situations that unite, even if only temporarily. One Minister described him as being 'never so relaxed and resolute as in a perilous situation' and as being 'sublime when facing a tragic one'.[57]

These were not the circumstances of 1968 or 1969, even although the May events at one moment got out of hand to the point of threatening temporarily the stability of the Government. Education, regionalism, the organization and functions of the Senate – these were not problems that could be dealt with by the mobilization of the nation behind a man of destiny entrusted with special powers. They called for governmental programmes, parliamentary debates and political campaigns, for the patience, skill and common sense that would enable ordinary political leaders to reach the compromises of ordinary, democratic, parliamentary politics. What was needed was the skills of an Edgar Faure, and it was, indeed, to him that General de Gaulle turned to deal with the problem of education. But what he did not realize – that is, if he did, in fact, regard the referendum of 1969 as a serious test of his political position – was that the conditions of success were not present. The issues themselves were not vital, nor was his continued presence at the head of the State. For, whether he had intended to do so or not, he had himself provided, in M. Pompidou, an acceptable successor, who had already announced that he would (at some time) be a candidate for the presidency.[58]

It seemed likely that President Pompidou would encounter problems calling for these normal qualities of political leadership rather than for the exceptional qualities of a de Gaulle. If so, then he was inheriting political machinery in some ways ill-adapted to the task of dealing with them. General de Gaulle's approach to the governmental process had been that of a soldier. He had seen it as a chain of command, in which policies were determined by the President and carried out by descending échelons of subordinate executives. Just after his death, one of his former Ministers described the General's relations with his Ministers as being 'essentially military':

> The kind of report that he preferred was one made by a young officer to his colonel: 'At such a time I learnt that . . . I therefore decided that . . . the consequence was as follows . . .' etc., and he did not care for others to make value judgements unless he asked for them . . . he disliked executive detail. He gave general directives, and it was then for the Minister to accept the responsibility for carrying them out.[59]

This technique no doubt has great advantages in a crisis when a national leader is sure that he has a united nation

behind him. It enables him to concentrate on essentials and
avoid being submerged by details. But in the absence of such a
crisis and of such a degree of national unity, a head of Government (or a head of State who treats himself as head of Government) needs a parliamentary majority party that can tell Ministers, and Ministers who can tell civil servants, what the public
will not stand. He needs therefore to be at the head of a team
of collaborators, not of a collection of executants. And that
implies understanding men. In an obituary article published
immediately after General de Gaulle's death, Louis Vallon, a
left-wing Gaullist, recalled the following opinion of General
de Gaulle expressed in 1942 by Georges Boris, who had worked
with him in London, as well as later in Paris:

> I think he would be a great man, even a very great man, if
> he understood men as well as he understands things, if he
> could make more contact with them and handle them better.
> It is no doubt because he despises them that there is such a
> contrast between the profundity of his philosophical world
> outlook and his poor knowledge of men. And this makes
> him politically better as a strategist than as a tactician . . .
> some people cannot see the wood for the trees. He is one
> of those who cannot see the trees for the wood.[60]

General de Gaulle never understood what made politicians
tick and was as contemptuous of them and of political parties
as he was of political ideologies. He regarded Ministers as being
there to carry out presidential decisions (sometimes without
even having been told in advance what they were). He regarded
Gaullist Deputies as being there to approve his decisions, and
opposition Deputies as 'grumblers, grousers and moaners'.
The result was that there were too often breaks in the chain of
command, both between Ministers and civil servants and between Ministers and Deputies. It may be true, as General de
Gaulle maintained, that he never used the words *'l'intendance
suit'*.[61] But he often behaved as if he had. He seemed unaware
that it was not safe to assume that when he had given an order
it had been carried out. Which no doubt helps to explain the
gulf between his own complacent account of the governmental

process in *Le Renouveau*[62] and the complaints of commentators who, like Jacques Fauvet, found it

> astonishing that a Government with so strong a head should have so weak a base, that authority should so often be lacking (except in the streets and the courts) and that even when the Government sees what ought to be done, it should take so many months to reach the most obvious decisions.[63]

It helps to explain too why a system that had always been regarded as bureaucratic came to be criticized so frequently as being technocratic, and why the French administration should have been able (as it had been often under previous régimes) to water down, change, and sometimes bury unpopular measures in the process of application. And it helps to explain the permanent *malaise* between Government and the Gaullist parliamentary group. The watchword of the party was 'efficiency', but General de Gaulle's methods sometimes contributed to a great deal of inefficiency.

M. Pompidou had clearly seen the need to transform the UDR into something more like a traditional party, which could have improved matters (though it would have required far more drastic changes in political habits to make much impact on the power of the French bureaucratic machine). But as Prime Minister he had encountered opposition from the section of the party described as 'the faithful Gaullists'. As President, he had not in 1969 and 1970 the authority to make any fundamental changes, even if he had wanted to do so, because he was himself in a difficult and delicate situation. Without either the exceptional record or the exceptional personal qualities of a de Gaulle, he had to create a new presidential image. But, as a faithful servant who had, for six years, conformed to General de Gaulle's conception of a Prime Minister, he could not, as a new President, immediately appear to be disloyal, nor were the faithful Gaullists any readier than they had been to accept the slightest deviation from the letter of the Gaullist word as they understood it to have been laid down by General de Gaulle. More important still, the founder of Gaullism was not dead, but only in retirement at Colombey-les-deux-Eglises. Who knew in 1969 and 1970 whether he might not at any moment break his silence, or even, if difficulties should arise, perhaps respond to a call for his return? The first years of the Pompidou septennate were, therefore, bound to be full of hesitations and uncertainties. Was this really the beginning of *l'après-Gaullisme*, or might General de Gaulle's *adieu* turn out after all to be only *au revoir*?

CHAPTER VI

Continuity or Change?

Disorder or chaos had often been predicted as the inevitable consequence of General de Gaulle's departure. In fact, the first reactions were a mixture of stupefaction, apprehension, relief and bereavement – depending on political viewpoints. But within a matter almost of hours, political life seemed, at least superficially, to have returned to normal. The acting President had taken up his residence in the Elysée, M. Pompidou had announced his intention to stand as candidate for the presidency, as had M. Gaston Defferre. And the country swung into the routine of preparation for a presidential election.

THE POLITICAL IMPORTANCE OF THE PRESIDENTIAL ELECTION

Nevertheless, this presidential election was bound to have a political importance quite different from that of the two previous ones. For eleven years, the personality of the President had dominated politics. Elections and referenda alike had been votes for and against General de Gaulle. The parties of the Left, whatever their differences, had all had as their primary aim to defeat Gaullism, while the Gaullist party had been a faithful expression of loyalty to General de Gaulle. Yet the first impression of the first electoral campaign to be conducted in his absence (physical as well as political, for he had gone to Ireland) was that he might never have existed. 'In a few weeks,' wrote the *Année politique* later, 'his style and his favourite themes had disappeared. The candidates talked only of bread-and-butter politics (*l'intendance*). Their priorities had changed.'[1] But whether or not this was merely a return to older and more familiar political attitudes that General de Gaulle had tried and failed to eradicate was not clear for some time.

What did appear certain was that the political battle was to be essentially between the Gaullist conception of the presidential rôle and the somewhat muted version offered by M. Pompidou's main opponent, M. Alain Poher. The latter was the interim President, a Centrist acceptable also to the Left, with a blameless record of political service in European organizations and Ministerial *cabinets*, with impeccable 'European' sympathies, and who, in 1968, had replaced M. Gaston Monnerville as President of the Senate. M. Poher appeared, indeed, an ideal President of the Fourth Republic.[2] He had made a highly popular début in his rôle of acting President by declaring that, as a temporary President only, who had not been 'invested' by the French people, it behoved him to be 'modest and decent'.[3] In accordance with this principle, he had delayed the declaration of his candidature until the last moment and announced that, in view of his rôle as acting President, he would not campaign actively, but merely use his allotted radio and television time.

At this stage, a number of factors were on his side. First, the remaining five candidates were all in one way or another fairly obvious non-starters. Three could be dismissed as having no intention or desire to win. M. Michel Rocard, secretary-general of the left-wing Socialist PSU, was regarded by the orthodox Socialist party as standing for the express purpose of dividing 'the democratic forces'.[4] He described himself as representing a conception of Socialism that involved 'the taking over by everybody – all workers and their organizations including trade unions and family associations – of the problems of daily life'.[5] M. Alain Krivine, a 1968 revolutionary still in his twenties and the founder a few weeks earlier of the Trotskyite movement, the *Ligue communiste*, described himself as being in favour of revolution, opposed to the Communist party, and to what the organ of his movement called 'the cretinism' of both Parliament and Leftists.[6] The third, M. Louis-Ferdinand Ducatel, was the inevitable 'individualist' or 'freak' candidate – the Barbu of 1969. He was in favour of private enterprise (thanks to which he was apparently a millionaire), opposed to bureaucracy and (comprehensibly) tax-collectors, and described himself as 'one of the discontented'. His own estimate of support for himself was 22 per cent. In fact he obtained 1·28 per cent of the votes cast, while MM. Rocard and Krivine obtained respectively 3·66 and 1·06 per cent.

The other two, M. Jacques Duclos, septuagenarian Communist Senator and elder statesman of the party, and M. Gaston Defferre, leader of the Socialist parliamentary group in the National Assembly, who had failed in 1965 to win acceptance of his candidature as the representative of a *'grande fédération'* including Centrists and Socialists, were standing in opposition to each other for purely tactical party reasons. Since the Socialist and Communist parties had been unable to reach the kind of electoral agreement that had made it possible for M. François Mitterrand to stand in 1965 as the presidential candidate of a united Left, each party was anxious to prove that it could attract more votes than the other. The Socialists calculated that a Socialist-cum-Communist candidate might well obtain second place in the first ballot, which (since only two candidates were allowed to stand in the event of a second ballot) would effectively ensure the election of M. Pompidou. For it was unlikely that the Centrists would supply the necessary votes for victory to a candidate closely associated with the Communist party. Socialists wanted, therefore, to ensure that they should come third (thus demonstrating their superior appeal to that of the Communists). They could then advise their supporters to vote for M. Poher at the second ballot.

Unfortunately for those who supported this plan, considerable sections of left-wing opinion (including M. Mitterrand's CIR and other groups in process of negotiating their fusion within a reorganized Socialist party) would have preferred a Socialist–Communist to a Socialist–Centrist line-up, and were opposed to M. Gaston Defferre owing to his 1965 activities.[7] M. Defferre also made a serious tactical error by taking the extraordinary step of presenting M. Mendès France as his intended Prime Minister, if he were to be elected President. The proposal was not actually unconstitutional, but it was unprecedented, politically inept, and generally criticized.[8] For M. Mendès France had consistently declared himself opposed to the system of presidential election which he was now implicitly supporting. These tactical manœuvres provided a classic picture of the 'party games' of 'the system' that General de Gaulle had so often castigated. As was pointed out by M. André Philip, a former Socialist who had become a left-wing Gaullist: 'Neither a single left-wing candidature, nor a Socialist–Centrist coalition makes sense without any decision regarding the purposes for which the alliance has been concluded.'[9]

M. Poher benefited initially from the contrast that he presented both to these left-wing rivals and to Gaullism. He had 'a more democratic air about him' than M. Pompidou.[10] He responded to a certain French need for 'a quiet life and reassurance'.[11] 'Nothing alarming,' wrote Pierre Viansson-Ponté. 'Nothing inspiring or really reassuring either. Everything is vague, colourless, fluid. Perhaps after all this is what the French really want.'[12] But this retiring modesty had its own problems. It immediately raised doubts regarding the utility of a weak President, in a situation in which the National Assembly could normally be counted on to have a massive Gaullist majority for the following three years. M. Poher took note of this difficulty and committed himself to a string of positive policy statements, some of which would have been unacceptable to any conceivable parliamentary majority, while others would certainly have been unacceptable to a Gaullist-dominated National Assembly. He was then faced with questions as to how he would deal with a situation of deadlock between President and National Assembly.[13]

The main dilemma of his opponent, M. Pompidou, was that only 100 per cent continuity would satisfy those Gaullists for whom Gaullist policy had to remain that previously decided by General de Gaulle, while only change would satisfy the more right-wing elements of the existing Gaullist majority in the National Assembly. Too much continuity risked the loss of too many votes, while too much change destroyed his own credibility, since he had been for six years the chief executant of Gaullist policies. While his more right-wing supporters intended to introduce more caution into participationist educational and industrial policies, left-wing Gaullists, such as MM. Vallon and Capitant, were already accusing him of intending to bury some of the reforms advocated by General de Gaulle.[14] His solution to the dilemma was, first, to conclude a firm alliance with the Giscardian conservatives, which he could do without committing himself to any very definite concessions because each needed the support of the other, and then to play the anti-Communist card that he had used so successfully in the general election the previous year. He also emphasized continuity by tributes to General de Gaulle,[15] and advocated change in cautious and general terms.

What really defeated M. Poher was less the appeal of M. Pompidou than his own hesitation and over-volubility, combined with the essential political weakness of his position, namely, the absence of any conceivable coherent parliamentary majority that would support the policies he advocated. The failure of M. Defferre's campaign (he received only 5·07 per cent of the votes cast in the first ballot) meant that M. Poher would not be able to count on receiving a sufficient number of Socialist votes at the second ballot to ensure his election, and the fact of his consequent dependence on some Communist support weakened his credibility as a moderate.

M. Pompidou's victory in the second ballot (in which he obtained 57·58 per cent of the vote, as against 42·42 per cent obtained by M. Poher) left unanswered the question of how he was to combine the requirements of continuity and change, and he was compelled for almost eighteen months to steer a cautious course under silent observation from Colombey-les-deux-Eglises. But he was faced with the immediate political problem of deciding exactly what his victory was for. In other words, he had to determine his relations with the Gaullist party and to discover his own presidential personality.

THE GAULLIST 'MALAISE'

While General de Gaulle was head of State, he had been able to impose his own will sufficiently to keep Gaullist differences and stresses within bounds. President Pompidou did not begin his septennate with this degree of unquestioned authority. He was well aware of this, and admitted before his election that he would be obliged to persuade and to establish a dialogue, where General de Gaulle had been able to command.[16] Moreover, as Prime Minister, he had been the leader of one of the 'clans' that General de Gaulle had managed to contain within what appeared as a coherent party, and so could not claim to be 'above the battle' as the General had always done (though not always with complete credibility). Two currents within the Gaullist movement were now agreed in feeling misgivings about M. Pompidou himself. He was a cautious and pragmatic conservative politician, but what might be called the 'historic' or 'fundamentalist' Gaullists – MM. Debré, Messmer, Vendroux, Couve de Murville, in particular – were conservative in a different sense. More Gaullist than de Gaulle, they were bent on protecting from any change or dilution the 'pure' spirit of Gaullism, as interpreted by themselves, and on maintaining the coherence and identity of the Gaullist movement. For M. Debré, the recognized keeper of the Gaullist soul or conscience,[17] the widening of the base of the Government coalition by the inclusion of three Ministers from the Centrist group, *Progrès et Démocratie moderne*, was already in itself a dilution of Gaullism. The immediate response of the 'fundamentalists' was, therefore, to revive the parliamentary *Amicale, Présence et Action du Gaullisme*, and to follow this up at the beginning of 1970 by the revival of the extra-parliamentary movement, the *Association Présence du Gaullisme*. The aim of both organizations was to act as watchdogs on behalf of the absent General, to see that there was no loss of the true Gaullist dynamic, and to ensure fidelity to 'the example and principles bequeathed by General de Gaulle'.[18]

This loyalist, or fundamentalist, approach was also characterized by a Jacobin nationalism, anti-Communism, and rigid adherence to the principles of Gaullist foreign policy as expressed by General de Gaulle, though apparently without any allowance for the considerable degree of pragmatic adaptation that he himself had introduced when he had found it useful to do so. In social policy, however, it was at times to the left of M. Pompidou and his supporters.

The second current of opinion, that of the left-wing Gaullists, was much more progressive as regards social policy, and enthusiastically in favour of the General's policy of participation that Pompidolist Gaullists regarded with some caution. But left-wing Gaullists shared the fundamentalists' adherence to the principles of foreign policy as outlined in Gaullist press conferences, and were even more fervently opposed, both to the policy of a more widely based Government coalition (*ouverture*), and to any attempt to transform the Gaullist movement into 'a party like the others'.

There were, however, important differences between the two wings. Debrétists saw Gaullism as a coherent, even monolithic, movement,[19] but left-wing Gaullists constituted a proliferation of small organizations, divided on the issue of their integration in or independence of the main movement. They were also much more openly opposed to M. Pompidou during the first year or so of his presidency, regarding him as being already in process of betraying Gaullism. In 1969, M. Louis Vallon, who had been, along with M. René Capitant, a leading left-wing Gaullist, published a book entitled *l'Anti-de Gaulle*, attacking M. Pompidou as an opponent of participation.[20] And the manifesto of the *Union gaulliste populaire*, formed by M. René Capitant and some of his supporters immediately after the referendum of 1969, attacked M. Pompidou's policy of *'ouverture'*, which it compared to the 'unnatural alliances' formed under the Fourth Republic's *'loi des apparentements'*. 'It is not possible', it maintained, 'to govern in association with everybody. Gaullism is a bloc.'[21] The Gaullist aim, declared a later statement by the movement, must be to fight for the transformation of a capitalist régime into one of participation.[22] The *Front des jeunes Progressistes* – another left-wing Gaullist splinter group – described the 'new society' advocated by the Prime Minister, M. Chaban-Delmas, as the policy of 'privileged members of a capitalist society', and called for the speedy application of the university-reform law.[23] This increasingly open dissension in the Gaullist ranks – personal as well as political, for MM. Debré, Frey, Messmer, Chaban-Delmas and Edgar Faure all had their 'clans'[24] – was largely responsible for the creation of an image of the Gaullist party during the months following the General's resignation as uncertain of itself, lacking in self-confidence.

What more than anything else made the Prime Minister's position difficult was the increased personal hostility that he met with from the party – and not only from the left wing and the loyalists. His reception at the National Council meeting at Versailles at the end of June 1970 was described as 'glacial'. And his reaction to the situation did nothing to improve matters. According to reports, he made a mediocre speech, in which he expressed the hope that he would not have to remind Gaullists that their 'fraternal family' depended on confidence.[25] Later, he was to complain of the 'moroseness' of the party.[26]

How far the criticisms denoted merely personal unpopularity and how far dissatisfaction with the Government it was difficult to say. There were certainly (as there had been during General de Gaulle's presidency) recurrent protests by the Gaullist parliamentary group that it was inadequately consulted by the Government, and that its conditions of work were unsatisfactory.[27] Some criticisms were clearly expressions of the nostalgia of the faithful, for whom Gaullism without the General remained inconceivable, and this element became even more vocal after the General's death. But during the first year or so, the mood was one of unease rather than disaffection.

The unease was reflected in attitudes to the President as well as to the Prime Minister and the Government. As has already been pointed out, M. Pompidou found himself in 1969 in an impossibly difficult situation. His aim, expressed both during his presidential campaign and in his first press conference, was to create a relationship between himself and both Government and public that would be 'more human, accessible and understandable'.[28] One of the ways in which he sought to do this was by a change in the style and tone of presidential press conferences.[29] It cannot be said that his efforts were wholly successful. To begin with, it was by no means certain that this Presidentialism 'with a human face' was what the French people really wanted, and it certainly created difficulties for him as President – difficulties that General de Gaulle had been able to avoid. For instance, answering questions at press conferences as they came – which at first he seemed to be doing – instead of having those that he intended to answer carefully planted, involved not only a wide range of heterogeneous questions (37 in the first and 41 in the third press conference), but also questions that were at times politically and even personally awkward, and that, therefore, sometimes made him appear to be on the defensive.[30] His simpler, more familiar and reasoned style, in contrast to the 'distant, regal and isolated' tone[31] and lofty generalizations of General de Gaulle, made him appear more vulnerable (and at least once perhaps even a little vulgar). It also removed some of the sense of occasion (as did the simpler ceremonial).[32] There was a lack of drama, not merely because the circumstances lacked drama, but because the General had always been able to provide his own drama if circumstances failed to provide it for him.[33]

Nor did the persistent rumours of disagreement between President and Prime Minister contribute to the image that the President was trying to build up. Such rumours in themselves put the relationship on a different footing from that between General de Gaulle and his Prime Ministers. M. Chaban-Delmas repeatedly reaffirmed the primacy of the President of the Republic, the need for complete confidence between President and Prime Minister, and the absence of any rift.[34] But these reiterated protestations only helped to weaken the authority of the Prime Minister, without increasing that of the President, and so contributed to the general impression of disorientation that at first characterized Gaullism without de Gaulle.

CIRCUMSTANCES AND UNCERTAINTIES (i) THE
ECONOMIC SITUATION AND REGIONALISM

Circumstances as well as personal factors played their part in increasing the difficulties of both Government and majority during the first years following General de Gaulle's resignation. The remaining years of the fourth Parliament of the Fifth Republic fall into two separate periods. In the first, which lasted up to about six months after the death of General de Gaulle in November 1970, the Government had to deal with immediate priorities, determined by circumstances, including the continuing consequences of the May events. In 1959, Raymond Aron had noted that General de Gaulle was presiding over French quarrels but not getting rid of them.[35] In 1969, the editor of *Le Monde* noted that his departure solved no problems.[36] The economic situation, educational reform and *participation* in universities, the continuing problem of disruption in schools as well as in universities were all problems that could not be shelved, but could not be quickly solved either. From 1971 onwards, new problems arose, and in an atmosphere that increased the difficulties of dealing with them. For the parties were already looking ahead and beginning to prepare for the first general election since 1958 to be held without General de Gaulle's overshadowing presence. Some of the new problems were also of a nature that risked weakening the Gaullist electoral appeal.

The Government's first priority was clearly to deal with the economic and monetary situation. By mid-1969, the former record figure of £3000 million (7000 million dollars) reserves had been reduced by half. France's competitive position, already weak, had been further weakened by the previous year's 15 per cent increase in wages (about 9 per cent in terms of real wages), and the unsatisfied claims of the trade unions for further increases did not promise any immediate improvement. The Bank rate was increased to 7 per cent in June (and to 8 per cent in October) and the Minister of Finance, M. Giscard d'Estaing, therefore introduced a seven-point plan aiming at stemming domestic demand, restoring the balance of payments within two years and encouraging industrial expansion, employment and exports.

Experts were not optimistic regarding the prospects of success.[37] General de Gaulle also had been faced with the need for a drastic austerity programme when he became President. But at that time he had had factors on his side that the new President did not have. One difficulty was that, in 1969 and 1970, it was not possible to expect the kind of response from industry and public that General de Gaulle had received when he introduced his austerity programme at the beginning of 1959. Neither production nor exports could be expanded rapidly, for industry had not enough capacity, and French prices were already too high to be competitive, even with the help of a devaluation of the franc by some 12 per cent, announced on 8 August. Nor could the public be counted on to avoid panic buying in an attempt to keep ahead of prices. There was no crisis atmosphere as there had been in 1958 and 1959. The increased purchasing power resulting from the 1968 wage increases was in itself enough to stimulate domestic demand. In addition, the Government was involved in high public spending, because it would have been politically impossible to reduce estimates for the social services, especially for education. Indeed, the veteran Radical Senator, M. Marcel Pellenc, who had specialized for years in the scrutiny of public expenditure, was launching a direct attack on the Government for its failure to spend enough.

> In eleven years the Fifth Republic has failed to solve the problems of housing, telephones, hospitals, education, motorways, full employment, social security, local finance, ex-servicemen and *rapatriés*, vocational training and private investment. The result is general discontent.[38]

These were some of the facts that went to make up the situation described by the new Prime Minister, M. Chaban-Delmas, as that of a 'stalemate society' (*la société bloquée*)[39] – a system hampered by conservative attitudes, caste-ridden structures and archaic methods. He proposed to replace this by a 'new society'. In presenting this idea in his declaration of general policy of 16 September 1969, he spoke in an atmosphere rendered more tense by a railway strike, an outbreak of wild-cat strikes on the Paris underground, discontent in the Post Office unions, threatened violence by small shopkeepers (going back to the previous February), and warnings from the CGT secretary-general, M. Georges Séguy, that the Government could expect a 'stormy autumn session' as a result of the devaluation of the franc and the introduction at the beginning of September of a programme of moderate austerity intended to arrest the rate of inflation.[40]

In the circumstances, it could not be said that the impact of M. Chaban-Delmas was discouraging. He obtained a massive majority (369 votes to 85), though his 'new society' was received with some scepticism, in the absence of any precise information regarding the methods by which it could be achieved.[41] Unfortunately for the Government, as previous ones had discovered, the sections of society most in need of change were precisely those determined to maintain, by violence if necessary, their own positions, which were essential elements in the 'blockage' that M. Chaban-Delmas wanted to get rid of. The result was that, though Centre and Right gave him credit at least for good intentions, M. François Mitterrand, speaking for the Left, summed up a fairly general opinion: 'Looking at you,' he said, 'I have no doubts as to your sincerity. But when I look at your majority, I have doubts regarding your success.'[42]

In fact, the Prime Minister was able to make considerable progress during the following months. There was relative industrial peace, assisted by the introduction of a new system of relating the minimum wage level to the cost of living, which involved less delay, and also by the introduction of a pioneer profit-sharing scheme in the nationalized Renault concern, and of measures to provide some 40 per cent of workers with the advantages associated with monthly instead of weekly wages.[43] *Contrats de progrès*, which were part of the Government's policy of *'concertation'*, that is contractual agreements covering both wages and prices, were in process of negotiation in the nationalized gas and electricity industries and already in application in the Paris transport system.

On 15 October 1970, in a second declaration of general policy, asking for the confidence of the National Assembly, M. Chaban-Delmas summed up these achievements with an impressive array of statistics in defence of the thirteen months of attempts to lay the foundations of his 'new society', and went on to outline the problems that still remained to be solved in 1971. They included pockets of unemployment, housing, inadequate occupational training, inequality of educational opportunity and over-centralization. The economic situation, though improved, was, he admitted, still fragile. He received, nevertheless, a no less impressive vote of confidence than he had done thirteen months earlier (382 votes to 89).[44]

If there had been discernible progress in the economic and social fields – though not such as to bring the 'new society' significantly nearer – the same could not be said of regionalization. It remained a popular idea in the country, but, though it was mentioned from time to time by the Prime Minister and the President, nothing was actually done. In December 1969, the Prime Minister even announced a series of reforms, including provisions for an experimental transfer of some State services to regional control, but did not intend to put them before Parliament until 1971.[45] In an interview given to journalists on 11 August 1970, the President undertook that the Government would submit 'genuine plans for *déconcentration* and decentralization, not eye-wash as has so often happened'. If by 'eye-wash' (*de la poudre aux yeux*) he meant public statements followed by no action, he had himself been as guilty of these as had his Prime Minister.[46] And the reasons for these tactics were simple. What the regionalists wanted was elected regional assemblies with some real powers of self-government. The most that the Gaullist party was prepared to contemplate was '*déconcentration*', and this purely administrative reform was regarded with suspicion by regionalists as being likely to make the situation worse rather than better.

By the end of 1970, however, the Government could no longer afford to appear to be stalling, and so what a well-known regionalist called 'a gesture of good will'[47] was made by the Prime Minister in his declaration of general policy, followed by the introduction of a Bill some eleven months later, the provisions of which would not be implemented until 1973. These included the creation of two regional assemblies, one to be indirectly elected by local elected representatives, the other to consist of advisory socio-professional appointees.

Their functions were to remain within the economic, social and cultural field. No regional local government was contemplated. In fact the only change of any importance was the provision that the regional Prefect was no longer to be also the Prefect of one of the *départements* within the region. He was, however, to be given no additional powers.[48]

This was in essentials the existing system. But it is difficult to see how any Government, of whatever political complexion, could have done anything else. For the truth is that regionalism is one of the perennial issues of French politics. It never dies, but never becomes practical politics. Regionalism will, no doubt, go on providing talking points and subjects for the theoretical exercises so popular with French political parties, especially centre parties. And M. Jean-Jacques Servan-Schreiber's ambitious plan in his Radical Manifesto of 1970 for regional decentralization in a European framework,[49] is likely to join in limbo the plans of the Gaullist 1960s and the acres of newsprint devoted to them. For without a revolution, no Government would voluntarily abandon any of its hold on the machinery of government. Administrators would not change their secular habits of thought, nor would they want to leave Paris in large numbers to live in the provinces. Deputies would not welcome a system in which their pressures would have to be exercised on strong regional officials instead of directly on Ministers. And ill-equipped regional Prefects, if entrusted with real functions, would be likely to increase rather than reduce the already long delays that characterize the relations of local and central administrators. Nor is it conceivable that any real local government could be based on between thirty and forty thousand small *communes*, with archaic financial systems, and which obstinately refuse to sink their identities in larger regions, and on *départements*, which are too small to provide suitable areas, yet to which French citizens and political parties remain no less obstinately attached.[50]

CIRCUMSTANCES AND UNCERTAINTIES
(ii) EDUCATIONAL PARTICIPATION AND THE
PERSISTENCE OF VIOLENCE

In the field of educational reform, there was certainly change, but it was accompanied by much criticism and by a degree of disturbance and disruption of university and even school life that created major political problems. For the first year, there were only provisional institutions, but during 1970 these were gradually replaced by those provided for in the 1968 Act, and the system was fully operative from 1971 onwards.

The opposition to the new system by revolutionaries and their sympathizers on the extreme Left did not, however, die down. Elections of student representatives to the new administrative bodies continued to be boycotted, except by moderates and Communists, and in many universities a number of student seats remained unfilled.[51] Disputes arose on points on which left-wing passions were easily aroused, and on which there were disagreements in the Gaullist camp between those who supported the line taken by M. Faure and those more conservative Gaullists who had welcomed his replacement at the Ministry of Education by M. Olivier Guichard.[52] There were disputes regarding the interpretation of certain provisions of the Act, and regarding certain ministerial decisions.[53] There were criticisms (by academics in particular) pointing out that the new system was not achieving what it set out to achieve, and especially that the transformation of the old Faculties into a large and heterogeneous collection of *Unités d'Enseignement et de Recherche* (UER) – roughly equivalent to British university departments, but varying enormously in size and range – had created inequalities, as well as intellectual and material confusion, and had often reduced instead of increasing the contacts between different fields of study (*pluridisciplinarité*) that had been one of the main purposes of their creation.[54]

Many of these educational shortcomings could perhaps be regarded as teething troubles inevitable in the circumstances. It was something of a miracle that a shake-up as profound as that introduced by the Faure Act had still not prevented most students from attending lectures and from sitting and passing their examinations. Within two years or so, 23 universities, each with the same five Faculties, had transformed themselves into 67 universities including 720 UER, and by 1970 there were (according to one calculation) already 70 different ways of passing the *licence en droit.*[55]

The fact remained, however, that in 1970 and 1971, when it was beginning to be possible to sort out temporary from more serious weaknesses and educational from political issues, there were four major criticisms of the new régime, and disillusion-ment was growing rather than diminishing. There were, first, an increasing number of objections to it on educational grounds,[56] which were also politically important because they helped to swell the now apparently endemic unrest and dis-turbance in universities and in some *lycées.* For the second criticism of the system was that students, instead of partici-pating, co-managing and discussing, were more and more demonstrating, occupying premises and declaring 'strikes' at the drop of a hat. 'The most trivial decision,' wrote the educa-tional correspondent of *Le Monde*, 'is enough to cause a storm.'[57] And according to another commentator, it had become '. . . a habit for those who have complaints or want to express some point of view to resort to the street or to go and bash opponents. . . .'[58]

The third criticism concerned the form taken by the violence in certain universities, especially in Paris, where it was fast developing into pitched battles between armed commandos of the Right and the Left. As has already been said, the Act had provided no means of dealing with this situation, since the university authorities remained responsible for maintaining order, but without any effective ways of enforcing their decis-ions. Police had to be called in when situations got out of hand, but, though arrests were often made, problems of identification made recourse to the courts largely ineffective. The recruitment of private security forces was resented and did not produce satisfactory results either.[59] In some universities, the only guarantee of sufficient order for classes to be held was provided by the Communist party, which had its own security service.

The worst troubles in the Paris region were in the peripheral university of Nanterre (Paris X), where the May events originated, and in the new experimental university of Vincennes (Paris VIII), though there were also violent clashes between Right and Left in the law departments housed in the Rue d'Assas (Paris II), while the other experimental university of Dauphine (Paris IX) was on strike for six weeks at the beginning of 1970 (mainly on educational grounds). During the 1969–70 session, teaching at Vincennes was possible only thanks to the Communist party's effective maintenance of order in the face of attempts at systematic disruption and destruction by leftists, to which were added the difficulties created by an overburdened and inadequate administration. 'To become a student at Vincennes,' wrote one correspondent, 'is not really recommended, except to those who want to study the theory and practice of guerilla warfare.'[60] Or, as the provisional administrator expressed it in a succinct notice over the door of his office, 'It is not necessary to be mad in order to work here, but it helps.'[61] In the University of Nanterre, offices of administrators were sacked, and one after the other the two Deans resigned, and were replaced only with difficulty. The material damage following one of the numerous incidents – that of March 1970 – was officially estimated at 400,000 francs. That following a Maoist incident at the University of Grenoble was estimated at 30,000 francs. March, April and May 1970 saw incidents in the University of Paris VI (where the Dean's office was ransacked), in Poitiers, where clashes with leftists caused casualties, in the law department housed in the Rue d'Assas, where there were clashes between leftists and rightists. In November 1970, three teachers at the University of Nanterre were physically attacked, the law lectures delivered by the former Gaullist Minister, M. Jean Foyer, interrupted and the university closed for a time. The following spring, there was arson by extremists at that most intellectual of establishments, the *Ecole normale supérieure* of the Rue d'Ulm, following leftist indiscipline leading to the resignation of its Director.[62] These were only a few of the incidents reported in the press almost daily.

The fourth criticism was that leftist movements and sectional organizations were responsible for recurrent violent incidents outside universities. In the month of March 1970 alone, Maoist extremists attacked a Town Hall in the Paris suburbs and organized meetings regarded by the Prefect of Police as intended to demoralize the army, while demonstrations by the militant tradesmen's organization, the CID–UNATI, led by M. Gérard Nicoud, caused a traffic jam in Paris and called for a tax strike. Lorry drivers blocked the gates of Paris for several days running. In May, explosives were used in Grenoble and, in Paris, the premises of the well-known confectioners, Fauchon, were invaded by leftists and smashed up.[63] These incidents were admittedly the responsibility of small groups of extremists or sectional interests, but, after all the disturbances of the past two years, the public had had enough of disorder and by now expected Ministers to do more about it than make periodic statements asserting that the Government would not tolerate violence.[64]

Some action was indeed taken during the year. In May, the two directors of the Maoist paper, *La Cause du Peuple*, were prosecuted, leading to an intensification of extremist action and further prosecutions of Maoists, of which the most important was that of M. Alain Geismar, the young revolutionary university teacher of 1968, who now led the Maoist movement, *La Gauche prolétarienne*. This movement was dissolved by the Government. M. Geismar's promise in June of 'a hot summer'[65] was fulfilled by more acts of vandalism, by the prosecution of other Maoists, associated with the papers *Vive la Révolution* and *l'Idiot international*, and by Maoist demonstrations, which included hunger strikes.

More far-reaching general measures to deal with the problem of violence were taken by the Government's Bill 'to prevent certain forms of delinquency', better known as the 'anti-smashers' Bill'.[66] Its aims were (i) to make the occupation and breaking up by armed commandos of the offices of public servants, such as university administrators, a punishable offence that could be speedily and severely dealt with; (ii) to punish the organizers and leaders of illegal demonstrations that degenerated into violence; (iii) to deal with all participants in such demonstrations; and (iv) to make adequate compensation payable. The Bill encountered hostility from the Left, partly on the ground that adequate means of dealing with these cases already existed, but mainly because it was feared that the law would be used to prevent trade-union or left-wing demonstrations, freedom for which was regarded by the Left (and not only by the Left) as being one of the fundamental constitutional rights. Objections more widely held included fears that the Bill would not enable the authorities to prevent *agents provocateurs* from transforming a legal and peaceful demonstration into an illegal and violent one, against the intentions of the organizers. Nor was this difficulty really overcome by the provision in the Bill that only those organizers should be punished who failed to order the dispersal of a demonstration when violence occurred, for they might not always be physically able to do this. The definition of a participant as one who decided to remain (even as an onlooker) after an order of dispersal had been given, was, therefore, not wholly satisfactory either, and critics argued that the payers might very easily be those who had not really been the smashers.[67]

GAULLIST MISFORTUNES OR MISMANAGEMENT?

During the two years leading up to the general election of March 1973, a number of factors combined to create new problems for the Gaullists. The death of General de Gaulle affected the Gaullist party in ways that were only gradually perceptible, but were none the less important. Jacques Fauvet's comment on the President's first press conference after de Gaulle's death was that 'it was as if a silent but oppressive shadow had disappeared, leaving him freer and more master of himself'.[68] In reality, M. Pompidou's confidence and authority had been steadily increasing for some time. But that he had by no means taken the place of his predecessor was made evident by the evolution of the party during the two years after de Gaulle's death. In spite of the Prime Minister's immediate appeal to the party to remain united,[69] a number of Gaullist fundamentalists resigned from the party during the following year, feeling, in the words of one of them, M. Christian Fouchet, that 'the great book of Gaullism' had been closed and sealed by the General's death.[70] Another, M. David Rousset, a left-wing Gaullist, accused the party of being 'a spreading bureaucracy' and of having 'gone back to the capitalism of grandfather'.[71] M. Jean-Marcel Jeanneney, the architect of the defeated regional plan and one of the General's most faithful supporters, resigned from the party, and made a number of criticisms of its policies, attributing what he regarded as its failures to the fact that *'le père n'est plus là'*.[72] M. Edgar Faure, who, from the back benches, was seeking to unite the various left-wing Gaullist movements, succeeded only in helping to produce two rival organizations.[73] He and his *Comité d'étude pour un nouveau contrat social* were suspected by some of hoping to form a possible third 'Faurist wing' – a suspicion strengthened by his announcement on 12 May 1971 that he intended to be a candidate for the presidency in 1976.

It was not merely, as Maurice Duverger suggested, that 'without its Victor Hugo' the party became 'increasingly bogged down in dull platitudes about routine matters and the maintenance of public order',[74] though there was something in that. It was rather that the would-be defenders of the pure Gaullist gospel had neither the appeal nor the talent to contribute what the General had contributed to the attraction and credibility of Gaullism. As one of *Le Monde*'s contributors to its well-known ironic 'Au jour le jour' column put it:

> When the lion died, the party that had supported him claimed to be his spiritual and political heir. Lionism was to be for ever pure and strong.
>
> After some time, doubts assailed some of the faithful. . . . We do not roar as he did, said a horse. I shall leave this party of howlers, barkers and bleaters.[75]

If the loss of de Gaulle had been the only misfortune of the party this initial sense of loss of unity and purpose might have been overcome. For none of those who resigned was a front-rank politician who carried real weight in the party. But there were other difficulties. A number of major problems confronted the Government, and some of them suggested mismanagement rather than misfortune. One was the recurrent problem of tensions within the party and within the Government coalition. In spite of the President's and the Prime Minister's initial good intentions, relations between Government and parliamentary group remained far from harmonious, and in July 1971 five presidents of the National Assembly's parliamentary Commissions, together with the leader of the parliamentary *Amicale*, M. Hubert Germain, launched a direct attack on the Government. In addition to the usual complaints of bad working relations between Government and Deputies, they accused the Government of paying undue attention to pressure groups, of failure to answer written parliamentary questions within a reasonable time or to answer them adequately, and of insufficient State intervention in the field of economic policy.[76] The Government made efforts to improve its relations with Parliament by making one or two minor procedural concessions, but by the end of the year, the president of the National Assembly's Finance Commission had returned to the charge that Parliament was not receiving enough information.

In the meantime, other problems had arisen. The suggestion by M. Alexandre Sanguinetti that the Gaullist party should have its president, like any other party, drew a tart response from the Prime Minister, who described himself as the leader of the majority, and so, in effect, of the UDR.[77] The secretary-general of the *Républicains indépendants*, M. Michel Poniatowski, proposed that *Républicains indépendants* should present their own candidates in the first ballot in the forthcoming elections, and followed this up with a proposal for a '*grande fédération*' including Centrists. This was hastily rejected by the UDR, which had not been consulted.[78] By the end of the year, not only was the UDR itself divided, but the parliamentary majority was beginning to look more and more like one of the quarrelling coalitions of the Fourth Republic.

The UDR [wrote André Passeron] do not know where to look for a guide – to the General's shade, the historic

Gaullists, the President of the Republic, the Government and its head, the secretary-general of the movement, or elsewhere.[79]

The most damaging effect on the party's image, however, was made by the revelation, from the middle of 1971 onwards, of a series of scandals, mainly fraudulent transactions by property-development companies. These exhibited the classic symptoms of scandals, described in Chapter I. Rumours were numerous. The processes of the law were slow, and the press devoted columns of newsprint to the subject over a period of some months.[80] Political, legal and criminal implications were complex and confusing. And since the politicians involved appeared to be all Gaullists, politicization of the affairs was unavoidable. At the end of 1971, a tax inspector convicted of fraud was revealed to have a brother who had at one time been a member of the *cabinet* of M. Chaban-Delmas and, at about the same time, the press published a facsimile of a tax demand addressed to the Prime Minister, which led to hints (though never to direct accusations) of possible tax avoidance* on his part. Though this was recognized within a relatively short time to be a 'non-affair', the unwelcome publicity to which the Prime Minister had been subjected certainly contributed to (if it was not wholly responsible for) his replacement the following July. In September 1972, there followed what became known as 'the Aranda affair', involving allegations by a civil servant that he and his friends possessed 136 documents implicating 48 well-known personalities in irregular transactions, mainly, it appeared, concerned with requests for favours from Ministers. This, too, entered on a long period of investigation.

As has always happened in French financial scandals, real or imaginary, the facts were used to make political capital. Both the Prime Minister and the Minister of Finance made it abundantly clear that the tax rebate responsible for reducing the Prime Minister's income-tax liability to negligible amounts

* What was in question was not tax *evasion*, that is illegal avoidance of tax liabilities, but only legal methods of *avoiding* tax in certain circumstances.

over a period of four years was perfectly legal, and had been introduced as far back as 1966 in order to encourage saving. This did not prevent the Communist party's acting secretary-general, M. Georges Marchais, from attacking what he called 'a fiscal system for cheats',[81] and the Radical party bureau from describing the measure as 'iniquitous'. The figures were used to show that this particular concession benefited the rich but not wage-earners and provided a peg on which to hang statistics showing the comparative ease with which certain categories could avoid taxation, while others could not.[82] The *comité directeur* of the Socialist party regarded the scandals as emphasizing the links between the Gaullists and land speculators and called for a parliamentary enquiry. With a general election a year away at most, the whole business provided valuable ammunition to the opposition in what was already by 1971 a period of electoral pre-negotiation.[83] And not only to the opposition. The Gaullists' partners in the Government, the *Républicains indépendants*, were not above emphasizing that their party came out of it all with an apparently unblemished reputation.

The affairs led also to prolonged and complicated controversies in the National Assembly and between the National Assembly and the Senate regarding the application and revision of the rules governing incompatibility between membership of Parliament and directorships of business concerns. The involvement in the scandals of a Gaullist Deputy, M. André Rives-Henrÿs,[84] created three major problems. The first was that raised by the charge that he had allowed his parliamentary title as a Deputy to be used for purposes of business publicity. This was a political offence for which the penalty was the loss of his seat. It was also a criminal offence. The political and criminal procedures were distinct, but not simultaneous. The Minister of Justice intended to submit the case to the Constitutional Council. If he had done so without delay, a decision that the Deputy was ineligible to sit would have had to be applied immediately, that is before the court had decided whether or not he was guilty of a penal offence on the same count. It was also possible that the court would be influenced by the Constitutional Council's decision. On the highly unlikely assumption that the court were to find him not guilty, however, he would already have been unseated for an offence that the court decided he had not committed, and, since there is no appeal from a decision of the Constitutional Council, his re-instatement would be impossible.

These arguments, both in the National Assembly and in the press, on the pros and cons of the decision of the Minister of Justice to wait for the court's decision before dealing with the political problem of M. André Rives-Henrÿs' ineligibility were complicated, however, by a problem of political expediency. If he were to be unseated, a by-election would normally follow. It was difficult to imagine a less auspicious moment for one, from the Gaullist point of view. But if the decision were to be delayed until the beginning of April 1972, the by-election would be avoided, under the rule forbidding by-elections within the twelve months preceding a general election. Whatever the legal arguments, therefore – and those put forward by the Minister were not unconvincing[85] – his decision was certainly politically helpful to the Government.

A third problem was that raised by the Bill introduced by the Government in November 1971 to tighten up the rules governing the parliamentary incompatibilities. It was criticized as being too closely related to the affairs then *sub judice*, as going too far, and as not going far enough. The majority in the Senate regarded it as too restrictive, with the result that it shuttled between the two assemblies until the end of the session, when a compromise was finally reached, allowing the Bill to be passed on the fourth vote in the National Assembly. It was then submitted to the Constitutional Council, which promptly ruled parts of it to be unconstitutional. It was therefore promulgated (without the offending parts) only on 24 January 1972.[86]

What the law actually does is to widen the area of incompatibility, in order to prevent Deputies from holding directorships in companies dealing with the buying and selling of building land, and to make it obligatory for Deputies and Senators to declare to the *bureau* of their assembly all outside activities that they intend to retain or to take up while in office.

The *bureau* judges whether these are incompatible with membership of Parliament. In cases of doubt, the Minister of Justice or the parliamentary assembly itself submits the matter to the Constitutional Council, which decides where there is incompatibility. The Deputy or Senator must regularize the situation within 150 days.

Neither the debates nor the Bill itself did much to restore the Government's shaken prestige. Divested of the articles declared to be unconstitutional, it was understandably regarded as a legislative mouse, and the debates merely helped to keep alive publicity about scandals that could not be other than damaging to the Government.

Nor was much encouragement forthcoming in other fields. In view of the continuing agitation in schools and universities, the Government introduced new disciplinary measures in universities, by the amendment of certain provisions of the Faure Act, most of them technical in nature, but capable, as had been demonstrated, of creating a great deal of friction and opposition.[87] A proposed amendment to the 1901 law on associations was intended to enable the Government to take more effective action to prevent the reconstitution of leftist movements that had been dissolved. Since the Constitutional Council also ruled unconstitutional the main point of controversy in this Bill, it is not necessary to discuss it in any detail.[88] Neither measure produced much effect. The agitation in universities continued. The Centre Censier (which includes parts of three universities – Paris I, III and VII) had to be closed for much of the month of April 1972. Students were still showing very little interest in the bodies on which they were supposed to be represented, and the number of non-voters in the 1971–2 session revealed even more apathy than had the figures for the previous session.[89] Most student and teachers' unions remained dominated by unrepresentative, politicized and divided left-wing movements, while the vast majority of both students and staff remained apathetic and discontented with the new system as well as with their own material situations and prospects. One of the non-extremist unions, the *Syndicat autonome du personnel enseignant des ex-facultés des lettres* (a revealing title in itself), gave the following description of the situation in the second term of the second year of the new system:

> ... teaching repeatedly prevented by minorities, sometimes for long periods and on differing pretexts, hundreds of lectures irretrievably lost, unrepresentative elected assemblies holding political debates, numbers of teachers discouraged, frequent interruptions of work, violent incidents, teachers attacked, as at Nantes, fires, as at Tours, students seriously wounded, as at Nanterre, scandalous judgments by disciplinary Councils, as at Caen. Those guilty always escape with impunity.
>
> In many universities the situation is becoming one of chronic anarchy. The alternative is for the university to be run by a single political party. Even if they want to maintain order, university authorities have not the means at their disposal to enforce respect for the law, freedom to work, non-denominational teaching or personal protection. Our universities are like foreign countries in which the laws of the Republic are no longer applied.[90]

General inertia within the universities was, however, accompanied by some weakening of the appeal of leftists in general. This was probably due more to their continuing publicized quarrels than to any positive reaction against them. Even some of their own members condemned a deliberate kidnapping in March 1972 as 'a serious political error, unhelpful to the revolutionary cause'.[91] But this atmosphere had at least one positive advantage. It made possible the passage of the long-awaited review of the 1959 Debré law providing for continued aid to Catholic schools.[92] At the end of 1969, when renewal was due, it would no doubt have created a storm in parties and trade unions as well as in universities and some schools. As it was, apart from a token strike or two by educational unions, the Bill (which in effect merely conferred permanence on the provisions of the 1959 law) was debated and passed without incident, and without more than a few minor amendments.[93] It seemed hardly possible that this almost century-old sore was finally healed, and somewhat ironic, if it were so, that the revolutionaries of 1968 had helped involuntarily to achieve one positive result that they would unanimously have resisted, if, in 1972, they had been thinking about it!

The economic situation was one of 'moroseness' rather than apathy, because, although the 'new society' had become an empty word, no indication of any acceptable alternative policy was in sight. The Prime Minister made relatively optimistic declarations of policy in April 1971 and in May 1972, the first followed by a motion of censure and the second by a vote of confidence.[94] The opposition achieved 95 votes in the first and 96 in the second. But this massive vote of confidence meant nothing, as was clearly evident when the President 'accepted the resignation' of the Prime Minister only six weeks later. No reason was given at the time for what was clearly a dismissal and was later admitted by the President to have been one. But the National Assembly, without protest, accepted the President's nomination of a not very well-known Minister, M. Pierre Messmer, the man mainly responsible for the formation and revival of the parliamentary *Amicale, Présence et Action du Gaullisme*, a man whose Gaullist *bona fides*, if not his political capacities, were equal to those of M. Michel Debré.

The main economic problem was that, in spite of France's relatively high growth rate, the reconstitution of her reserves, the improvement in her trade balance, the progress of contractual policies and of the policy of 'profit-sharing', the basic fragilities of the economy remained unchanged, and so therefore did the basic discontents and potential political unrest. The Sixth National Plan, unenthusiastically agreed to by the National Assembly in June 1971, had been criticized for its timidity by the CGT and the CFDT, and especially for its failure to deal with housing and transport. The reluctance of some sections on the Government side to show less timidity in the fields of participation and contractual agreement was, however, matched by that of the CGT and the CFDT, which continued to prefer the traditional methods of wage demands, demonstrations and token strikes. Though exports had increased, the improvement was attributable more to heavily subsidized agricultural exports, to the 1969 devaluation and to the revaluation of the Deutschmark than to a real effort to improve France's share in foreign markets. The international monetary situation from the middle of 1971 onwards had increased pessimism among the experts, though the Government's adoption of a double exchange rate (for commercial and financial transactions respectively) had certainly helped to insulate France temporarily from its effects, as did the Government's efforts to keep prices down. But by the autumn of 1972, prices were rising at a higher rate than for the past ten years. The final rate of increase for the year threatened to be about 50 per cent higher than had been estimated.

There remained, too, the permanent problems that no Government had been able to eliminate to the point at which they ceased to be a threat to economic and perhaps to political stability – unemployment, estimated to have reached the half-million mark in 1972, the special difficulties of regions such as Alsace-Lorraine and Brittany, the non-competitiveness of the too numerous small farms and small shops, with the consequent recurrent outbursts of discontent and violence by peasants' and militant tradesmen's organizations such as CID–UNATI. Though economists pointed out the dangers of doing nothing to check the price rise, the Government, as everybody really knew, was helpless, because, with a general election only a few months away, what was economically necessary would have been politically suicidal. By the middle of 1972, the CGT and the CFDT had already launched the popular slogan of 'a thousand francs a month for a forty-hour week', a demand which, if accepted, would have had an immediate and possibly disastrous effect on French costs.[95] M. Chaban-Delmas had tried to avert a clash by promising that this level would be achieved by 1973, a statement neither credible nor acceptable. M. Messmer started off by praising his predecessor's social policy and promising to continue it, which brought the following comment from *Le Monde*'s political correspondent:

To continue the social policy of M. Chaban-Delmas, and at the same time conserve the support and approval of those who attacked it, constitutes a problem that not many men would feel capable of resolving.[96]

By the end of the year, there were few in any party who believed that M. Messmer was the man to do it. After a declaration of general policy, several television appearances, two trips to the provinces and two press conferences, the new Prime Minister still created, as he had done in July, an impression of 'inflexible insignificance'. One query at least was no longer heard. There was quite certainly now no dyarchy at the top! 'Everything,' wrote one commentator, 'now depends on the mind of the head of State.'[97]

CHANGE OR PERPLEXITY?

The long period of pre-electoralism that began about the middle of 1971 was carried on, however, in general ignorance of what was in the mind of the President. After a long, painful, complicated and well-publicized gestation, the Socialist and Communist parties eventually gave birth, on 27 June 1972, to something called a 'common programme'. Its terms were to form their common electoral manifesto, and, in case of a Socialist–Communist victory in the elections, to form their agreed Government programme. It consisted of a long and detailed document, to be added to, but not to replace, the separate programmes of the two parties, that of the Communist party, *Programme pour un Gouvernement démocratique d'Union populaire*, published in October 1971 and that of the Socialist party, *Changer le Vie*, published in January 1972 and, after prolonged discussion, agreed to at a special conference the following March.[98]

In spite of the fact that it had taken months of negotiation, following years of acrimonious argument, to reach an agreed statement, its contents proved to be the least important thing about it. It followed fairly closely the lines of the party programmes, omitting the considerable divergencies between them, and was not unfairly described by the Radical weekly, *l'Express*, as expressing 'union without agreement'.[99] The measures proposed included the democratization of institutions, involving a number of constitutional amendments, some of which would greatly limit presidential power, the pursuit of a foreign policy of independence of the two blocs, involving partial disarmament in Europe, support for a democratized European Community, and a 'shopping-list' of nationalizations, reduced from the 26 included in the Communist party programme to about a dozen. The programme remained silent regarding the importance to be given to centralized State control on the one hand, and on the other to industrial democracy (*autogestion*), on which the two signatories were irreconcilably divided.

The agreement was limited to the extent of common ground that both could accept as a programme covering the length of a Parliament, and any concessions had been made only on subsidiary points, leaving unresolved fundamental disagreements on questions such as European policy, attitudes to the Atlantic Alliance, the scope and methods of nationalization, the electoral system, and Soviet policy in Czechoslovakia. Each party tried to claim the document as representing its own policy (which was made possible by its deliberate ambiguities, vagueness and omissions), and hoped to attract more votes than its co-signatory – which explained why it was decided that it should be presented to the electorate, not by joint Socialist–Communist candidates in each constituency, but by Socialist and Communist candidates who would oppose each other in the first ballot.

> Our main objective [said the Socialist party leader, M. François Mitterrand] is to rebuild the great Socialist party, by recovering the ground now occupied by the Communist party, in order to demonstrate that of the five million Communist electors, three million can vote Socialist.[100]

To anyone not familiar with the history of French Socialist–Communist relations, this might seem a curious demonstration of unity, as might the decision to set up a liaison committee between the two ostensibly united parties.[101] The subsequent pre-electoral manœuvres of both parties in fact revealed the need for a liaison committee. There were constant quarrels

about the methods of publicizing the common programme.
The Socialists feared a kind of take-over by the more active
and efficient Communist party machine, in the form, for
instance, of presentations of the programme in terms favourable to Communist theses, and of publicity given mainly to
joint meetings, which was what the Communists wanted and
the Socialists did not. The result was that, in October, the
Socialist executive committee decided to have 'as much of the
common programme as possible, as little common action as
possible'.[102]

By far the most generally discussed question was the extent
to which the Socialist–Communist programme did or did not
provide an explicit acceptance by the Communist party of
the Socialist demand for an undertaking to respect the principle
(oddly described as '*l'alternance au pouvoir*') that Government
resignation is obligatory on defeat in the National Assembly
or in a general election. The following two sentences came in
for particular scrutiny:

> If the confidence of the country were to be withdrawn from
> the majority parties, they would renounce power in order to
> continue the struggle in opposition. But the main task of
> democratic government, whose existence implies the support
> of the majority of the people, will be to satisfy the working
> masses, and it will, therefore, be justified by their ever more
> active confidence.[103]

They raised a number of queries. The juxtaposition of two
sentences which, taken together, appear to be either in contradiction or meaningless, is in the classic tradition of French
left-wing compromises. When the same two sentences had
been published in the 'balance-sheet' of Socialist–Communist
conversations at the end of 1970, they had represented divergent
views. The Socialists had emphasized their acceptance of the
first, the Communists the importance of the second.

The Socialist interpretation was that the Communists now
did accept the Socialist view.[104] In that case, what was the
precise meaning of 'But'? Did it mean that the Communists

accepted the principle, but in view of their claim to represent 'the working masses' were taking back with the left hand what they had just conceded with the right?[105] Or did it mean, as an ingenious article in the Communist paper, *l'Humanité*, indicated, that the confidence of 'the working masses' would be enough to prevent a conservative Government from undoing the work of a left-wing Government in the field, say, of nationalizations?[106] Or was the second sentence merely an expression of confident hope that, given the support of the masses, etc., it was reasonable to assume that the situation envisaged in the first sentence would never occur? If so, then the divergence was still there, with the result that the document really provided no reassurance at all.

Criticisms of the Socialist–Communist agreement and allegations that a Government that included Communists could not be relied on to resign if defeated in the National Assembly proved strong weapons in the Gaullist propaganda armoury. Gaullist spokesmen denied the possibility of a normal working of the democratic 'pendulum' if Communists formed part of the Government coalition. Some of their less subtle propagandists expressed views that were, from the democratic point of view, no less open to challenge than those that they attributed to Communists. The secretary-general of the party, M. Alain Peyrefitte, even seemed to be suggesting that the UDR itself should refuse to resign if defeated, because Communists in power could not be relied on to do so![107] A more subtle approach was that of the former Gaullist Government spokesman, M. Léo Hamon, who, having reaffirmed the necessity for Gaullists to comply with the decision of the electorate, as General de Gaulle had done in 1969, added that, since it was inconceivable that the French people would elect a Socialist–Communist majority, Gaullists had an obligation to represent, in addition to their own supporters, those who would be the victims of a Socialist–Communist coalition, condemned to remain permanently in opposition. This might, he thought, make it desirable, in certain circumstances and conditions not defined, to include Socialists in the Government coalition. He appeared not to be considering the difficulties that would arise if his assumption of the impossibility of a Socialist–Communist victory should prove to be ill-founded.[108]

These political arguments were no doubt useful tactical weapons in an election campaign. But, as so often happens, political arguments were complicated by constitutional considerations. The President, questioned in press conferences regarding his own interpretation of his constitutional obligations in such a situation, gave non-committal answers.[109] Gaullist and opposition politicians and commentators gave their own interpretations.[110] The whole question became a confused tactical battle about hypothetical situations.[111]

The opposition Centre groups were no less obsessed with tactics than were Socialists and Communists. The *Mouvement réformateur*, led by MM. Jean Lecanuet and Jean-Jacques Servan-Schreiber, did produce a brief programme.[112] But some of M. Lecanuet's statements showed that he at least was not ruling out the possibility of allowing himself to be tempted in certain circumstances, and on certain conditions, to support Government candidates, and perhaps even a Gaullist-dominated Government coalition. He hinted that, although M. Pompidou could not count on him to support his present policies, if these were to be changed then it would be 'the duty of Centrists to help the Government to succeed'. And he followed this up with a statement that, contrary to the commitment in its Charter, the *Mouvement réformateur* would not automatically withdraw from participation in the second ballot in cases when its own candidate could not win, but would consider cases on their merits.[113]

The announcement that the former Gaullist Minister, M. Jean-Marcel Jeanneney, had joined the *Mouvement réformateur*, and, with the approval of the movement, formed a study group, *Réformes et Participation*, as a kind of 'true-Gaullist' enclave within it, had inevitably strengthened the impression that Centrists were by no means implacably opposed to the Government, but were primarily interested in convincing the electors that Centrism was a force to be reckoned with. This was a difficult task, because Centrists were a small and heterogeneous formation and the UDR could afford to ignore them in most constituencies, counting on the opposition of Centrists to the Socialist–Communist coalition to attract their votes to itself at the second ballot. The Gaullist calculation was, as Georges Vedel put it, that 'at the second ballot, the Centrist vote could be counted on to follow the UDR (as automatically as the commissariat follows the troops), without the UDR having to make more than a few trifling concessions'.[114]

The *Républicains indépendants*, as partners of the Gaullists in the Government, committed to a single joint candidate with the UDR in most constituencies, were both worse and better placed to assert their own individuality. They were, for the time being, compelled to remain loyal, since they constituted very much the minor partner, and had everything to gain by biding their time. Nobody expected the Gaullists to repeat their spectacular electoral victory of 1968, and a much smaller Gaullist party could provide them with the opportunity to play a more important rôle. Writing in the Socialist weekly, *l'Unité*, M. Mitterrand expressed their position perfectly. He was sure, he said, that M. Giscard d'Estaing prayed every night to the All-Highest, 'to give the Left enough seats . . . but not too many, to ensure that he, Valéry, had the upper hand in a National Assembly in which the UDR had lost its absolute majority'.[115]

All these tactical manœuvres filled the pages of the press during the months preceding the opening of the official election campaign, to the exclusion of serious policy considerations. Indeed, neither Gaullists nor their conservative partners had produced any policy statement by the end of 1972, though the Prime Minister announced in January 1973 the forthcoming publication of a detailed statement of Gaullist priorities, accompanied by an estimate of their cost. Costs, he emphasized, had been noticeably omitted from the common programme:

> . . . their little red and black book* is intended to appeal to the faithful and win votes from some who are taken in by

---

* The common programme. The Communist programme had been published in a 'little orange book'.

the fallacious precision of their proposals. But to Frenchmen with common sense, its contents will cause nothing but dismay: a catalogue of economic and social measures that would cost at least four times the estimated amount of the national revenue: a foreign policy that nobody believes in, since the authors themselves are not agreed on the main problems. . . . Everything points to the dominance . . . and the intolerance . . . of the more powerful and determined of the two partners.[116]

There were influential Socialists who came very near to expressing similar views. For instance, in a powerful article in *Le Monde*, M. Arthur Notebart challenged not only the reality of the Communist conversion to the democratic doctrine of *l'alternance au pouvoir*, but also the sincerity of other beliefs to which they had subscribed in the common programme. If they really believed in the principles of individual liberty and of non-interference in the affairs of other States, why were they so reluctant to condemn the Prague trials, and why did they refuse to be represented at the demonstration called by the Socialists to protest against Soviet interference in Czechoslovakia? Socialists believed in Europe, French membership of the Atlantic Alliance, the right to conclude defensive treaties, and the retention by France of her nuclear arms. If the Communists had changed their minds on these issues, they should say so clearly. If they had not, then the agreement was no more than a confidence trick (*un marché de dupes*).[117] In any case, asked a correspondent, why should Socialists want to sign a common programme with Communists, when their party was so much weaker than the Communist party? The answer was simple – 'Because the election made it necessary'.[118]

What Gaullism represented was no clearer. According to an article in *l'Express* at the end of 1972, there were at least eight brands of Gaullism, all in search of a leader and a programme.

Pending the production of this breviary [wrote the author], everybody sings his own credo.

The leaders of the majority – from the muscular Gaullism

of M. Messmer to the ecumenical Gaullism of M. Edgar Faure – rack their brains to find the exact points on which they differ. Nobody, they say, has the right to speak in the name of General de Gaulle. Nobody? All of them have been doing so unceasingly since last September.[119]

The elector could be counted on to recognize at least three distinct brands. The first, the 'historic' Gaullists, men of action, such as the Prime Minister, or men of faith and ideas, such as M. Debré, or unquestioning disciples, such as MM. Couve de Murville and Pierre Lefranc, still saw Gaullism as an inspiration, a bond between a leader, a faithful band of lieutenants and a mass *rassemblement* of followers. Primarily interested in maintaining the movement's uniqueness and its internal cohesion, they saw electoral compromises as too much like the regrettable practices of the Fourth Republic. Winning the election was less important than saving the Gaullist soul. The second, the institutionalists, – including younger, backbench Gaullists who were coming to regard 'historic' Gaullists as historic monuments – believed that winning the election was crucial. In fact the desire to retain power seemed in itself sufficient inspiration. It was the secretary-general, M. Alain Peyrefitte who, in 1970, long before he acceded to that office, had said: 'We are in power for thirty years, if we can avoid doing anything stupid'.[120] For these Gaullists, tactics and organization were essential. Though constituting the strongest element in the party, they were not strong enough to do without the support of M. Giscard d'Estaing's *Républicains indépendants*, whom both the other main brands of Gaullism regarded as largely responsible for what left-wing Gaullists described as the party's 'slide to the right' under M. Pompidou's presidency. Since M. Pompidou was a cautious politician, he kept his options open and tried to keep a balance, both by including Centrists in the Government and by replacing M. Chaban-Delmas, once the 'new society' had lost its appeal, by a 'historic' Gaullist. The third brand of Gaullism – the various 'progressive' and 'participationist' groups – were only on the fringes of the power battle. Their best-known personality,

M. Edgar Faure, even more than M. Giscard d'Estaing, was compelled to toe the line and bide his time.

Whether because he was by temperament as well as by necessity a conciliator rather than a man of action and decision, or because he was intellectually and politically better equipped to be a Prime Minister than a President,[121] M. Pompidou had not succeeded by 1973 in establishing over the movement the kind of ascendency that he had established over the Government. He could not provide a Grand Design, such as that of General de Gaulle, which, despite its unrealism, offered a politically coherent objective and, to some, an inspiring vision. Nor could he achieve the apparent remoteness from party politics that General de Gaulle could claim, as someone who had never been a member of the Gaullist party, or indeed of any other.

Nor could he use the field of foreign policy for spectacular acts or statements, as General de Gaulle had done – deriving political capital at home from his activities, whether they were aggressive, conciliatory or purely verbal. M. Pompidou clearly did not seek to be aggressive. But, as is discussed in the following chapters, whatever he might have wanted to do, his opportunities, where foreign policy was concerned, were severely limited. Some of General de Gaulle's policies had closed certain doors, perhaps permanently. Other doors had been closed by the evolution of the international situation. If France had been represented at the two European summits of 1969 and 1972 by General de Gaulle instead of by President Pompidou, there is no guarantee that the former would have had any greater impact.

Whatever the cause, however, the political consequences of Gaullist uncertainties and of the President's apparent perplexities and doubts were important factors in the pre-electoral atmosphere. Under the Fifth Republic, interest had been focused on, and responsibility attributed to, presidential leadership. In its apparent absence, it was natural that politicians should begin to think seriously about filling the gap. After all, Presidents have been known to die in office or retire prematurely. And, even if M. Pompidou were to remain for his full term and then seek re-election, the presidential election was only just over three years away. The result was that, for all political parties except the Gaullist party, the 1973 election was concerned more with future Presidents than with future policies. The favourite (according to the opinion polls),[122] M. Giscard d'Estaing, derived a great advantage from his existing position, and hoped to improve his chances by increasing the influence of his own party within the coalition, perhaps, as his secretary-general had been suggesting, by establishing closer relations with the Centrists. M. Mitterrand was counting on the Socialist–Communist coalition to do well enough to enable him to attract more left-wing votes in 1976 than he had done as the presidential candidate of the united Left in 1965. M. Lecanuet, M. Jean-Jacques Servan-Schreiber and M. Edgar Faure were all manœuvring in the wings, hoping to increase the respective bargaining powers of Centre, Radical and progressive Gaullist opinion.

The Government, however, could not afford to ignore the fact that the electors were living in 1973, and was compelled to take note of the possible effects on Gaullist prospects of the scandals, the disturbances in universities, the activities of leftists, and economic problems. In fact, the first three had surprisingly little influence. The scandals were dropping out of the news and, as invariably happened after a certain time, ceasing to interest the public. The 1972 autumn term had begun more quietly in both schools and universities than in any year since 1967. What incidents there were concerned practical questions such as shortage of premises and staff or the troubles of second-year medical students without places. Though there was social discontent, there was still no desire on the part of trade unions for a showdown with the Government. The combination of favourable export figures, an increasing growth rate, economic confidence caused by the up-swing of the economy in Common Market countries and the United States, and a general political climate of scepticism and inertia seemed to promise a quiet and uneventful election campaign.

The Government hoped to ensure this by a series of precautionary economic measures announced just before the end of the year. They included increases in family allowances, certain reductions in the amounts of tax payable under VAT, together with promises of help to the large numbers of small tradesmen who could not understand how it worked and resented having to pay it anyway. A Bill was promised to protect workers from wrongful dismissal (something that the trade unions had been requesting for a quarter of a century). None of these measures was likely to do anything to cure the persistent and disquieting rise of prices (by then rising faster than they had done in 1963), the continuing problem of unemployment, and the housing shortage. But anything like the 'stabilization plan' of 1963 would have been politically suicidal. The Government saw the main sources of its own strength in the public's apparent lack of faith in the capacity of any conceivable alternative Government to solve these problems or to maintain the rate of expansion and of economic modernization, as well as in the strength of fears of Communism, and in the likelihood that, if necessary, the Centre parties would vote for the Gaullists rather than for candidates allied with Communists.

It was not an inspiring appeal, but 1968–73 had not been a period of inspired politics and no party could hope to arouse much enthusiasm. At the beginning of 1972, Pierre Viansson-Ponté had described French politics as presenting to the world 'one enormous question mark'.[123] At the opening of the April session of Parliament, the right-wing Senator and ex-presidential candidate, M. Pierre Marcilhacy, had taken a more dismal view:

> In politics [he wrote], the Right no longer believes in its country, the Left is looking to action rather than to doctrine, parents say that they no longer understand their children, teachers do not know what to teach, priests no longer believe in God. In every field, men with faith in their mission are hard to find. Thus there is disorder in the hearts, minds and souls of men, at a time when order reigns in the streets, on the roads and in the workshop.[124]

Perhaps the key to the situation was that suggested implicitly by an academic observer of the political scene, M. Roger-Gérard Schwarzenberg:

> Nothing dissipates the disappointment, disillusionment and disarray. Neither the popularity of Ministers, nor the prestige of the Prime Minister, nor the dogma of presidential infallibility. Between Government and governed, the charm is broken . . . the political machine operates in a vacuum, without any real impact on the country.[125]

With all its faults, a Parliament whose members, whether in the majority or the opposition, were conscious that they had a job to do, and that the eyes of the country were on *them*, and not exclusively on the head of State, had perhaps more to be said for it after all than opponents of the Fourth Republic would admit. There was evidence at the end of the 1968–73 Parliament that a growing number of Gaullist Deputies were beginning to come round to this view.[126]

The official election campaign, which opened on 12 February, produced no new themes and no dramatic surprises, though, as the campaign progressed, a somewhat artificial atmosphere of tension was maintained by the frequent publication in the press of the results of opinion polls, accompanied by predictions of the ground apparently being gained by the united Left. The President followed General de Gaulle's example and made a final appeal to the electorate at the close of the campaign. This was criticized, as such appeals by General de Gaulle had been, as an unjustifiable intervention by the President in party politics.[127]

The results provided no dramatic surprises either, and indeed, could be regarded as something of an anti-climax. Though not statistically inconclusive, they were politically inconclusive, in that they gave all parties cause for reflection and some misgivings. The Gaullists undoubtedly did better than the more pessimistic of them had feared. With their Giscardian and Centre allies they had a majority of between twenty and fifty, without counting on any support from the *Réformateurs*. The only other election of the régime to have been held at the end of a normal parliamentary term and in a political atmosphere without any overriding preoccupation or threat of political crisis, that of 1967, had given the Gaullists and their allies only the barest of majorities.[128] Nevertheless, there was little complacency in the Gaullist ranks. The barrage of opinion polls predicting Socialist–Communist gains had given them a fright. They had felt obliged to match some of the promises of social benefits in the common programme with promises of their own, in spite of the fact that, if fulfilled with reasonable promptness, these were bound to create precisely the kind of difficulties that they had predicted in the event of a left-wing victory. Indeed, one of M. Mitterrand's first moves after the election was to suggest that the Government should immediately carry out those parts of M. Messmer's programme, as announced in his Provins speech, on which there was apparent agreement between Government and opposition parties! Even with the aid of these belated promises of social and economic benefits, the Gaullists did not succeed in avoiding the loss of nearly a hundred seats. This figure was not unexpected, but what perhaps gave cause for more concern was the fact that the Gaullist coalition lost over 3 per cent of its 1967 first-ballot votes.[129] Nor could this fall in votes be attributed either to the attraction of the *Mouvement réformateur* (for the Centre had done no more than hold its own) or to apathy (for there had been a high poll).[130] Beyond all doubt, the Government parties had lost some ground to the Left.

The two main opposition parties, however, had no real grounds for satisfaction either. The combined left-wing vote at the first ballot was 46·24 per cent of the votes cast. This figure included some 4·6 per cent of votes cast for the PSU and other left-wing candidates outside the coalition. It showed an increase of under 3 per cent on the combined left-wing vote in the first ballot of the 1967 election, when the PSU and independent left-wing vote had been much smaller. In terms of votes, the Left's increase of just under a million and a half was almost wholly accounted for by the increase in the electorate (over two million since 1967) and in the dissident left-wing vote. The UGSD and the Communists together

polled only just over three-quarters of a million more than
did the Communists and the FGDS in 1967 (41·47 per cent
of the vote cast in 1967 and 41·61 per cent in 1973). But the
Communist share of that total had increased by only some
126,000 and the Communist percentage of the total poll
actually fell from 22·51 in 1967 to 21·25 in 1973. The Socialist-
Radical UGSD at least had the satisfaction of having polled
three-quarters of a million more votes than the Federation
had received in 1967 and of having increased its percentage of
the total poll by about 1·5 per cent. But the Socialists had not
attained their objective of attracting more votes than the
Communist party. The latter still just topped the five-million
mark, while the Socialists, even with the help of something
over a quarter of a million Radicals, just failed to reach the
five-million mark.[131]

Nor was the 1973 situation any more encouraging from the
point of view of seats. With 102 seats (including 11 held by
Radicaux de gauche) the UGSD had doubled its strength in the
National Assembly, but had still not reached the figure for
representatives of the Federation in 1967. The Communists
had more than doubled their strength, but with 73 seats still
held only the number that they held in 1967.

The opposition Centre *Mouvement réformateur*, though it
doubled its representation in the National Assembly, achieved
only the bare minimum required to enable it to constitute
a recognized parliamentary group. Its total of 34 Deputies
was still well below the *Centre Démocrate*'s representation in
1967.[132] It was clear that M. Lecanuet would not be able to
realize his hopes of holding a balance between Government
and opposition coalitions.

All in all, these results were disappointing for all parties.
What they indicated in terms of the future evolution of the
politics of the Fifth Republic was by no means clear. In
accordance with French electoral tradition in normal periods,
foreign policy had played no part in the election. In the field
of internal policy, the election had solved no problems,
clarified no issues, made or unmade no reputations.[133] The
President had acquired no wider field of talent to help him to

revivify the Gaullist party image. Socialist and Communist parties were apparently faced with the prospect of five further years in opposition, during which all the existing frictions, whether between orthodox parties and dissident Leftists or between Socialists and Communists, could be expected to continue.

Nor had the election results contributed in any way to strengthening the prestige of the President himself, either as head of State or as France's spokesman within the European Community. The most that could be said was that France had demonstrated her capacity to survive the disappearance of General de Gaulle without any apparent threat of the kind of upheaval that he had so often predicted. As far as could be foreseen, the Gaullist régime could reasonably look forward to completing its second decade, and the President could expect to complete his presidential term.

The most important known event in the immediate future, the presidential election of 1976, promised, therefore, not only to provide something of a repetition of the 1973 electoral atmosphere, but also to be preceded by a similarly lengthy period of pre-electoral negotiation, with the consequent risk of increasing still farther the growing gulf between the pre-occupations of politicians and those of their electors. In its own way, the persistent 'electoralism' that had characterized the régime since 1962 was slowly creating an image of the Fifth Republic's internal politics which, if different from that of the Fourth Republic, was likely sooner or later to prove no more satisfactory to the electorate.

PART II

Foreign Policy

CHAPTER VII

Gaullism in the Pattern of French Foreign Policy

CONTINUITY AND CONSENSUS

There have been fewer issues in French foreign policy than in internal politics on which there has been acute party conflict, though when such issues do arise they can be no less divisive. It is not merely that there is more consciousness of what unites Frenchmen than of what divides them, but that there is also much less general interest in foreign than in internal affairs. As has already been said, it is a commonplace of French political life that elections are rarely won on foreign-policy issues. In 1849, Guizot claimed that '. . . foreign policy does not concern the French at all and will not be the cause of any important event. Governments can do what they please'.[1]

This has certainly not always been true, but it quite often has been. Throughout most of the Third Republic, foreign affairs were regarded, even by the majority of Deputies, as being the concern of the President of the Republic and the Minister of Foreign Affairs.[2] In more recent times, it has not been unknown for a Foreign Minister to present Deputies with what was virtually a *fait accompli* and for his Ministry to escape control by the Cabinet more easily than others.[3] General de Gaulle shared the general view that his compatriots were not primarily interested in foreign policy. Having outlined in his Memoirs the plans that he had had in 1945 for restoring France to her traditional status, he added:

I realized that my ideas regarding the status and rights of France were not shared by many leaders of opinion and that I should be less and less able to rely on their voices, pens, and influence in support of my ambitious policies for France. I admit that this initial dissent affected me deeply. . . .[4]

Lack of interest in foreign policy in general has not, however, prevented specific conflicts and incidents from leaving bitter and lasting memories that have influenced attitudes to subsequent relations, either between political parties with conflicting views or between France and the country or countries concerned. French memories have been no less long in foreign than in internal politics, and both Franco-British and Franco-American relations have been, and continue to be, affected by the atmosphere created as a result of such past feelings. For many years, Franco-American relations were coloured by a favourable bias going back to the Revolutionary era, and maintained by vague feelings of Republican solidarity. More recently, they have been coloured by fears of American dominance in the field of Western defence and of increasing United States investment in Europe. Franco-British relations would be incomprehensible without some knowledge of the resentments and suspicions that have been created in the course of a long history of wars, rivalries and misunderstandings, and that can be reawakened by some minor incident and magnify it out of all proportion. Memories of colonial rivalries, especially in Africa, made it possible at the beginning of the century for the French Foreign Minister, Jules Cambon, to suggest that some English statesmen were capable of going on from the Boer War to attack the French Empire.[5] The impact on French opinion of American reactions to the Suez affair in 1956,[6] and the violence of the French reaction to American and British offers of 'good offices' in 1958 during the Franco-Tunisian crisis, were explicable only in the context of a climate determined by past fears of 'Anglo-Saxon' attitudes or policies in relation to what France regarded as her national interests or her rightful status.

On questions of what ought to be France's rôle in the world, and of her main foreign-policy objectives, there has been and still is a high degree of continuity and consensus. General de Gaulle's view that France's vocation was to be a great power, a world power, and that this would always be her destiny,[7] has been largely shared by parties on the Left as well as on the Right, and so the sense of resentment in post-war France regarding France's subordinate position in NATO and the absence of a French finger on the nuclear trigger was hardly less deeply felt by M. Guy Mollet[8] than by General de Gaulle himself, who regarded it as 'intolerable for a great State to be dependent on the decisions and actions of another State, however friendly'.[9]

There has been agreement that the main field of activity of French foreign policy should be that of Europe, as it has been since the fourteenth century. The frontiers of that Europe have not, of course, always been the same, nor have the objectives of France's European policies. The Europe that Pierre Dubois sought to unite in the fourteenth century, and Eméric Crucé in the seventeenth, was that of Catholic Christendom. The Europe of Sully, Louis XIV and Louis XV was a framework for the realization of French nationalist ambitions. Up to the defeat of Napoleon, the dominant tradition of French foreign policy – the claim to certain 'natural frontiers' – though explicable in the light of the historical vulnerability of France's Eastern frontiers, served also as a justification for expansionist policies. But it could and did serve equally well as a justification for more idealistic aims.

> It is not possible [wrote Carlo Laroche] to say when the policy of French unification becomes a policy of conquest. . . . There is a whole school of thought that has sought a dominating rôle for France: every great country has its own messianism and believes itself called on to regenerate the world by ruling it. What is interesting is to see how it accomplishes its mission. In France, the tradition of conquest has always been accompanied by noble ideas – one would be tempted to call them utopian, if it were not for the fact that yesterday's utopia can be tomorrow's reality.[10]

The Revolutionaries certainly regarded themselves as inspired by noble ideas, but they none the less claimed the right to the same natural frontiers as had been claimed by Richelieu. 'The traditional and natural frontiers of France', said Carnot in 1794, 'are the Rhine, the Alps and the Pyrenees.' Danton had justified the annexation of Belgium the previous year on the same grounds:

> I maintain that there is no need to fear the Republic. Its frontiers have been laid down by nature. We shall reach them . . . the Rhine, the Ocean, the Alps. These should be the frontiers of our Republic and no power will be able to prevent us from reaching them.[11]

From 1815 onwards, the dominant tradition of French foreign policy became one of moderation or introversion – what has been described as that of 'natural equilibrium' – the attitude of a power whose territorial ambitions were basically satisfied and which was anxious to consolidate acquired positions, to ensure its own security, but not to annex territory. In his study of French foreign-policy changes since 1945, published in 1963, Jean-Baptiste Duroselle pointed out that

> no government in power since Louis XVIII has ever tried to go beyond these frontiers except that of Napoleon III, and even for him the goal of 'destroying the shameful treaties of 1815' was only acceptable if pursued by pacific means.[12]

Nevertheless, the idea of 'natural frontiers' remained in French minds and, in one form or another, it runs through French history from Richelieu to de Gaulle. But it has become a nostalgic formulation of an ideal guarantee of France's security, unattainable in practice, or alternatively a guarantee attainable only through some European concert of nations. The former view was expressed in Clemenceau's speech in the Chamber of Deputies in 1919:

> We all know instinctively that the drive to the Rhine was the tradition of our ancestors. . . . This was the traditional frontier, a real frontier defining French territory. . . That is where we ought to have ended up. It is not the fault of the Revolutionary armies that we did not stay there. . . . But

it is not our fault either if, today, when I want to go on to the Rhine, I encounter German territory between the Rhine and me, and am obliged to take account of that fact.[13]

General de Gaulle frequently expressed the latter point of view. It was, he said in 1948, France's 'duty and dignity' to be 'at the centre and in the key position of an agglomeration, whose arteries would be the North Sea, the Rhine and the Mediterranean'. And he spoke in his Memoirs of the plan that he had had at the time of the Liberation in 1944

> to achieve a political, economic and strategic grouping of the States bordering on the Rhine, the Alps and the Pyrenees. To make this organization one of the three great world powers and, if necessary, one day the arbiter between the Soviet and Anglo-Saxon camps.[14]

From 1870 onwards, France's foreign policy has been dominated by the fact that she saw Germany as the permanent threat to her security. The primary purpose of any treaty, agreement or European organization has been, therefore, to protect her from this danger. The means actually pursued have included peace treaties, collective action through the League of Nations, alliances with the countries of the 'little Entente' and with Russia and, after the 1939–45 war, especially though not exclusively, some form of European organization. Whatever the differing views of French parties regarding the possibility or desirability of creating organizations aiming at European unity, all of them, without exception, have shared the view that the permanent, overriding priority of French foreign policy was the solution of the German problem. And so, whatever else it might be, the idea of Europe was primarily in French minds a device for rendering Germany harmless, by including her in the larger European framework, just as it was possible to overcome French opposition to German rearmament only by including Germany in the Atlantic framework. In both cases, the intention was to prevent the possibility of Germany's ever again regaining a dominant position from which she could threaten France.

The colonialism of the late nineteenth and early twentieth centuries provided a field of action outside Europe for French foreign policy. At first, there was by no means wholehearted support for colonial expansion, but well before the problem of colonial nationalism became a political problem the principles of French colonial rule had been generally accepted. Though the Empire was regarded as having economic advantages for France, its value lay much more in the political and cultural fields. It was seen as a contribution to France's great-power status, and even more as a civilizing mission. French administrators were to teach French methods of government, while French doctors and teachers, in French-supplied hospitals and schools, were to play a vital rôle in anchoring the political loyalties of the educated classes in the overseas dependencies to the Republic. There was never any real support – either before or after the 1944 Brazzaville Declaration[15] – for the idea that these territories should evolve towards eventual independence. What was envisaged was, at most, 'autonomy', which meant a limited area of self-government within a framework of French control of vital services, especially finance and foreign affairs.

When decolonization became inevitable, France tried at first to replace these institutional bonds by others that would ensure the maintenance of the close relationship. The attempt to define Moroccan and Tunisian independence as *'l'indépendance dans l'interdépendance'* failed, and the invention of the concept of the Community – which was a form of 'autonomy'[16] – was replaced by full independence before the institutions had begun to function as they were intended. But whatever the objections of former dependencies to the idea of some degree of continued dependence on France, the fact of it was inescapable, for they were not, or at least could not be for years, economically viable, and they had, in addition, administratively, culturally and politically a very real 'special relationship' with France. It was therefore possible for France, under the Gaullist régime, still to claim to include within France's sphere of influence the former French territories in French-speaking Africa. Under the leadership of General de Gaulle,

France also sought to establish or maintain special cultural and economic links between France and countries that, though not former dependencies, could plausibly be regarded as having either linguistic, cultural, or traditional links with France. This much vaguer and less realistic conception of France's sphere of influence was intended to prolong the 'civilizing mission' of colonialism in a form more suited to the twentieth century. As expressed in the more grandiloquent phraseology of General de Gaulle, France saw herself, not merely as 'the guardian of the Rhine', but as 'the starting point of a road from the Western world to Africa and the East'.[17] This aspect of foreign policy was not only accepted by all parties, but was in many ways the most generally popular of Gaullist foreign-policy objectives.

THE IMPORTANCE OF THE FOURTH REPUBLIC

One of the many traumatic effects of the second world war was the creation for France of at least two major problems of foreign policy that she was politically, economically and psychologically ill-equipped to deal with. First, she found herself in an unaccustomed and uncomfortable position of material and psychological inferiority within the Western defence system. If, as has been suggested, there has traditionally been in France's relations with her allies and neighbours a strong element of 'touchiness', it must be admitted that, during the decade following the war, she had a great deal to be touchy about. The feeling of being a liberated, not a liberating power, her absence from Yalta and Potsdam (something that General de Gaulle never either forgot or forgave), the belated *de jure* recognition of the de Gaulle provisional Government by the allies on 23 October 1944, the grudging agreement by her allies to allow France a share in the occupation of Germany – so grudging that it made her 'an occupying power by courtesy rather than by right'[18] – all these created feelings of humiliation and resentment that were only slowly and only partially dissipated. They were to be an important element in the friction with the United States which was the most notable characteristic of the foreign policy of the Fifth Republic. And differences of attitude towards the United States were to add yet another to the already considerable frictions and misunderstandings between France and Britain.

The second problem was that, although there was general agreement (except of course for the Communists) on the principle of the need for European unity as being the only effective way of dealing with the German threat, the immediate problem of the creation of European institutions was one on which there was agreement neither between Britain and France nor between French parties themselves. Between 1948 and 1954, indeed, this problem was the most divisive issue in French politics, and party conflicts on the Left were further exacerbated by the existence of a powerful Communist party, preoccupied primarily with promoting good relations with the Soviet Union, and therefore suspicious of 'Europeanism'.

The most obvious achievements of the Fourth Republic in the field of foreign policy were therefore the negative ones of increasing France's disagreements with her allies, and of actually weakening her influence within the Atlantic Alliance. Her material contribution to defence was lessened by the demands of the Algerian war and her political contribution was weakened by persistent Government instability and indecision resulting from party divisions on foreign policy. Positive contributions (though less obvious perhaps to her allies) were the Fourth Republic's impressive record in reconstruction, and the progress made in programmes for economic modernization, without which General de Gaulle could not have begun to carry out his own ambitious foreign policy.

THE IMPORTANCE OF FRANCO-BRITISH RELATIONS

The Fourth Republic also bequeathed to the Fifth a persistent problem of bad Franco-British relations. It is impossible, of course, to isolate this aspect of France's foreign policy from her attitude to the United States and NATO, and to the construction of a united Europe. But Franco-British relations do nevertheless constitute a complex problem in themselves, for frictions and misunderstandings go back a long way and go deep. In 1944, General de Gaulle said in a letter to Marshal Stalin: 'Between France and the Soviet Union there are no matters in direct dispute. Between France and Great Britain, there always have been and there always will be.'[19] The second statement was certainly true and is, indeed, an understatement. For, in addition to matters of direct dispute, both past and present – from a history of war 'for 54 of the 126 years preceding the Revolution'[20] to disagreements regarding the organization of Europe since 1948 – there have been many matters of indirect dispute, together with deep-seated temperamental incompatibilities that have helped to perpetuate what Bertrand de Jouvenel called 'the injection of shrillness' into Franco-British relations.[21] And because Europe has been the centre of French foreign policy, France's conception of the rôle of Britain in Europe has been and still is one of the main points of political controversy, within France, as well as between France and Britain.

Up to the second world war, Britain remained half part of Europe and half unwilling to be committed to the Continent. She had responded only 'cautiously' to Briand's 1930 proposals for European Federal Union. But in the post-war years, most of French opinion counted on Britain to become part of the new supranational Europe, an organization that would protect France against future threats from Germany. Britain's reluctance to agree to French proposals, however, led to a great deal of ill-feeling between 1948 and 1954. General de Gaulle of course shared both the well-known British dislike of supranational institutions and the French belief in the central place of Europe in French foreign policy, but resented Britain's Atlanticism. He never forgot the Churchillian statement of the British position made to him in 1944, recorded in his Memoirs as a kind of manifesto of British subservience to the United States: '. . . every time we have to choose between Europe and the open sea', Churchill had said, 'we shall always choose the open sea. And whenever I have to choose between you and Roosevelt, I shall always choose Roosevelt.'[22]

In reality, Franco-British disagreements included, along with 'matters of direct dispute', such as rivalries in areas that each country regarded as being in its own legitimate sphere of influence (especially in the Middle East), disagreements regarding European policy and Europe's relations with the United States. There were also some less easily definable political incompatibilities attributable to history and national psychology rather than to specific issues.

Just as in French internal politics constitutions that include detailed and precise obligations reflect a basic political and constitutional insecurity, so in foreign policy the French sense of national insecurity is reflected in a preference for treaties and agreements that lay down not only principles and goals, but also precise routes that must be taken to reach the goals. There is also an intellectual as well as a temperamental liking for logical and legalistic formulations of what are often purely political issues. Thus, between 1960 and 1965, French opposition to United Nations peace-keeping activities was buttressed by references to the legal obligations imposed by the Charter,[23] France's withdrawal from NATO was officially justified by a series of juridical arguments that nobody really believed,[24] and French objections to a meeting of the WEU in 1969, though couched in juridical terms, were known to be really political objections having little or nothing to do with either the WEU or the proposed agenda of the meeting.[25] In all these cases, France and Britain were on opposite sides.

In Franco-British relations, the French liking for clear statements and precise commitments – at the risk of being obliged to find ways of evading such commitments, if they turn out to be inapplicable in unforeseen circumstances – comes into conflict with the British liking for a cautious pragmatism that has often led France to conclude either that the British have no clear foreign policy, or that they are deliberately obscuring their real purposes in a nebulous haze. The result has been the creation of a climate of built-in distrust. In fact, throughout the present century, France and Britain have practically never been in step. When, in the years before the 1914 war, the French wanted an alliance, the British were prepared for no more than an entente, which the French regarded as too imprecise. Yet the British regarded the Briand proposal of 1930 as too imprecise – and also as being 'penetrated with a vague and puzzling idealism'.[26] Exactly twenty years later, France's proposal for a European Coal and Steel Community met with a refusal from Great Britain, which did not want to be definitely committed to a principle without knowing what precise obligations would be involved. In the years immediately following the two world wars, France's demands had been clear enough, but had been unacceptable to her allies.

> After 1919 [wrote Raymond Aron] the French had, and could have, only one passion: to conserve the fruits of a dearly won victory, to safeguard a European system that had, by a miracle, weakened 'the hereditary enemy', to stop history there, as some have said.[27]

This was also France's first passion after the 1939–45 war. At almost no point, however, either during the inter-war period or in the years from 1945 onwards, were France and Britain on the same wavelength. In the 1920s, France believed that security should precede disarmament, while Britain held that security was unachievable without disarmament. Britain was readier than France to envisage a reduction in land forces, but less ready to accept naval disarmament. Later, when the British wanted to apply sanctions at the time of the Italo-Abyssinian war, the French were unwilling. When Germany reoccupied the Rhineland, Britain did nothing, because she was determined to prevent a war. When the Spanish civil war posed the problem of non-intervention, each country was preoccupied with its own internal pressures and problems. After the second world war, difficulties between the allies regarding the possible and desirable means of containing Germany were fought out all over again. After the French launched the first post-war proposals for a European organization, France and Britain disagreed at every stage – on the principle of integration, on the relations of European and Atlantic organizations, on the need for additional military guarantees by Britain and the United States. The list is long enough without the addition of ten years of argument regarding the desirability or possibility of British membership of the Common Market.

Yet, in spite of persistent disagreements, there has been, since the eighteenth century, a permanent attraction between the two countries which makes their relationship essentially ambivalent. The attraction is no doubt based on their increasing conviction that the first condition of any lasting security in Europe is that they should stand together – a conviction cemented by their experiences of two world wars in alliance. There is, too, a long-standing British admiration for France's achievements in the field of political ideas, and for her intellectual and cultural brilliance, and on the French side an unwilling admiration for British political and parliamentary institutions that have, up to now, worked rather better than those of France. Unfortunately, these sentiments tend to come to the fore mainly in times of war, and, with the return of peace, are soon submerged in the familiar sequences of discord, misunderstanding and estrangement.

THE NATURE OF GAULLIST FOREIGN POLICY

Since the objectives of Gaullist foreign policy were essentially traditional, divergences between France and Britain continued, as was to be expected, and were indeed intensified under the Fifth Republic. Nor is it easy to believe that, in a European Community of nine, these differences can avoid adding to the existing obstacles to greater unity.

Can it be said then that there is any specifically Gaullist contribution to French foreign policy? Its originality up to now has been mainly in methods rather than objectives, and it has been mainly to its methods that political opponents have objected. These have been new, in that the President has personally directed foreign policy, and has chosen to make many of his most important statements at presidential press conferences (an innovation of the Fifth Republic). This method has given great publicity to presidential views – views which were often expressed by General de Gaulle in deliberately provocative terms. This method certainly created, both in France and outside, a new image to replace the *'immobilisme'* and hesitation that had been characteristic of the foreign policy of the Fourth Republic. It was a powerful political weapon in that it helped to restore France's confidence in her own international status, as well as to strengthen the President's internal position.

All the same, it has been suggested – explicitly or implicitly – by opponents of Gaullism that its main contribution as far as foreign policy was concerned was, under the presidency of General de Gaulle, the successful propagation of a number of temporarily useful myths.[28] The different aspects of Gaullist foreign policy discussed in the following chapters reveal it as going through three distinct phases. In the first, which lasted up to the end of the Algerian war, it was inevitably negative, in that although France's *attitudes* were those of increasing distance from NATO and from Great Britain, these could not yet be translated into actions. In the second phase, there was action, and France not only withdrew from NATO, but also *de facto* excluded Great Britain for the second time from membership of the European Community. But the withdrawal from NATO meant withdrawal into a notional and as yet non-existent Europe, whose members were not then, and have not been since, agreed on where they are going or even seeking to go. The third phase, from 1969 onwards, which saw the reversal of the French attitude regarding British membership of the European Community, brought new uncertainties for a Community of nine, and also brought into question some of the hitherto most popular themes of Gaullist foreign policy outside Europe, but without providing alternative ones.

CHAPTER VIII

France and Europe – The Search for Security and Leadership

THE LEGACY OF THE FOURTH REPUBLIC

In an often quoted *boutade*, General de Gaulle accused the Fourth Republic of having no foreign policy.[1] If by that he meant that its leaders had no coherent objective, then his accusation was unjustified. The Fourth Republic had one overriding obsession and some say only one creative idea. The obsession was the overwhelming fear of a renewed threat of aggression from Germany, together with the assumption that some political formula or recipe could be found that would eliminate the threat. As André Fontaine wrote in 1952, 'France cannot be reproached for having no foreign policy. One could even say that her German policy *is* her foreign policy.' And he headed the section of the article in which he made this affirmation: 'France has a German policy: she has no other'.[2] The one creative idea of the Fourth Republic was that the magic formula was to be something called 'Europe'. General de Gaulle inherited from the Fourth Republic organizations that were intended to provide a framework within which West Germany could be, so to speak, anchored to the West, while remaining divided from East Germany until some time in the far distant future when she might be regarded as no longer constituting a threat to European peace and security.

That the post-war European movement was dominated by the desire for security from Germany is a fact that French politicians made no attempt to hide. Robert Schuman spoke in 1953 of the Coal–Steel Pool as offering a concrete solution of both the Franco-German and the European problems. Edouard

Herriot thought that the solution of the German problem must precede the construction of Europe. In 1949, General de Gaulle had laid down as the condition for the construction of Europe an agreement between Frenchmen and Germans, though at that time he had not envisaged the re-creation of a German national Government, but only a loose federation of States, with the Ruhr remaining under European control.[3] And he had already described the Europe that would be built on that basis as including France's African territories, as being supported by the United States, and as forming the nucleus of a wider, historical Europe that would include a Russia assumed by then to have abandoned the Communist system.

The 'Europe of the Six', accepted by France in the 'fifties, had not been originally envisaged by Governments of the Fourth Republic, but had followed from the failure of earlier efforts to achieve security from Germany. The first had been the traditional method of alliances and the containment of Germany through international control of the Ruhr arsenal, the economic attachment of the Saar to France, the occupation of the Rhineland, and the prevention for as long as possible of the creation of a West German State. Three of these four 'bastions' of French security had had to be abandoned by 1949, owing to differences between the four occupying powers. And so, in 1948, France was already turning to the second method, that of 'Europe' – a Europe that was seen at first as grouping all the countries of Western Europe, but that, in 1949, succeeded only in forming the Council of Europe, a body with minimal functions unable to provide any of the guarantees of security sought by France.

By 1951, the idea of 'little Europe' – a Europe of six that would eventually form a supranational entity within which Germany would be not so much anchored as enmeshed – had taken a strong hold in most of the political parties in France. This objective was, however, divisive as well as obsessive. For if French opinion was unanimous on the need to eliminate the threat of German aggression, it was far from united on either the desirability or the possibility of a united Western Europe. The Communists, of course, looked primarily to the

Soviet Union and so did not want to see a rehabilitated West German State committed either to a West European 'capitalist' group of nations or to an Atlantic organization dominated by the United States. The reactionary Right remained traditionally nationalist and afraid of a renaissance of German national power, particularly in the economic field. The Christian Democrat MRP was wholly in favour of the European idea and, in a Europe dominated at that time by three Catholic leaders, de Gasperi, Adenauer and Schumann, this undiluted enthusiasm helped to make the MRP even more suspect to the French Left.

Neutralist opinion, which was strong in left-wing circles at the beginning of the 'fifties, was particularly suspicious of the extension of the European idea to the field of defence. All blocs, whether on the Right or the Left, were regarded by neutralists, and indeed by much French opinion on the Left in general, as likely to be ineffective methods of preventing war, and German rearmament was especially feared as being more likely to weaken than to strengthen the defence position of the West. The moderate Right, the Radicals and the Socialists were on the whole in favour of the European idea, but there were divisions both within and between parties. In particular, there were divisions regarding the conditions in which a supranational Europe including Germany could be made safe from the dangers presented by a Germany with recovered economic strength, regarding the desirability or otherwise of British membership of such a Europe, and regarding the ways (if any) in which German rearmament could be made acceptable to France. Parties were divided also on the need for a European military force (if it ever proved possible to create one), to be controlled by a European political authority, and on the methods of creating such an authority.

With the exception of the Communist party and the MRP, then, all parties were to a greater or lesser extent divided on the issue of European integration, and even more divided on proposals to create a European defence force that would include German units. Indeed, the four-year discussion from

1950 to 1954 over the plans for the European Defence Community (EDC) involved more political controversy than had any other single issue since the Dreyfus affair or the separation of Church and State. The problem was finally settled by the rejection of the whole plan by the French National Assembly in August 1954 and by the conclusion, within a few months, of the Paris and London agreements. These provided for a German national army under the direct control of NATO, and for British and American forces to be stationed in France under the aegis of NATO for a period of at least twenty years.

The route to Europe, laid down in 1957 by the Treaty of Rome (accepted enthusiastically by some and apprehensively by others), was in a short time generally agreed on as the framework within which a 'European' foreign policy would be pursued. When General de Gaulle returned to power in 1958, his acceptance of France's obligations under the treaty reassured those who had feared that 'Europeanism' would be abandoned under Gaullist rule, while the General's interpretation of those obligations reassured his own supporters. From 1958 onwards, therefore, with the exception of the Communists, all sections of opinion were agreed in defending the EEC, the Gaullists for old-fashioned nationalist reasons, the ardent 'Europeans' because they persuaded themselves that it could be the initial stage of a dream Europe, 'a Europe not merely united but integrated . . . a European super-nation above nations'.[4]

GENERAL DE GAULLE AND THE EUROPEAN
ECONOMIC COMMUNITY

General de Gaulle consistently rejected the whole idea of supranationalism, not only because it would, in his view, mean submerging the French personality in a 'technocratic', or 'faceless', community system, but also because it would prevent France from regaining what he saw as her rightful position in Europe. His aim was that France should be the leader of a far older 'Europe', whose geographical boundaries were wider than those of the Community of the Six. He had, nevertheless, inherited from the Fourth Republic the obligations subscribed to by France in the Treaty of Rome. Since all parties saw in the treaty possibilities of economic advantages for France, both Government and opposition parties were able to travel the road together, in so far as the specific requirements of the treaty were concerned, in spite of their widely differing conceptions of the ultimate 'European' goal. General de Gaulle was also able to use the appeal of older European ideas. His skilful exploitation of more grandiose conceptions was comforting to his own supporters and, as soon became clear, acceptable to large sections of the French public, which welcomed promises of a Europe in which France could hope to achieve security and the status of a great power, as well as material economic advantages.

In French history and foreign policy, 'Europe' has meant three different things and something of all three persists in the political attitudes of the Fifth Republic. It has been an expression of French universalism, of belief in the existence of a common European religion, culture and history, and this is a theme to which General de Gaulle often returned. '*Our* Europe', he claimed, 'is the main centre of modern civilization.'[5] When he was in the United States in 1960, he referred to 'the nations that were the creators and have remained the custodians of modern civilization', adding: 'That means the whole of Europe, and America, her daughter.'[6] Europe has also been seen throughout French history as a theatre in which France's rôle is dominant and sometimes dominating – a thin disguise for French nationalism, but a nationalism that claims to be seeking peace rather than conquest. As one writer put it:

> Except during brief periods of her history, France has not sought hegemony for herself, but only to defend herself against foreign domination. . . . All plans for hegemony that we know of are plans for perpetual peace; revolutionary conquest itself is a crusade.[7]

The two themes, indeed, were often combined by General de Gaulle. The 'physical and moral centre' of Western Europe must be France.[8] But at the same time, it was to be 'Europe from the Atlantic to the Urals, Europe, all those old countries where modern civilization grew up, that will decide the future of the world . . . .'[9]

In 1959, such responsibilities looked a long way away. The third theme, that of the European road back to great-power status, as well as to France's security from German aggression, was one that was shared by many supranational 'Europeans' in France as well as by nationalist Gaullists. To both, the EEC represented a first stage, and one, moreover, that at least had the advantage of assisting France's economic recovery and development, without which future dreams of power in Europe must remain unrealized. 'We have', said General de Gaulle in 1962, 'with several States of Western Europe, created an economic community which is beginning to produce results that will be to France's advantage.'[10]

To General de Gaulle, 'Europeanism' within the EEC meant essentially three things. It meant, first, using the Treaty of Rome and the organization of the European Community to provide economic advantages for France. Second, it meant using the institution as a basis from which to go on to develop political as well as economic co-operation. And third, it meant preventing Europe, either within the EEC or outside it, from developing supranational institutions. The first test of whether it was worth France's while to remain a member of the EEC was, therefore, the extent to which the latter could be persuaded to meet her demands regarding the common agricultural policy. This was also the test by which the majority of French citizens judged General de Gaulle's success or failure.

Before the Presidential election of 1965 [wrote a prominent Gaullist in 1970], what did we not hear about the General's intransigence and the way it was sabotaging Europe, while, all the time, he was defending what has certainly been vital for France: the inclusion of French agriculture in the common market.[11]

In the long struggle on this issue between 1961 and 1966, and again – though against less opposition – between 1969 and 1970, the Government was seen no less by its opponents than by its supporters as ably fighting for French national interests, and as justifiably doing so, since agricultural advantage was generally seen as legitimate compensation for what was expected to be the high price to French industry of competition within the Common Market. A similar test was applied by almost all French opinion to the issue of British membership of the EEC. In France's view, Great Britain must accept not only the terms of the Treaty of Rome, but also those of the agricultural settlement reached by the Six, before her application for membership could be seriously considered. It was not possible, wrote a left-wing French economist in 1963, for Britain 'to enter Europe and continue to buy from the Antipodes at the expense of a partner whose agriculture vitally needs to export'.[12]

Already, by 1960, however, General de Gaulle had begun to prepare the way for what he saw as the second function of the EEC, which was to provide a ready-made framework within which France could begin to pursue the Gaullist primary objective of regaining political leadership in Europe. In what became known as the Fouchet Plans, France proposed an institutional basis similar to that of the EEC as the French saw it, but which would provide for political co-operation, and was intended to lead to co-ordinated foreign and defence policies, though without introducing any element of supranationalism. The proposals went through two stages. The first was a failure. Between 1960 and 1962, a committee of the Six, presided over by M. Christian Fouchet, put forward a plan for inter-governmental meetings at regular intervals, and for the setting up of a Ministerial Council whose decisions would require unanimity. There was also to be a parliamentary assembly with purely advisory functions, together with a Commission which was to be what General de Gaulle believed that of the EEC ought to be, namely, a purely executive body entrusted with the carrying out of ministerial decisions. After several amendments to meet criticisms, the whole plan was eventually dropped in April 1962 for a number of reasons, of which the main one was the opposition of France's five partners to the purely inter-governmental basis of the proposed

political organization insisted on by France. They also feared
that it might be the prelude to an attempt by France to undermine the would-be supranational character of the EEC and to
weaken NATO, and they lacked confidence in France's willingness to extend the right of membership of this 'political'
Europe to Britain.[13]

THE FRANCO-GERMAN AXIS

The Gaullist plan for a political Europe had, therefore, to be
modified by the substitution for the Fouchet Plans of a more
acceptable but less ambitious bilateral arrangement between
France and Germany, described by the Foreign Minister,
M. Couve de Murville, as 'a first application . . . of the famous
Fouchet Plan'.[14] The Franco-German treaty of January 1963
had the advantage that it could be presented to the public as
evidence of progress towards a settlement of the German
problem, since it aimed at the replacement of fear and suspicion
by a system of permanent co-operation and consultation between the two countries, through regular meetings of heads
of State, Ministers and officials, and through collaboration on
questions of mutual interest. Such questions were intended to
include transport, defence (including research), cultural exchanges and so on, together with co-operation in providing
aid to developing countries.

In reality, the following years saw very little Franco-German
collaboration, and not even any significant degree of consultation. For instance, Germany was not consulted on either of
the two presidential vetos of British membership of the EEC,
on the President's statements on the Vietnam war, on monetary problems, or on his references, during his visit to Poland
in 1967 to the town of Zabrze (the former German Hinden-
burg) as 'the most Polish of all Polish cities'. Nor was there
any sign that the two countries were moving closer to each
other on foreign-policy questions generally. On the contrary,
in his press conference of 23 July 1964, the President had to
admit that, up to then, the treaty had produced no common
political line.

This was, in fact, a considerable understatement, as he himself went on to demonstrate by listing disagreements between France and Germany – on defence and the organization of NATO, on attitudes towards the East European countries, frontier questions in Central and Eastern Europe, the recognition of China, the problem of peace in Indo-China, the question of aid to underdeveloped countries in Africa, Asia and Latin America, and finally (and clearly the point that rankled most) the settlement of the Common Market agricultural policy, without which, he pointed out, the future of the Community remained problematical.

The existence of a Franco-German axis at least helped to ensure German acceptance of French demands in the EEC, and so contributed to General de Gaulle's success in achieving his third objective, which was the prevention of the development of any effective degree of European supranationalism. In June 1965, the EEC Commission put forward two proposals in connection with the financing of the common agricultural policy. The first was that, since funds were likely to be considerably in excess of current needs, the Commission should control the use of the surplus. The second was that the European Assembly should exercise supervision over the Commissions' administration. Though the two proposals were immediately withdrawn in the face of French opposition, the French resented what they regarded as an attempt by their partners to compel them to accept an advance towards supranationalism (even if only a minor advance) in order to obtain the benefits of the agricultural settlement. French representatives, therefore, refused to attend further meetings of the EEC without guarantees against any possibility of France's being obliged to accept decisions that she might regard as being contrary to her vital national interests.

Such guarantees involved, in the first place, a modification of some procedures agreed under the treaty. From January 1966, decisions on many important issues were due to be taken by qualified majority – which meant that France would require, as a minimum, the support of at least one country (other than Luxembourg) to block any decision. France was not prepared to accept these conditions without reservation. In the second place, the Commission's proposals provided a pretext for a French attempt to reduce the importance of its rôle in the Community. There was certainly some basis for France's belief that there had been an attempt by the Commission to force a decision on her. There was a general convention in the Community that, even where qualified-majority decisions were provided for, these should not be imposed on an unwilling partner, and Germany had actually obtained an undertaking in 1964 that the qualified-majority rule would not be used to change the cereal prices agreed on in December 1964. It was also generally understood that, before making proposals on major matters, the Commission should endeavour to reach agreement with national Governments. But this particular Commission proposal had overridden the votes of both the French members of the Commission, who, though not representatives, usually expected their advice on probable reactions in their own countries to be heeded. It dealt, moreover, with a matter on which the treaty required no decision until 1970, and so could legitimately be regarded as not strictly relevant to the main issue (as some representatives of the Six agreed). Leaving out of account the question of the desirability or otherwise in principle of according supranational powers to a body such as the Commission, there were certainly cogent practical reasons for considering the European Assembly, as it was constituted, an unsuitable body to exercise real powers.

Whatever may have been the merits of the arguments on either side, however, the upshot was that the main work of the EEC was virtually brought to a halt for seven months, and that the final settlement, though described as a compromise, was, in the view of the French, a victory for their case. For in addition to France's insistence on maintaining her position on the issue of the qualified-majority vote, seven out of ten new points raised by France, most of which involved minor reductions of the importance of the Commission, were accepted. The so-called agreement of January 1966 merely registered the failure of the Six to agree on the question of the application of the qualified-majority vote. In any case involving the vital interests of a member, the Six undertook to try to reach agreement, but without stating what was to happen if they failed.

The French maintained, however, that they would exercise what they insisted was their right to refuse to accept any decision made by a qualified-majority vote if it was contrary to what they regarded as a vital national interest. They also decided that they would exercise their undoubted right to defeat a proposal held by any other member to be contrary to his own country's national interests, presumably by simply adding their own vote to that of the member concerned. This meant that France could, *de facto*, prevent the working of the qualified-majority rule, since the vote of any two members (excluding Luxembourg) could prevent the achievement of a qualified majority. France had, therefore, succeeded in blocking even the small advance towards supranationalism authorized under the treaty. In practice, however, things went on much as before, and France continued to accept qualified-majority decisions where no vital national interest seemed to her to be at stake.[15]

The Franco-German axis was also used by France to serve Gaullist interests in preventing the development of supranationalism outside the field of the EEC. For General de Gaulle chose to regard the issue of integrated defence within NATO, and in particular the American proposal for multilateral nuclear forces, as a test case of German 'Europeanism'. Just as Britain must accept the agricultural policy desired by France in order to qualify for membership of the EEC, so Germany must accept the French definition of 'European Europe' as meaning a Europe independent of the United States.[16]

The discussion in the Gaullist press of France's conception of her own rôle in the nuclear defence of Europe did nothing to improve Franco-German relations. On the one hand, the participation of Germany in a proposed multilateral NATO nuclear force was unacceptable to France, as being contrary to the principle of 'European Europe', and the Prime Minister, M. Pompidou, even hinted that it might be contrary to the terms of the Franco-German treaty.

If [he said] the multilateral force were to lead to the creation of a kind of Germano-American military alliance . . . we should not consider this to be entirely compatible with our relations with the Federal Republic resulting from the Franco-German treaty . . . nor with the conception of European defence held by both the French Government and the opposition.[17]

On the other hand, this French 'conception of European defence' did not provide for any other German nuclear rôle in the foreseeable future. The following 'timetable' provided by Michel Debré is typical of many articles appearing in the Gaullist press in 1964:

France is the key to European security, and indeed the essential key for the Western half of the continent. She must, therefore, be able to defend herself, and that means that she must have the weapons essential to modern defence. She must also retain responsibility for her own forces if patriotism is to be assured.

If Europe is to be treated as an unequal partner, Europe will not take shape, and some nations will turn to neutralism. That will give Germany the right to possess nuclear arms or to share in their attribution. There must first be forged, in accordance with the requirements imposed by the facts, that is to say progressively and under the leadership of Governments, a European policy and a European authority. If the effort succeeds, then the time will come for a European patriotism. But the sequence of events must not be interfered with.[18]

If this 'sequence of events' were to be adhered to, then Germany was likely to have to wait a very long time indeed for the right to a nuclear rôle. Meanwhile, she was presumably to remain an unequal partner in a Europe which had no political or defence organization of its own and showed no signs of any willingness or ability to begin to create one. M. Debré was writing in 1965, five years after the Fouchet Plans for political and defence co-operation had first been proposed.

Not interfering with the course of events laid down by him apparently implied that, in the interim period while there was no 'European policy' or 'European authority', 'European Europe' must rely on France's embryonic nuclear deterrent for her defence, an assumption that none of France's partners in the European Community was prepared to make.

In the event, to France's satisfaction, the United States dropped the proposal for a multilateral force. But the general tone of the debate about it could hardly have been expected to assist Franco-German détente and co-operation. In fact, relations between the two countries actually deteriorated during the years following the signature of the Franco-German treaty. The personal sympathy that had existed between General de Gaulle and Chancellor Adenauer was lacking in the relations with his successor, Chancellor Erhard. Between 1966 and 1969, during the chancellorship of Dr Kiesinger, there was at least some increase in Franco-German cordiality, though still little discernible community of interest, beyond the fact that, for reasons of her own, of which political acceptance in Europe was the most important, Germany still felt it worth her while to continue to pay the high economic price implicit in the French conditions for the European agricultural settlement, and to play a conciliatory rôle, avoiding any open disagreement with France. But there was real friction, disquiet, and at times German resentment, both concerning General de Gaulle's continued lack of support for German reunification[19] and concerning contradictions in existing political circumstances between the French policy of détente with the Soviet Union and that of Franco-German entente. Though there was an increase in Franco-German cultural exchanges, this meant only that many more German students were coming to France than there were French students going to Germany.[20] There was virtually no co-operation in defence, no significant co-operation in scientific and technical research, which by 1967 had not got beyond the planning stage and was no more advanced in 1972. And nothing had come of the General's obvious desire for German co-operation in what he had hoped to present as 'European' aid to the third world.

FRANCO-BRITISH RELATIONS AND THE EUROPEAN COMMUNITY DURING GENERAL DE GAULLE'S PRESIDENCY

Throughout the Fifth Republic there was persistent friction between France and Great Britain on European policies, and these were also a source of recurrent friction between France and her partners in the Community. Franco-British differences, indeed, went back to the Fourth Republic, and General de Gaulle, in his criticisms of British attitudes and policies, more than once recalled the earlier differences during the period when, for much of French opinion, a supranational Europe had seemed to offer the only solution to the German problem. He never at any moment shared the belief in supranationalism, but, as has been said, the Community system was useful to him for other purposes, and, in his arguments against British entry, the survival of a very real French resentment of British policies and attitudes towards the Community was an additional weapon in his armoury.

Leaving out of account the specific points of disagreement on the conditions of British membership that were so exhaustively discussed in the Brussels negotiations of 1961 to 1963, and again between 1970 and 1971, there were, from the beginning, three fundamental differences of approach between the two countries on the European question. The first, on supranational methods and the goal of a supranational Europe, had ceased before the mid-sixties to have more than symbolic importance. It was, by then, clear that progress towards economic unity was going to be very slow and that no progress at all was being made towards political unity. In France, fidelity to the idea of a supranational Europe had by then become a ritual *'profession de foi'* in French opposition and Centre parties. But calls to 'abandon out-dated nationalism and move towards the Europe of the Community'[21] or statements that 'European unity is the only means of preventing America from dominating the West'[22] were more and more ceasing to carry conviction. According to an opinion poll published early in 1968, 43 per cent of French people questioned thought that European integration would be achieved *by the end of the century*, while 43 per cent thought that it would not, and the views of non-French 'Europeans' questioned were even more pessimistic.[23] It looked as if M. Mitterrand's conclusion that the Gaullists had won two-thirds of the battle against Europe was not unjustified, at least as far as a supranational Europe was concerned.[24] For, in the 1968 French general election, over 62 per cent of the votes cast were for Gaullist or Communist candidates, and these two parties were agreed at least in their hostility to European integration.

By 1970, even as convinced a 'European' as Chancellor Brandt could admit, without causing a raised eyebrow anywhere, that 'the time when co-operation can include some supranationalism has not yet come, far from it'.[25] But what had survived from the era of Franco-British divergencies in the 1950s on the objective of supranationalism was a very real suspicion of British motives in the field of European policy. The British were still regarded as potential wreckers, the possible 'Trojan horse' of the Community. There was also a recurrent French irritation throughout the Fifth Republic with the other five members, both on the ground that they continually sought to associate Great Britain with any political discussions within the Community (as happened during the negotiations regarding the Fouchet Plans, and in 1969 in relation to political discussions in the Western European Union), and also on the ground that, within the Community, they used the issues of supranationalism and of British membership as debating points intended to put pressure on France. During the 1965–6 quarrel between France and the five, M. Couve de Murville expressed this irritation with great frankness.

> No member of a responsible Government [he said] talks seriously of supranationality, which is a myth, used only to fight out-of-date battles – as is shown by the fact that such ideas are always associated with affirmations of the need for Great Britain's participation.[26]

Both in 1963 and in 1967, in his press conferences announcing a *de facto* veto on negotiations regarding British membership,

General de Gaulle explicitly criticized the early attempts of British Governments to get agreement on an alternative European organization to that provided for under the Treaty of Rome.

> While the Community was in process of formation [he said in November 1967], England at first refused to join it and adopted a hostile attitude, as if she saw in it an economic and political threat. She then tried to negotiate conditions of entry, which, if accepted, would have stifled the Community. This attempt having failed, the British Government affirmed that it no longer wished to join the Community and concentrated on strengthening its links with the Commonwealth, and with other European countries in a free-trade area. Now, having apparently changed her attitude, England declares that she is prepared to accept the Treaty of Rome, provided exceptions can be made to allow her a long transitional period, and provided essential changes can be made in its application to her.[27]

The second fundamental difference of approach between Britain and France concerned the relationship between Europe and the United States. The British never shared the Gaullist conviction (held by a great many French non-Gaullists as well) that the European continent was, as a Gaullist Deputy put it, 'the natural and legitimate framework of the Six'.[28] They had steadfastly refused to recognize that membership of any European organization need involve sacrificing the British special relationship with the Commonwealth or British commitments to the Atlantic Alliance and NATO. General de Gaulle, together with a surprising proportion of opposition politicians, resented France's dependence on Atlantic integrated defence, resented American domination of the organization, and resented what he and many sections of French opinion regarded as a 'special', privileged relationship between Britain and the United States, which made Britain a member of, and excluded France from, the 'club' of nuclear powers.

The consequences of this attitude towards the United States in the field of French defence policy are discussed in the following chapter. In the field of France's European policy it made her regard Britain as an undesirable partner for a number of reasons. First, France was alone among the Six in resenting the Atlantic organization. Her five partners remained loyal to it and, as has already been mentioned, Germany for a time hoped to take part in a multilateral Atlantic nuclear force, while retaining the 'special relationship' between France and Germany intended to be created as a result of the signature of the Franco-German treaty. While France remained the dominant essential partner in the Community, General de Gaulle could hope to persuade his partners to accept his own conception of 'European Europe', independent of, and claiming equality with, the United States. On this issue, his position in France was far stronger than many British observers were prepared to admit. He could count not only on the anti-Americanism of the Communists, but also on that of considerable sections of French opinion on the Left – an anti-Americanism that had made the Fourth Republic a reluctant and sometimes resentful member of the Atlantic Alliance and that was increased by growing fears of American economic hegemony.

The third fundamental difference between France and Britain was that their economic interests were in conflict. As has already been said, for General de Gaulle and for the majority of the French, the European Community meant, first and foremost, economic advantages for France, especially for French agriculture, and the test of its success was, therefore, the creation by the Six of a common agricultural policy acceptable to France. This, to quote General de Gaulle's own words, would

ensure that the countries of the Community are self-supporting in foodstuffs, any advantages derived from the import of cheaper food from outside being compensated for by 'financial levies'. But a high proportion of England's food is derived from buying cheaply from anywhere in the world, and especially from the Commonwealth. If she agrees to the rules of the Six, then her balance of payments will be destroyed by 'levies', yet she will be obliged to increase the price of her foodstuffs to the level of the continent, and so to increase the wages of her workers, thus making her goods dearer and markets more difficult to obtain.

And, in case it should be thought that General de Gaulle's refusal to accept British membership was in any way dictated by sympathy for this British predicament, it should be emphasized that his conclusion was that

> If she joins the Community without accepting the agricultural system of the Six, then this system will collapse forthwith, thus upsetting entirely the equilibrium of the Common Market and depriving France of one of her main reasons for belonging to it.[29]

The strength of General de Gaulle's position was, first, that this was the principal reason for the French people's support of the Common Market, as well as for that of the French Government, and second that, although Germany and Holland would have preferred a less protectionist system, the latter was too small to carry weight, and the former too anxious for political reasons to form part of the Community to do other than accept French conditions. If Britain were a member of the Community, as he predicted consistently, it would change its nature, by which he meant that France's ability to impose the agricultural policy would be jeopardized. It would also become politically less independent of the United States than he intended it to be, since the influence of Britain would undoubtedly lead to a strengthening of Atlantic links.

General de Gaulle's attitude to British membership remained perfectly consistent, and his successive statements really did no more than repeat this thesis.[30] Within the framework of Gaullist European policy it made sense. What requires some explanation is the consistent support (in principle) for British membership that appeared to be forthcoming from French opposition parties and from France's five partners, in spite of their disagreements with Britain regarding supranationalism, and in spite of the fact that French opposition parties shared the President's attitude towards the Community's economic policies and especially as they related to French agriculture.

There were also British politicians who continued to preach the need for British solidarity both with the Commonwealth and within the Atlantic Alliance, but who, nevertheless, declared themselves convinced Europeans.

One explanation of these apparent inconsistencies is that, on both sides of the Channel, supporters of British membership made assumptions, sometimes only implicitly, that the Gaullists did not make. British Europeans continued, up to a relatively recent date, to assume that it *would* be possible for Britain to retain Commonwealth links and to negotiate precisely the kind of 'privileged' position for her own agricultural interests (at least for a fairly prolonged period) that General de Gaulle had consistently ruled out. French supporters of British entry assumed, on the contrary, that this would *not* be possible, and that Great Britain would sooner or later have to resign herself to accepting French conditions. Yet even as late as 1967, Mr Wilson's formal acceptance in the House of Commons of the Treaty of Rome was accompanied by a proviso regarding the need for 'necessary adjustments' in order to meet British requirements.

It has sometimes been suggested that the first French veto of the British application for membership of the European Community was really caused by the President's anger at British readiness, immediately following the meeting in December 1962 between General de Gaulle and the British Prime Minister, Mr Macmillan, to accept the American nuclear proposals in the Nassau Agreement. This, it has been suggested, finally convinced him that Britain's subservience to the United States was incurable, and so would defeat his plans for Europe if Britain were to become a member of the Community. It seems more probable that Nassau was not a determining factor, but a pretext – an additional irritant that affected the tone, and perhaps also the timing, but not the basic argument of his press conference the following January. For one thing, there is no evidence that the President had not foreseen some such development as the Nassau Agreement from the time of the December meeting with the British Prime Minister at Rambouillet. In his own reconstruction of the sequence of events, the diplomatic editor of *Le Monde*, André Fontaine, claims that, at this meeting, the President was informed of British nuclear problems and that he then told Mr Macmillan that he did not consider Britain ready (*mûre*) to enter the Community, and that he had gone on to quote in support of that view the Churchillian statement of British attitudes to America that had so impressed him in 1944 and that he had subsequently included in the Memoirs.[31]

There is a good deal of evidence pointing to the conclusion that the strongest specific reason for the veto was the British objection to the agricultural policy of the Community. Both then and later, Gaullist spokesmen, and particularly the President himself, consistently emphasized the vital importance for France of the agricultural policy. A number of influential Ministers or ex-Ministers went farther, and stated categorically that this was the main problem.[32] And even in 1969, the former Minister of Agriculture, M. Edgard Pisani, a left-wing Gaullist, who was himself in favour of British entry, was still explaining that this would be impossible unless Britain subscribed to the common agricultural policy. He believed the policy to be unsound, and its imposition on Britain of a contribution then estimated to amount to about 50 per cent of the Community's expenditure on agriculture to be inequitable. But the most that he could do was to hold out a vague hope that, once Britain had become a member, the Community *might* be induced to 'question the objectives of its agricultural policy'.[33] In the light of the years of negotiation that the Six had required in order to reach agreement, this was cold comfort. Perhaps the most indicative fact is that the negotiations on the third British application did not get seriously under way until 1970, *after* the Six had reached final agreement on the financial implications of the agricultural policy.

What also seems clear, however, is that, in addition to the specific advantages sought by General de Gaulle from the Community, his general overriding purpose was that France should retain both political and economic leadership and control of it. This would necessarily involve preventing Great Britain from becoming a member, whether or not she fulfilled specific conditions of entry. It would explain why, in 1967,

when the British Prime Minister appeared to be at last prepared to comply with the economic conditions, General de
Gaulle and his Foreign Minister, M. Couve de Murville,
promptly produced fresh objections. It is noteworthy that Mr
Wilson's statement in the House of Commons, indicating
Britain's willingness to comply with the conditions of the
Treaty of Rome, was made on 2 May 1967 and that on 16 May,
in a press conference, General de Gaulle, after a restatement
of the familiar conditions, added two more. First, the British
financial situation was, he said, incompatible with membership.
(The following year, France's financial situation was no less
serious, but no suggestion was made from any quarter that
this fact disqualified France from membership of the Community!) The second new condition was that the continued
existence of the sterling balances and sterling's rôle as a
reserve currency were both inadmissible. This issue had, it is
true, been raised by General de Gaulle before, though not as a
specific bar to membership. In July 1967, M. Couve de
Murville even suggested that British membership might constitute a hindrance to the progress of East–West détente.[34] At
the meeting of the Council of Ministers of the Community on
23–4 October, he echoed General de Gaulle's May demands.

On 27 November, the President himself settled the matter by
ruling out *de facto* even the opening of negotiations, a move
which a Frenchman, author of one of the most comprehensive
studies of the foreign policies of France, explained as follows:

> It was [wrote Guy de Carmoy in 1968] precisely because
> England accepted the main economic and monetary condi-
> tions laid down by France that de Gaulle vetoed, not
> England's entry into the Community, but rather any nego-
> tiation prior to her entry. His refusal to negotiate limited
> the possibility of a debate among the Six on the unspoken
> political reason for the rejection of Great Britain's candida-
> ture: England's presence would change the balance of power
> within an enlarged Community.[35]

It is difficult to quarrel with this interpretation in the light
of the evidence now available. The President's own account of

his attitude in the last volume but one of his Memoirs has none of the supposed 'ambiguity' of his statements in successive press conferences. It is perhaps worth quoting in some detail, if only to provide a background to the later discussions under the presidency of M. Pompidou. As far back as September 1958, he was outlining his policy regarding the EEC and British membership in conversations with Chancellor Adenauer. And already he was foreseeing what would happen:

> Difficulties would arise [he said] for the European Economic Community from the problem of agriculture, a solution to which was essential for France, and Britain's application for membership, which France felt must be turned down as long as Britain remained economically and politically what she was.

During a visit two months later to Chancellor Adenauer he had recorded the agreement of the French and German Governments 'to put an end to the negotiations conducted by Reginald Maudling which were calculated to submerge the Community of the Six at the outset in a vast free-trade area with England and eventually the whole of the West'. Writing of the situation as it was in 1962, he had described the negotiations between Great Britain and the Community as 'fruitless bargaining', revealing to the Community 'that good intentions are not enough to reconcile the irreconcilable'. The Treaty of Rome, he wrote, did not, as it stood, meet France's requirements, owing to the fact that the negotiators in 1957 had not felt it their duty to insist that such a crucial French interest as agriculture should receive satisfaction from the outset. It would, therefore, be necessary, either to obtain it *en route* or to liquidate the Common Market. And he recalled conversations with the British Prime Minister, Mr Macmillan, in the course of which he had said: 'My Government made it clear that it would not agree to anything which did not include the common external tariff and an agricultural agreement.'

France's methods of getting her own way, namely to threaten to liquidate the Common Market if she did not, were clearly not open to Britain, whose request for the consideration of special relationships and special interests was ruled out from the start. But nor were they open to France's five partners. For de Gaulle notes that, since they refused to share his view that the negotiations were 'the squaring of the circle', France would have to make that decision for them.

> I realized [he says] that, in order to integrate agriculture effectively in the Community, we should have to take a firm line with our partners, whose interests in this matter were not the same as ours. But I held that this was a *sine qua non* of our membership. In order to *impose* [author's italics] on the Common Market as it developed what we regarded as necessary in this respect, we had to make the most desperate efforts, at times going to the point of threatening to leave the organization. However, we succeeded.[36]

All that General de Gaulle said from then on was wholly consistent with what he reports himself as having said or decided between 1958 and 1962. He was still saying it in 1967, and in virtually the same words, and only wishful thinking could have interpreted his words differently. What finally made France change her mind may well have been a combination of two factors: first, a change in the conditions within the Community itself that made the French Government decide that France had more to gain than to lose by British entry; and second, the realization that circumstances in Britain were by then such that France was in a position to obtain the conditions laid down by General de Gaulle all along.

THE WEU QUARREL AND THE 'SOAMES AFFAIR'

Before negotiations on the third British application could get under way, however, there was a long period of acute Franco-British misunderstanding. The only major point on which France's five partners in the Community had successfully resisted the wishes of the French Government was that of the conditions under which the Six should form a political organization. The Fouchet Plans had had to be dropped and, in spite of hints dropped from time to time by General de Gaulle indicating that he was open to consider proposals to revive them or something like them, nothing was done for the following seven years. But in 1969, the five returned to their own offensive and agreed, in spite of French objections, to political discussions within the Western European Union. At the February meeting in Luxembourg of the Council of WEU, a proposal that the organization should hold regular discussions on foreign-policy issues before decisions were taken was opposed by France, partly perhaps on the general ground that such political discussions in the WEU could not form a basis for decisions, but certainly mainly because the French Government feared that the proposal was a pretext for reintroducing a debate on British membership of the Community and, moreover, in a body in which Britain was able to make her own views clear.[37] The French Government, therefore, decided to boycott the special WEU meeting called on 14 February at the request of Britain to discuss the problem of the Middle East.

The question of the Middle East had, of course, in itself no relevance to the problem of Britain's entry into the Common Market. But the French had a number of juridical objections to the meeting, and discussion of these led to a complicated legal wrangle of the kind that they have shown themselves to be adepts at sustaining – not only within the Community, but also in the United Nations, as well as in relation to the circumstances in which France withdrew from NATO.

France's first objection was that the question of the Middle East was one that concerned the Security Council rather than the WEU. To this, the British replied that there was no reason why the views of countries not represented in the Security Council should not be elicited, and especially the views of Germany, which was not even a member of the United Nations. The second objection put forward by France was that the terms of the WEU Treaty did not authorize the calling of the meeting. Article VIII (4) of the treaty (as revised in 1954) required all decisions of the WEU to be unanimous. The French interpreted this rule to cover also the *calling* of a meeting at which decisions might be taken. The Germans, who had already found the French veto of November 1967 a strain on the Franco-German axis, found this conflict embarrassing. They tried as usual to play a conciliatory rôle, but to avoid anything that looked like open disagreement with France. They sided at first with the British interpretation, then wavered, and conceded that a meeting called in the absence of unanimity ought to avoid the discussion of 'abnormal' items. This of course raised the further problem as to what exactly constituted 'routine' and what 'abnormal' matters. The third French objection was that the primary function of the WEU was to discuss matters concerning security. The British (relying on article VIII (1) and (3)) held that the treaty provided for the calling of a meeting by any member in order to discuss a situation likely to threaten peace or endanger economic stability, and that this provision clearly covered a debate on the Middle East.[38] The dispute led to a decision by the French Government not to attend subsequent meetings of the WEU, which it boycotted for fifteen months.

It was in the atmosphere of Franco-British disagreement and suspicion created by this dispute that what was called the 'Soames affair' occurred. It arose out of an interview between General de Gaulle and the British Ambassador in Paris on 4 February 1969, in the course of which the President suggested conversations between the French and British Governments on the future evolution of the European Community. Subsequent disagreements between the two Governments, on both facts and tactics, transformed what ought to have been at most a very small storm in a small diplomatic teacup into a major incident, arousing resentment on both sides. There had been, to begin with, some uncertainty in British minds as to the scope of the intended conversations. Was the intention to discuss proposals for changes in the Community system, or (as seemed, on the evidence of what appeared in the press on both sides of the Channel, to be far more likely) to afford an opportunity for a wide-ranging, forward-looking, general survey, perhaps taking up the suggestions made in the President's November 1967 press conference regarding the changes in the Community's organization that would become necessary, if ever Great Britain were to become a member?

This point could perhaps have been cleared up, if the talks had ever taken place. Several things prevented them from being held. The first was that General de Gaulle had intended them to be, at first, bilateral and private, but the British Government had decided against this and communicated information regarding the proposal, first to the German Government, and then (following a leakage to the French press) to the other members of the Community, and to the British press. This procedure was resented by the French Government, while the British Government resented French protests that the British account was inaccurate and misrepresented what the President had said. British explanations of the reasons for making the proposals public made the diplomatic situation worse rather than better, for they were unconvincing, except on the assumption (which had clearly been made) that the offer was in some way a French diplomatic trap intended to create trouble between Britain and the other five members of the Community.[39] The degree of French exacerbation was explicable only on the assumption (which had equally clearly been made) that the British were 'once again' trying to make trouble in the Community.[40] In addition, one of the President's reported suggestions (held by the French to be a misrepresentation of what he had actually said) was for a European 'four-power directorate'. As reported, this suggestion could have been expected to annoy the smaller countries, and did in fact do so.[41]

A meeting the following month between General de Gaulle and Chancellor Kiesinger enabled the President to clear up any misapprehensions, but the fundamental divergence between France and the other members on the enlargement of the Community to include Great Britain remained. So, for some months, did the Franco-British estrangement.

FRANCO-BRITISH RELATIONS AND THE EUROPEAN
COMMUNITY AFTER DE GAULLE

With the resignation of General de Gaulle on 28 April 1969, there was at first a widespread feeling in Great Britain, to some extent echoed in the European Community, that his successor might be more 'flexible' or more 'pragmatic' on the question of the enlargement of the Community. In a moment of euphoria, the Dutch Foreign Minister, Dr Luns, even concluded that the word 'veto' had disappeared from French diplomatic language.[42] But whatever the language used, the French attitude under the presidency of M. Pompidou appeared for some months to remain unchanged. Both he and his first Foreign Minister, M. Maurice Schumann, outlined untiringly the Gaullist programme for the future of the European Community, which meant merely spelling out in somewhat more prosaic and simple language the essential points made by General de Gaulle in his press conference of 1967.

It is true that, in 1969 and 1970, the British financial situation no longer seemed to rule out in advance any resumption of negotiations. But the three preliminary conditions repeatedly laid down by the President and the Foreign Minister remained invariable. They were described as 'completion, consolidation, and broadening (*achèvement, approfondissement, élargissement*)'. First, the financing of the agricultural policy must be definitely agreed on. Second, the Community's organization must be strengthened in order to enable it to withstand the strains that an enlargement of membership would impose – by which was meant that it must become a real community. There must be a development in depth (*approfondissement*) through Europeanization in technical and scientific fields, in transport, company law and monetary policy. The list of desiderata seemed, indeed, capable of indefinite extension and the Community had made no more than a tentative start in any of these fields. Nor did it seem likely that the Six would be able to agree sufficiently to make any significant progress in any of them in the near future. The third condition was that agreement among the Six themselves on the conditions of a broadening of its membership (*élargissement*) must precede actual negotiations.[43]

The first condition was met by the middle of 1970. Agreement on the financing of the Community's agricultural policy had been reached in fact by 22 December 1969, but a number of points had been left to be cleared up, and so the French Parliament finally ratified it only on 22 June 1970.[44] Negotiations with Britain were formally opened a week later, on 30 June. But this did not mean that all the difficulties regarding agriculture were ended. Britain could no longer call the agreement in question, but it remained to settle exactly how its terms were to apply to her and, on this, French and British views were very soon seen to be widely different. The level of the British contribution to the Community's agricultural fund was seen by France in terms of the aid that it could supply to her own continuing problems of farm surpluses and of out-of-date small farms, whereas to Britain it represented an increase in her own industrial costs that could seriously diminish her competitiveness within the Community. If the opening of talks, therefore, justified the comment that the era of 'No' had ended, it also justified the conclusion that the era of conditions was only just beginning.

There were those, however, who believed that, by then, France's attitude was far more one of apprehension regarding Germany's increasing economic strength within the Community than of fears either of British industrial competition or of British political ambitions. Though this certainly appeared to be the case, it by no means justified optimism regarding French conditions for British entry. Though there was no formal common front of the Six, in reality, as everybody knew, France was the only negotiator who really counted. Germany was clearly in favour of British entry, and also of the inclusion of Britain in political talks before the completion of the negotiations of her membership of the Common Market. But the fragility of Chancellor Brandt's Government coalition and his dependence at that time on President Pompidou's support for his *Ostpolitik* equally clearly ruled out any possibility in practice of German opposition to French views. The result was that France was able to get her own way, as she had always done in the past, on issues that she considered of vital importance to her. There were indeed times when, as one commentator put it, the negotiations over British entry reached an absurd situation in which four of the members were negotiating with

France on issues which ought to have been the subject of bargaining between the Six and Britain.[45]

As for the second condition – consolidation, or the development of the Community in depth – this had, by common consent, dropped out of sight, except for the patching up of the political controversy within the WEU, and for some tentative and not very successful endeavours to find ways of surmounting the immediate practical problems created by the disunity and even conflict between the Six over current monetary problems. Preparatory discussions on a possible political Community had been held by the six Ministers of Foreign Affairs, and these had helped to lessen the risk of further clashes in the WEU, because the Six had at least agreed on the need henceforth for regular consultations on political matters within the framework of the European Community. It was decided that each meeting (and these were to take place twice a year) would be followed by a meeting of ten, to enable the four candidates for membership of the Community to be 'kept informed' of the positions of the Six and to express their own views.[46]

This decision, together with France's resumption in June 1970 of her seat on the WEU Council of Ministers, certainly contributed to an improvement in Franco-British relations, though it was no more than a tentative revival of the defunct Fouchet Plans and had even more modest objectives. It would certainly have been unrealistic to read much into it, and nobody did. It was quite clear that the French attitude to political discussion in the WEU was unchanged, and the return of the French Foreign Minister in June 1970 merely provided the occasion for a restatement of the only conditions on which France was prepared to accept the WEU as a forum for political discussion. The French Minister insisted that the agenda for future WEU meetings should be agreed unanimously by the permanent representatives, that matters should be treated as urgent only on the request of the Foreign Minister of the country concerned, and should be considered by the following meeting of permanent representatives only if no member had raised any objection. These requirements were 'noted', though not specifically agreed to, by the other six members, which merely meant that face had been saved all round and the status quo restored. On the subject of monetary and economic union, the Six had agreed on a target date of 1980. But the first stage, which was to be the co-ordination and harmonization of their budgetary procedures, had already reached a state of deadlock, and little or no progress was made throughout 1971 and 1972.[47]

Nor was there throughout 1970 any discernible progress in the British negotiations, as the President himself commented in a press conference in January 1971. In answer to a question on the subject he replied:

> The English are recognized to have, among other qualities, those of humour, tenacity and realism. I sometimes think that we have not yet got beyond the stage of humour.
>
> I do not doubt that tenacity will follow. I hope that realism will finally triumph.[48]

In view of an earlier remark that British entry depended essentially on Britain herself, this could only mean that, at that stage, France considered Britain as being still unwilling to pay the price of entry to the Common Market Club, or, in other words, saw the concessions that she was asking for – regarding among other things, the level of British contributions to the Community funds during the transition period – as not to be taken seriously, but hoped that eventually Britain would realize that she would have to accept the views of France.

In a specially televised interview on 17 May, President Pompidou still appeared to be reiterating France's familiar basic conditions, without giving an inch. The United Kingdom, he said, must show herself truly European, which meant accepting the rules of the Community, and especially the rule regarding Community preference. 'This', he said, 'is a fundamental rule and, therefore, Britain will have to accept it fully.' He went on to ask the familiar question: Was Britain ready for the changes that economic and monetary union would demand? He dismissed Commonwealth sugar and New Zealand dairy produce as questions to be settled in Brussels, adding only that Britain's relationship with New Zealand was 'sentimental rather than commercial'. France's interests as a butter producer were, however, in his view, 'not wholly sentimental', a fact that the British negotiators were shortly to discover for themselves.[49] He concluded that it was now for Britain to choose Europe instead of 'the open sea', together with all the changes that this would bring in the *British* way of life and in *Britain's* relations with the outside world [author's italics].

What looked for months like an only too predictable deadlock was, however, spectacularly broken in May and June, following the summit meeting between M. Pompidou and Mr Heath, held in Paris on 20 and 21 May. The decisions reached at it were not made public, but it was widely assumed that they had a great deal to do with the fact that five weeks later, agreement on most of the outstanding major points was reached and, on 28 October, the British Parliament approved 'the decision of principle to join the European Community on the basis of the arrangements negotiated'. Had there been a significant change in French attitudes, or was it, as some anti-Marketeers in Britain maintained, that the British Government had adopted the French definition of 'realism' and given way to French demands all along the line? Certainly French opinion was evidently satisfied with the terms, and the President himself wasted no time in pointing out to French dairy farmers the opportunities offered to them by the terms relating to New Zealand dairy produce. In a speech at St Flour (a cheese-producing area) he said: 'Britain is importing 75,000 tons of cheese every year from New Zealand. But under Common Market rules, these imports will decrease and tend to disappear. This offers you new opportunities that you will have to seize.'[50]

A number of explanations have been put forward, and others could be suggested, of what appeared to be France's change of attitude towards British membership during the first half of 1971, a change expressed dramatically in the May 'summit' at which the French President and the British Prime Minister seemed to be publicly inaugurating what from then onwards was taken for granted as the inevitably successful outcome of the negotiations. It has been suggested that one reason for the French President's apparent change of attitude was that, having agreed in principle at The Hague to enlargement, and later reaffirmed the sincerity of his assurances that France would not veto British entry, he could not afford to be seen to be, in effect, imposing a veto, by refusing to allow the negotiations to begin, once the agricultural finance agreement had been concluded. Another suggestion, which could be additional rather than an alternative, was that he was under heavy pressure from the other five (mainly from Germany and Holland) during the final stages of negotiation of the financial settlement – pressure that had amounted to an implicit if not explicit threat to refuse to accept it, except in return for France's agreement to enlargement. On either of these theses, France could have decided to accept the opening of negotiations, relying on a long series of tough conditions that would either prove unacceptable to Britain, or at least enable France to obtain as many concessions as possible. In that case, the President might well have come to the conclusion, by the spring of 1971, that the negotiations had almost reached the latter point, and that all that was needed was a last push that a Franco-British summit could help to provide.[51]

Whether or not either of these suggestions is well-founded, there were certainly long periods when it was by no means clear to British negotiators, or to observers and commentators, that France was not trying to bring about the breakdown of the negotiations. And the effect of the renewed French demand in March 1971 for Britain to abandon the privileged position of sterling helped to increase feelings that she was.[52] General de Gaulle had of course objected to the use of sterling as a reserve currency as far back as 1965, and the issue of sterling had similarly been reintroduced by France in 1967, a few months before the second veto. This time, it did not appear to play a major rôle, partly no doubt because Britain was able to convince the French that the relinquishment of this heavy responsibility was not unacceptable, and that the run-down of the sterling balances need not prove an obstacle to agreement.

One question that was much discussed at the time was the extent to which the issue of possible Franco-British nuclear co-operation had been important. The British negotiator denied that the subject had formed any part of the negotiations, but this need not have prevented the question from being discussed at the May summit. Questioned on the point in his interview on Panorama on 17 May, the President had merely replied that there were no objections on his side, but that Britain might have some – an allusion, no doubt, to the problems presented by the MacMahon Act.[53] Later, in reply to a question in the House of Commons, Mr Heath replied categorically that defence had been only briefly mentioned during his meeting with the President and that, not only was no agreement reached, but he was not asked for any offer and had made none.[54]

Two other considerations, of a more general nature, could also have helped to change France's attitude to enlargement. The first was the fear of Germany's growing economic power and of her consequent eventual domination of the Community, a fear perhaps exacerbated by Germany's recent demonstrations of unwillingness to continue docilely to accept policies desired by France, especially monetary policies. That this was certainly at the back of some French minds was indicated by Chancellor Brandt's speech at The Hague, in which he had put forward among other reasons for agreeing to enlargement that 'anyone who fears that the economic strength of the Federal Republic of Germany could cause an imbalance within the Community ought to be in favour of enlargement for that very reason'.[55] The second general reason which might have influenced President Pompidou was the stagnation of the Community itself during these years. Though the British press paid little or no attention to this argument – perhaps because it might have damped still more the failing ardour of the British public as the negotiations dragged on – there was a great deal of comment on the subject from 1968 onwards, and there was confirmation of French reasons for pessimism from Brussels as well. The Brussels Commission, for instance, in its report for 1968, spoke of 'a general deterioration of the atmosphere in the Community',[56] while, on the eve of the Hague summit, a well-known French commentator noted that 'the apparent inability of the Six either to strengthen their own links or to extend these to other countries raises doubts regarding the capacity of the Economic Community to survive'.[57] Another had described the Pompidou triptych as 'words, words, words' and gone on to predict that, if no progress was made at the Hague summit, Europe as it existed would 'run out of steam'.[58]

As many comments made clear, French politicians had already run out of enthusiasm, and the reasons for this pessimism regarding the future of the Community – a pessimism by no means restricted to France[59] – were both political and economic. French economic grievances were contributing to the French Government's difficulties, especially the growing gap between the large prosperous farms and the small uneconomic ones – a gap that the Community's agricultural policy was actually helping to widen. There were gloomy comments regarding the impossibility of achieving anything like the degree of rationalization of either agriculture or industry that France would need in order to stand up to the full rigour of competition within the Common Market from 1970 onward. There was criticism of the Community's slow and clumsy machinery, and of the fact that 70 to 80 per cent of ministerial meetings had been concerned with agriculture,[60] though it accounted for only 7 per cent of the production of the Community.

By 1971, criticism of the working – or rather of the ineffective working – of Community institutions was creating still more pessimism, and even among French politicians and journalists known for their former enthusiasm for the Common Market. Critics deplored the Community's failure to develop any real common policies. A UDR Deputy wrote in January 1971:

The Six have achieved no real common policies, not even in research. We are still waiting for any attempt to achieve specialization in national products. The 'common agricultural policy' is in reality no more than a scale of prices fixed sometimes too low, sometimes too high. . . . The devaluation of the franc and the revaluation of the Mark in the space of a few weeks revealed the total absence of any agreement in the monetary field.[61]

Ten months later, the conservative President of the National Assembly Committee of Foreign Affairs, M. Jean de Broglie, advised delegates at the Congress of the *Républicains indépendants* to have no illusions. 'The Community', he said, 'is today virtually a ruin, temporarily habitable, but from which every morning somebody removes a few stones to build a house elsewhere. Monetary union is its only chance of survival.'[62] And of monetary union, one of the two French members of the Brussels Commission, M. Jean-François Deniau, wrote bluntly a week later, 'The creation of a European currency is not possible in the foreseeable future.'[63]

Perhaps all these factors may have had something to do with the decision to hold the Pompidou–Heath summit. It must be remembered too that the Soames affair may really have been an attempt on the part of General de Gaulle to find some way of coming round to a similar decision. President Pompidou himself gave no indication between 1969 and May 1970 of his own intentions or of his own feelings with regard to the progress of the negotiations. But from the moment that the May summit was decided on, the successful outcome of the negotiations was a virtual certainty, for neither participant could afford to see the negotiations end in failure. What could be done, however, was to use the summit to obtain the fulfilment of France's remaining essential conditions, of which the most important was British acceptance of Community preference, and her consequent willingness to make the substantial contribution to Community funds that France needed in order to prevent trouble from her marginal farmers. This was settled by a compromise *à la française* shortly afterwards.[64] And for good measure, the communiqué issued at the end of the summit meeting expressed British willingness to support France's interpretation of the use of the veto, as stated in the Luxembourg 'agreement' of January 1966. It was, as Uwe Kitzinger pointed out in his very well-documented reconstruction of the course of the negotiations, *Diplomacy and Persuasion*, no source of satisfaction to France's partners in the Community that 'the new candidate had, as it were, as the price of not being blackballed, agreed to support a virtual modification of one of the EEC's rules, and one originally thought vital to it'.[65]

THE STRENGTH AND WEAKNESS OF GAULLIST EUROPEAN POLICIES

What was perhaps happening in 1971 was that France and Britain both felt unable to cure their own economic ills, and so each was counting on association with the other within the Community to provide the needed but hitherto unattainable cure. But whether this was so or not, the fact remained that, at a time when most of the British press and most politicians on the Government side were optimistically looking forward to increased British economic dynamism in the Community, French critics were deploring the Community's loss of dynamism. There were, however, significant differences in the attitudes of the two countries to the Common Market. Whereas British opinion was divided regarding the desirability of Britain's membership, the pessimism expressed in certain influential circles, along the lines just quoted, did not reflect the verdict of the ordinary French citizen. All parties had welcomed the extent to which French economic interests had been furthered by France's domination of the Community. Even the Communists, in spite of their ritual denunciations of the Community's 'capitalistic' and 'monopolistic' structures, had always been careful not to suggest that France should not use these to defend her national interests, and especially the interests of her farmers. There was quasi-universal support for Gaullist economic policies in the Common Market.

On the political side, as his opponents had pointed out, General de Gaulle had not achieved his objectives. France had entered the 1970s without the concerted European foreign policy that it had been his main purpose to achieve. But the opposition parties had had no alternative policy to propose. From the Centre to the Socialists, there was merely continued repetition of the ritual affirmations of the need to build a united Europe, a process that even one of the most enthusiastic of the Socialist 'Europeans' had admitted to be likely to take at least fifteen to twenty years.[66] It was not surprising that General de Gaulle should have ridiculed this kind of 'Europeanism' as pure verbiage,[67] or that, by 1970, much of the dream was fading.

Among the opposition parties, only the Communists had a coherent European policy, and that was nearer to Gaullism than to that of the other left-wing parties with which they had been trying since 1961 to agree on a common electoral anti-Gaullist platform. The Communists were opposed to either a political or a military 'Europe', and so to the existence of either a French or a so-called 'European' nuclear force. They opposed British membership of the Community, except on the condition that Britain would leave the Atlantic Alliance and abandon her 'special relationship' with the USA.[68] They were opposed to both European and Atlantic supranationalism and shared with the Gaullists the belief that France should be able to 'decide her destiny in full sovereignty'.[69]

The European policies of non-Communist opposition parties could be summed up as: (i) claims for Europe's equality of status with the USA (at some unspecified date); (ii) general support (in principle) for European supranationalism; (iii) support, either for Europe's membership of an Atlantic alliance, reorganized in some way (unspecified) that would be more acceptable to France, or else for a kind of neutralism, based on the assumption of a gradual disappearance of both NATO and Warsaw blocs; (iv) attitudes to British membership of the Community based on ambiguities and unspecified assumptions; and (v) support for what was described as a 'European' deterrent, which, in existing conditions, amounted to a plea for control of a non-credible French deterrent by a non-existent 'Europe'.

As against Communist negativism and the utopianism of the non-Communist Left, Gaullist 'Europeanism' had at least the merit of seeking concrete advantages for France, in the political as well as in the economic field. There was, too, a considerable measure of support in France, even among opponents of Gaullists, for certain Gaullist attitudes, especially for the wider Europeanism associated with the Gaullist policy of détente with the Soviet Union and the countries of Eastern Europe, and for the anti-Americanism that characterized both that and Gaullist Atlantic policies. On the other hand, the evolution of the Community had itself helped to create new problems. One was, by the end of the 1960s, the increasing French dissatisfaction with its working, because, as the conflicts between national economic interests became more complex and difficult, the highly rigid and cumbrous structure of Community institutions demanded more and more time and effort in order to permit of even minimal agreement. In 1957, Dr Erhard had described the EEC as being

> like an armoured car, heavily protected against attack from outside, with an allotted place for everybody inside, outsize brakes and an under-sized engine, which will stall more often than it runs. [70]

By 1968, more enthusiastic Europeans than Dr Erhard had discovered the truth of that prophetic statement, and it was difficult to believe that the difficulties of the 'deepening' process (*approfondissement*) and the increase in the number of members of the Community would not make such problems even more frustrating, particularly for France, with her large farming population, dependent on the Community's agricultural policy.

The second problem was that, though the Community had failed to create any 'European' industries, large numbers of industrial concentrations cutting across Community frontiers had been created – most of them American. French opinion was especially afraid of the increasing invasion of American investment, as was made clear by the popularity of M. Jean-Jacques Servan-Schreiber's book, *Le Défi américain*. Yet it was reasonable to ask whether the process might not already have gone too far to be controlled, and so have rendered irrevocably out of date the French objective of an economic Europe able to compete with the United States.[71]

The third problem, and certainly the most obvious in 1971 and 1972, was that the increasing proportion of intra-Community trade might entail the risk of the partners' exporting their economic crises to each other, or at least the risk of their creating increasing difficulties for each other by their inability to agree on a policy in periods of economic difficulty. By 1969, over 50 per cent of France's imports were coming from the Community and 47·8 per cent of her exports going to her partners.[72] By 1971, one-fifth of French exports were going to Germany.[73] In 1963, the French recession had certainly been in part attributable to the falling off of Germany's imports from France, owing to her own recession. In 1971, the monetary crisis had revealed the extent to which independent action by one member of the Community could affect the others. The problem of monetary instability was described in October by M. Jean-François Deniau as being 'a temporary and negative expedient' which, if it were to continue, would 'lead to a cumulative process of decline in the Community'. There were, indeed, major differences of opinion on how to deal with the problem, and France was both out of step and vulnerable – out of step because she alone among the Six wanted a fundamental monetary reorganization which would include revaluation of the dollar, and vulnerable because of her farmers, her export situation and her unemployment problem. Nor could she afford, in a pre-electoral period, to risk a revival of the kind of financial speculation that had occurred in 1969 in anticipation of the revaluation of the Mark.

To these problems, there was added from 1972 onwards the further complication of a new and difficult transition period from a Community of six, forming a relatively homogeneous even if disunited family, to a more heterogeneous group of nine – a transition period that would be characterized by exceedingly complex, difficult and perhaps crucial conflicts. To quote M. Jean-François Deniau once again, the Community had reached 'a stage of transformation, even hesitation'. 'If', he said, 'European construction were in practice to be halted at its present stage, American criticisms would, generally speaking, be justified, for the process of decline and ultimate dissolution would be unavoidable.'[74] Whether or not this was what General de Gaulle had foreseen, it certainly looked as if one of his predictions at least would be realized. The enlargement of the Community must involve it in a sea-change, the nature and scope of which it was impossible to estimate.

FRANCE IN A COMMUNITY OF NINE

First impressions were rather of a curious, ineffective continuity of Gaullist policies. General de Gaulle's Fouchet Plans of 1960 to 1962 had failed. So did M. Pompidou's proposal in 1972 for the creation of a 'technical secretariat' to consider political co-operation. As originally put forward at the end of February 1972, during the regular six-monthly Franco-German summit meeting, the proposal had been accompanied by a vague reference to a possible French plan for a 'confederation' that could provide a basis for discussion – an echo of General de Gaulle's 'imposing confederation', presented between 1952 and 1960 as an ultimate European objective. As announced in the President's press conference of 16 March, it was accompanied by an equally vague suggestion, applying to some possible future date (*éventuellement*), for a permanent Council of 'Secretaries of State for European affairs'.[75]

The method, as well as the proposal itself, was in the authentic Gaullist tradition – an idea thrown out half casually, as General de Gaulle had thrown out hints from time to time that he would welcome suggestions for the revival of something like the Fouchet Plans, and itself a pale shadow of the Fouchet Plans, even sooner lost to sight, owing to the inability of the nine to surmount the first preliminary hurdle, which was the location of the headquarters of the secretariat. The French naturally wanted Paris. Most of the other members wanted Brussels. The result was that, when the matter was discussed at the European summit in October, there was deadlock, and the whole idea was dropped, or at least shelved for the time being.

It was overshadowed by two events in the field of European policy, the President's announcement of a referendum in France on the membership of Britain and the other three candidates, and the European summit, finally held in October, after some hesitation on the part of the French Government.[76] The referendum, held on 23 April 1972, asked for approval 'in the light of the new possibilities open to Europe, of the Bill submitted by the President of the Republic to the French people, to authorize the ratification of the treaty admitting Great Britain, Denmark, Ireland and Norway to membership of the European Communities.'[77] This too was an authentic Gaullist gesture – indeed, as it turned out, far more so than the President had intended. For this was not the 'solemn European referendum' that President de Gaulle advocated in 1960, but a purely French referendum that recalled in several ways the last Gaullist referendum of 1969. Like that measure, its exact purpose was not clear. Since the treaty had already been signed the previous January, and would undoubtedly have been ratified by Parliament, a referendum seemed unnecessary. Moreover, since there was no significant opposition to the membership of the new candidates (except of course from the historic Gaullists, still living in the 1967 Gaullist period), it was obvious that the answer would be Yes. Unlike the 1969 referendum, however, it was not so much a referendum as an opinion poll, for it committed nobody to anything.

The referendum, therefore, immediately became, and remained, a matter of political controversy, the upshot of which was a general view that it had three main purposes, none of which had any direct relevance to European policy, but all of which were directly relevant to M. Pompidou's own position as President. The first was to demonstrate to historic Gaullists, by the most impeccably Gaullist of methods, the referendum, that the President had the majority of the nation behind him. In fact, it merely convinced them that he was using Gaullist methods in the service of anti-Gaullist policies.[78] Second, it was intended to present to the electorate a picture of strong and united Government parties, which could help to eradicate the unfortunate repercussions of the various scandals with which Gaullist names had been associated. This seemed a likely result, for he could reasonably count on the votes of the integrationist Europeans of the Centre parties. At the same time, he hoped to present a picture of opposition disunity, and in this he succeeded. For the Socialists and Communists, engaged on what then looked like a hopeless quest for a 'common programme', could not even agree sufficiently to present a common front on the referendum. Third, as the President explained himself, he hoped to use the 'impressive majority' that he was asking for to demonstrate that he had 'a solemn mandate' to speak for France at the European summit, and to give him added authority in his efforts within the European Community to preserve France's essential interests, and to ensure a European policy 'of independence vis-à-vis all and co-operation with all'.[79]

If, as it appeared, this was a bid for French leadership of the Community of nine, then the results of the referendum were not likely to be of much help to him. For 39·52 per cent of the electors did not vote and 17·22 per cent voted No. Only 36·12 per cent voted Yes. The fact that it was a fine Sunday, and that Frenchmen had preferred, as was suggested, to go fishing, was hardly likely to provide much consolation for a higher abstention rate than had been seen since 1815![80]

Nor did the autumn summit provide any comfort. The nine showed themselves in profound disagreement on monetary questions, on attitudes to scientific and industrial co-operation and to the third world, and also regarding the future evolution of the Community itself. The President was irritated by the continuing integrationist tendencies of the other five original members, and especially by the Dutch.[81] No decisions were reached (except to agree on dates at which future decisions would in principle be taken). The year ended without any progress towards Franco-German monetary agreement being reached, and 1973 began with the first meeting of the Council of Ministers to be attended by the new members. Its proceedings, which did not normally attract much attention, were therefore this time reported on at length, thus giving publicity to an immediate disagreement between the British and French

Ministers on what ought to be the functions of the Council. It was impossible not to conclude that a long and difficult period of adjustment was going to be needed before any confident predictions could be made regarding the future evolution of the Community in its new form. In the meantime, M. Pompidou had clearly not succeeded in establishing his first deliberate claim to a specific Pompidolian rôle and status in Europe.

CHAPTER IX

Atlantic and Defence Policies – The Search for Status

THE LEGACY OF THE FOURTH REPUBLIC

One of General de Gaulle's greatest assets was that his whole approach to foreign policy was positive, where that of his predecessors under the Fourth Republic had often been hesitant and negative. He had a clear conception of what ought to be and could become France's foreign policy, if France were properly led. He was therefore able to present to his compatriots a coherent picture of the stages that were to lead to his ultimate goal. Although, between 1958 and 1962, he was only too clearly the prisoner of facts, and especially of the fact of the Algerian war, he could at least begin to prepare for future positive action. Where the Fourth Republic had too often appeared to be the victim of events, the Fifth was made by General de Gaulle to appear, under his leadership, to be gradually but surely assuming control of them.

There are, as Alfred Grosser pointed out, two methods of submitting to facts:

> One method is to analyse a situation, extrapolate its data and then, in the light of the analysis, take decisions related to the political objective. The other method is to let the facts decide and adapt policies in consequence. It must be admitted that the Fourth Republic almost always adopted the second.[1]

The facts that General de Gaulle had to face were difficult enough. The bulk of the French army was tied up in Algeria, fighting an out-of-date colonial-type war. In the field of defence policy and of attitudes to the Atlantic Alliance, there were the same basic divisions between Gaullist and opposition parties as there were regarding the rôle of the EEC. The former rejected and the latter advocated (at least in principle) supranational forms of control in NATO. The former advocated and the latter rejected (again in principle) the development by France of an independent national nuclear deterrent.

General de Gaulle was, however, assisted by several facts that he was able to exploit with great political adroitness. One was the existence in France of a fairly wide area of common ground between the parties. Both Gaullists and opposition parties believed that Europe ought to have a far larger share in Atlantic decision-making, including decisions on nuclear policy and the control of the nuclear deterrent. Both were agreed in their determination that Germany must not become a nuclear power. And both were afraid of American economic as well as military dominance in Europe. The difference between them was further reduced by the fact that, once the decision had been taken that France should develop a nuclear capacity, it inevitably became in practice irreversible. For no French Government, whatever its political colouring, could afford deliberately to sacrifice the research and expense that had been undertaken in order to develop nuclear power.[2] Opposition parties would have resented no less than Gaullists the reduction of status that would have resulted from the abandonment of nuclear production, just as they resented no less than the Gaullists France's exclusion from the 'Anglo-Saxon' nuclear 'club' within the Atlantic Alliance. For the Left no less than for the Right, French nuclear power was also a reassuring guarantee of French military superiority over Germany.

Another fact that assisted General de Gaulle was his ability to exploit certain political sentiments that had developed during the Fourth Republic. One of these was the widespread resentment in France of British and American criticisms (in the United Nations as well as in NATO) of French policies in North Africa. Another was French resentment of Britain's so-called special relationship with the US in NATO by virtue of her nuclear capacity and her access to American nuclear information under the revised MacMahon Act. The following statement made by the Socialist leader, M. Guy Mollet, in 1959 reflected widely-held French views. Inequality within the alliance, he said, ' . . . divides the partners into second-class allies, whose freedom of action is limited, and first-class allies, whose rôle is to lead the free world'.[3] The reaction of a French left-wing newspaper to the revision of the MacMahon Act had been similar. It predicted 'the creation of an Anglo-US atomic directorate' which could 'only make more apparent and more burdensome the hegemony of the English-speaking peoples at the heart of the Atlantic Alliance'.[4]

The national 'touchiness' that was so often the expression of these feelings of resentment became, in General de Gaulle's hands, a political weapon that helped him to increase his prestige among his fellow-countrymen to the extent that he succeeded in exasperating his allies. This was a tactic that he had learnt in London during the war, when it had greatly helped to mitigate a much more serious French sense of weakness and humiliation. Under the Fifth Republic, anti-Americanism, suspicion of British and American hegemony in the Atlantic Alliance, accusations of British subservience to the United States, resentment of American attitudes to the Suez affair – all these helped to increase support for French claims to equality within the Atlantic organization. During the years 1958–62, when de Gaulle had little to offer his compatriots except words, his words on these themes were widely welcomed, sometimes in the most unlikely quarters. At a time when France had taken the decision to become a nuclear power, but was still without any operational nuclear capacity, the prestige he derived from Gaullist assertions of France's right to be treated as a great power was, therefore, far from negligible. After all, 'negative prestige is still prestige'.[5]

THE IMPORTANCE OF THE 'GAULLIST GRAND DESIGN'

Some understanding of this psychological context is essential in any attempt to assess the importance of the long-term aims of Gaullist foreign policy. What has often been called the Gaullist 'Grand Design' was, in the first place, addressed to men's minds. Whatever it was in General de Gaulle's mind, it was certainly nothing so precise as a programme. There is no evidence, indeed, that he believed the objectives could ever be attained, or even that he would be able in his lifetime to make discernible progress towards the goal. But the definition of the objectives did supply him with a coherent policy, capable of rallying support for complicated manœuvres and sometimes for measures unpopular in themselves, precisely because it was positive and aimed at building up national morale.

As he said over and over again, the central aim of his foreign policy was to create a grouping of nations that he described as 'Europe from the Atlantic to the Urals'. This goal was realizable only on one basic assumption, together with a number of conditions and stages. The assumption was that the permanent destiny of France was to be a power 'in the front rank'[6] and that it was consequently her duty to conduct herself in such a way as to make the fulfilment of that destiny possible. The conditions of success, or the stages of progress towards the goal, were essentially four. First, France must herself be economically and politically strong, in order to be able to exercise her historic function of leadership in Western Europe. This implied the integration of her foreign and internal policies. It is possible to argue, either that General de Gaulle's internal policy was geared to his foreign-policy objectives, or, on the other hand, that he deliberately used his foreign policy to strengthen his hand at home, but in either case they were in fact inseparable.

The second condition, or the second stage, was the building up of an association of Western European States under French leadership. The European Community was to be only a starting point in this process, which required political as well as economic association, together with the rejection of 'any kind of dependence',[7] by which he meant, among other things, any form of integration in which France would be absorbed in a supranational organization. The third stage was the breaking down of the barriers constituted by the iron curtain, and the gradual re-formation of the historic frontiers of Europe 'from the Atlantic to the Urals', which would involve the disappearance of the two blocs formed by the super-powers and their allies, dependencies and satellites. A hazily outlined fourth stage – perhaps only the ultimate achievement of the third, but clearly envisaged as achievable only at some undefined date in the far distant future – would be what he called 'fraternal Europe', 'which we have never seen'.[8] This would be possible only when the process of détente and co-operation between countries on both sides of the iron curtain had led to the return to the European fold of a Soviet Union which had abandoned Communist totalitarian ideology.

For practical purposes, only the first three stages could be regarded as forming part of foreign policy in the normal meaning of the term. The first demanded the economic modernization of France (and particularly of her agriculture) through the institutions of the Common Market, the stability of the political régime, through the working of the new Constitution under Gaullist leadership, and the restoration of France's military strength, including the creation of a national nuclear force. The second required the consolidation of France's position in the EEC, together with the formation of a European political association, as soon as France's partners were prepared to accept Gaullist conditions. The third, announced in his press conference of 31 January 1964, consisted of attempts to create a wider Europe, by increased co-operation with the Soviet Union and the East European satellites, and by the gradual strengthening of the world image of this Europe through the development of a world rôle for France (and eventually for Europe) in the hitherto uncommitted and underdeveloped 'third world'.

The 'European' implications of the design have been discussed in the preceding chapter. What remained to be done was to ensure that the Gaullist 'European Europe' should be free from integration in the Atlantic Alliance and, as far as possible in the circumstances, from the appearance of dependence on the United States in the determination of defence policy. Since it was patently obvious to everybody in France as well as to France's partners in Europe that American nuclear and conventional forces were, and would be in the foreseeable future, essential to the defence of Europe, this Gaullist policy of so-called 'independence' was entirely verbal. And since General de Gaulle did not succeed in detaching France's partners in the Community from their loyalty to NATO, or even in getting them to press for the reorganization of NATO along lines more acceptable to him, he could ensure the withdrawal only of France from the integrated organizations of NATO. Indeed, it is clear that he would not have wanted the other partners in the Community to follow his example, not only because he was himself enough of a realist to recognize that Western Europe could not afford to break up the alliance, but also because he did not in practice believe any more than they did in the possibility of their being independent in the field of defence, but hoped to create circumstances in which they would eventually be dependent on France rather than on the United States.

The constant assertion of French independence of the United States, through the expression of opposition to specific American policies, especially those that were unpopular with the Soviet Union and the 'third world', also served a useful purpose in helping him to build up good relations with the Eastern bloc and with the uncommitted nations, in preparation for the so-called 'world rôle' of France, which is discussed in the following chapter.

THE RETREAT FROM NATO

During the first four years of his presidency, General de Gaulle's Atlantic policy was relatively cautious. The first French nuclear test did not take place until February 1960. The decision to create a French nuclear striking force was taken only at the end of that year, and after a hard-fought parliamentary battle. During these years, most of the French army was tied up in Algeria, and so the process of military reorganization, decided on in January 1959, could not yet be put into application. Moreover, these were the years of the

Berlin air-lift, the construction of the Berlin wall, and the Cuba crisis. Even General de Gaulle would not have been able to persuade his countrymen to abandon the American nuclear umbrella, nor did he himself wish to do so. It was by no means certain up to the end of 1962 that he would even be able to command the loyalty of the French army, as was made clear by the military insurrection in Algeria in April 1961.[9] His position at home, once the Algerian affair was settled, might well be precarious, as he was himself well aware. Indeed, he explains in the final volume of his Memoirs that he had expected 'the parties' to try to get rid of him and had made plans to prevent this.

> With the settlement of the Algerian problem, with the incontrovertible affirmation of the loyalty of the army and the suppression of terrorist subversion, the different strands of the opposition combined and reinforced each other. It became evident that the 'wait and hope' policy that they had observed up to then was about to cease.[10]

The success of General de Gaulle's plans was in large part due to the use that he had made of the previous four years to consolidate his own position and to strengthen that of France, including, in the field of foreign policy, the process of decolonization and the establishment of close Franco-African relations. He had also begun to prepare the way for future policies towards NATO. In September 1958, in a much-discussed memorandum to President Eisenhower, he challenged the adequacy of NATO in its existing form to guarantee the security of France and of the free world, and suggested the creation of a tripartite directorate consisting of the United States, France and Great Britain, which would be responsible for joint decisions on questions concerning world security and for the drawing up and application of strategic plans, including those involving the use of nuclear weapons.[11] The proposed directorate was to extend its activities in the field of defence beyond the areas covered by the Atlantic Alliance.[12] The President also stated that France's future attitude towards NATO would depend on the response to this proposal.

Whether General de Gaulle ever expected these proposals to be taken seriously by Washington is open to considerable doubt. He himself said, though only very much later, that he did not. It by no means follows, as has been alleged in some quarters, that he was deliberately courting a snub and that, on this occasion as in all his anti-NATO activities, 'his intention was never for a single moment to reform NATO, but rather to bury it',[13] secure in the certainty that the United States was bound to defend France in her own strategic interests. It seems much more likely that he was using tactics that he had so often used in London in a position of much greater weakness and inferiority, namely the use of intransigence as a bargaining weapon which, even if it achieved little or nothing as far as the specific issue was concerned, nevertheless helped to build up his own prestige in French opinion. In other words, when France was unable to have a positive foreign policy of her own, national frustration could be used as an instrument of internal policy. In situations of weakness during his presidency, and especially during the Algerian war, he often resorted, too, to tactics of 'mystification', issuing statements couched in vague or ambiguous terms that committed him to nothing, but ensured wide publicity and discussion. For they were accompanied by often contradictory ministerial and press interpretations, which revealed that, whatever his real purposes might be, they had certainly not been communicated to his Ministers.

The 1958 Memorandum combined both these tactics. It was intransigent on a very sore point with French opinion – France's subordinate position in the alliance; and its exact meaning was unclear. The result was contradictory 'glosses' from the Foreign Minister, M. Couve de Murville, who stated both that the President was asking for the right to a nuclear veto, and also that he was not, but was merely asking for closer consultation.[14] Similar 'mystification' tactics were also evident in the President's press conference of 5 September 1960, when he returned to the proposal for extra-European activities by the Western nuclear powers. The Atlantic Alliance, he then said, ought not to be limited to Europe. The world powers of the Western alliance should undertake 'some organized political and ultimately strategic action outside Europe, and especially in the Middle East and in Africa, with which these three powers are continually involved'.[15]

The 1958 proposals certainly aroused wide interest. It was alleged by an American writer, in 1970, that the President had himself engineered this by communicating the terms of the memorandum (which was never published), not only to the British Government, but also to the West German and Italian Ambassadors in Paris and to M. Paul-Henri Spaak, these last three being obviously bound to oppose what could only appear as a French demand for a share in a nuclear veto that would certainly not be accorded to their own countries.[16] Whether or not this allegation was true, the contents of the memorandum were certainly rapidly leaked to both the French and the German press, the accuracy of whose reports of the contents of the memorandum was never seriously challenged.[17]

This initial skirmish (or declaration of intent) was followed during the next three years by a cautious but consistent process of withdrawal of French forces from involvement in the integrated structure of NATO, though without any direct indication by the President that France intended to sever her connection with the organization. On 7 March 1959, it was announced that units of the French Mediterranean fleet would no longer be available to NATO in time of war.[18] In June, the President refused to allow the stock-piling of missiles by American troops stationed in France, and the setting up of launching platforms.[19] In 1960, the decision to create a French nuclear force, which would remain under national control, was approved by Parliament, though the debate revealed considerable misgivings outside Gaullist circles. This decision had been foreshadowed in the much-publicized address by the President the previous November to the students of the *Centre des hautes études militaires*, in which he had said that

> . . . If a country like France makes war, it must be *her* war and *her* war effort. . . . The so-called system of 'integration' . . . has had its day. . . . The philosophical basis of your

centres and your schools must be the conception of a defence of France and of the Community that will be a French defence. . . . It follows clearly that, in the coming years, we must produce what is called a 'striking force' that can be used on our own behalf anywhere and at any time. And it goes without saying that it must be a force equipped with atomic weapons which – whether we produce or buy them – will belong to us. In circumstances in which France risks destruction from any part of the world, we must have a defence that can act anywhere in the world.[20]

In 1962, on the conclusion of the Algerian war, French troops previously removed from Germany, where they had been serving under NATO command, were repatriated to France and remained under national control. By 1963, France had only two divisions in Germany at full strength and only in air defence was there any remaining integration. The movement had, however, not been entirely one way, for France had agreed in 1960 to a unified early-warning system, and to a certain degree of co-ordination of air defence within the inter-allied system. She had also agreed to have German supply and training bases on French soil and, in 1961, to the training of French troops in the use of nuclear weapons – though not in France, while the warheads remained under American control. Up to 1963, therefore, France was merely living up to M. Couve de Murville's description of her as 'a difficult ally'.[21]

The second phase of the President's NATO policy, from 1963 to 1966, was much more aggressive. Whether he had, by then, really decided on the eventual break, or whether he was merely becoming more intransigent owing to changes in the international situation and in France's military and strategic position was, at that time, not clear. What is certain is that, from about 1963 onwards, the 'nuclear stalemate' seemed to most Frenchmen to have made a nuclear war between the two great nuclear powers an increasingly remote possibility. On the Right no less than on the Left, there was a genuine belief (or a genuine desire to believe) that the USSR was now seeking a détente between East and West. The Gaullists, together with a surprisingly large number of French politicians on the Left, accepted General de Gaulle's claim that France was eminently fitted to further this détente. On the Left, there was the traditional hankering for good relations with the Soviet Union, and on both Right and Left the traditional hankering for a Franco-Russian entente as an additional insurance against any threat of a revival of German aggressiveness. For both sides too, this policy, definitively launched by the President in his press conference of 31 January 1964, provided France with something that could be presented as an independent international rôle for France. And that was a welcome change from the sense of subordination and inferiority that, in the field of foreign policy, had characterized so much of French opinion since the war.

There was also, from 1963 onwards, a change in the position of the Gaullist régime that made an increased assertiveness possible. It was politically stronger, owing to the end of the Algerian war, the Gaullist victory in the general election at the end of 1962, and the constitutional revision that had preceded it, and which had given the President the additional strength and prestige of election by universal suffrage. It was militarily stronger, because the modernization of the armed forces, planned as far back as 1959, was by then actually in progress, and reorganization had included effective steps to prevent any recurrence of threats by dissident army elements against the authority of the State. The army had returned to its traditional rôle of *la grande muette*, and the OAS and plots by 'colonels' were both things of the past. Withdrawal came, therefore, as the culmination of a series of decisions taken between 1963 and 1966, which continued the process begun in 1959. In 1963, the French Atlantic fleet was withdrawn from NATO command. The 'Stikker' plan for long-range study of NATO's strategic requirements was objected to by France, on the ground that this was a matter for which Governments and not officials were responsible. In 1964, American proposals for a multilateral mixed-manned nuclear Atlantic force (MLF) and a British proposal for a multinational Atlantic force (ANF) were both rejected by France. Gaullists and their opponents alike considered such schemes as militarily ineffective and politically undesirable,[22] in that they made no real change in the system of American control of the use of the nuclear deterrent. French naval officers at NATO headquarters were accredited from 1964 onwards as national representatives. In 1965, France refused to accede to the McNamara proposal for a restricted committee to study the possibilities of increased allied consultations on nuclear strategy. In 1966, she refused to participate in the 'Fallex' NATO exercise, because it was regarded as being an exercise within the framework of a strategic concept that did not correspond to that of massive reprisals agreed on in 1956.[23] By then the stage was set for the third phase of Gaullist Atlantic policy, the severance of all links with NATO.

GAULLIST STRATEGIC THEORIES

From 1963 onwards, another change in France's situation was the development, not merely of the small nuclear striking force of Mirages IV, due to become operational from 1965, but also of a national nuclear strategy that could be popularized and publicized by Gaullist politicians and journalists as justifying a French claim to 'independence' in the field of national defence. Nobody who knew anything about the facts really believed that France's embryo deterrent could defend France against aggression by a major nuclear power, but the widespread belief in the existence of a nuclear stalemate, and in a Soviet desire for détente with Europe, provided the opportunity to make such claims without creating serious fears of endangering French security.

It is worth while looking a little more closely at these theories, not in their military, but in their political context, for they served Gaullist purposes in a number of ways, and a great deal was written about them in the press as well as in military journals. The more technical arguments were, in the main, put forward by Gaullist soldiers and politicians. The President himself referred to them usually only in general terms, leaving the more fantastic claims to his supporters.[24]

And his approach emphasized political and diplomatic rather than purely military considerations. As he put it, first in his press conference of 14 January 1963, and frequently in later press conferences or broadcasts, the new situation of 'nuclear stalemate', in which the United States and the Soviet Union had a nuclear capacity that enabled each to annihilate the other, while it ruled out the possibility of a major nuclear war, had made small and medium powers more vulnerable to attack. They could not retaliate, yet they were at the same time less able to count on the automatic support of the major nuclear power, which was unlikely to be willing to risk escalation into a major war unless its own territory was directly threatened. It followed, therefore, that the defence of Europe could no longer be regarded as a primary interest of the United States, and Europe must consequently look more and more to her own nuclear defence. Since France was the only continental power that had any nuclear capacity, this meant that she must be able to rely on her own nuclear deterrent to protect her own (and eventually Western Europe's) vital interests. 'The French nuclear force,' he said, ' . . . will have the dire and terrible capacity to destroy millions and millions of men in a few seconds. This fact cannot fail to influence in some degree the intentions of a possible aggressor.'[25]

As expounded by Gaullist spokesmen, the argument was more colourful and circumstantial. One of the most enthusiastic of these, General Pierre Gallois, put it in this way:

> Like sorcerers' apprentices, both the Americans and the Russians have invented and brought into widespread use a weapon which ensures their own security, but which at the same time paralyses their rôle in the world, because no government can seriously believe that either of them can lead a coalition or share its power with members of a coalition, or risk its existence for the sake of its allies.[26]

The deductions to be made from the existence of this state of affairs were that substitutes for United States nuclear defence, such as defence by conventional weapons only, the pursuit of political agreements on the 'de-nuclearization' of certain parts of the world (on the model of the Rapacki plan), or the device of 'multilateral' fleets of submarines or surface vessels, could all be dismissed, in the Gaullist view, as unrealistic and unacceptable. If the Soviet Union believed that aggression in some area was militarily worth while, then it would not submit to defeat in a conventional war, when recourse to nuclear weapons could bring victory. Nor would it be deterred by political agreements, and even less by any Atlantic force. While such a force remained under American control, it would not be used except to defend American territory. But the use of a deterrent *not* under American control would be an act of collective suicide unless the users could be sure of persuading the Soviet Union either that its use could ensure United States intervention, or else that it could inflict enough damage to make the kind of limited aggression that could bring it into action an unprofitable adventure.

The so-called 'theory of relative nuclear invulnerability', or 'proportionate deterrence', developed by Gaullist strategists with the aid of a formidable array of diagrams, was an attempt to provide an answer to the second of these problems. Briefly summarized, the theory was that, in order to deter aggression, a minor power needed only to be able to inflict an amount of nuclear damage sufficient to cancel out the advantages sought by the potential aggressor. As developed by the Gaullist politician, Louis Vallon, the theory was that

> the value of dissuasion is not measured in bombs or megatons; it depends on the relationship in the mind of the potential aggressor between the benefits and risks of the operation. Only that amount of force is needed which is capable of discouraging a possible aggressor.
>
> The dissuasive potential of the Mirages IV A-bombers and the first nuclear submarines will certainly not be comparable to that of the American and Russian arsenals. But the equalizing power of the atom must not be left out of account. A single thermo-nuclear projectile can totally destroy an essential objective, and so a small number would be sufficient to threaten the vital centres of a great country.

Soviet Russia has a restricted number of key objectives constituting a high proportion of the country's economic potential. Would it be reasonable of her, merely in order to wipe out France, to adopt a strategy that involved the possible destruction of this potential and thus her reduction for many years to a position of total inferiority to the United States?[27]

This theory has been quoted at some length, and in the words of a Gaullist expounder, because to most British readers the whole case will appear to be as full of holes as a sieve. And this is, indeed, how it appeared to many Frenchmen, by no means all of whom were unsympathetic to Gaullism. To deal with only the most glaringly obvious objections, the theory, to be credible, relied on three assumptions that could certainly not be justified on the basis of known facts, and were, on any hypothesis, highly unrealistic. The first was the assumption that the French deterrent was in actual fact capable of inflicting the required amount of damage. The second was that the French command could be relied on to get its sums right, that is, to assess accurately, not only the nuclear potential needed, but also, and more important, the exact balance of risk and advantage *in the mind of the potential aggressor*. The third was that the potential aggressor would believe, not merely in the credibility of the French deterrent, but also in the willingness of the French actually to put their theories to the test by using it.

There was no objective method of assessing the extent to which the second and third conditions or assumptions could be fulfilled. As far as the first was concerned, the facts were far from encouraging. The French deterrent consisted of a striking force of some 50–60 Mirages IV A-bombers, only half of which were to be operational by the end of 1965. Their range was too limited to enable them to reach the Soviet Union without being refuelled in flight by tankers bought from the United States, a fact that, in itself, made nonsense of the whole idea of 'independence'. They were, moreover, considered by all but Gaullist spokesmen to be highly vulnerable to attack by ballistic missiles, so that only a small number could be relied on to reach their target and deliver their bombs – which were then not yet thermo-nuclear, and still were not at the beginning of the 'seventies. The 'terrible destruction' predicted by General de Gaulle and his supporters could, therefore, be inflicted, if at all, only on cities and by a single strike. The following estimate was given by Raymond Aron of the probable consequences of an attempt to use the French deterrent:

> If the French Government takes upon itself to send some thirty Mirages IV (the maximum number likely to be available . . .), it will be asking for the total destruction of the French nation. For this would undoubtedly be the response to the destruction inflicted by France's bombs. With such a weapon, the French Government would not be able to deter the Soviet leaders in circumstances in which the United States themselves were unable to deter them, unless it had convinced them that it had become totally insane.[28]

The case against the French deterrent was also put eloquently to the President himself, in a personal interview accorded to the Socialist leader, M. Jules Moch – a resister and former Minister (who had been Minister of Defence at the time of the entry into application of the Atlantic Alliance):

> Finally, what I said to him was substantially this. Our striking force will not deter any major nuclear power, and for two reasons: if we are attacked, since we are at the centre of the nuclear world, whereas the United States and the Soviet Union are each far away from the potential enemy, our country will be destroyed before it can use its nuclear force in reply. If, on the other hand, we threaten to attack and to use our inevitably limited nuclear force in order to destroy some two to four millions of civilians in enemy cities, then our potential enemy can be sure that we shall not carry out the threat, because our own Government is aware that a quarter of an hour after our attack no Frenchman would be

alive. In both cases there is no dissuasion and our little striking force represents only milliards of wasted francs and increased danger for France. We might as well brandish 'a wooden sword'.[29]

It is not possible within the framework of the present book to discuss in detail the various technical and military arguments for and against the Gaullist theories of deterrence.[30] Nor is it necessary, for the simple reason that the claims made for it between 1963 and 1966 were demonstrably political rather than military. To the great majority unaware of the facts, they helped to bolster up Gaullist claims to membership of 'the nuclear club', to justify General de Gaulle's objections to integration in NATO while the American finger was on the nuclear trigger, and finally to present a French withdrawal from NATO as reasonable.[31] What, in reality, made the withdrawal possible was the fact that, in 1966, it seemed militarily safe for France to go her own way, regardless of the effect of her actions on the military efficiency of NATO, on which France herself would depend as much as any of her allies.

Gaullist nuclear theories also had the advantage, in French eyes, of providing additional arguments against the acquisition by the German Federal Republic of a nuclear capacity. General de Gaulle's political objections to German participation in the proposed Atlantic nuclear mixed-manned force, as being inconsistent with the Gaullist conception of 'Europe', have already been mentioned in the preceding chapter. The attempt by Gaullist propagandists to present the French deterrent as the nucleus of a future European system, and thus as a protection for Germany eventually replacing that of the United States, was even less convincing than Gaullist claims for the efficiency of the deterrent. There is no evidence, however, that these were ever intended to convince any but French opinion and, as French opponents pointed out, the arguments were inconsistent as well as unconvincing. In the debate in the National Assembly at the end of 1964, the Radical leader, Maurice Faure, asked the Prime Minister (then M. Pompidou) whether he was seriously suggesting that the French deterrent should be regarded as a protection for other European countries. He added:

> You justify the French deterrent by the argument that a nation today will use its deterrent only in its own defence. And yet you are asking Italy, Germany and Belgium to place in us the confidence that you are refusing to the United States.[32]

A more convincing case in favour of the French deterrent was put forward by the Prime Minister himself, in a speech in the National Assembly. If France were to give up her nuclear programme, he said, she would, in ten, fifteen, or at most twenty years, be reduced to the status of an underdeveloped country.[33] There is no doubt that the pace and cost of nuclear development would make a fresh start technically as well as financially impossible for any country that sacrificed its nuclear know-how. Even the Socialists were eventually susceptible to this argument. In 1963, they had been among the most vociferous opponents of a national deterrent. But both the 1972 Socialist programme and the Socialist–Communist 'common programme' combined anti-nuclear decisions of principle with cautious provisos as to the time schedule of their application, and with contradictory assurances of the need for national defence.[34] One practical reason for the Government's excessive claims for the deterrent was no doubt the hope of making its steadily escalating cost more palatable to the taxpayer.

If the French Government had ever shared the view, expressed by Raymond Aron in 1963, that, though useless against the USSR, the French nuclear deterrent could be 'a diplomatic trump-card against the USA',[35] it had become clear long before the end of the 1960s that the diplomatic dividends were negligible. In some quarters, however, there was support for the view that its real dissuasive value lay in the threat of its use to 'trigger-off' United States intervention, or rather the threat of United States intervention, on issues of vital importance to France. On this hypothesis, a French threat to use the deterrent could deter the Soviet Union from a contemplated aggression through fear that this would bring a threat of American reprisals. The deterrent would thus merely ensure a French voice in the circumstances in which United States aid would be forthcoming. The logical weaknesses of this case were obvious.[36] If Gaullists were justified in alleging the unreliability of United States defence of Europe, except in the presence of a direct threat to American territory, then it followed logically that such 'triggering-off' devices must, of necessity, prove equally unreliable. Similarly, it followed logically that the Germans could be expected to be as sceptical of Gaullist claims that the French deterrent was a potential European deterrent capable of defending Germany as the French were of American willingness to defend Europe.

THE WITHDRAWAL FROM NATO

The President had hinted in his 1958 Memorandum that France might feel obliged to reconsider her participation in NATO. In 1965, he had stated quite plainly that he intended to end integration in NATO, at latest in 1969.[37] Nevertheless, his decision to do so in 1966 came as a surprise to many. In his press conference of February, he had announced that France would take steps between then and 1969 to restore her sovereignty over 'all that is French'.[38] But the official announcement of the withdrawal came less than a month later, in an exchange of letters between himself and President Johnson.[39] In the memorandum communicated to the NATO allies he replied in advance to criticisms of this unilateral action by affirming that it would have been futile to consult France's partners, since all were in favour of the status quo.[40] He did not consult Germany either, although consultation was required under the 1963 Franco-German treaty of co-operation, and he informed only three of his Ministers in advance. In fact, however, all of them approved the decision at the meeting of the Council of Ministers on 9 March.[41]

Comments in the French press and statements by politicians all gave a number of reasons for the decision, some quasi-juridical, others political. The decision itself was presented to the general public essentially as an important step towards the objective of 'national independence' in the framework of the policy of détente and co-operation with the Soviet Union and the East European satellites, announced by the President in his press conference of 31 January 1964. And it was this approach which more than anything else made it acceptable to much of public opinion as well as to considerable elements among the opposition parties represented in Parliament. The tone of Gaullist political comment is well illustrated by the following statement made by a Gaullist delegate to the WEU Parliamentary Assembly the following June: 'The 7th of March', he said, 'marks the end of an epoch, that of monolithic alliances, of the system of blocs, of the cold war, of Russo-American nuclear bipolarism and of a Europe under external protection.'[42]

The extent of general support in France for General de Gaulle's foreign policy had already been revealed by his successful defiance of traditional electoral mythology (according to which French elections are never won on issues of foreign policy), in the presidential election of the previous December, when his campaign slogan had been 'national independence'. The attitude of the Communist party towards the President's desire for co-operation with the Soviet Union was echoed on the non-Communist Left, even though Socialists had little sympathy with the Gaullist defence of national sovereignty. But in the Radical and Centre groups in the National Assembly, there were serious misgivings regarding the effects, both on the Alliance and on French security, of the withdrawal from NATO. M. René Pleven (*Centre démocrate*), in a much-remarked speech during the debate on the Government's general policy in April, accused it of acting precipitately without reflecting on

the repercussions that our withdrawal from NATO might have on our own security, and – what is morally even more serious – on the security of our allies. You often accuse us [he went on] of giving way to an irrational belief (*une mystique*) in integration; I fear you are giving way to an irrational belief in total national independence. If integration does not solve all problems, total independence is even less capable of solving them, especially in the field of defence. . . . Our withdrawal from NATO will involve a lamentable waste of forces, money and men, whereas the central problem of NATO ought to have been the rational organization of the production of nuclear arms and the avoidance of their proliferation.[43]

Later in the debate, speaking on the censure motion tabled by left-wing parties (excluding the Communists), the president of the Radical party, M. Maurice Faure, regretted that the Government should be 'destroying one balance without having found another to replace it and without knowing exactly what kind of balance to substitute for it'.[44] The Catholic Democrat paper, *Témoignage chrétien*, accused the Government of weakening the Alliance and of leaving NATO without itself being able to ensure French security.[45] And M. Pleven, returning to the charge, asked:

If the other thirteen countries in the alliance were to use the same arguments, what would be left of the alliance? What would be the effect on European security?[46]

M. Mitterrand launched a more general attack on the President's isolationism, asking whether it was in the interests of peace to demolish the Alliance without forming others, to dismantle Europe, to refuse to sign the test-ban treaty? This policy could, he said, be defined as 'a kind of Poujadism on a world-wide scale'.[47] M. Guy Mollet emphasized the President's failure to consult Parliament and his abusive interpretations of the Constitution.[48]

To succeed, the motion of censure would have needed 242 votes. It received only 137, of which 70 were cast by members of Radical and Centre groups, and 64 by Socialists. A third of the Centre groups did not vote, nor did the Communist party.[49] The fact was that there was on the Left no real fear of a Soviet threat, that the détente policy was popular and the United States unpopular. The criticisms of *Témoignage chrétien*, for instance, were tempered by the remark that the French

Government's action was, in actual fact, not likely to endanger France or her allies, because 'the threats to the Western world, and especially to Europe . . . are no longer as dangerous as they were'. Maurice Duverger went so far as to argue that the USA could not afford *not* to defend France and consequently that even neutrality would not endanger French security.[50] Left-wing opponents were hardly less preoccupied than were the Gaullists themselves by the dangers of 'economic colonization' by America, as the enthusiastic reception the following year of M. Jean-Jacques Servan-Schreiber's *Défi américain* revealed, and both Maurice Duverger and *Témoignage chrétien* expressed this fear.

For many on the Left, a pertinent criticism was that of Robert Escarpit, whose comment in *Le Monde* on M. Mitterrand's criticisms of Gaullist 'Poujadism' was that 'to call this Poujadism is very flattering to M. Poujade. . . . Chesterton said of the Puritans that they used a just indignation in the service of unjust causes. Could it not be said that Gaullist diplomacy uses dubious indignation in the service of a just cause?'[51] It was mainly this undisputed acceptance by the Left of the justice and rightness of the French Government's objectives of equal status for France in the Atlantic Alliance, of 'independence' of America (even if largely symbolic), and of détente and co-operation with the Eastern bloc, that helped to explain the absence of any demand by the Left during the following years that France should return to NATO. André Philip (a former Socialist Minister who had become a left-wing Gaullist) wrote in 1966:

> It is a fact that General de Gaulle's demand for a European Europe is supported by the great majority of French opinion, which wants no protectorate, whether American or Russian, economic or political; it is a fact that, even when he is no longer there, and whatever the results of elections, there will be no majority in favour of returning to NATO.[52]

His prediction proved correct. In 1972, the draft programme of the Socialist party was advocating a foreign policy based on hopes of 'the progressive and simultaneous disappearance of the Atlantic Treaty and the Warsaw Pact', and of the creation of a system of European collective security.[53]

Nor were the 'Europeans' who supported France's continued membership of NATO any more realistic. The main spokesman of the *Centre démocrate*, Jean Lecanuet, was as convinced as were both Gaullists and left-wing parties of the need for the reorganization of NATO and the elimination of the two blocs.

> Only a united Europe [he said], that is, a Europe economic-ally and militarily integrated, could counterbalance the power of the United States in the alliance. As we see it, the Atlantic Alliance would then consist of two partners equal in rights and responsibilities.[54]

Of the three main currents of opinion – Gaullist nationalism, Centre and Socialist 'Europeanism', and left-wing neutralism or near-neutralism – it would be difficult to decide which was the most unrealistic.

The main arguments put forward officially by the French Government at the time of the withdrawal were, as has been said, juridical, or quasi-juridical, as well as political. They included: (i) the reiteration of French claims that the United States had ignored French requests for the organizational reform of NATO; (ii) the claim that, with the recession of the danger of nuclear war in Europe and the increasing threat from the East presented by the Vietnam war, France was risking being drawn into this conflict against her will so long as NATO and American bases remained on her soil; (iii) the accusation that the McNamara strategy of a graduated nuclear response was juridically invalid, in that it had been decided by the United States unilaterally, contrary to the agreed strategy of NATO, which had been one of massive reprisals.[55]

As opponents pointed out, there were obvious weaknesses in these arguments. In the first place, none of the objections to the NATO structure was new. The treaty laid down regular procedures that France could have used before withdrawing unilaterally. In reply to French suggestions that the United States had refused to listen to the French Government's pro-posals, Dean Rusk stated categorically that, in spite of repeated

American requests, the United States had never received any precise proposals from France.[56] The Americans also pointed out (as indeed did some French politicians – in particular, M. Pleven) that the argument relating to the danger of an escalation of the Vietnam war that could involve France was invalid, since her obligations under the treaty covered only Europe and Algeria. Any escalation of the war likely to involve France would, therefore, have to be decided by all members of the Alliance. And, since France had elected to remain a member of the Alliance, her obligations under the treaty were unaffected by her withdrawal from NATO.

The argument used by General de Gaulle in the press conference of February 1966, in which he invoked in effect the principle of *rebus sic stantibus*, was of course more difficult to counter. 'Nothing', he then said,

> can maintain a treaty's validity when its purposes have changed. Nothing can make an alliance remain the same, when the conditions in which it was concluded have changed. ... It is evident that, owing to the internal and external evolution of the Eastern countries, the Western world is today no longer threatened as it was at the time when the American protectorate was organized in Europe under the cloak (*sous le couvert*) of NATO.

The change which in his view invalidated the treaty (though he did not explain why it should do so) was that the nuclear stalemate, by reducing the certainty of American nuclear aid to Europe, had removed 'at a blow, the justification (at least for France) for integration, though not for the alliance itself'.[57]

The French Government's objections to the McNamara doctrine of graduated response were at least comprehensible, though politically untenable, since fourteen of the fifteen members of NATO had agreed to it, and this fact considerably weakened the force of the Gaullist complaint that the United States was acting unilaterally (a complaint that the French were in any case hardly in a position to make when France was in process of withdrawing from NATO by unilateral action). As the Prime Minister, M. Pompidou, explained in the National

Assembly, France believed that the adoption of the McNamara doctrine would increase the risks to her, in the event of a threatened nuclear aggression:

> Inside NATO itself [he said] we have witnessed the gradual replacement, without our agreement, of the initial strategy which was based on deterrence – and therefore on the immediate use of nuclear reprisal – by a so-called 'flexible' strategy which, on the pretext of reducing the risk of total war, in fact enables the United States to limit the field of initial operations by sparing the territory of the potential main aggressor.
>
> Such a method cannot be satisfactory to us, for it increases the dangers for France. The conventional forces of the alliance, which alone are integrated, even if equipped with tactical nuclear weapons (which can still be used only on American orders), cannot be certain of halting an attack from the East. Such a strategy risks exposing us, first to nuclear air-raids and then to invasion.[58]

Even Frenchmen who accepted the inevitable dominance of NATO by the United States were uneasy regarding the repercussions on smaller powers of the American nuclear strategy. That strategy certainly deprived the small French deterrent of whatever credibility it might have been held to possess, for it was capable only of a single, massive 'anti-city' strike. American strategy assumed a defensive capacity of NATO conventional forces that did not exist and was unlikely to be attained in the near future (especially as France had admittedly neglected provision for conventional defence, partly owing to the demands of the Algerian war, partly because tactical nuclear weapons were available only under American control). This situation might well prove a temptation to an aggressor to regard

> the territory between the Soviet frontier and the Atlantic as ... a theatre of operations within which hostilities could be confined, just as Korea was the territory between the sanctuaries of Manchuria and Japan, within which North

Koreans supported by the Chinese and South Koreans supported by the Americans fought out a drawn match for three years. [59]

Even if an agreement could be reached that could take account of European fears on these points, there still remained for Gaullists an unbridgeable gulf. The 'American finger still remained alone on the trigger' in the case of tactical no less than of strategic nuclear weapons.

How far these arguments were causes and how far pretexts must remain matters for speculation. They certainly do not explain why General de Gaulle decided to withdraw from NATO in 1966 rather than in 1969, when its organization was to come normally under review. If we are to believe what de Gaulle says of his NATO policy in the last complete volume of his Memoirs, he had decided as early as 1958 to leave NATO, but to time the operation with circumspection, owing to France's lack of nuclear capacity, her involvement in the Algerian war, and his uncertainty regarding the intentions of the Soviet Union during the first years of his presidency. Shortly before his death, he wrote regarding his intentions in 1958:

> My aim, then, was to disengage France, not from the Atlantic Alliance, which I intended to maintain by way of ultimate precaution, but from the integration realized by NATO under American command. . . . But I was anxious to proceed gradually, linking each stage with overall developments and continuing to cultivate France's traditional friendships. [60]

He also said that, if he did not succeed in his efforts to place the Alliance under a triple instead of a dual directorate, he had already decided in 1958 that France would reserve the right, under article 12 of the treaty, 'either to ask for its reform or to leave it'. Article 12, however, does not provide for any such action, but merely for 'consultations' on revision at the request of any member. Article 13 (not mentioned by the General) does provide for a member to leave the Alliance, but only after 1969, and with one year's advance notice. But, in the General's view, since his preliminary condition of American acceptance of his proposed tripartite directorate had not been met – and he himself reveals in the same volume of the Memoirs that he had never expected that it would be – there was nothing to prevent France from withdrawing from NATO whenever he chose.[61] His Foreign Minister, M. Couve de Murville, however, was clearly under the impression, as late as October 1965, that France's withdrawal would not take place until 1969, for he said in the debate of October in that year that 'we say now, in 1965, that reforms are necessary before 1969'.[62]

The real reasons for the President's choice of 1966 to announce France's withdrawal from NATO must, therefore, remain a matter for conjecture. It may be that he thought that the withdrawal would please the Soviet Union and so help his policy of détente, and perhaps also enhance his prestige in the third world, where his apparent anti-Americanism was popular. He was due to visit Moscow the following June and so, if he was to break with NATO in the near future, it was obviously desirable to do so before the visit rather than subsequently, when it might appear that he had done so under pressure from Moscow. Or it may be that he had all along intended to withdraw at the first moment at which he felt in a strong enough position to do so. In which case, 1966 was a comprehensible date, for he had been re-elected to a second septennate the previous December, and could be reasonably confident that the public would support his foreign policy. At that time it was clear, too, that the political claims of France to equality within the alliance and to independence of America were popular enough to outweigh any considerations of their unreality in military terms, and that he had considerable support in the ranks of the opposition (especially in the Communist party) as well as among the general public. It is also possible that to a man of his age, the inevitably irreversible nature of the decision was attractive.[63] If he had not made much headway with the construction of a Gaullist-dominated Europe, he could at least ensure at one blow the avoidance of Atlantic integration, which he regarded as a major obstacle to the emergence of a European Europe.

Whatever the reasons, however, they had certainly little or nothing to do with any real intention that France should rely on a national, independent, defence force, which, though operational, was regarded by influential politicians and strategists as unable to reach its targets, and too small to inflict any significant damage on a possible enemy. General de Gaulle's claim in 1965 that '*si grand que soit le verre que l'on nous tend du dehors nous préférons boire dans le nôtre*',[64] though a popular electoral slogan, sounded less impressive in the light of General Jousse's claim that the USSR could destroy the whole of France with 0·14 per cent of her nuclear potential, and so without impairing her defence against the United States. His statement that, in the event of a nuclear war, French territory would be, not a marginal advantage (as some Gaullist strategists had assumed in their expositions), but on the contrary, a vital strategic need and, as such, well worth the price of any nuclear damage that France might be capable of inflicting on the aggressor,[65] was not alarming to most Frenchmen, though only because they assumed that this would also be the conclusion of the United States, and because they had no serious fears that the nuclear stalemate would end. If this had not been the case, it is hard to see why French opinion should have accepted with such equanimity a cut-back in the 1970 defence estimates involving the deferment for some years of the date at which French nuclear submarines and missiles would be expected to come into service in replacement of the by then obsolescent Mirages IV.

AFTER THE WITHDRAWAL

From 1966, although remaining a member of the Alliance, France ceased to take part in NATO operations. By 1 July 1966, all French forces had reverted to French command. All foreign forces were required to leave France by 1 April 1967. From 7 September 1966, France no longer contributed to NATO military costs. There were, however, several exceptions to this last rule. It was agreed, in particular, that France should continue to use the NATO early-warning system, and should share in the new, long-range, radar network (NATO Air Defence Ground Environment, or NADGE). For her part, France agreed in 1967 that allied planes could fly over French territory.

These exceptions were, of course, essential, both for the continued functioning of NATO and for the retention of any semblance of credibility for France's nuclear deterrent. For, as René Pleven remarked in the National Assembly, without the NATO early-warning system the French deterrent would have been blind and deaf and would have risked being destroyed on the ground.[66] France continued too to rely on the United States jet tankers, without which, as has already been pointed out, her small force of nuclear bombers, even if it could get off the ground, had no hope of reaching its targets.

The negotiation, in December 1966, of a Franco-German working agreement, whereby French forces under national command would co-operate with German forces under NATO command, provided a settlement in principle of the main problem created for the conventional forces of the Atlantic Alliance stationed in Europe. It was agreed that French forces could be stationed in Germany only with the consent of the Federal Government, and France informed the NATO Commander-in-Chief that French forces posted to Germany would co-operate with the allied armies, when, in the view of the French Government, a clear act of aggression had occurred. What was far from clear, however, was what the precise functions of the French forces would be, and these were left for the military commanders to work out.

As far as political decisions were concerned, these were still made in the Atlantic Council in conjunction with France, which meant, of course, that France retained a veto. Thus, France accepted the Harmel report of December 1967 on the future tasks of the Alliance in relation to East–West détente and the suggestions the following June for balanced, mutual, force reductions by East and West. It was assumed by some sections of French opinion, as well as by much opinion outside France, that in 1969, when the terms of the treaty permitted withdrawal from the Alliance, France might leave it, and some ardent Gaullists argued in favour of such a decision as being the logical continuation of French resistance to American leadership of Western Europe.[67] The French Communist party was, of course, also in favour of France's withdrawal from the Alliance.

This did not happen. The practical problems posed by the French withdrawal from NATO were naturally difficult and expensive for her allies, involving as they did a decrease in the numbers of troops under NATO command in Europe and the creation of new systems of deployment of allied troops in a Central European sector no longer including France. But since the nuclear balance remained, as anticipated by French opinion, unaltered, and there was no significant change in the relations between the super-powers, these difficulties did not prove insuperable or confront NATO with any immediate dangers. What did happen was that, from the autumn of 1968 onwards, a number of changes occurred, of which the first, and perhaps the most important, was in the European political situation. Though the Soviet invasion of Czechoslovakia in the summer of 1968 was played down by General de Gaulle in his next press conference as being in the nature of 'a little local incident' that need not affect France's policy of détente with the Eastern bloc,[68] it is doubtful whether he succeeded in convincing many of his hearers, or indeed, whether he had, in reality, convinced himself that this could be so. It was certainly a harsh reminder of how little France had counted in the so-called Franco-Soviet *rapprochement*.

A number of changes followed, and it is reasonable to assume, if impossible to prove, that the Soviet action had a good deal to do with them. The following November, France signed the communiqué, published after the meeting of the Atlantic Council, which, though it reaffirmed the political objective of the fifteen Ministers as being the establishment of stable and peaceful relations between East and West, nevertheless stated that the invasion of Czechoslovakia risked compromising some of the results already achieved in the field of détente. The French representative, the Minister of Defence, M. Debré, also announced that, given the international situation and the 'element of balance represented by the Atlantic Alliance', France intended to remain a member.[69] On 5 December, the French Minister for the Armed Forces, M. Messmer, ended two years of speculation regarding France's intentions by announcing categorically in the French National Assembly: 'We are in the Atlantic Alliance and we intend to remain in it.'[70] This decision was later reaffirmed by President Pompidou in a broadcast on 10 June 1970.[71]

Another change was that the French official strategy of 'massive reprisals', consistently defended by both the Minister for the Armed Forces and the Foreign Minister, M. Couve de Murville, from 1964 onwards, was officially dropped in 1969. The equally unrealistic theory of 'all-round defence' (*la défense tous azimuths*), defended from 1967 onwards[72] and reaffirmed by both the Chief of Staff, General Ailleret, and by General de Gaulle himself as late as January 1968, was also quietly abandoned. In his speech to the *Centre des hautes Etudes militaires* on 27 January 1968, the President had proclaimed that

Vauban fortified all our frontiers, the Pyrenees, the Alps, our ports and even Belgium. We were present everywhere, we made war everywhere. There is no reason why this strategy, which has always protected us against everything, should not continue to be ours.[73]

Yet, in May 1969, following General Ailleret's death, the new Chief of Staff, General Fourquet, gave a lecture confirming its abandonment.[74]

A third change was the increasing unofficial co-operation between French and NATO forces. Naval and air-force reconnaissance units were already co-operating in the Mediterranean in 1969. And on his return from Europe in the spring of 1969, Mr Nixon indicated in a press conference in Washington that he was hopeful of more consultation as well as military co-operation.[75]

Some of these changes preceded General de Gaulle's

resignation – the official change in strategy, for instance – and there is no clear evidence that his replacement by M. Pompidou made much difference. During the early years of the latter's presidency, he was certainly less temperamentally inclined to use General de Gaulle's often spectacular methods, and was less politically free to use them even if he had been so inclined. But there was no evidence that he had any desire to move away from the general direction of General de Gaulle's foreign policy. As Prime Minister, he had been a faithful executant and echo of the President's opinions for six years. As President, he continually reaffirmed his loyalty to these policies and specifically to that of withdrawal from NATO.[76] It is probable, therefore, that he regarded himself as merely continuing what General de Gaulle had already begun, though contributing a characteristic tone of his own.

There were, moreover, practical reasons that could help to explain the change of emphasis in Atlantic and defence attitudes, and these would have existed if General de Gaulle had remained in power. Among them were the continuing financial problems following the events of May 1968, together with the problems that nuclear expenditure was creating within the army. The former alone would have made some slowing down of nuclear production unavoidable, since universities, schools, and trade unions were all rival claimants for attention in the budget. A strategy of 'all-round defence' would have meant increased military estimates as well, and so would an effort to achieve the targets set for the coming into operation of the new generation of nuclear weapons. In addition, events in Czechoslovakia had highlighted the need to improve the equipment of conventional forces, which meant buying tactical nuclear weapons from the United States, since French ones would not be available before 1973.

The result of the competition for funds between the Ministry of Defence and the Prime Minister, who was concentrating on the 'new society', was predictable. The military estimates had been cut back in 1969, and in 1970 there were further cuts, partly owing to growing criticisms of the cost of nuclear arms in terms of neglect of conventional forces, and partly owing to the escalating costs of the new nuclear weapons. There were complaints, even among Gaullists, of inadequate equipment and training, and consequently of poor morale in the conventional forces.[77] By 1972, the Gaullist president of the National Assembly's Defence Commission was arguing that the first necessity for France was to ensure that her conventional forces were sufficiently well equipped to be able to protect her nuclear arms, and admitting that French conventional forces were much weaker than those of Great Britain and Germany because they had been neglected in favour of the nuclear arm.[78]

There were also increasing delays in the completion of the nuclear programme. By the end of the 1960s, the striking force was already obsolescent. Its life was prolonged beyond 1972 by technical improvements which included an increase in its bomb-carrying capacity, but it was still regarded by many critics as constituting too small a force to be viable. This criticism was applicable *a fortiori* to the newer weapons scheduled to come into operation in the 1970s. Of the five nuclear submarines planned, only two were operational by the end of 1972. Two more were under construction, but nobody expected them to be operational in the near future.[79] There were grave doubts regarding the effectiveness of French missiles, which had a shorter range than the Polaris ones. Of the first generation of ground-to-ground missiles, only nine of the planned total of eighteen were in service by 1971.[80] In 1972, the president of the National Assembly Defence Commission was arguing in favour of a target of six submarines and twenty-seven missiles.[81] But ICBMs were not expected to be in service before the 1980s.[82]

In the early 1970s, however, public interest in defence problems seemed to be, at least for the time being, at a low ebb. The 1968 economic crisis that had followed the May events had concentrated French attention on economic and social problems. The announcement in December 1972 by the Defence Minister, M. Michel Debré, of an ambitious fifteen-year plan for the modernization of the French strategic nuclear force seemed of less importance than the continuing need for the slowing down of nuclear production, in order to meet the demands for increased social spending. M. Debré expressed his regret that France's nuclear effort did not seem to interest either her allies or her European partners. He announced several plans for European collaboration in the construction of aircraft, but nobody was likely to forget that there had been others that had come to nothing, and that the new ones were still only in the planning stage. As for Euratom, it continued to be, as it had been for a number of years, on the verge of collapse, owing to national conflicts on policy and to inadequate funds.[83] For the time being, what interest there was in foreign affairs seemed to be focused on the Europe of nine and on international monetary questions.

CHAPTER X

The Search for a World Rôle

THE CONCEPT OF THE WORLD RÔLE

In a speech at the Ecole militaire in June 1970, the French Defence Minister, Michel Debré, described Gaullist foreign policy as having four principles.[1] The first – to retain France's freedom of decision – has been discussed in the two preceding chapters. The other three all related to France's rôle outside the European and Atlantic fields. The second – to establish good relations with the super-powers – was interpreted in practice by Governments of the Fifth Republic up to 1963 as implying resistance to the threat of aggression from one super-power and reluctant and increasingly critical support of the other, on which the country relied wholly for its defence. From 1963 onwards, it took the form of progressive severance of all formal defence links with the allied super-power, and of increasingly conciliatory approaches to the other. French official statements assumed that in the long run the Soviet Union would be amenable to persuasion (exercised through a French policy of détente and co-operation with the Eastern bloc) to the point of considering the desirability of a dissolution of both blocs. M. Debré's third principle – to encourage peaceful co-operation in areas concerned directly with France's security – proved in practice difficult to distinguish from his fourth – the need for France to play a part in peaceful co-operation throughout the world. For the areas which France seemed to regard as of direct concern to her own security included both Vietnam and the Middle East.

General de Gaulle himself continually emphasized the relationship between France's vocation to help to maintain peace and the possibility of a change of heart in the Eastern bloc, of

> ... an evolution that will make it possible for us to establish one day, from the Atlantic to the Urals, a détente, perhaps an entente, and, who knows, at some future date co-operation, because, after all, men are the same everywhere, and we can hope that one day beyond all ideologies, ambitions and tyrannies, the great movement bringing men together to make peace will take place.[2]

The spirit and methods associated with this aspect of his foreign policy were thus very different from those that characterized his European and Atlantic policies. He defended the latter with an assertiveness and intransigence in conformity with what he himself had postulated on the opening page of his early work on leadership, *Le Fil de l'Epée*, as an essential principle of greatness in a leader. The actual phrase with which he headed his preface: '*Etre grand c'est soutenir une grande querelle*', though attributed to Hamlet, is, in reality, a mistranslation and distorts Shakespeare's meaning out of all recognition.[3] But it does provide an accurate enough picture of what often appeared to be his motto both in the Community and as a member of the Atlantic Alliance. His aggressively anti-Soviet period lasted up to the months following the Cuba crisis, and from then on he adopted towards the Soviet Union a consistently conciliatory attitude that even the Czech intervention of 1968 did not openly weaken. Though it must be added that he never compromised on the essential points of divergence between French and Soviet policies with regard to East Germany.

The essence of his conception of France's world rôle was best expressed by him during the presidential election campaign of 1965. France, he said, had 'given up domination' and was trying to promote international co-operation. And he went on,

> That is our ambition. But for that we should have none, and a country needs ambition. We seek the good of man and the future of mankind. France alone can play this rôle and France is the only country playing it.[4]

More pragmatically, President Pompidou defined the rôle as being

> first to maintain good relations with all, and then to try, wherever possible, to protect lives and interests, especially cultural interests. We put France's interests first, but we consider the interests of others wherever possible.[5]

In practice, this rôle can be seen as consisting of a series of activities carried out by France in different arenas, and with differing intensity at different times, with the aim of making her influence felt outside the European and Atlantic fields. The first arena was the French-speaking world, *la Francophonie*, that is, primarily the former French overseas territories that, between 1959 and 1961, became independent countries, and with which France sought to maintain close links. This area was extended to include certain independent countries that had formerly been French possessions (in particular Canada), or that might be considered to have some special affinities with France, whether linguistic or cultural. Similar policies were also adopted in a number of countries in which France hoped to extend her influence by means of trade and aid, and of cultural and technical co-operation, including efforts to encourage the teaching of French and knowledge of French literature. This sphere of activity, both wide and heterogeneous, was described ironically by one commentator as 'France from Japan to Paraguay'.

The second arena was provided by the world organization of the United Nations, which General de Gaulle saw essentially as offering to all its members a forum for the expression of opinion on world issues, but which, he insisted, had conferred only on the permanent members of the Security Council the responsibility for maintaining peace. He saw France's rôle, therefore, as being to try to limit the activities of the United Nations when these appeared to him to infringe national sovereignty.

A third arena included the countries behind the iron curtain, with which he was seeking to establish a relationship on which to base his hoped-for détente and co-operation, as a prelude to the dissolution of the super-power blocs, and the creation of Europe from the Atlantic to the Urals. A fourth consisted of areas in relation to which France felt that she had a special immediate contribution to make as a peace-maker, by virtue of her past history and experience. In Vietnam, for instance, France had been a former colonial power, and had fought an eight-year war. In the Middle East, she had a long tradition of involvement, both in Syria and in the Lebanon. The continuance of close links with the former North African dependencies, which were directly interested in good relations with Arab countries, increased her interest in the Arab world in general and in Mediterranean countries in particular.

This so-called peace-keeping rôle, however, inevitably overlapped with M. Debré's third principle (namely, that France had an important part to play in areas closely concerned with her own security), because General de Gaulle had always regarded security as being bound up with the theory of spheres of influence, and he considered that France's 'natural' sphere of influence was Europe, extended by Africa and the Middle Eastern connection, while the Pacific was the natural sphere of influence of the United States and 'East of Suez' that of Britain.[6]

LA FRANCOPHONIE

During the early years of the régime, the dominant interest of the Algerian war restricted French initiative in these wider fields, as it did in the Atlantic field. In any case, the conditions of the cold war ruled out any policy of détente and co-operation. The only field open to French activities was that of her own overseas possessions then claiming the right granted under the new Constitution to accede to independence. French policy was to maintain a 'presence' in these newly-independent countries by negotiating with them agreements for continued aid – economic, technical, administrative and, wherever possible, military. French Governments frequently emphasized the fact that, of all Western countries, France was devoting the highest proportion of her national resources to supplying aid to underdeveloped territories.[7] But almost all of it was channelled to former French possessions, and without the tens of thousands of teachers, civil servants and technicians provided by France, it is difficult to see how these territories would have survived the first years of independence. It was, however, a policy that also served the interests of France's world policy, for the links of a common language and common educational and administrative traditions, together with the economic advantages provided by technical and financial aid, helped to replace the severed colonial links by others that ensured for France the continuation of her traditional special relationship with these countries. It also supplied an assured market for French exports.

The idea of *la Francophonie* was not, however, restricted to former French possessions, although it was not for some years that the wider approach could be developed in practice. Gaullists intended it to be a French form of 'special relationship' based on the encouragement of linguistic and cultural links wherever they existed or could be encouraged, but mainly, of course, in French-speaking areas. What might, perhaps, be described as the 'Grand Design' of *la Francophonie* was expounded as far back as 1959 by two young Gaullist civil servants, one of whom was later to be called on to help to carry out the policy in French-speaking Canada. 'The future of French culture and traditions', they wrote, 'will be decided, not merely in Dakar, but also in São Paulo and even more in Quebec and New Brunswick.' They saw the spread of French influence 'as a series of concentric circles':

> At the centre, Paris and metropolitan France; farther afield, Africa and the Community; farther still, people of the French-speaking world; and finally, the as yet unexplored galaxies of the Latin culture.[8]

The search for solidarity based on French language and Latin culture, whether expressed through France's relations with her former colonial territories, through the visits of General de Gaulle to the hitherto 'unexplored galaxies' of the ten Latin-American Republics in 1964, or through his even more eventful, if briefer, visit to French-speaking Canada in

1967, had the same basic pattern. There were exchanges of official visitors, speeches by General de Gaulle stressing the links between France and the different countries visited, followed by a series of agreements for increased technical and cultural co-operation. That the policy was welcome to, and achieved a great deal in, French-speaking Africa is beyond all doubt. There was also plentiful evidence of the survival of a genuine attachment to France in these countries, as distinct from the desire for the material benefits that they derived from French aid and trade.[9]

Nevertheless, the appeal for the institutionalization of these links launched in 1965 by President Senghor of Senegal and President Bourguiba of Tunisia (both of them powerful pro-French influences, and striking examples of the strength of French cultural penetration) did not make much headway. They sought what the latter described as 'a kind of Commonwealth, a Community that respects the sovereignty of each member and harmonizes the action of all'.[10] Some African States did not want to go as far as that and saw dangers in the renewal of an institutional structure following the rapid collapse of the Community created under the 1958 Constitution. The President of Guinea, who had opted out of that Community, denounced the Senghor–Bourguiba proposals for a *Communauté francophone* as neo-colonialism. Nor was the French Government's response very encouraging. French reserve was, no doubt, in part due to the desire to avoid controversy between African States on this matter – for some of them, Morocco and Algeria in particular, had their own reservations – but also in part perhaps to the problem of the political instability of the African States and perhaps, too, to the vaguely supranational overtones of the proposal, and its emphasis on 'the African voice'. The primary aim of France in creating *la Francophonie* was, after all, to make her own voice better heard! But though nothing came of this plan, the sense of solidarity that it expressed did find expression in the creation of a number of specialized agencies on a French-speaking basis, including organizations of linguists, historians, geographers and civil servants.

The genuine popularity of this policy in France, and no less on the opposition than on the Government side, was due more to the general belief that it contributed to France's prestige in the world than to any specific political or economic advantages that she might derive from it. It is much more difficult to assess the political advantages and disadvantages of French actions in the wider fields of French-speaking Canada and Latin America. In his press conference of 31 January 1964, General de Gaulle defined the general principles of this aspect of *la Francophonie* as being to go beyond the African framework and to be concerned with

> other countries in other continents which naturally and instinctively attract us, because they are to a greater or lesser extent developing countries, that desire help of the kind that we can supply, and may desire to associate themselves with what France stands for.[11]

His vocabulary and methods sometimes seemed to defeat these ends. And they certainly made it hard at times to regard the wider French-speaking solidarity campaign (even though it could obviously be exonerated from any charge of old-fashioned colonialism) as being wholly devoid of what might be called shadow empire-building.

General de Gaulle's apparent encouragement of French-Canadian separatism, exemplified by his cry of *Vive le Québec libre!* in Montreal in 1967, brought an outcry from the Canadian press and Government. And however much truth there was in the French Foreign Minister's later implication that it was all no more than a storm in a teacup, the fact that the President's official visit to Canada was abruptly cut short without a visit to Ottawa, and that relations between Canada and France remained strained for almost three years, must surely be regarded as cancelling out some of the advantages of Franco-Canadian *rapprochement* in Quebec and New Brunswick. In his press conference of 27 November 1967, the General seemed indeed to be going out of his way to eliminate the possibility of more acceptable interpretations of his attitude. For he appeared to be advocating (or envisaging) constitutional changes in Canada that would enable Quebec to accede to 'the rank of a sovereign State, master of its national existence', and also to be asserting the need for 'organized solidarity' of 'the French community on both sides of the Atlantic'.[12] Added to all this, there was the anxiety created in some other countries by the President's behaviour in relation to French-speaking minorities. One commentator, for example, pointed out that Belgians were uneasy lest the General's *Vive le Québec libre!* should be a prelude to *Vive la Wallonie libre!*[13]

Many French believers in the solidarity of French-speaking territories were critical of the General's rôle in this Canadian incident, pointing out that, by his own standards, this was at best unwarrantable intervention in Canadian affairs and at worst deliberate trouble-making. In either case, it was, as the Canadian Prime Minister expressed it, 'unacceptable'. It would be a mistake, however, to allow General de Gaulle's vague, grandiloquent, didactic and often ambiguous style to obscure the positive cultural aspects of the policy, particularly in the field of education, where, under the Gaullist régime, provision for exchange of teachers between Quebec and France and for scholarships and French aid was considerably increased. And what Alfred Grosser defined as *francocentrisme*[14] – a kind of cultural imperialism based on a general assumption of French excellence, and in itself justifying a certain Americanophobia – undoubtedly contributed to the Government's prestige at home, since it was an attitude shared by large elements of the French population.

It was in this context of more general cultural expansion that the President's marathon visit to Latin America belonged. In this case there was no claim to linguistic links, but only to the common bond of a Latin culture and to a common desire for political independence. The latter aspiration was referred to throughout the President's visit in general terms and without any explicit reference to the United States or to 'American hegemony'.[15] French critics, however, regarded the evidence of the facts themselves as sufficiently present in the minds of the hosts to render mention of them unnecessary. All the aid that France could offer was no more than a pale shadow of what

these countries were already receiving from the United States.
As Pierre Mendès France remarked:

> There was applause in the street and the squares, the bishops
> were on the steps of the cathedral, and gold-braided generals
> on the airfields, but, for all these unfortunate people, once
> the lights were out, the alternatives remained the same. It was
> still Johnson or Castro.[16]

For France, the importance of the visit was, as the President
himself put it, his appearance in Latin America, 'in the forefront of the world stage'.[17] He certainly succeeded in keeping
his visit in the forefront of the news almost uninterruptedly
for a month. A Socialist-inspired periodical described the visit
as useless, adding: 'When this "historic" (and costly) journey
is over, nothing will remain.'[18] A few months later, however,
the President based a difficult, but successful, presidential
election campaign mainly on the issue of foreign policy, claiming that, under the Gaullist régime, France now counted for
something in the world, and emphasizing the importance of
France's task in increasing or recreating her links with Asia,
Africa, Latin America and the East.

> This [he said] is how a France that has become herself again,
> with her ambitions for humanity and her eternal genius, must
> help the world to recover the equilibrium that alone can be
> the voice of peace.[19]

There is no doubt that, rightly or wrongly, the pursuit of
world-wide cultural links, the increase in the number of children learning French in *lycées* abroad, and of adults reading
French literature in the institutes and cultural centres being
set up from Luxembourg to Libya and from Kuwait to Japan,
were important in French minds as contributions towards
putting France back on the political map. This view is borne
out, for instance, by the importance attached by Gaullist
Governments to providing statistical evidence of French
cultural achievements. By 1968, the Foreign Minister was quoting figures of half a million books sent to centres abroad, of
over half a million children abroad being taught the French

language by French methods, and of the supply of between 25 and 30 thousand teachers.[20]

It has been said earlier that, wherever possible, General de Gaulle's attitude to foreign policy was positive, even during the first four years of his presidency, when positive French initiatives were restricted by the cold war and France's military dependence on the United States, by the military and political problem of Algeria, and by the still uncertain hold of the Gaullists on power. But just as, during these years, the popularity in France of the idea of European integration obliged General de Gaulle to adopt a mainly negative policy of persistent resistance to any extension of integration in practice, so he felt obliged to take a similarly resistant attitude to what he regarded as both juridically and politically unsound bases for collective action through the United Nations. The tone of his objections was often determined by more subjective criteria. For Governments of the Fourth Republic, and the majority of Frenchmen with them, had strongly resented criticisms in the United Nations of what they regarded as national policies outside the competence of that organization. Derogatory remarks in presidential press conferences about 'the so-called united nations', or 'the united, or disunited, nations' were thus generally popular.[21]

The basic Gaullist conception of the proper function of the United Nations was legalistic and logical. It was also politically comprehensible in the light of the increasing political activity of more recent members of the United Nations, anxious to exploit to the full the advantages of the political forum provided by United Nations debates, but without any capacity themselves to contribute much to the solution of problems that they brought before that body. It was based on a strict interpretation of the provisions of the Charter, according to which the use of armed personnel, other than for observation and investigation, must be authorized by a decision of the Security Council. In General de Gaulle's view, of course, this provision was politically as well as juridically correct, since only the great powers with adequate military (including nuclear) resources were able to keep the peace, and then only if they were in agreement, as the Charter required them to be.

In application of this principle, the French denied the validity of any action taken under the General Assembly's 1950 'uniting for peace' resolution, passed in order to overcome the obstacle of the Soviet veto in the Security Council. For the same reason, they rejected the decision of the International Court of Justice in 1962, which recognized the General Assembly's right in this case to apply article 17(2) of the Charter, and thus allow the apportionment among members of the expenses of military intervention undertaken in pursuance of a decision by the General Assembly in the absence of a Security Council decision. France, said General de Gaulle in his press conference of 11 April 1961, had 'no desire to provide either her money or her men for any existing or future actions taken by that organization – or disorganization.'[22] In accordance with this position, even a Gaullist Government would have accepted the validity of the decision to intervene in Korea in 1950, since it was based on a Security Council resolution, fortuitously unanimous in the absence of the Soviet member. But the French Government refused to contribute to the expenses of the Congo expedition, on the ground that they could not properly be authorized by virtue of article 17 alone.

It did not follow, in the French view, that military intervention, even when authorized by a Security Council resolution, was necessarily expedient. In his speech to the General Assembly on 29 September 1965, the French Foreign Minister expressed the opinion that, wherever possible, intervention should be political rather than military, and should be limited to supervision and observation, partly because the United Nations had not the means to take effective military action, and partly because any action involving force was bound to increase international disunity and so risk weakening the authority of the Security Council. France also insisted on strict adherence to the terms of the Charter concerning United Nations' incompetence to intervene in the domestic affairs of any State, or in disputes between sovereign States, when these were capable of being settled by the parties themselves. On these principles, France denied the right of the United Nations to intervene in the Franco-Tunisian dispute in 1961,[23] although Tunisia had appealed to the Security Council. The French Government considered that the Cyprus question, too, ought to be settled bilaterally.[24] France also refused to vote for intervention in the Rhodesian dispute, on the ground that this was a domestic dispute and therefore outside the competence of the Security Council, even though the British Foreign Secretary had appealed to the Security Council to support measures taken against the illegal Smith régime, and had ruled out military action.[25]

What then, in the Gaullist view, ought to be the function of the United Nations? In 1965, U Thant complained that it was in danger of degenerating into a mere debating society.[26] In his press conference of 4 February 1965, General de Gaulle had made it plain that in his opinion the United Nations *had* degenerated, but precisely because it had ceased to regard itself as a debating society, and had taken on functions that were not only illegal, but had 'cost the organization its unity, prestige and capacity to work properly'.

> In 1950 [he said], the General Assembly arrogated to itself the right to decide on the use of force, which made it the scene of quarrels between the two rivals. Through the disorder thus created the then Secretary-General was allowed to set himself up as a superior person with excessive authority.[27]

Only by returning to a conception of its functions based on a strict application of the Charter would the United Nations, in the French Government's view, be able to recover its former position. And part of the return to normality was the abandonment of the 'personalization' of the rôle of the Secretary-General, which had permitted personal initiatives on the lines of the intervention of Dag Hammarskjöld in the Tunisian affair. In the Gaullist view, the Secretary-General was neither a mediator nor a spokesman on behalf of an organization that in any case had none of the attributes of a super-State. He was merely the general administrator of a heterogeneous assembly of sovereign States whose function ought to be to constitute 'a forum for the discussion of world affairs'.[28] It was because France assumed that the United Nations intended to restrict its functions to something nearer this rôle, said the French Foreign Minister in 1965, that France had decided to return after three years of non-participation in General Assembly debates.

If the United Nations existed only for discussion and debate, it followed logically that disarmament, which was a subject for negotiation and decision, could not usefully be considered by a large United Nations conference. Although France had taken part in all disarmament conferences up to 1961, she refused to attend the 18-nation Conference decided on in December 1961, on the ground that it would be no more than a propaganda platform, and that negotiations ought to be between the five nuclear powers.[29]

Whether or not the President was using juridical and quasi-juridical arguments to obscure what was in reality merely the expression of his general objection to any organization that interfered with the rights of sovereign States, some of his criticisms were undoubtedly pertinent as well as caustic. In this field as in others, General de Gaulle had his own methods of pointing out unpalatable truths, even if this involved him in policies that appeared to be almost wholly negative.

DÉTENTE AND CO-OPERATION

In his policy of détente and co-operation with countries behind the iron curtain, on the other hand, the President was encouraging national illusions and avoiding unpalatable truths. The results of the economic and cultural measures comprising the general policy described as *la Francophonie* were certainly far more modest than those claimed for it or even expected from it. But the claim to a world political rôle based on a policy of détente and co-operation with the Soviet Union and tne East European satellites rested on far more precarious foundations. It could, indeed, be fairly described as an illusion based on the assumption of the accuracy of the Gaullist view of history, according to which the Communist ideology was destined sooner or later to disappear, permitting the eventual re-integration of Russia and the East European satellites in the European family of nations. It implied the further assumption that it was possible to judge when the time was ripe for under-taking the task of accelerating the process by encouraging peaceful co-operation wherever possible with countries behind the iron curtain. Up to 1963, the General had been as bluntly critical of the Soviet Union as any European or American statesman, and as firm in his resistance to Soviet policy during both the Berlin and Cuba crises. France, he had consistently maintained, was 'not prepared to yield to the threats of the totalitarian Empire'.[30] In 1963, he noted the possibility that various factors, including what he called 'human evolution' in Communist countries, their social and economic difficulties, and increasing Sino-Soviet tension, might bring a new climate in which the Kremlin might genuinely seek peaceful co-existence.[31] By 1964 he had decided that the time for détente and co-operation had arrived. The illusion was the claim (whether or not it was a genuine belief is open to doubt) that France had a special vocation to help to bring about or acceler-ate this evolution, and that this task would enable her to play an important rôle in world politics.

In practice, the policy of détente and co-operation added up to little more than the extension to the Soviet and Eastern European theatres of the procedures used in the pursuit of *la Francophonie*. From 1964 onwards, there was the familiar pattern of streams of State visits, followed by trade agreements, and by cultural co-operation involving the setting up of read-ing rooms in Poland, Rumania, Yugoslavia, Hungary and Bulgaria. Though there was a considerable increase in French trade with countries behind the iron curtain, which almost doubled between 1964 and 1967, the actual volume of trade remained small in relation to France's trade with either Europe or America, and accounted for only a very small proportion of her total foreign trade.[32] But no great importance was attached to trade figures, since the Government's primary aim was explicitly stated to be political – to help to create a better political climate in Europe.[33]

In this it could hardly be said to have succeeded. The USSR's invasion of Czechoslovakia in 1968 could leave no single lingering doubt that the 'breaking-down of blocs' was a pure illusion, and that the détente existed only in the fields, and to the extent, that suited the purposes of the USSR. Nor could supporters of the myth derive any comfort from the temporary convergence of French and Soviet views on certain issues. If both were agreed in opposing German re-unification and on the undesirability of a German nuclear rôle, their reasons were contradictory. They disagreed on what ought to be the status of East Germany, for the French accepted a distant prospect of German re-unification within a European framework, while the Soviet Union did not. If they were agreed in opposing the war in Vietnam, they disagreed on what ought to be the status of Vietnam. The Gaullists believed in neutralization, the Communists in a Vietnam that would form part of the Eastern bloc. There was no evidence that, for the Soviet Union, France was ever more than a minor adjunct in the propaganda war against the United States. It suited both temporarily to rock the Atlantic boat. Neither was under any illusion that France really wanted to overturn it.

This is not to say that France derived no advantages from the policy. It was, certainly, the most generally popular of Gaullist foreign policies. Declarations of detachment from the USA and proclamations of pro-Soviet attitudes helped to give France a special position vis-à-vis the countries of the uncommitted world, which in itself encouraged the illusion of increasing French influence in the world.[34] The real advantages were, however, perceptible more in the internal than in the external field. The détente policy was acceptable to all those (and their number was increased by disappointments regarding the achievements of the Franco-German treaty) who shared the traditional French reliance on *rapprochement* with Poland and Russia as additional safeguards against the threat of a resurgent Germany. It was acceptable to that section of left-wing opinion that was indulging in the 1960s in a kind of wishful thinking (in its way as negative and unrealistic as the neutralism of the 1950s had been) that was anti-American, anti-NATO, and still basically anti-German, without being in favour of any realistic positive foreign policy. There were those who were counting on the emergence at some indefinite future date of a supranational Europe. There were also those whose conception of such a Europe was anti-capitalist, and who were, therefore, counting on finding enough common ground with the Communist party to make an electoral alliance with the Left a practical proposition. They regarded détente with the Soviet Union and the East European countries as being likely to make this task easier. The assumption proved to be mistaken.

Other contradictions of the détente policy were bound to make it, in any case, little more than a gesture. If, as French critics pointed out, with Bonn as his ally, General de Gaulle was not an acceptable ally for the USSR, it was even more certain that a détente with the USSR would not make for acceptable relations between France and Communist China. The lengthy and diffuse historical survey which preceded the President's announcement on 31 January 1964 of the decision to restore diplomatic relations with China did not really explain what he hoped to gain from this step. He merely stated that the French objective of peace in South-East Asia would be unattainable without China's agreement.[35] This opinion was also reiterated in a statement made by the Prime Minister a month later. In the years that followed the exchange of ambassadors, however, there was no perceptible change in Franco-Chinese relations, which continued to be characterized by a total lack of either détente or co-operation.[36]

THE PEACE-MAKING RÔLE

Both General de Gaulle and Gaullist spokesmen continually emphasized that the policy of détente and co-operation was intended to contribute to the establishment everywhere of 'the climate of détente, stability and peace' that France held to be indispensable to world equilibrium.[37] And although the Foreign Minister, M. Schumann, in his speech to the UN

General Assembly shortly after his appointment in 1969, mentioned only three objectives of French foreign policy – hostility to blocs, the extension of European horizons beyond the EEC and aid to developing countries[38] – French Governments also had a fourth objective, which was to try wherever possible to propose methods of obtaining and guaranteeing peace in areas suffering from tensions or actually at war.

In the Gaullist view, peace could be maintained only by the great powers, which meant by the nuclear powers, eventually including China. As far back as 1960, France had put forward suggestions, though admittedly only in vague terms, for peace-keeping action by the Western great powers within the Atlantic Alliance[39] and, as has already been said, General de Gaulle consistently expressed the view that only the great powers within the United Nations, that is, the permanent members of the Security Council, could legitimately play a positive peace-keeping rôle. France's particular rôle was, in the Gaullist view, that of an arbitrator, in the sense that, not being directly involved in either the Vietnam or the Middle Eastern wars, she was in a position to put forward peace proposals.

In neither case can it be said that France's initiatives made any significant impact, mainly because the suggestions themselves were known in advance to be unacceptable to combatants on both sides, as well as to one or more of the great powers either directly or indirectly concerned. As a would-be peace-maker, France was also, where the Vietnam war was concerned, doubly disqualified from playing an influential rôle. In the first place, neither side regarded her as an 'honest broker'. Even those critics of the President who shared his view that the Vietnam war could not be won by military means, and who believed that France could have a mission to encourage peaceful settlement (and these were numerous), felt obliged to point out that, as a member of the Atlantic Alliance, France's objectivity was suspect to both the USSR and North Vietnam, and yet no less suspect to the USA, owing to the quasi-neutralism, at times more than tinged with active anti-Americanism, that had characterized General de Gaulle's and his Ministers' pronouncements on Vietnam from 1964 onwards.

France's proposals included open advocacy of the neutralization of a unified Vietnam, a policy that even some Gaullist members of parliament had regarded as the inevitable prelude to a Communist take-over in Vietnam,[40] together with suggestions for the withdrawal of US forces as a preliminary condition for the opening of peace talks. On the General's own admission the time was not ripe for such a move, and the proposals were put forward, especially in his speech at Pnom Penh on 1 September 1966, in a manner that could not but be interpreted in the USA as anti-American, since he roundly criticized American policy, but remained silent on any possible shortcomings of the other side. To describe French policy as 'a policy of peace', as M. Couve de Murville had done, wrote a prominent right-wing critic of the General, was to misuse the word. It was 'a policy which, far from leading to mediation, the appeasement of passions and a search for solutions acceptable to all, denounces one side and is at times even more intransigent than the other'.[41] France's second disqualification was, as opponents also frequently pointed out, that she had neither the economic nor the military resources to be able to claim with any verisimilitude the influence that General de Gaulle himself always asserted belonged only to great powers. Nor was there at any time the slightest indication that France's views carried any weight with the Soviet Union.[42]

Gaullist attempts at peace-making in the Middle East met with no more success. The background to France's Middle Eastern policies was more complex and the French position essentially more difficult. On the eve of the six-day war, however, France could still legitimately be described as objective, in the sense that her own direct interests as well as her principle of helping to maintain the peace demanded the avoidance of an Arab–Israeli conflict. The French Government did indeed actively try to prevent Israel from beginning hostilities. Once war had become a fact, French policy was to prevent it from escalating and to find some *modus vivendi* that could be imposed on the combatants. The French Government's proposals, put forward repeatedly from 1967 onwards, were consistent. They were that the four powers should take the initiative, at least to the extent of holding a meeting to discuss the problem; that the terms for a cease-fire should include the evacuation by Israel of the conquered territories, and permission for the Palestinian refugees either to be repatriated to Israel or settled in other countries, in return for recognition of Israel's right to exist and international guarantees of her frontiers; that such guarantees should include the presence of United Nations forces, which should not be withdrawn except by decision of the Security Council.

The difficulties in the way of any application of this plan were obvious, and the French press did not hesitate to point them out. There seemed no likelihood of Israel's agreeing to the prior evacuation of the conquered territories, in the absence of confidence in the reality of the proposed guarantee. After all, Israel had counted on a Western guarantee of her frontiers after the evacuation of Sinai in 1957. There seemed even less likelihood that the Arabs would agree to recognize Israel, and a settlement imposed against the will of the Arabs could not be expected to work.

THE MEDITERRANEAN AS A SPHERE OF INFLUENCE

By 1970, there had been a kind of 'escalation' in the degree of France's involvement in the arguments about the war. She was no longer playing primarily a peace-making rôle (if indeed she could be said ever to have played one), but rather that of a great power concerned with the future of a traditional sphere of influence. The countries of the Middle East have traditionally been regarded by French Governments, whatever their political complexion, as French spheres of influence. During and after the 1939–45 war, Syria and the Lebanon were regarded as French spheres of influence from which Britain was trying to oust the French.[43] British and American decisions to supply arms to Tunisia in 1957 were resented by France (although Tunisia was by then independent), as was the despatch the following year of British and American troops to the Lebanon without consultations with France. What was essentially a pro-Arab policy had been undermined during the Algerian war by French hostility to President Nasser's actively pro-Algerian sympathies and activities, and by a strong pro-Israeli feeling that developed in France, partly as a result of the Nazi persecution of the Jews. This pro-Israeli sentiment had been evident during the Suez adventure, which had helped to consolidate it, although the Suez expedition itself had been primarily seen as an anti-Nasser campaign to weaken Arab support for the Algerian nationalists.[44]

With the end of the Algerian war, a pro-Arab policy became imperative, if the Gaullist policy of friendship with former dependencies bordering on the Mediterranean was to succeed. These countries were all, to a greater or lesser degree, anti-Israel (though President Bourguiba made repeated efforts to win support for more moderate pro-Arab policies). But a 'special relationship' with Israel also existed by virtue of the latter's dependence on France for a regular supply of arms. The announcement at the beginning of 1970 that the French Government was to sell 100 Mirages (of various types) to Libya, therefore, caused serious protests in France, where the public had remained sympathetic to Israel in spite of a general desire to remain on good terms with the Arab world.[45] The announcement in itself seemed to make nonsense of the official policy of non-involvement, particularly as the embargo imposed a year earlier on the delivery of 50 Mirages to Israel (already paid for) was still in force. In 1972 the purchase price was refunded to Israel.

The explanations put forward by the Minister of Defence, M. Michel Debré, did nothing to help matters.[46] The distinction between sales of arms to 'direct' and 'indirect' participants in the war, the French Government's assurances that Libya had undertaken that the arms would not be used in the war, and alternatively that Libyans, in the French view, could not use the arms, since they would be delivered only over a long period of time, all failed to convince the critics. Nor was public opinion in France appeased by considerations of *Realpolitik*, such as the argument that, while no agreement existed to prevent the sale of arms to the combatants, Libya could obtain them in even greater quantities elsewhere, or that a French 'presence' in Libya was preferable to the alternative of a Soviet 'presence', or that France needed the export sales.

The 'Mirages affair' was important in two ways. It became to a certain extent a symbol. It provided comforting evidence to uncritical Gaullists that, under the presidency of M. Pompidou, French foreign policy remained essentially unchanged. It provided disquieting evidence to critical opponents that M. Pompidou could make authentically Gaullist errors of judgement. 'Gaullist foreign policy', wrote Jacques Fauvet, 'has rediscovered a taste for the spectacular, not to say the outrageous. Libya is M. Pompidou's "free Quebec".'[47] It also created a general conviction in France that the real aim of France was not to play the peace-maker, however important the restoration of peace might be to her, but to strengthen her influence in the area, to achieve General de Gaulle's aim of a Europe 'extended to Africa', not merely by maintaining French ascendancy in former colonial territories, but also by ensuring French predominance in the Mediterranean.

There were certainly indications pointing in this direction, in particular the attempts to normalize relations between France and the Maghreb countries. Franco-Moroccan relations had been strained since the Ben Barka affair in 1965, and Franco-Tunisian relations since 1964. Though President Bourguiba had made more than one overture to France, these had met hitherto with little response. Franco-Algerian relations had been in difficulties for years. Yet, by the beginning of 1970, a spectacular improvement was perceptible in the relations between France and former French North African countries. Diplomatic relations between France and Morocco, suspended in 1966 as a result of the Ben Barka affair, were resumed at the end of 1969. There were talks in April with a view to settling outstanding Franco-Moroccan difficulties and extending co-operation. There was also a new effort to improve relations between the North African countries themselves. The long-standing frontier problem between Morocco and Algeria was finally settled,[48] as was that of the Tunisian–Algerian frontier.[49] The problem of Franco-Algerian relations was admittedly the hardest nut to crack, but in January 1970, President

Boumedienne was expressing the hope that the page had been turned, and even that increased military co-operation between France and Algeria would be possible. Algeria, he said, wanted no foreign fleets in the Mediterranean, but did want co-operation between States bordering on the Mediterranean.[50]

Hopes were also being expressed regarding the possibility of extending to Algeria the association with the EEC already provided for in the case of Tunisia and Morocco. By the summer of 1970, then, it seemed possible that, for the first time, harmony might reign not only between France and all three North African countries, but also between the three countries themselves. Efforts to increase co-operation between Mediterranean States were also extended to the Iberian peninsula. In June 1970, the French Foreign Minister visited Lisbon, and the Defence Minister concluded a military agreement with Spain, following on the promise the previous February to sell her 30 Mirages III. The Defence Minister, M. Debré, described the agreement as 'another step along the road towards the strengthening of the French presence in the Mediterranean'.[51] In this context, the Mirages affair could be presented to the French public as making political sense from the point of view of future French interests, if not from that of reducing tension in the Middle East in the immediate future. The Mediterranean, said the Minister of Agriculture commenting on the Libyan deal, was 'one of the few areas in which independent and concerted action by Europe would have positive significance'.[52] President Pompidou spoke of the need 'to improve Europe's equilibrium by making Mediterranean and Latin influences more clearly apparent'.[53]

The Prime Minister described France's Middle Eastern policy in two words, 'peace', and 'presence'.[54] But it looked as if, failing the possibility of combining these two objectives, the French Government was preparing in the 1970s to give priority to the second. In the 1950s, French foreign policy had been characterized by a reluctant Atlanticism, and dominated, often to the exclusion of all other considerations, by the repercussions at home and abroad of the Algerian war. In the 1960s, it had been characterized by the progressive weakening and finally the severance of Atlantic links, and by the projection by General de Gaulle of a highly unrealistic image of an independent France, destined to be the leader of Europe – of a Europe that, except for France's embryonic nuclear deterrent, was non-nuclear, and seemed likely to remain politically, militarily and economically disunited.

If the 1970s were to see a serious bid by France for the leadership of the countries bordering on the Mediterranean, then she would be faced with a difficult choice, and one that General de Gaulle could no longer make for her. It would be a choice that at least one highly qualified commentator spelled out with some misgiving. 'The France of M. Pompidou', wrote Jacques Fauvet in January 1970,

> has gone back to her natural position and dimensions. She knows that she can compete neither with Asia nor with the two Americas. She counted in the world only ephemerally, by virtue of the importance accorded to her, thanks to the prestige of General de Gaulle. The same France now realizes that, if Europe ever does come into being, it will be neither the French nor the Franco-German Europe that the General had hoped for. Whether or not Great Britain joins it, it will certainly be more German than truly European. What, then, is left for France except the Mediterranean and those African countries to the south of it. . . . In this area, it is perhaps less difficult to achieve a policy of independence vis-à-vis the 'blocs'. But such a policy assumes radical choices, beginning with the sacrifice of the friendship of Israel.[55]

The next three years were to supply no answers to these questions, and no evidence of any significant French rôle in the Mediterranean.

FRANCO-AMERICAN RELATIONS AND THE WORLD RÔLE

Any study of Gaullist foreign policy must raise questions regarding the precise relationship, whether in General de Gaulle's mind or in the minds of French politicians and public, between French foreign-policy objectives and Franco-American relations in general. There were, throughout General de Gaulle's presidency, perpetual divergences between France and the United States on policies not directly concerned with either the European or the Atlantic policies hitherto discussed. Some of these arose from France's assertion of her right to be regarded as a great power, able to intervene effectively in wider political issues, such as United Nations policies and problems associated with the Vietnam and the Middle Eastern wars. This would-be world rôle was bound to create further tensions in Franco-American relations, if only because General de Gaulle challenged what he saw as the United States conception of her own world rôle. To quote only one example, in the volume of his Memoirs published in 1970 only shortly before his death, he described his criticisms in 1959 of President Eisenhower's attitudes to world problems. The United States, he said, took it for granted that, 'in the free world, whether in the realm of security, economics, finance, science, technology or anything else, the fundamental if not the sole reality was that of America'.[56] This was precisely the objection (*mutatis mutandis*) of his opponents to his own attitudes, namely, that his approach to world problems was dominated by his single-minded pursuit of French interests as he saw them. At times, indeed, he quite frankly admitted that he considered this attitude normal. For example, he specifically denied any intention of reproaching the United States for her late entry into the first world war, because he recognized that each nation must put its own interests first.[57]

On some Franco-American differences, however, and especially those on monetary policy and the American involvement in the Vietnam war, the President's public statements ranged from reasoned and often statesmanlike analyses of the essential difficulties of the problem to what at times appeared to be biased and even provocative points of view that could not avoid exacerbating relations between the two countries, and which sometimes seemed to have that express purpose. For instance, his own account of what he said to President Kennedy in 1960 about the Vietnam war was clearly based on the French experience of an eight-year struggle ending in defeat, and reflected his well-known views regarding the relative strengths in the long run of ideologies and nationalism.

> You will find [he said] that intervention in this area will be an endless entanglement. Once a nation has been aroused, no foreign power, however strong, can impose its will upon it. You will discover this for yourselves . . . the more you become involved against Communism, the more the Communists will appear as the champions of national independence, and the more support they will receive, if only from despair. We French have had experience of it.[58]

These sentiments were unexceptionable, even if they did not make any significant contribution to resolving the American political and military dilemma in Vietnam. But the tone here was a far cry from that of his speech at Pnom Penh in 1966, in which he stated that France condemned what was going on in Vietnam, recalled France's example in ending the war in Algeria, expressed himself in favour of an agreement intended 'to restore and guarantee the neutrality of the peoples of Indo-China and their right to self-determination', and declared that the possibility of negotiations with a view to reaching an agreement 'would evidently depend on a prior commitment by America to withdraw her troops within a reasonable and specified time'. Reaffirming this position in his press conference the following October, he spoke of 'the bombing of a small nation by a large one', and repeated his previous conclusions that peace was not in sight, that France had no peace plan to propose, but that the conditions that might make such an agreement possible must include an American decision to recognize the principle of the right to self-determination of 'the Vietnam people'. He then added that he very sincerely believed that it would be to the advantage of France's American friends to follow France's advice on Vietnam, Europe, NATO and currency questions.[59] He could hardly have sincerely believed that the White House and the Pentagon would share this belief, or that his speech could conceivably have any effect other than to exacerbate American opinion and create the impression that he had either become converted to the theses of North Vietnam or else was simply trying to make mischief.[60]

There was a similar apparent contradiction between the President's analysis of international monetary problems and the French Government's actions in the monetary field. In his press conference of 4 February 1965, he drew attention to the existence of a real problem, namely, the possibilities open to the United States (and in theory to Great Britain as well) to use her position as holder of a reserve currency in order to run payments deficits with impunity, thus benefiting from a privileged freedom of action denied to European countries. There was a good deal of support in France for this point of view:

> There is no reason [wrote one commentator in *Le Monde*] why the rest of the world should transfer to the United States twenty milliard dollars' worth of capital in return for credit notes on the Federal Reserve Bank, when this body cannot even guarantee the conversion rate.[61]

It was legitimate for the President to go on to recommend a cure that looked like a plea for a return to the gold standard, even if this was criticizable on technical grounds (and it did meet with a flood of criticism in France), and even if this policy was one that suited France – which had amassed a large gold reserve – much better than it did any other country. But the French action of converting dollars into gold and withdrawing in 1967 from the gold pool appeared to some of his opponents as part of a deliberate attempt to increase United States difficulties.

Was it true, as Guy de Carmoy has affirmed, that 'by 1967 a real anti-American obsession could be discerned'?[62] It is hardly surprising that some percipient American critics should have thought so. The years 1965–7 certainly constituted a low-water mark in Franco-American relations, for the 1965 monetary controversy was followed by the 1966 withdrawal from NATO and the 1967 monetary campaign, described by a former United States Under-Secretary of the Treasury as 'mischief-making'.[63] In his book, *De Gaulle and the Anglo-Saxons*, the American author, John Newhouse, even concludes that 'there was never any possibility of doing serious business with de Gaulle on reasonable terms' and that he never considered himself an ally of the United States, 'except in the most limited and pragmatic sense'. 'If the source of the disagreement did not exist', he says, 'then the pretext for disagreement was called up.'[64]

This conclusion does not really explain Gaullist anti-Americanism, and M. de Carmoy's suggestion of an 'obsession' in 1967 understates the problem. For if General de Gaulle was obsessed by anti-Americanism – and he himself always denied being anti-American – then the obsession dated from long before then. A reader of the two final volumes of the Memoirs who was unacquainted with his rôle in French history and politics, with the idiosyncrasies and very personal style of his accounts of this rôle, and with the tone and vocabulary of his many speeches and press conferences, would be forgiven for concluding that he had been anti-American throughout his political life. The following sentiments, for instance, could certainly justify such a conclusion.

> ... was it not primarily the Anglo-Saxons' cry of 'Halt' that brought the sudden cessation of hostilities on 11 November 1918, at the very moment that we were about to pluck the fruits of victory? Were not the wishes and promises of the American President the dominant factor in the Treaty of Versailles. ... And afterwards, was it not to gratify the wishes of Washington and London that the Government in Paris surrendered the guarantee we had secured and renounced the reparations which Germany owed us in exchange for specious schemes offered to us by America?[65]

Even the abortive EDC, which was a purely European plan, would, according to this account, have meant 'handing over the command of this stateless assemblage lock, stock and barrel to the United States of America'. NATO was a system in which 'an American generalissimo with headquarters near Versailles exercised over the old world the military authority of the new'. Suez was an expedition which 'London and Paris undertook against Nasser', but in which 'French forces of every kind and at every level were placed under the orders of the British, and the latter had only to decide to recall theirs at the behest of Washington and Moscow' for the French forces to be withdrawn as well.[66] If France's European partners favoured the idea of European integration, this was because they themselves sought subordination to America. For

> a stateless system, incapable by its very nature of having its own defence or foreign policy, would inevitably be obliged to follow the dictates of America. If, in the absence of a supranational technocracy, they were anxious to see the Community join the British Commonwealth, it was because that path also led to the position of Washington's Protectorate.[67]

There is, of course, another side to the picture. At the time of the Cuba crisis, the General did not hesitate an instant to come down decisively on the side of Washington.[68] In spite of all the talk about 'détente and co-operation', he never for an instant left any doubt in Soviet minds regarding his commitment to the defence system of the Western alliance.[69] And in spite of all his criticisms of America, and his recognition that his own Atlantic and defence policies had earned France 'a great deal of reproach and invective in many quarters of America', he affirmed (though not wholly accurately) that these had 'never led to a rupture or even an estrangement between the two Governments'.[70]

The truth is that, although the General was hostile to any American policies that appeared to thwart his own plans, he was, in foreign policy (as indeed in all things), essentially a realist and a pragmatist. As a nationalist, he was perpetually resentful of the impact on his own nationalist policies of the nationalist policies of others. And just as Frenchmen were for him an irritating though necessary element of France, so other nations were irritating obstacles to his foreign policy. Yet he was, nevertheless, obliged to take them into account. His anti-Americanism (like his anti-British policies and attitudes) was thus essentially ancillary and opportunist, though this may not always have been apparent. On this point, says Mr Newhouse, 'France's interest, as he defined it, might one day require close relations with America. Thus anti-Americanism, though a useful chord to strike from time to time, was not to be formalized as a policy.'[71] It often looked as if it was a policy, because, throughout his political life, General de Gaulle rarely had sufficient choice of 'useful chords' to strike. He was in power only at moments of danger and difficulty, and for most of the time had formidable problems to contend with, and inadequate military or political assets with which to set about solving them.

There are at least two important factors that must be taken into account in any attempt to assess the real motivation of the President's policies in relation to the United States. The first is that there were always strong and genuine differences between French and American priorities in foreign policy, and that in this matter, the President was in reality speaking for the bulk of the French nation, including those opponents who had little or no sympathy with the grandiose Gaullist conceptions in which he liked to clothe his policies. For the United States, the immediate potential enemy was the Soviet Union. For the French President, as for the whole of France, the main threat never ceased to be that of Germany, and the overriding pre-occupation of French foreign policy was, under the Fifth as under the Fourth Republic, the need to ensure French security from that threat. Even in the years of the Berlin air-lift and the building of the Berlin wall, when General de Gaulle was adopting an intransigent line towards the Soviet Union, the central preoccupation of all French political parties still remained Western Europe and France's place within it. The changed climate from 1963 onwards widened the gap between France and the United States, because it enabled the French to discount the need for American defence, without ceasing in practice to rely on it. It thus enabled those parties that had always hoped for *rapprochement* with the Soviet Union, either for ideological reasons (as in the case of the Communist party) or for a mixture of ideological and tactical reasons (as in the case of the Socialist party) to feel free to look Eastwards.

Nor was it only on the Left that the *rapprochement* with the

Soviet Union and the East European satellites was popular.
Right and Left felt equally free to pursue traditional policies of
Franco-Russian friendship as an additional means of containing
Germany, for the Soviet Union was among the most fervent
opponents of any policy envisaging an eventual re-unification
of Germany. General de Gaulle's détente policy, whatever its
long-term objectives, had as its most important immediate
objective to make Europe safe from Germany. It was he who,
in 1944, had said that the Rhine was the key to France's
future.[72] It was he who, in 1959, had explained to President
Eisenhower (if the account given in his Memoirs can be
relied on) that the solution to the problems of East and West
was not 'a technical deal on armaments between Washington
and Moscow, but a *rapprochement* between one European nation
and another', with a view to 'dismantling the iron curtain piece
by piece', and who had claimed that France was ideally placed
to bring this about, since she had no quarrel with the Soviet
Union, towards which she had always been specially attracted.
His expressed intention in inviting Khrushchev to France in
1960 was to discuss the need to keep Germany divided in the
absence of any general European settlement, and this was
wholly in tune with French priorities in all parties, from Right
to Left.[73]

The second factor which affected General de Gaulle's
declared position in relation to America during the first decade
of the Fifth Republic was the very small scope for independent
action open to any French Government in the field of foreign
policy. As has been said, General de Gaulle was in power during
two extremely difficult periods of French history, when France
was, in fact, inescapably dependent on America, and when this
dependence was resented by a country whose great-power
status had been equally inescapably undermined by war. The
inadequacies of French defence and the backwardness of the
economy combined to make him dependent on American technology as well as on American defence. All that the President
had to offer as a substitute for the status and power that he
sought was a symbolic independence compounded almost
entirely of words. In the field of Franco-American relations,

his only decisive action – the withdrawal from NATO – was carried out in the 1963–7 climate in which French opinion had ceased to believe in the reality of a Soviet threat. In other words, it was intended to be a gesture entailing no actual weakening of American defence. His words found echoes in all political parties because they fed old resentments – Free French resentment of American recognition of the Vichy Government, France's resentment of her exclusion from Yalta, of American criticisms of North African policies, and of the Suez adventure, her resentment of her subordinate position in NATO and her fears of an American economic 'take-over'.

So receptive was French opinion to this kind of verbal and essentially unrealistic anti-Americanism that, to many observers, one of the most obvious indications of a thaw in Franco-American relations from 1969 onwards was the disappearance from the French press – and in particular from the loyal and uncritical Gaullist sections of it – of the more exaggerated expressions of anti-Americanism. In 1958, shortly before he became Prime Minister, Michel Debré wrote that: 'The official position of the United States can be summarized as follows: it does not want France to be an atomic power. It has no desire for France to recover her political independence'.[74] Some ten years later, the left-wing Gaullist weekly, *Notre République*, was expressing the view that 'For a country like France, the only policy is to cut the White House down to size'.[75]

From 1969 onwards, possibly in large part as a consequence of the Soviet intervention in Czechoslovakia, which had shaken even French complacency regarding the peaceful intentions of Russia, there was quite clearly a general desire to halt the long deterioration in Franco-American relations. It had led Paul Reynaud to protest as far back as 1963 against

> an isolated France, the rejection of the Entente cordiale that has saved us twice in thirty years; discord in the Atlantic Alliance; American irritation, indeed hostility to us, although their presence in Europe safeguards our liberty. . . .[76]

In 1970, M. Pompidou made his first (and not wholly happy) presidential visit to the United States. It came as the climax to a series of exchanges of visits by French and American politicians and personalities (including President Nixon's visit to Paris) that *Le Monde* had considered significant enough to be listed under the heading: 'A year of cordiality'.[77] It was followed by a statement in which the President expressed his conviction that President Nixon had now accepted the fact that France had an independent rôle to play.

> I felt [he said] that France counted. She counts because of her geographical situation, her intellectual quality and, I believe, her moral quality.[78]

It may seem, perhaps, that an increase in cordiality and co-operation was not enough to counterbalance France's reaffirmed intention of remaining outside NATO and inside the Alliance, and that increased optimism regarding the possibilities of reaching agreement on international monetary problems, following the Pompidou–Nixon meeting in the Azores at the end of 1971, was a slight basis on which to build any exaggerated hopes for better Franco-American relations in the 1970s. The general feeling in France that something was changing probably owed more to a change of presidential style than to anything else. But it certainly owed something, too, to the changing focus of French foreign policy, following on the growing realization that the very popular Gaullist 'world rôle', as seen by General de Gaulle, was likely to prove no less elusive than 'independence'.

PART III

Reflections by Way of Conclusion

CHAPTER XI

Politics and the Republic

From 1958 to about 1967, the Fifth Republic was regularly referred to, both inside and outside France, as 'de Gaulle's Republic'.[1] From 1967 onwards, this attitude was gradually replaced by speculation about what the post-Gaullist era would be like, and the speculation continued under the presidency of M. Pompidou. The claim, in 1971, by the then secretary-general of the Gaullist party, M. René Tomasini, that France had entered a new period 'in which M. Pompidou is the incarnation of Gaullism'[2] was, as has been seen, not accepted by all Gaullists. Nor was it accepted by all observers outside the Gaullist party. 'Gaullism is creeping away on tiptoe,' wrote Raymond Barrillon in 1971. 'Pompidolism is slipping in soundlessly'.[3] There were others who seemed less sure of this. For though opinion polls reported that some 60 per cent or more of those questioned expressed themselves satisfied with M. Pompidou, the vote in the 1972 referendum, on which he had appealed for a demonstration of personal support, was clearly disappointing to him.[4] And his speech welcoming Great Britain into the European Community seemed to reveal some uncertainty regarding the state of the Republic, for having praised the stability of British democracy, he added: 'I hope we shall not infect it with the old virus of instability that has resisted Gaullist antibiotics.'[5]

The ineffectiveness of Gaullist antibiotics against the old virus of electoralism was patent. Surveying electoral prospects in 1973, M. François Mitterrand claimed that France was still in the Fourth Republic.

> The Fourth? But we are still in it! [he wrote]. Unless there is a victory for the Left, the next Assembly will be dominated

by hinge-groups and marginal groups, whose sole aim will be to get future conservative and Centre rivals into orbit for the presidential election.[6]

And contemplating with some cynicism the pre-electoral declarations of various political leaders, a well-known commentator, Alain Duhamel, concluded that French politics was still in 1900, and that in a France that was changing in every other field, only politics remained unchanging.[7]

After fourteen years, exactly how much of that kind of family resemblance was there between political life in the Fifth Republic and that of its predecessors? And if there were to be a change of régime, what would be the legacy of the Fifth Republic to its successor? Of the three Republics that France has known in the course of the present century, the Third Republic has undoubtedly had the greatest impact on French political habits. After a century of constitutional experiment, it created something that was lost in 1940 and has not yet been recovered, namely, a sense of permanence – of '*la durée*'. In the first two decades of the century, France came nearer than she had ever done before or has done since to the American and British situation, in which the continuance of the régime is something that can be taken for granted. The Fourth Republic began to look impermanent before its Constitution had begun to be applied. And, after fourteen years of the most stable government that any French Republic has known, the Fifth Republic still had a curiously impermanent look. The possibility of a challenge to the régime in the near or not too distant future was still being evoked by commentators in 1973, partly no doubt because the events of 1968 were too recent to have been forgotten, but partly also because the person for whom the régime had been designed had disappeared.

The Third Republic also bequeathed to its successors certain lasting political habits and ways of life – the *commune*, the *département* and the constituency as the basic centres of party activity; the key position of the Deputy within the political system, and the continued importance of the Prefect within the administrative system; reliance on the *Conseil d'Etat* as a

controller and guide of local administration and, in the relations between State and citizen, as the protector of both the
individual citizen and the civil servant; the strength of the
desire for uniformity and State control both in education and
in local administration; the crystallization of the main political
issues and the identity of the main 'political families' about
which and by which a basically static, though superficially
'effervescent', party struggle was carried on.[8] It can at least
be said in favour of M. Duhamel's thesis that French politics
was still in 1900 that, if a Frenchman were to return in 1973
from some isolated island in which he had been exiled for
72 years, and drop in to his local departmental Socialist, Communist or Radical party meeting, he would be far more at home
than was the Japanese citizen who discovered post-war Japan
after an exile of only twenty-five years.

The Third Republic, then, gave France a workable parliamentary machine, consolidated her political habits and party
organizations, and strengthened attitudes to the State that were,
at least up to the 1930s, shared by the bulk of the population.
The Fourth Republic was from the start a Republic of illusions.[9] The parties constituting the parliamentary majority in
1945 and 1946 were victims of at least three major French
illusions – the eighteenth-century illusion that institutions
alone are capable of creating political habits, the illusion derived from it that a series of fresh constitutional starts is something that can help to do this, and the recurrent left-wing
illusion that, if political power is unattainable by the Left while
Socialists and Communists remain divided, then there must be
some way of enabling them to reach sufficient agreement to be
able to govern together.

But the Fourth Republic rapidly became one of disillusion-
ment and frustration, because Socialist–Communist unity
proved unattainable, and because new political habits were
not created. By the beginning of the 1950s, there was already
pressure for the reform of a Constitution whose provisions had
been fought over for a year, and then accepted unenthusiastically by only a third of the electorate. Political divisions, not
the Constitution, made the system unworkable, and the frustra-

tions caused by these had created in less than five years a two-fold opposition of Gaullists and Communists, opposed to each other and to any conceivable Government majority. Frustration was caused, too, by the economic consequences of a world war, combined with the legacy of the Third Republic's economically as well as politically static system, and of a colonial system unadapted to the changing colonial world of the 1950s. It was perhaps not surprising that the Fourth Republic should have succumbed under the weight of its problems and should have disappeared in 1958 without a shot being fired in its defence.

Though a temporary Republic – often described from 1950 onwards as an 'interlude' – it did, nevertheless, present its successor with important positive as well as negative legacies. It had, if not a generally accepted foreign policy, at least common attitudes regarding the need for a policy based on the search for European unity in one form or another, and for a start based on the economic co-operation of the contiguous countries of Western Europe. It left an economy firmly and irrevocably committed to modernization and planning, a comprehensive system of social insurance, and some belated preparation for the gradual evolution of colonial territories towards self-government, together with two already independent North African States.

The Fifth Republic began its life as one intended by all but a small number of convinced Gaullists to be only temporary – a *régime de salut public*. It also became in some ways a Republic of illusions and a Republic of myths, though the illusions were those of General de Gaulle rather than of Parliament or parties. Its institutions were intended by him to provide an instrument by which new constitutional and political habits could be created. And his leadership was intended to make possible a foreign policy that would restore as much as could be achieved of France's historic rôle as one of the great powers and give her a dominant place in Europe. Neither of these aims was achieved, though the myths of French power and greatness on which his foreign policy was based served at least the useful purpose of re-creating a national confidence badly shaken by the events of 1939 to 1945 and by the apparently insoluble post-war problems.

The Fifth Republic certainly created new political habits, though not those that General de Gaulle had hoped to see. The acceptance by the Left of the system of presidential election by universal suffrage was not due to any general conversion to General de Gaulle's constitutional theories, but to the establishment of *de facto* presidential control of Government policies and the consequent need for presidential power to be based on universal suffrage. The presidency thus became more than a rival power citadel to Parliament. It became the primary prize in the political battle. The result was that elections and electoral tactics played an even larger rôle than before, which was the exact opposite of what General de Gaulle had intended.

Nor was there any sign of the development of the political bi-polarization that Gaullists had hoped for, as indeed had left-wing supporters of a quasi- or fully presidential system. There was bi-polarization to the extent imposed by the rules governing the second ballot of the presidential election, but no permanent *rapprochement* within the main political formations. Pro-Government parties, Centre groups and left-wing parties each formed electoral coalitions, but retained their identities, so that the number of parties was no less than under the Fourth Republic. And as far as party practices were concerned, the Gaullists were influenced by opposition tactics, instead of themselves establishing new practices. The incompatibility rule, for instance, though formally respected, was in reality circumvented, and Gaullist Ministers and Deputies were no less representatives of their constituency and of the interests of party members than were those of the '*système des partis*'. Proxy voting and empty seats in the National Assembly still existed. Electoral agreements between the Gaullists and their Giscardian allies were much the same as those concluded by parties under the previous régime, except that the Gaullists were much stronger than any previous single party and so could dictate terms more favourable to themselves, and except that, under the leadership of M. Giscard d'Estaing, the

Républicains indépendants were a more disciplined party than hitherto. But it is doubtful whether this latter change had anything to do with Gaullist principles.

It is in this context that the 1972 Socialist-cum-Communist 'common programme' should be seen. Their only previous common Government programme, that of 1936, had, it is true, led to a Popular Front Government, but not to the inclusion of Communist Ministers in it. The Governments of post-war France, between 1945 and 1947, had included Communist Ministers, but there had been no common programme. There was, however, in the immediate post-war years, more real belief in the possibility of achieving lasting Socialist–Communist co-operation, both inside and outside Parliament, than has ever existed since. A prolonged effort was made to unite the two parties. The two trade-union movements, Communist-dominated and Socialistic, did achieve organizational unity for a brief period from 1943, under the German occupation, but only at the cost of increasing strain and friction. It lasted only until 1947. Communist Ministers left the Government four months after the Constitution had come into operation, and the strikes of 1947 ended the period of trade-union fusion. With the return of the Fifth Republic to the system of election that had existed throughout most of the Third Republic there was a return to the former habit of electoral agreements at the second ballot, but the parties always opposed each other at the first ballot. The respective trade-union confederations remained rivals. Given this background, and eleven years of unsuccessful conversations between Socialists and Communists, an agreement reached only when the election was under a year away, and under which the two signatories continued to oppose each other at the first ballot, looked unimpressive, and some scepticism regarding the likelihood of its survival for long after the election was permissible.[10]

The most important change in political life under the Fifth Republic, the demotion of Parliament, with the consequent apathy and absenteeism of Deputies, stagnation of parties and proliferation of study groups and Clubs that preferred to remain on the fringe of parties or outside them altogether, meant that, in spite of the frequently expressed desire of left-wing parties for new members and new thinking, they attracted only old members and old thinking. The Communist party was a partial exception to this rule in that its members got younger, but their periods of membership appeared to get shorter; for year after year, the official figures showed several thousands of new members, but the total membership remained virtually unchanged.[11] This 'depolitization' of a formerly highly politicized society was accompanied, as seen in the first volume, by a profusion of 'leftist' revolutionary groups declaring themselves opposed to the whole system of what they called 'bourgeois' democracy, and regarding both the Communist party and the Communist-dominated trade-union movement as part of bourgeois democracy. The result of this twofold development was that the opposition parties became increasingly impotent and atomized.

In fourteen years, however, Gaullism had greatly increased the difficulties in the way of any left-wing attempt to dislodge the Gaullist majority in the National Assembly. The Fifth Republic had not merely brought about changes in the political climate, but had also changed much of the context of politics. France had been transformed from a colonial empire under challenge to a community of French-speaking independent States, from an economically backward to a modern industrial State, and from an insular, protectionist economy to an influential member of a West European Common Market. The clerical issue that had been for so long a rallying point for the Left seemed at last to be disappearing. The formerly predominantly Catholic trade-union confederation had abandoned all denominational associations, and the Christian Democrat MRP had ceased to exist as an organized political force. The hemicycle of the National Assembly had been transformed, from one in which solid blocks of Communists, Socialists and MRP faced smaller and less organized Centre and right-wing parties, to one in which a solid phalanx of Gaullists and *Républicains indépendants* faced a hundred or so Socialists and Communists and some thirty members of a divided Centre. If all these changes had not yet brought the degree of permanence that characterized the best years of the Third Republic, then the explanation must lie within the system itself.

One thing that had not changed was the impossibility of taking the Constitution for granted. No less than under the Fourth Republic, constitutional questions were themselves matters of controversy, and what ought to have been purely political controversies were perpetually complicated by constitutional implications. In 1960, 1961, 1962, 1963 and 1969, it was the President's interpretations of the constitutional provisions that were challenged, mainly by opposition parties, the *Conseil d'Etat*, and a certain number of lawyers and political scientists, but also by some Centre and right-wing politicians. In 1960 and 1962, the primary issue was constitutional and, in 1963, 1967, 1969 and 1971, constitutional and political issues were inter-mingled. There was no sustained demand for substantial con-stitutional revision, as there had been under the Fourth Repub-lic, but there was a recurrent preoccupation with constitutional uncertainties. What seemed to outside observers an uncon-scionable amount of time and energy was devoted to complex and often hair-splitting argument about constitutional points.

The most important of these uncertainties arose not from actual but from potential conflicts. What M. Chaban-Delmas called the Constitution's 'Achilles heel' has already been men-tioned in relation to both the 1969 presidential election and the general election of 1973. But it remained a permanent problem, because the Constitution itself offered no solution, if a conflict between President and National Assembly were to arise.[12]

A further factor creating uncertainty under the Fifth Repub-lic was the evolution of the presidential office. This could, in certain circumstances, render the problem of the 'Achilles heel' even more serious. The fact that M. Pompidou was clearly seen to be the leader of the majority party and the effective head of the Government, and not merely the 'arbiter' as des-cribed in article 5 of the Constitution (at first thought to be

General de Gaulle's own conception of the presidential function), made the personality of the President of supreme political
importance. If, as seemed evident in 1973, his powers could be
curbed only by an internal revolt in the majority party or by
the kind of clash between President and Assembly that could
lead to unforeseen dangers affecting the régime, then the course
of constitutional history might perhaps be determined by the
fact that the holder of the presidential office at the time of such
a crisis was either a weak or a power-hungry man. It was no
doubt to be regretted that President Lebrun had been a weak
President at a critical moment of French history, in 1940. But
it is doubtful whether, even if he had been a man of strong
personality, he could have made very much difference. A
President with the ambitions of a Napoleon III might be in a
powerful position to achieve his ends, if faced with a situation
in which the Constitution offered no solution to a clash between
President and National Assembly.

These considerations were at least at the back of the minds of
those who pressed the President in 1973 to give his own views
on what the Constitution would require him to do. Although
the left-wing parties seemed more preoccupied with the problem, it could concern both sides. A left-wing opposition wanted
to know what its victory in the parliamentary election would
be worth, with a Gaullist President in the Elysée. But a
Gaullist minority would be no less interested to know whether
a left-wing majority might not radically change the nature of
the presidential office (as the authors of the common programme had said they would do) and whether a Government
including Communists could be relied on to resign and go into
opposition if defeated in the National Assembly, and what the
President would do if either of these things happened.

Such hypothetical examples make it clear that the prospects
of constitutional controversy were by no means remote. The
Constitution of the Fifth Republic was still not universally
regarded as the definitive constitution of France, and no
Frenchman in 1973 could face the chance of an electoral swing
of the pendulum with the confidence felt by Conservative and
Labour voters in Britain and Democrat and Republican electors

in the United States that, whichever side won, the Constitution would not be affected.

The rôle of Parliament in the Fifth Republic was a subject of profound dissatisfaction in the ranks of opposition parties, and of some anxiety and questioning on the Gaullist side. As has already been mentioned in the previous volume,[13] some of the opposition Deputies objected to the Gaullist system because they had a nostalgic desire to return to old and familiar ways, perhaps even including the Third and Fourth Republic habits of obstructing parliamentary business, introducing a profusion of Private Members' Bills, and bringing down Governments without providing any viable alternative. The Gaullist 'malaise' was a much more complex phenomenon. The dissatisfaction of Gaullist Deputies really existed at three levels, though their expression of it did not always make this clear. Some of it was irritation regarding procedural inadequacies, which led to reiterated complaints addressed at the end of each session to the president of the National Assembly. Similar complaints were expressed on behalf of the Senate by its president. The 1971 manifesto of the five Gaullist presidents of Assembly Commissions falls into this category. But it also expressed a deeper dissatisfaction. One of the five, M. Alexandre Sanguinetti, president of the National Defence Commission, described it a few weeks later as being essentially part of the process of adaptation to the post-Gaullist era. The acceptance of 'a certain style of Government' under the presidency of General de Gaulle had, he said, been justified by his personality and by special circumstances, among which he mentioned the habit, prior to the Gaullist régime, of legislative domination of the executive (*le régime d'assemblée*). Now that 'de Gaulle, the giant' was no longer there, 'unconditional obedience' was no longer justified.

'The time has come', he said, 'to revive Parliament.'[14] But how? And to what end? If, as some Gaullists affirmed, the Gaullist party intended to inaugurate a new epoch, in which 'a dominant party' could expect to hold power for long periods, either alone or in coalition, then it would have to do two things, neither of which had been done by 1973. It must find a more satisfying rôle for its backbenchers, and it must make clear to its supporters and electors the basic principles of Gaullism.

In the chapter of his book, *The Gaullist Phenomenon*, in which he discusses the concept of the dominant party, Jean Charlot seems to deny the need for any basic principles. He rejects both the ideological dogmatism of the left-wing *parti de masses* and the kind of pragmatic leadership that characterizes what he calls *partis de notables* and *partis de cadres*, that is, parties run by dominant local personalities or by a small number of political leaders. He sees the Gaullist party as being none of these, but as an 'elector-based party' (*un parti d'électeurs*), that is, one held together by acceptance of General de Gaulle's conception of France (*une certaine idée de la France*), organized on the basis of a *rassemblement* that unites (as against parties that divide) and preaching a non-doctrinaire, practical approach to politics, based on electoral opportunism. 'Gaullist ideology', he says, 'is no more than the belief that ideologies pass. Nations remain as the motive force of history, and politics must be national.' Gaullist party policy, therefore, needs to be based only on 'common values, covering a wide enough area to rally to it a maximum number of supporters'.[15]

What such values were and how wide the area they should cover were questions to which the Gaullist party supplied no convincing answers. M. Charlot rejects the Debré doctrine of the State, the Capitant belief in social democracy and the former MRP's belief in the common good, as constituting 'doctrinal strait-jackets'. He sees Gaullism, however, as playing in France a rôle analogous to that played in Britain by the Conservative and Labour parties. Neither, however, has ever sought to base its appeal to the electors solely on evocations of Disraeli and Macmillan, or of Keir Hardie and Attlee, or to base its policies purely on electoral opportunism. Indeed, from the moment that a parliamentary party seeks to be associated with policy-making, instead of merely saying Aye to Government proposals, even the most pragmatic policy needs some formulation in terms of general principles, however vague. There must be something between ideology and electoral opportunism. It could be argued, too, that a *rassemblement* is not a suitable framework for democratic politics, except in moments of national crisis when there are a few simple overriding preoccupations on which agreement is possible, at least for a time.

General de Gaulle undoubtedly disagreed with this last argument, but he did perceive the need for something more than a blind belief in his leadership coupled with electoral opportunism. He produced the idea of participation. The signatories of the manifesto published in October 1972 by 'Five Deputies in search of a Parliament'[16] believed in 'democracy through participation', but they also saw the rôle of Parliament as being in need of adaptation to meet the challenge presented by the acceleration of technical change. They noted the growing gulf between executives and legislatures, and the growing power of technocrats, administrators and communications media, a power that was creating a 'Republic of Silence' in which the individual would no longer feel any sense of responsibility for politics.

On this third level of questioning, there was as yet little positive contribution from Gaullist party leaders. Indeed, the party was open to charges of succumbing to technocracy instead of resisting it. It could be argued, too, that the last years of General de Gaulle's presidency did not encourage any belief in the attractive force of the idea of participation. Nor was it certain that those Deputies who shared M. Sanguinetti's demand for a more active rôle for Parliament would have shared the five Deputies' view that Parliaments in the modern world should play a smaller legislative rôle and become rather organs of 'enquiry and control'. But the dissatisfaction with the rôle of Parliament did indicate that the disappearance of de Gaulle and the realization that M. Pompidou had not provided a replacement for him had led to doubts regarding the adequacy as a rallying point for Gaullists of the idea of 'efficiency' (*efficacité*). The question: Efficiency for what? was perhaps what lay behind the malaise and the disillusionment regarding

M. Chaban-Delmas' 'new society', which, by 1973, had ceased to appear new enough.

While Gaullists proclaimed their unwillingness to create an ideological party, parties of the Left demonstrated their unwillingness to abandon ideology. And while Gaullists thought almost exclusively about power, Socialists and Communists were not thinking enough about power and its responsibilities. The 'common programme' intensified this backward-looking attitude. As long as Socialists and Communists remained rivals for the support of the same sections of the community, each was tempted to outdo the other in the use of familiar, old-fashioned and, it was hoped, vote-winning clichés. Electors who asked themselves in 1973 how each side was intending to use the power it was asking for were given no really satisfying answers, for, while one side offered familiar, distant utopias, the other seemed to look no farther ahead than the next budget.

Only in the field of foreign policy was there something nearer to a consensus, and that was due to the fact that, in the absence of a de Gaulle and the presence of an international situation which offered only the slenderest margin of independent action to second-class powers, foreign policy had lost much of its importance. Differences of opinion regarding the precise institutional form of a far-distant, and as yet hypothetical united Europe, or regarding the relative attractions of a policy of 'national independence' and one based on the assumption of a 'progressive dissolution of the two blocs', had become purely academic, and mattered little to most electors, who were more interested in the price of beef and the incidence of VAT. Or at least the Gaullist party was counting on that being the case.

It was easy enough to conclude, as some critics did, that

> a Government faced by *contestation* on the one hand and technocracy on the other is probably mistaken in assuming that its best ally is a weak Parliament.[17]

But with France's political background, and in the absence of clear-cut practical policies, of strong party organizations in the country, and of political interest on the part of the electors, it was difficult to see how Parliament could be significantly strengthened in the immediate future. The Gaullists were still largely under the spell of de Gaulle. The main opposition parties were still under the spell of nineteenth-century ideas, on the interpretation of which they had been quarrelling for over half a century.

POLITICS AND PROBLEMS

Political problems, too, were in some ways more difficult, even if they presented fewer obviously and immediately insoluble dilemmas than those that the Fourth Republic had had to face. For the achievements of the Fifth Republic brought their own problems, and these appeared by the 1970s to be creating a series of interlocking dilemmas stretching far into the future. What General de Gaulle had regarded as the prior condition for France's recovery of great-power status had been fulfilled. The 'economic renewal' that he had so tirelessly – and lengthily – preached in his press conferences was a fact. In 1953, France had been spoken of as 'the sick man of Europe'. In 1973, economists were debating the likelihood that she would, by 1985, have the most powerful economy in Europe.[18] But part of the cost of the economic revolution had been the creation of a number of obdurate economic problems that statesmen were wrestling with unsuccessfully, and that were, therefore, potential political problems. Economic disparities between the prosperity of different regions, between public and private sectors, between prosperous modern farmers and small family farmers and retailers – all these and other signs of economic disequilibrium were compelling Governments to temper economically desirable policies with politically unavoidable palliatives.

France's economic prospects in 1985, and perhaps even in 1975, could not therefore be accurately predicted solely on the basis of existing economic trends. These could be profoundly affected by weaknesses of the economic, administrative and political machinery, and this in turn could be rendered ineffective by political stresses generated by economic and social discontents. The revolution of 1968 constituted a salutary reminder of the speed with which a particular conjunction of economic, social and political factors could produce a political explosion, whose effects went far beyond the fields in which its immediate causes were to be found. If politicians are often too unaware of the impact of economics on political attitudes, economists too often extrapolate economic data, without allowing for the extent to which, in the last resort, economics depends on politics.

There were, too, additional long-range problems, the effects of which on the political and economic situation were unpredictable in the early 1970s, and might remain so for a long time. The first concerned France's place in the world, and the impact of the international situation on domestic politics. General de Gaulle's grandiose forecasts of France's recovery of international status and influence had not been, and could not be, realized. They provided a temporary breakwater, delaying the full impact of the effects on French minds of loss of Empire, loss of defence potential in a nuclear world, and loss of influence in a world increasingly dominated by the two giants. It was clear before the end of his presidency that, in the international society, France had reached a 'stalemate' even more serious, and certainly more permanent, than the economic 'stalemate' that had given birth in the domestic field to plans for a 'new society'. European integration was no nearer than it had been a decade earlier, and conflicts within the Community of Nine were already threatening to reduce its advance in any direction from, at best, a slow and painful crawl to, at worst, an immobile or even a disintegrating Europe. If the dream of a possible European defence system was, by then, as dead as the 1950s dream of the EDC, France's position in a curious limbo, half in and half out of an Atlantic Alliance that no longer appeared to have any clear purposes, represented no real advance on her situation in the 1950s and 1960s as a reluctant and sleeping partner of NATO.

Outside the field of Europe and the Atlantic, the dream of 'Europe from the Atlantic to the Urals' was dead (if indeed it had ever really existed, even in General de Gaulle's mind, as more than a useful propaganda instrument), and the abortive

Gaullist 'détente with the Eastern bloc' had been stationary since 1968, limited to the plane of minor trade agreements, arranged in the course of periodic State visits. And the only visible result of M. Pompidou's attempt to substitute for this now obviously non-existent sphere of influence what he called 'a French presence in the Mediterranean' had been the presence of some 100 Mirages in Libya instead of 50 in Israel, and considerable disquiet both in France and among her allies regarding what looked like a Franco-Arab axis. Nor had it even achieved any real improvement in the relations between France and the Arab North African States. The links between France and all her former possessions were, in any case, like those of the Commonwealth, gradually being loosened.

This process was no doubt inevitable, and France was not alone in having lost an Empire without discovering a rôle. Great Britain, indeed, seemed several paces behind France, in that she had begun her search for a European rôle at the precise moment when, both in the Community as well as in France, doubts regarding its future were clearly evident, even among the most enthusiastic Europeans. A second long-range problem, however, was one that, though it affected all Western industrialized States, seemed likely to bring peculiar difficulties for France. The spread of changing attitudes to hitherto generally accepted principles of parliamentary government, and the failure of democratic political systems to keep pace with the rate of technical change, were phenomena that reacted on each other, producing symptoms such as the violence of minorities, the apathy of majorities, and the scepticism of the politically minded regarding the adequacy of parliamentary systems. France's political system was still relatively new, and already under heavy criticism by left-wing political parties. The previous fourteen years had brought too many traumatic political experiences for political parties to contend with – the Algerian war, with its accompaniment of insurrections and terrorism, the May revolution, the revolutionary changes in traditional economic and social structures, and the disappearance of a man of destiny to whom the direction of the State had been confided for over a decade.

These institutional and political problems were intensified by continuing uncertainties regarding the President himself – his personality, his conception of his office, his policies – to which were added in 1973 uncertainties created by persistent concern about his state of health. The result was to make the future of the Fifth Republic itself even less predictable and a matter for continued speculation.

M. Pompidou once remarked, when he was Prime Minister, that, to some people, General de Gaulle's presidency was merely 'an unpleasant interlude' (*un mauvais moment à passer*). To many, however, it may well appear in retrospect as a comfortable interlude that postponed some uncomfortable moments of truth. For, to a country that, in 1958, had been on the verge of civil war, and perhaps of anarchy, he had brought a new Republic, new hopes of national independence and greatness, decisive action in moments of immediate crisis and reminders every six months, on the 'grand occasions' that he called press conferences, of the country's steady progress. He had created a picture of 'a France eternally serene, pursuing her destiny along a road that ran straight ahead'.[19] He was no longer there to supply dreams in default of solutions to the complicated problems of the 1970s. It was M. Pompidou who described France on 10 November 1970 as 'widowed'. In 1973, she was still suffering from the self-questioning, uncertainties and anxieties that widows have to face.

Notes

Note: Where the place of publication is not cited, the work was published in Paris or London.

PART I

CHAPTER I

1. Charles Morazé, *Les Français et la République* (Armand Colin, 1956), p. 98.
2. Albert Thibaudet, *La République des Professeurs* (Grasset, 1927). The phrase refers to the victory in the elections of May 1924 of the Cartel led by Herriot, Painlevé and Blum, 'which suggested a parliamentary State led by three *Normaliens*' (p. 14).
3. *v.* for instance, the parliamentary battles over electoral reform in 1950 and 1951 and again in 1955. There were disagreements in 1950 on the proposal to amend 11 articles of the Constitution, and on amendments to the Bill put forward in the two assemblies in 1953 and 1954. Further proposals to amend 27 articles were made in 1955. There was an abortive Bill in March 1958, and a Bill was actually under discussion in the National Assembly when the Fourth Republic fell.
4. Morazé, op. cit., p. 15.
5. On some institutional differences, *v.* Vol. I, pp. 6–7 and 20–4. On electoral differences, *v.* ibid., pp. 25 and 36–44.
6. *La IVe République et sa Politique extérieure* (Armand Colin, 1961), p. 398.
7. Broadcast of 13 June 1958 (*Année politique*, Presses universitaires de France, 1958), p. 545.
8. *v.* also Chapter VII, pp. 222–6.
9. André Siegfried, *Tableau des Partis en France* (Grasset, 1930), p. 63.
10. Quoted in J. M. Thompson, *Leaders of the French Revolution* (Oxford, Basil Blackwell, 1932), p. 225.
11. *v.* Chapters VIII and IX for examples in the field of foreign affairs.

12. *v.* Chapters II, III and V, pp. 67, 111, 146.

13. *v.* Chapter V, pp. 154, 416.

14. Siegfried, op. cit., p. 60.

15. *v.* Vol. I, pp. 159 and 372.

16. Morazé, op. cit., p. 44.

17. Ibid., p. 47.

18. Ibid. pp. 47–132.

19. *v.* pp. 157, 433.

20. *v. Le Monde*, 22–3 April 1972, which reports a number of dis-turbances by the CID–UNATI movement at meetings addressed during the referendum campaign by Ministers and prominent UDR personalities. This movement also distributed leaflets at Thionville during the presidential tour of Lorraine.

21. *La République des Professeurs* (Grasset, 1927), p. 256.

22. Siegfried, op. cit., p. 55.

23. Morazé, op. cit., p. 22.

24. Philip M. Williams, *Wars, Plots and Scandals in Post-war France* (Cambridge U.P., 1970), p. 3.

25. Douglas Johnson, *France and the Dreyfus Affair* (Blandford Press, 1966), p. 4. *v.* also the description of scandals under the Fourth Republic given by Georgette Elgey in *La République des Illusions* (Fayard, 1965), p. 189. Mr Williams gives a trans-lation of this passage on the opening page of his *Wars, Plots and Scandals in Post-war France.*

26. Pierre Viansson-Ponté, *Histoire de la République Gaullienne* (Fayard, Vol. I, 1970, Vol. II, 1971), Vol. II, pp. 206–7.

27. *Année politique*, 1966, p. 410.

28. Ibid., 1967, p. 51.

29. *v.* for instance, M. Pompidou's remark in an interview in *l'Express* (5 September 1967): '*Vous le savez aussi bien que moi, ce pays est à peu près ingouvernable.*' *v.* also Jacques Fauvet's remark in *La France déchirée* (Fayard, 1957), p. 22: '. . . four-teen undisciplined Parliamentary groups and forty million opinions'.

30. Philip Williams, op. cit., pp. 3 and 7.
    As Philip Williams recognizes in his book, the phenomenon of scandals is really very complicated. He attempts a classification into the following four main categories (p. 5):

    (i) those concerned with the private lives of politicians;
    (ii) those that are primarily financial;

(iii) plots to overthrow the Republic;
(iv) accusations of treason and espionage.

He himself demonstrates convincingly that such a classification can be only a rough guide. Some affairs do not fit into it – for example, the Mitterrand affair of 1959, in which M. Mitterrand stated that he had been the victim of an attempted assassination. This was transformed into a counter-accusation that he had himself arranged the apparent attempt for political reasons, and then into an accusation by M. Mitterrand that he had been the victim of a police plot. The *Action française* in the 1930s was certainly an organization whose aim was to destroy the Republic. It was not a plot, but a recognized political party, highly respected in many quarters. There is no doubt, however, that members of it were involved in a plot to assassinate Léon Blum in 1936. The Ben Barka affair of 1965 began as a simple case of the suspected murder or abduction of the Moroccan leader, but developed into a scandal involving the organization and behaviour of certain branches of the police and secret police services. The best-known affair of all, the Dreyfus affair, began as an ill-founded accusation of espionage against a Jewish army officer. It developed into a national political issue between the anti-clerical Left and the Catholic and conservative 'Establishment', which, though not aimed at overthrowing the Republic, certainly seriously weakened it for a time.

31. *v.* accounts of these in *Le Monde*, 17 and 19 February 1972.

32. *v.* for instance, Pierre Viansson-Ponté, 'Les raisons profondes', in *Le Monde*, 23 March 1972. There were reports at the time that the Prime Minister's 'departure' had been 'increasingly canvassed in Gaullist circles' (Charles Hargrove in *The Times*, 23 May 1972). The President was asked in his press conference of 16 March whether he was 'still satisfied with his Prime Minister'—a question admittedly put by the representative of a left-wing paper (*Le Monde*, 18 March 1972). In fact, he was dropped a few months later.

33. In 1936, a Socialist Minister, Roger Salengro, committed suicide following false accusations that he had deserted during the first world war.

34. This was the 'Touvier affair'. M. Paul Touvier had been twice sentenced to death in his absence (1945 and 1947). After his

pardon, he was reported to be living in terror of private vengeance from resisters who had suffered at the hands of the militia.

35. *v.* Odette Keun, *I Discover the English* (John Lane the Bodley Head, 1934), p. 221: 'The English themselves cannot analyse their classes . . . but they have a sixth sense about them. They know a class and they place a person in it immediately and unerringly – by instinct.'

36. Quoted by Jean-Marie Cotteret and René Moreno in *Le Vocabulaire du Général de Gaulle* (Armand Colin, 1969). The authors base this statement on an analysis of 62,471 words used by General de Gaulle in 46 speeches and interviews between 1956 and 1965 (*v.* review of this book by Alain Duhamel in *Le Monde*, 23 January 1972).

37. M. Mollet's exact words in a speech to a Socialist conference in July 1958 were:

> . . . this man, of whom it has been said – and rightly, as I have myself said a hundred times in public meetings – that he was not brought up as a Republican [*il n'était pas un Républicain de formation*], nevertheless realized that at one time he had saved the nation that he served, because the Republicans were on his side, and for that reason he became a Republican.

Cf. also M. Mollet's letter to General de Gaulle of 25 May 1958, in which he said: 'Even in the calmest hours of the Republic that you restored to us, I proclaimed my conviction that you do not want dictatorship, because you refused it when it was offered to you.' (*v.* text of this letter in *The Thirteenth of May: The Advent of de Gaulle's Republic*, ed. Charles S. Maier and Dan S. White, Oxford U.P., 1968, p. 310.)

38. On this *v.* André Siegfried, op. cit., p. 57, 'Les Partis en tant qu'issus de la Révolution française.'
v. also Jean Guéhenno, *Jeunesse de la France* (Grasset, 1936), pp. 60–1:

> France, the France of today, is young, quite young. Her history goes back no more than 150 years. The Revolution made her. . . . Renan used to say that it would soon be necessary to teach two brands of ancient history. He meant that the history of Europe before the Revolution

would soon seem to us as ancient as that of the Greeks and Romans. . . .

39. *v.* Guéhenno, op. cit.: 'The fundamental uniqueness of the French people, as I see it, is the union in their minds of aristocratic feeling and democratic ideas, of respect for personal merit and faith in equality.'

40. *Le Monde*, 27 May 1972.

CHAPTER II

1. Gaullists in the National Assembly numbered only 20 in 1958. Pierre Viansson-Ponté, in his *Histoire de la République Gaullienne* (Fayard, 1970, Vol. I, p. 28), quotes the results of a questionnaire carried out by *Paris-Presse* (10 May 1958), in which 34 prominent politicians and political personalities were asked whether they were in favour of an appeal to General de Gaulle. Four were categorically against; four refused to commit themselves; six would not do so without more information regarding General de Gaulle's opinion on current political issues. These included at least four former Prime Ministers and a politician about to become the next Prime Minister of the Fourth Republic. Only one – the right-wing Deputy, Paul Antier, who had been among the first to rally to de Gaulle in 1940 – expressed himself as explicitly in favour.

2. Viansson-Ponté, op. cit., Vol. I, p. 41.

3. *Mémoires d'Espoir, Le Renouveau* (Plon, 1970), p. 37 (English translation, *Memoirs of Hope*, Weidenfeld & Nicolson, 1971, p. 33).
   v. also *L'Effort*, p. 35 (English translation, p. 312), where he says that in 1962, the opposition of politicians to the referendum was strengthened by the fact that his success would 'put paid to the hopes they cherished of seeing me depart'.

4. For accounts of the events of and following 13 May, *v.* in particular, Charles de Gaulle, *Mémoires d'Espoir, Le Renouveau*; Charles S. Maier and Dan S. White (eds), *The Thirteenth of May*; *The Advent of de Gaulle's Republic*; *Problems in European History*: a documentary collection (Oxford U.P., 1968); Philip M. Williams and Martin Harrison, *De Gaulle's Republic* (Longmans, 1960), Part II; Jules Moch, *Rencontres avec . . . de Gaulle* (Plon, 1971), Part II. Among journalistic accounts, *v.* Alexander Werth, *The De Gaulle Revolution* (Robert Hale,

1960); Sirius, *Le Suicide de la IVe République* (Editions du Cerf, 1958); Jean Ferniot, *Les Ides de Mai* (Plon, 1958); Viansson-Ponté, op. cit., Vol. I, Chapters 1–3. Among accounts by political scientists, *v.* Jacques Chapsal, *La Vie politique en France depuis 1940* (Presses universitaires de France, 1966), Part I, Chapter VIII, Part II, Chapter I, which include useful bibliographies. Among accounts by politicians, *v.* Léo Hamon, *De Gaulle dans la République* (Plon, 1958); Guy Mollet, *13 mai 1958–13 mai 1962* (Plon, 1962). Among accounts by biographers, *v.* Paul-Marie de la Gorce, *De Gaulle entre deux Mondes* (Fayard, 1964), Chapters 14–17; Aidan Crawley, *De Gaulle* (Collins, 1969), Chapters XX and XXI.

5. For accounts of this aspect of the events, *v.* Serge and Merry Bromberger, *Les treize Complots du treize mai* (Fayard, 1959); Jean-Raymond Tournoux, *Secrets d'Etat* (Plon, 1960), Part III.

6. The 329 included 42 Socialists out of 95, 70 members of the Christian Democrat MRP out of 74, 24 Radicals out of 42, 40 members of various left-centre groups, 15 out of 20 Social Republicans (Gaullists), 103 out of 108 members of conservative groups, 30 Poujadists and 3 Deputies on the extreme Right. The 224 who voted against included 141 out of 142 Communists, 6 near-Communists, 49 Socialists together with 2 African Socialists, 18 Radicals, 3 MRP, 5 left-centre and 2 conservatives (*Année politique*, 1958, p. 71).

7. Viansson-Ponté, op. cit., Vol. I, p. 59.

8. On 8 August to the Consultative Constitutional Committee (11th session) (*Travaux préparatoires de la Constitution, Avis et Débats*, La Documentation française, 1960), p. 118.

9. Maier and White, op. cit., p. 274.

10. The prime-ministerial declaration was the shortest in Republican history – between 500 and 600 words. General de Gaulle did not remain in the National Assembly for the following debate, though he did return the following day and took part in the debate on the Bill to amend article 90 of the Constitution. He did not present a list of his proposed Ministers, as article 45 of the 1946 Constitution (as amended) required.

11. *v. 13 mai 1958–13 mai 1962* (p. 29). In his letter to General de Gaulle giving the reasons for his resignation from the Government, he wrote: 'I regret none of my decisions since May. I am happy and proud to have been able to help you to re-establish Republican institutions on a more solid basis. . . .'

12. For the text of this press conference, *v. Année politique*, 1958, p. 534. Maier and White, op. cit., give an English translation (p. 287).

13. For results of the referendum and of the general elections, *v. Année Politique*, 1958, pp. 591 and 145.

14. Preface to ibid., 1958, p. xv.

15. *v. Mémoires d'Espoir, Le Renouveau*, p. 21 (English translation, p. 17): 'I had played no part whatsoever either in the local agitation, or the military movement, or the political schemes which provoked it, and I had no connection with any elements on the spot or any minister in Paris. . . . It is true that two or three enterprising individuals, who had participated in my public activity at the time when I still engaged in it, spent their time in Algeria spreading the idea that one day the fate of the country would have to be entrusted to me. But they did it without my endorsement and without having even consulted me.'

v. also the evidence of Jules Moch (op. cit., p. 160), who was Minister of the Interior in M. Pflimlin's Government from 15 May onwards: 'Did General de Gaulle inspire these barely legal activities (*à la limite de la légalité*)? There is no justification for believing that he did, and I do not believe it.'

v. also André Siegfried (*Année politique*, 1958, p. x): 'Foreigners have sometimes suspected this great Frenchman of being a plotter. That is not and never has been true . . . he makes no secret of the fact that, if he is to accede to power, it must be following a delegation within the framework of existing regular institutions. . . .'

16. On General de Gaulle's own conception of his 'legitimacy', *v.* Vol. I, pp. 135–6.

17. *v.* Jules Moch, op. cit., p. 258, where he reports that the Generals commanding the four Southern military regions (Bordeaux, Toulouse, Marseilles and Lyons) were all openly sympathetic to the Algiers insurgents. M. Moch reports also (p. 267) that the Minister of National Defence had given the Prime Minister the following information: '. . . although apparently disciplined, the army is in a state of moral rebellion. Nor can the police be counted on to be wholly loyal.' *v.* also ibid., p. 278.

18. Ibid., p. 278.

The visits to Colombey-les-deux-Eglises included one by the

former conservative Prime Minister, M. Antoine Pinay (22 May), meetings between the Prime Minister, M. Pierre Pflimlin and General de Gaulle (26 May) and between the latter and the presidents of the two parliamentary assemblies (28 May), the visits to General de Gaulle of the former President of the Republic, M. Vincent Auriol (28 May), and of the secretary-general of the Socialist party, M. Guy Mollet, accompanied by M. Maurice Deixonne (30 May). Letters to General de Gaulle from M. Guy Mollet (25 May) and M. Vincent Auriol (26 May), together with the General's replies, were communicated to the *comité directeur* of the Socialist party on 30 and 31 May, along with oral reports of these meetings. Taken in conjunction with the President of the Republic's message to Parliament on 29 May, this coming and going (most of which was known to a fairly wide circle) was bound to create rumours and anxiety. (*v.* ibid., p. 283.)

19. Reported in ibid., p. 273.
20. The texts of these three declarations are given in annexe of *Année politique*, 1958, pp. 534 and 539. The letters of MM. Auriol and Mollet to General de Gaulle, and the replies, are given on pp. 537–9.
21. *v.* Moch, op. cit., pp. 260 and 270.
22. *v.* ibid., pp. 298, 300 and 306. M. Moch states that his account is reproduced textually from notes taken by him at the meeting. He reports M. Guy Mollet as saying:

> De Gaulle began by analysing the situation. . . . The system is in his view solely responsible. That is his first preoccupation.
>
> The second is to put our house in order, especially the army, which must be made to obey. He did not disavow the soldiers, he said, because he was anxious to restore order rather than to denounce disorder. He was brutally severe in his references to the men of Ajaccio and even to the men of Algiers. (p. 197)
>
> . . . The authorities bear a heavy responsibility; but he does not put them all in the same basket (*il ne les met pas toutes dans le même sac*). . . . There will be tremendous difficulties in restoring order. As for the basic problem, the ultras will no longer cry '*Vive de Gaulle!*' when they realize what he wants to do. (p. 300)

M. Vincent Auriol, he says, reported de Gaulle as saying: 'The men of Algiers know that I do not take orders from the Generals (*je ne suis pas l'homme des généraux*).'

23. *v. Mémoires d'Espoir, Le Renouveau*, p. 90 (English translation, p. 84): 'Most of the officials and soldiers responsible for carrying out policy, whether on the spot or in Paris, felt that my authority was necessary and must be obeyed. But familiar illusions about Algeria died hard. . . . Michel Debré himself in all loyalty took responsibility for all my proposals. He was in any case aware that in matters of State it is reason that must prevail. But he suffered and did not hide it. On the morning when I showed him, before delivering it, the speech in which I predicted that "one day there will be an Algerian Republic", he could not contain his chagrin.'

24. Speech made at the meeting of the *Conseil national de la Résistance* on 12 September 1944 (*Année politique*, 1944–5, p. 441).

25. *Le Monde*, 31 July 1963.

26. *Année politique*, 1944–5, p. 440.

27. In this connection, the reactions of both M. Guy Mollet and M. Jules Moch to an observation made by the President of the Republic, M. René Coty, are perhaps interesting. In his report to the executive of the Socialist party of his interview with the President, M. Mollet (as reported by Jules Moch) quoted the President as commenting on General de Gaulle's suggestions regarding the procedure for amending article 90 of the existing Constitution as follows: 'General de Gaulle's ideas on this subject are somewhat nebulous. He is not a lawyer. If he had been a jurist, he would not have been the man of 18 June.'

'This phrase [said M. Moch] impressed Guy Mollet and seemed to me, too, to be correct as well as profound' (op. cit., p. 296). In other words, both men, although anxious that General de Gaulle's return to power should be seen to be in accordance with legal and constitutional requirements, were more interested in obtaining satisfaction on certain broad basic principles than in insisting rigidly on the dotting of every 'i' and the crossing of every procedural 't'. But for them, as for the majority of Frenchmen, as, indeed, for General de Gaulle himself, the verdict of 'universal suffrage' was and remained the ultimate test.

28. *Mémoires d'Espoir, Le Renouveau*, p. 42 (English translation, p. 38).

29. Ibid., pp. 42–4 (English translation, pp. 38–40).

30. Five small territories (later increased to six) opted to remain within the Republic.
31. This possibility was offered to the African States verbally by General de Gaulle during his tour of these countries in August 1958.
32. The States obtained preference for their exports in French markets and accorded French exports preference in their own markets. They negotiated a fresh agreement with the Six in order to remain associated with the Common Market, and this agreement, signed at Yaoundé in 1963, was renewed for a further five years in 1969. The agreement gives them considerable protection from competition from the English-speaking African States, and these advantages were written into the Accession Treaty signed by Great Britain in 1972 (*Protocol 22*, Part II, paragraph 2).
33. *Mémoires d'Espoir, Le Renouveau*, p. 49 (English translation, p. 45).
34. Ibid, pp. 49–50 (English translation, pp. 45–6).
35. Quoted by Jules Moch (op. cit., pp. 307 and 306), as reported by M. Auriol to the Socialist party executive on 31 May 1958. cf. the report made by the Socialist secretary-general, M. Guy Mollet, to the party executive of his own interview with General de Gaulle on 30 May, in the course of which the General had said, apropos of Algeria:

> The eventual solution is a federal Algeria (*le fédéralisme interne*). I am thinking of an Algeria that will be a federation of ethnic communities: Kabyles, Arabs, Mozabites, Berbers, Europeans and Jews. All this will be done in such a way that no majority will be able to impose its will on the minority constituted by one of these communities. (ibid., pp. 300–1)

36. Ibid., pp. 50–1 (English translation, p. 46).
37. Ibid., p. 49 (English translation, p. 44).
    The following extract from General de Gaulle's instructions to the newly appointed Delegate-General for Algeria in December 1958 illustrates the application of his principle of pragmatism:

> The Algerian problem is a matter between the entire French nation and Algeria as she really is, not between France and

sections of the Algerian population seeking either to compel France to desert Algeria or to impose an arbitrary solution. The Government's purpose, despite delays and ordeals, is that the French nation shall enable the real Algeria to take shape.

38. For a more detailed study of the stages leading to the ending of the Algerian war, *v.* the author's *Algeria and France* (Methuen, 1963, and New York, Praeger, 1963).

39. The offer of the so-called *paix des braves* was made in General de Gaulle's broadcast just before the 1958 election. He called on the Algerian nationalists to lay down their arms and seek an honourable peace. The offer was refused, as it was bound to be. The nationalists could not afford to lay down their arms without guarantees that the French would not turn a cease-fire into a French military victory.

40. Municipal elections were held in 85 per cent of Algeria's 1485 *communes*, and 60 per cent of the electors voted. Of some 14,000 Councillors elected, over 11,000 were Moslems. Moslem women (who had not voted until the general election of 1958) were also able to become accustomed to voting.

41. For text of this declaration, *v. Année politique*, 1959, pp. 629–30. The declaration was followed by a message from the President to the army in Algeria emphasizing that, after a period 'which would probably be some years away', a referendum would be held that would constitute 'a wholly free choice', and that he was counting on the army's loyal discipline and acceptance of his decisions.

42. General de Gaulle paid a visit to the army in Algeria in the weeks following the revolt. This was considered as part of the setback by many who favoured a progressive solution in Algeria and were counting on the General to obtain one. It was popularly known as *la tournée des popottes* (the round of visits to officers' messes) and, though no communiqués were issued giving details of what he said in the course of these visits, reports that leaked out gave the impression that he had made some verbal concessions to supporters of *Algérie française*. He himself denied that this was so. (*v. Le Renouveau*, p. 92, English translation, p. 86.)

43. The gradual evolution of French opinion on the representativeness of the GPRA is illustrated by Jacques Chapsal, who points out that it was first referred to in the French press as

the so-called GPRA, then as the GPRA in inverted commas, and finally simply as the GPRA without inverted commas. (*La Vie politique en France*, Presses universitaires de France, 1966, p. 415n.)

44. *v.* for instance, his press conferences of 11 April and 5 September 1961 and broadcast of 2 October of the same year (*Année politique*, 1961, pp. 646, 667 and 674). The reference to Algeria in the first is clearly expressive of irritation:

> If the Algerian people finally decide to allow themselves to to be persuaded to choose a rupture with France that would involve our ceasing to take further interest in their future, we shall raise no objection. We shall naturally cease forthwith to sacrifice our men, our resources and our money in a hopeless enterprise. We shall ask those of our nationals still living in Algeria, and who will be at too much risk, to leave, and we shall return to their own country those Algerians living in France who will then have ceased to be French. If this happens, some residents in Algeria (and we have a reasonable idea of the areas in which they live) will probably wish to remain French. They have as much right to self-determination as the others. They would have no obligations to a new country to which they did not belong, to an Algerian sovereignty that had never existed, or to an Algerian State that had still to be born. We should, therefore, in the first instance, 'regroup' these people in order to be able to protect them. As for the future, we should have to wait and see.

45. For instance, the demonstration at the Salle de la Mutualité in Paris of 27 October 1960, expressions of protest by religious opinion both Catholic and Protestant on 1 November, the demonstration in favour of negotiation by eleven 'democratic organizations' (trade unions and left-wing parties, excluding Communists and PSU) on 19 January 1961, the 'anti OAS day' in favour of peace called by trade unions in Paris on 19 December 1961. There were also demonstrations by Moslems in Paris, especially on 17 October 1961.

46. The signatories of the Manifesto (originally 121) included Jean-Paul Sartre, Simone de Beauvoir, Vercors, and left-wing writers, including well-known fellow travellers. It was signed in July 1960, and its contents were published on 6 September in the national press.

47. A few weeks earlier, a number of Moslem Deputies and Senators had come out openly in favour of negotiations with the FLN.

48. The trial of the Abbé Davezies in 1962 was especially important, in that witnesses included highly respected political personalities and officials, one of whom, M. Paul Teitgen, had actually resigned from his post as head of the Algiers police, owing to the evidence that he possessed of the existence of the practice of torture by French authorities. The allegation had been made earlier, and especially in *La Question* (Editions de Minuit, 1958) by Henri Alleg, the Communist editor of *Alger républicain*, which described how he himself had been tortured. The evidence of a high official such as M. Paul Teitgen was, however, impressive and incontrovertible. On this, *v.* Pierre Vidal-Nacquet, *Torture: Cancer of Democracy* (Harmondsworth, Penguin Special, 1963). He was a signatory of the Manifesto of 121, and was a well-known member of the extreme Left, whose sympathies were wholly on the side of the nationalists (as were those of Henri Alleg), but he does quote a great deal of very impressive evidence from sources in no way suspect of Communist sympathies. *v.* also the book published later by General Massu (*La Bataille d'Alger*) in which he defended the use of torture by the French army in Algeria.

49. On this *v.* the following extract from an anonymous report by nine national-servicemen:

> One has to have heard one's comrades – good chaps – describe, sometimes with a conspiratorial smile, the horrors they have witnessed or taken part in: torture, summary executions, reprisals. Sometimes they try hurriedly to justify themselves: 'we are rotters, but then so are the FLN. This is a ruthless war. It's inevitable.'
>
> One has to have heard them in order to grasp the kind of situation they find themselves in, and how it weighs on them. . . . Consciences deteriorate with frightening rapidity. Perhaps, looking back when they have returned to France, they will be able to face these problems squarely again, to ask themselves if they had not gone too far. Will they have breakdowns as a result? Will they be able to forget? Ought they to forget? (Quoted in *Esprit*, 1961, pp. 19–20).

For a moving account of the moral problems created by the use of terrorism and violence on both sides, *v.* Germaine Tillion, *Les Ennemis complémentaires* (Editions de Minuit, 1960).

50. These OAS attacks began in April 1961 and by August of that year there had been over 1000 incidents in Algeria. By October there had been 726 in France. On 23 November 1961, there were 13 '*plasticages*' in Paris in a single day. (Viansson-Ponté, op. cit., Vol. I, pp. 534, 538, 540 and 541.)

51. Figures given by the Government spokesman, following the meeting of the Council of Ministers of 31 March 1966 (*Le Monde*, 1 April 1966). *v.* also figures given in ibid. of 2, 22 and 23 March 1966. FLN prisoners held by France were released in 1962 on the application of the Evian agreement.

52. These interests were by no means politically agreed. In the referendum of April 1972, the three main associations of *rapatriés*, the FNR (*Front national des Rapatriés*), the ANFANOMA (*Association nationale des Français d'Afrique du Nord d'Outre-Mer et leurs Amis*) and the RANFRAN (*Rassemblement national des Français d'Afrique du Nord*), all gave different advice to their members on how to vote. The first advised abstention, the second 'Yes' and the third left members to decide for themselves. (*v. Le Monde*, 22 April 1972.)

53. *v.* Michel Legris, 'Les Rapatriés: Un parti sans parti', in *Le Monde*, 30 and 31 May and 1 June 1972. He mentions, among towns most likely to have at least one candidate representing *rapatriés*: Toulouse, Toulon, Avignon, Montpellier, Nice.

54. Ibid., 30 May 1972 – 'Des Statistiques difficiles'. *v.* also Robert Buron ('Algériens d'Algérie et Algériens français' in *Le Monde*, 30 May 1972), who points out that later arrivals from Algeria often had difficulty in obtaining French citizenship, owing to the fact that the provisions of the 1962 law giving those of French origin automatic right to French citizenship lapsed in 1967, and that some Moslems who were in France and elected to remain there had not necessarily wanted at first to become French citizens, and so encountered difficulties later when they changed their minds.

55. *v.* Chapter III, pp. 71–4.

56. *v.* pp. 118–21 and 361.

57. Ordinance of 7 February 1959. At that time only 12 towns had

populations of 120,000 and over. For the following municipal elections in 1965, the law was to be changed again. Under a law of 16 June 1964, the list system with two ballots was to be used for municipal elections in all towns, but for towns of over 30,000, lists were to be 'blocked', that is, they could not be modified either by *panachage* (inserting names from another list) or by preferential votes. This reform met with some criticism, because *'listes bloquées'* meant, in practice, that electoral alliances had to be concluded at the first ballot, which leaves much less room for electoral manœuvring. In the 1965 elections, too, the three largest towns, Paris, Lyons and Marseilles, were divided into sectors.

58. The main provisions of the Ordinance of 7 January 1959 were to give the Government the right to declare a state of alert (*la mise en garde*) without having to consult Parliament, the extension of the period of military service from 18 to 24 months and the establishment of a new Defence Committee headed by the President of the Republic. The *loi-programme*, voted on 8 December, after three motions of censure in the National Assembly (24–5 October, 22 November and 6 December) and two defeats in the Senate (9–10 November, 30 November), met with hostility, almost exclusively owing to the provisions for an independent, national, nuclear force, though it was also concerned with a comprehensive reorganization and modernization of conventional forces. It provided for a three-tier organization of national defence: the *Défense opérationnelle du territoire* (DOT); the *Forces d'intervention*; and the *Force nucléaire stratégique*. The first was, as its title suggested, essentially a home-defence force; the second was intended for frontier defence, co-operation with NATO, and use overseas.

59. This list includes only the main social and economic plans, which aroused political and parliamentary interest and controversy. There were also, in the early months as well as during the following years, a number of reforms, mainly of a technical and non-controversial character, most of which were of little general interest. They included, for instance, plans for the re-siting of the Paris fruit and vegetable markets, for the extension of health insurance to agriculture, the encouragement of scientific research, electrification. . . . In all, the years 1959–61 saw the passage of 231 laws; some of these were comprehensive, long-term *'lois de programme'*, concerned with

the reform and development of the administrative, social and economic systems.

60. In his speech of 28 December 1958, General de Gaulle described and defended these measures. The situation, he said, remained precarious.

> With my Government, I have, therefore, decided to put our affairs truly and thoroughly in order. . . . We have taken, and shall apply, a whole series of financial, economic and social measures to place the nation on a basis of truth and severity, which alone can enable it to build up prosperity. I do not pretend that this will not impose hardship on our country. But the restoration that we are aiming at will well repay the cost.

The general aim, he went on, was to prevent inflation and encourage investment. The specific measures taken would include

> . . . increases in company tax and taxes on high incomes; taxes on wine, spirits and tobacco; the suppression of a number of State subsidies, especially on consumption goods; reduction of expenditure on nationalized industries, especially railways; the elimination of the deficit in the social-insurance funds; the suppression of ex-servicemen's pensions, except in cases of need or ill-health (though pensions to widows, orphans and cripples would naturally be unchanged); the abolition of those '*indexations*' of prices that are really expressions of lack of confidence in our currency. . . . (*Année politique*, 1958, p. 568)

61. Ibid., 1962, p. 700.
62. Ibid., 1961, pp. 673, 681; 1962, pp. 625, 700.
63. Ibid., 1961, p. 681.
64. Ibid., 1959, p. 603.
65. Ibid., 1958, p. 638.
66. In January 1958, the Prime Minister, M. Félix Gaillard, had been obliged to agree to a debate on this subject, in spite of the fact that his proposal for annual instead of quarterly payments had already been voted in principle. The Government, having made the agenda a question of confidence, was bound to win, but two days were wasted in debate in order to allow Deputies to explain to their constituents that their hand had

been forced. The amount of the pension at that time, in the words of the *Manchester Guardian*'s Paris correspondent Darsie Gillie, scarcely sufficed 'for a quarterly round of drinks' (15 January 1958). Some 4½ million payments were made (which meant in reality that 3½ million people received them, since some people received more than one payment). Reductions in the total amounts payable were made in the 1959 budget (which was passed by ordinance, and so without any discussion in Parliament). When it came to voting the 1960 budget at the end of 1959, Deputies objected to the fact that only partial restoration of payments had been made. 35 new francs per head were to be paid to those over 65 who had been deprived of pensions the previous year – the cost to the revenue being 20 million new francs. The estimated increase in civil expenditure alone amounted in 1960 to 2240 million new francs (*Année politique*, 1959, pp. 180–1 and 136). The Parliamentary Commission was asking for the restoration of the full payment to those over 65, amounting to 143 new francs per head per annum.

67. These sought to restrict the privilege to '*bona fide*' producers – a provision that would have cut out a considerable element of the clandestine trade in duty-free spirits.

68. For a detailed account of the prolonged battle between Government and Parliament on this issue, *v.* Philip Williams, *The French Parliament 1958–1967* (Allen & Unwin, 1968), pp. 85–9.

69. Between 1951 and 1959, only some 5000 million francs out of a total subsidy of 33,000 millions had gone to Catholic schools. The rest had gone to the State schools, because anti-clericals refused to agree to a subsidy for Catholic schools unless the State schools also received one. The subsidy to State schools provided considerable funds for improving school equipment.

70. Prefectoral reports commented, as did many Deputies, on the strength of feeling on this issue in the country.

71. M. Pierre-Olivier Lapie, a well-known resister appointed by General de Gaulle to be Governor of Chad in 1940, had been a member of the Consultative Assembly in Algiers, Socialist Deputy for Nancy, from 1946–56, a Minister in the short-lived Blum Government of December 1946 and Minister of Education in the Pleven and Queuille Governments of 1950–1. He was appointed President of the Com-

mission on 23 June 1959 and expelled from the party by the *Commission des Conflits* in October. (*Année politique*, 1959, p. 126.)

72. *v.* text of M. Debré's speeches, both in the National Assembly and the Senate, in *Documents relatifs à la loi scolaire du 31 décembre 1959* (Documentation française, 1960, p. 23), which also gives the text of the law and of the decree applying its provisions.

73. For M. Guy Mollet's statement in the National Assembly, *v.* report in *Année politique*, 1959, p. 154.

74. For the constitutional aspects, *v.* Vol. I, pp. 117–18 and 128.

75. An INSEE (*Institut national de la Statistique et des Etudes économiques*) study at the end of 1959 had stated that farmers' incomes were increasing at only half the rate of incomes in other sectors (*Le Monde*, 1 January 1960).
   The farmers calculated that, though they constituted 26·5 per cent of the active population, they received only 10·5 per cent of the national income.

76. *Année politique*, 1961, p. 87 (quoting *Candide*).

77. *v.* for instance, quotations in ibid., 1961, p. 101. The problems at issue and the Government's efforts to deal with them are discussed in some detail, pp. 177–82 and 221–4.

78. *Rural Revolution in France. The Peasantry in the Twentieth Century* (Oxford U.P., 1964), p. 169.

79. These included decrees of 31 July to increase funds available for improving market facilities, to fix prices for cereals and for southern wine growers. Social benefits were also promised, including an increase in farmers' family allowances and old-age pensions and in aid for young farmers, together with a diminution in health-insurance contributions payable by farmers.

80. Quoted in *Année politique*, 1961, p. 707.

81. This 'Pisani Charter' of 10 August 1962 was criticized by the Right, because State intervention to eliminate peasant farmers smacked of Socialism, and also by the extreme Left, which regarded it as a capitalist measure directed against the small farmer. As usual the plan had to be watered down somewhat to be acceptable.

82. *Année politique*, 1961, p. 681.

83. The only strikes involving a number of industries were a

one day strike on 1 February 1960 and an hour's stoppage on 23 April 1961. Both of these were political and concerned with the Algerian affair.

84. In 1962, prices increased by 4·50 per cent (on the basis of the index used, which covered 179 items), while wages rose by about 10 per cent, but there were variations as between one category and another. Increases in the private sector were in general larger than in the public sector, and those of skilled personnel larger than those of other categories.

85. For text of the Prime Minister's declaration to the National Assembly, *v. Année politique*, 1962, p. 694.

86. Ibid., p. 686.

87. *13 mai 1958–13 mai 1962*, p. 240. M. Mollet originally made the statement in a slightly different form in May 1961, when he said that 80 per cent of the French were for the President on Algeria, and 85 per cent against him on everything else.

88. *v.* Vol. I, pp. 21–3.

89. On the constitutional issues raised by the referendum of 1962, *v.* Vol. I, pp. 118–22.

90. *Année politique*, 1962, p. 678.

91. *v.* the following passage from his broadcast of 4 October (ibid.): 'Once again the result will express the nation's decision on an essential matter. . . . It is your answers that will decide on 28 October whether I can and should pursue my task in the service of France.'

92. Abstentions in the constitutional referendum of 13 October 1946 had reached 31·4 per cent. The weather was said to have been bad on the day of the referendum. The Constitution which the electors were being asked to approve was also not popular, being the result of compromises made necessary by the defeat of the first draft the previous April.

93. That the Left was very conscious of this fact is indicated by post mortems within the party. *v.* for instance, the suggestions of André Philip (*Le Monde*, 30 November 1962, 'Les fautes de la Gauche') that the reasons for the Left's failure were the majority's abuse of its right to use the radio, the rôle of General de Gaulle (who made four televised broadcasts during October, in which he appeared as a party leader rather than an arbiter), the depolitization of the voters and the negativism of the left-wing Cartel. He wanted new approaches more appealing to the young and new (and presumably younger)

faces in control of the party, together with a positive programme.
94. *Le Monde*, 29 November 1962.

CHAPTER III

1. *Année politique*, 1962, p. 700; ibid., 1963, p. 422.
2. *Mémoires d'Espoir, L'Effort* (Plon, 1971), p. 108 (English
   translation, *Memoirs of Hope*, Weidenfeld & Nicolson, 1971,
   p. 338).
3. *v. Année politique*, 1963, p. 18. Sub-heading: '*Les débats bud-
   gétaires ont-ils encore un intérêt?*'
4. *v.* speech by M. Gaston Monnerville to the Senate on 9
   October:

   > In a democracy, government is not by monologue. There is
   > an imperative, moral obligation to respect the country's
   > laws. It is a rule that applies to all French citizens, and in
   > the first place to the first among them, whose function it is
   > to see that the Constitution remains unassailable. (*Année
   > politique*, 1962, p. 682.)

   v. also speech to the Radical Party Congress on 30 September:

   > To the attempt to hold a plebiscite, now in process, my
   > personal reply is No. . . . It is No, because there is inten-
   > tional, deliberate, calculated and outrageous violation of the
   > Constitution of the Fifth Republic. . . . May I say that I
   > consider the motion of censure to be a direct, legal, consti-
   > tutional reply to what I call *forfaiture*. (*Année politique*, 1962,
   > p. 105.)

   The term *forfaiture* is used in French penal law to describe a
   serious criminal offence involving a dereliction of duty which,
   in the case of a President of the Republic, would be in the
   nature of treason.
5. It was reported that, following the defeat of the Government
   on 5 October 1962, the President's meeting with the presidents
   of the two assemblies consisted of a thirty-five minute interview with M. Chaban-Delmas and a three-minute interview
   with M. Monnerville, and that when, after the following
   election, the Senate *bureau* requested the normal audience with
   the President, it was informed that this would be granted only

if it were not led by its president. (*v.* Pierre Viansson-Ponté, *Histoire de la République Gaullienne* (Fayard, Vol. I, 1970, Vol. II, 1971), Vol. II, pp. 43 and 88.)

6. On the *Conseil d'Etat*'s doctrine of 'the general principles of law', *v. Conseil d'Etat, Etudes et Documents* (Imprimerie nationale, 1951), Fascicule 5, p. 28.

7. *v. L'Effort*, pp. 76–7 (English translation, p. 327).

> To accept such an injunction, especially in a matter of this kind, would clearly be to acquiesce in an intolerable usurpation. As Head of State I have a legitimacy conferred by the hardest facts of history, a mandate by virtue of my function, and a legislative mission authorized by the people's vote in a referendum. These cannot and should not be judged by a body which has no authority in law to do so, which is, on the contrary, challenging the law and has clearly been led by political circumstances to exceed its powers. For these reasons I hold the *Conseil d'Etat*'s ruling to be null and void.

8. There were objections, too, on the ground that the offences to be dealt with by the court – '*les crimes et délits de nature à porter atteinte à l'autorité de l'Etat*' – were not precisely defined in the Bill and were not defined either in the penal code. But some degree of vagueness is inherent in the definition of political crimes, such as sedition and treason. The Commission had provided a more precise definition, namely that the '*crimes et délits*' must be in connection with an individual or collective enterprise aimed at substituting an illegal authority for that of the State, which the *rapporteur* described as the first precise definition of what constituted an attack on the State.

9. *v.* extracts from M. Mitterrand's speech in the National Assembly on 3 January (quoted in *Année politique*, 1963, p. 11).

10. For an account of these devices, *v.* ibid., pp. 13–14.

11. The Bill was voted on 11 January, after some concessions had been made on one of the three main points at issue. The period during which a suspect could be held without a charge being made (*la garde à vue*) was reduced from 15 to 10 days. The vote revealed that even some Deputies belonging to Government parties had doubts regarding some of the Bill's provisions, with the result that the Bill had to go to a mixed Commission

of the two assemblies, and the final vote in the National Assembly, which followed the Commission's failure to agree on a compromise, was obtained only by the use of the *vote bloqué*.

12. It should be said also that there had previously been objections by lawyers to the abolition by the President of the *Haut Tribunal militaire*, as well as to the constitution of the *Cour militaire de Justice*. Maître Garçon, a well-known liberal lawyer, wrote in *Le Monde* (3 April 1962) on the dissolution of the *Haut Tribunal*:

> What is serious . . . is that a verdict recognizing extenuating circumstances in the case of an accused person should lead to the abolition of the court. This decision proves that the special court was set up not to judge, but to sentence, and to pronounce a specific sentence.

It is worth noting perhaps that, however justified the condemnation of the court might be, it was, in practice, due to disappear anyway at latest in July 1962 (*v.* final *décision* of 30 September 1961 on the ending of the President's special powers under article 16).

The *Conseil de l'Ordre des avocats de la Cour de Paris* condemned the ordinance setting up the *Cour militaire de Justice* in the following terms: 'It is not a court that provides citizens with the normal guarantees of justice.' (*Le Monde*, 10 November 1962.) Maître Garçon had also criticized the Act setting up the *Cour de Sûreté de l'Etat*, describing the provisions for the *garde à vue* as restoring 'the procedure of the Inquisition' (*Année politique*, 1963, p. 13).

13. Quoted in ibid., p. 11.

This cannot be rendered adequately in English. The use of the term *'le pouvoir'* was often deliberate. Under the French Constitution, the President remains irresponsible. All attacks on what is universally recognized as presidential policy (and claimed by the President himself as his policy) are, therefore, theoretically addressed to the Government. The term *'le pouvoir'* (the public authorities) can apply to both. It was often used with the intention of being understood as applying to the President.

In the speech made by M. Gaston Monnerville on 9 October (from which an extract is quoted in note 4), he was clearly referring at many points to the President of the Republic and not to the Government. *v.* for instance, the following extract:

> ... Parliament is deliberately by-passed; the authorities (*le pouvoir*) are thus violating precise and unambiguous provisions of the constitutional charter.
>
> In his recent televised talk, the President of the Republic said: 'I have the right'. With all due respect to his office, but seriously and firmly, I reply: No, Mr President, you do not *have* the right. You are *taking* it. (*Année politique, 1962,* p. 682.)

14. *v.* the account given in Viansson-Ponté, op. cit., Vol. II, p. 18. The two others condemned to death along with Lieutenant-Colonel Bastien-Thiry were reprieved and finally amnestied in 1968. André Canal, whose case was the occasion for the *Conseil d'Etat*'s ruling on the legality of the *Cour militaire*, was reprieved by the President on 28 November 1962.
15. *v. L'Effort*, pp. 46–7 (English translation, pp. 316–17).
16. Ibid., pp. 74–8 (English translation, pp. 326–8).
17. The *Conseil* regarded measures taken to apply *décisions* as belonging also to the executive field, and some of the decrees in application of *décisions*, therefore, came within their jurisdiction. *v.* examples quoted in Philip Williams and Martin Harrison, *Politics and Society in de Gaulle's Republic* (London, Longman, 1971), pp. 190–1.
18. For the ruling of the *Conseil*, together with the statement of the case, *v. Les grands Arrêts de la Jurisprudence administrative* (Sirey, 1969), No. 105, p. 504 seq.
19. *L'Effort*, p. 46 (English translation, p. 316).
20. Ibid., p. 77 (English translation, p. 327).
21. For text of these reforms, *v. Journal Officiel*, 1 August 1963, Décrets No. 63-766 of 30 July, and No. 63-767, pp. 7017 and 7113.

    But *v.* General de Gaulle's reference in *L'Effort* (p. 78): 'the necessary reform of this officious (*abusif*) body must be carried out by law'. This certainly provides confirmation of the general view that, at that time, he had intended to carry out a reform going much farther than those included in the above-mentioned decrees. The report of the body set up in January did, indeed, include reforms affecting the functions of the *Conseil*. (*v. Année politique*, 1963, pp. 39–40.)

22. Order of 3 March (signed by the President). In answer to a question at his press conference of 20 January 1967 on which of his decisions he considered the most unfortunate, the Prime Minister replied that it was the requisitioning of the miners in 1963. (*v.* Viansson-Ponté, op. cit., Vol. II, p. 104. M. Viansson-Ponté himself was the questioner.)

23. The Council of Ministers had also decided at the same meeting, on 13 March, to appoint a General Secretary to work out an energy policy, and the Minister of Finance undertook to study the effects on the budget of increased wages for nationalized industries. These two decisions had, of course, no immediate influence on the strike.

24. The general attitude was expressed in an answer to a written Parliamentary Question (*v. Journal Officiel*, A.N. 17 January 1958), which stated that the *Conseil d'Etat* recognized that Ministers could, in given circumstances, forbid strikes by civil servants, either by virtue of their functions, or because their presence at work was necessary for the continuity of services, the security of persons or property, or for official contracts necessary in essential national services. For the *Conseil d'Etat*'s important ruling in the Dehaene case in 1950, *v. Les grands Arrêts de la Jurisprudence administrative*, p. 398 seq.

25. Some trade unions were also opposed to these strikes. The FO Transport Federation dissociated itself from the 'lightning' strikes in Paris in June 1963, on the ground that they were 'inefficient, unpopular, and failed to consider the interests of passengers' (quoted in *Année politique*, 1963, p. 170).

26. On this *v.* for instance, articles in *Le Monde*, 10–11 February 1963, and *The Economist*, 23 March and 1 June.

27. *v. The Guardian*, 27 June 1963.

28. *v.* his statement to the National Assembly of 7 May 1963. Price increases amounted to 5·2 per cent in 1962. Increases in wages included a 4 per cent increase in the basic minimum wage (*salaire minimum interprofessionnel garanti*, or SMIG) applying directly to some half a million very poorly paid workers. Among special factors responsible for price increases were the increased consumption as a result of a long winter and the influx of Algerians. The price increases in the public services in fact cancelled out the benefits of the wage increases and the increases in pensions, but there was some

reduction of taxation of small taxpayers and some increase of taxation of business firms (*v.* statement by the Prime Minister to the National Assembly on 14 May 1963).

29. Quoted in *Candide*, 19–26 September 1963.

30. *v.* OECD Report on France, published in September 1963, and also Report of September 1964, which reiterates this view, attributing French inflation mainly to temporary factors, such as the increased demand by Algerian repatriates, higher railway fares in 1962 and 1963 and increasing costs owing to wage increases. The OECD reports held that the inflation was not necessarily permanent and so the various short-term measures taken by the stabilization plan in September 1963 might make the situation worse rather than better. Price blocking and failure to encourage investment might, in these circumstances, well result in the discouragement of private industries and, if there were to be a fall of demand, they might not be able to maintain employment. This was to some extent what had happened, or was happening by the middle of 1964.

31. According to the Bank of France, French expenditure on hire purchase was still far lower than that of other industrialized countries. *v.* for instance, figures quoted in *The Economist* (9 February 1963) which gives hire purchase as accounting for only 1·5 per cent of GNP as against 1·8 per cent in Germany, 2·3 per cent in Great Britain, and 7·2 per cent in the USA. It was nevertheless increasing in 1962 at a faster rate in France than in other countries.

32. The average Frenchman's standard of living increased by about 4·6 per cent in 1962. According to the Minister of Finance (statement in the National Assembly of 7 May 1963) the volume of consumption had increased by 13 per cent in 1962, while the number of consumers had increased by two million, or about 4 per cent. Increased wages and social-security payments were estimated to have led to an 11 per cent increase of spending in 1962, though GNP had increased by only 9 per cent during that year.

33. *L'Express*, 19 September 1963.

34. *Figaro*, 3 September 1963.

35. The Toutée Commission was appointed in October 1963 to study ways of improving methods of wage negotiation in the public sector. Its report was published in January 1964. *v. Notes et Etudes documentaires*, 2 March 1964, No. 3069 (La

Documentation française). An Incomes Conference was appointed at the same time under the chairmanship of M. Pierre Massé to put forward, in collaboration with trade-union and employers' organizations, suggestions for an incomes policy. It produced its report at the beginning of February.

36. Quoted in *Année politique*, 1964, p. 182.

37. By the autumn of 1964, the gap between wages in the public and private sectors was said by representatives of the former to have increased to between 6 and 7 per cent.

   The motion of censure of 27 October 1964 received 209 votes. This was the tenth censure motion of the régime, and the fifth tabled on the initiative of Deputies. *v.* Vol. I, pp. 86–7.

38. The normal economic consequences of such a policy were, of course, to some extent evaded, owing to France's ability to impose her own conceptions of Community agricultural policy on her five partners between 1965 and 1966.

39. INSEE (*Institut national de la Statistique et des Études économiques*) reports showed a slowing-down of production from July 1964 onwards. For instance, Peugeot-Sochaux was working only a 32-hour week in September 1964 and had five days' production of cars in stock. The electrical and construction industries were also suffering from a falling-off of demand.

40. Press conference of 27 December 1963 (*Le Monde*, 28 December 1963).

41. For a report of M. Giscard d'Estaing's speech, on 26 March 1965, to the Association of Economic and Financial Journalists, *v. Le Monde*, 27 March 1965. For expressions of more pessimistic views, *v.* the following: M. Antoine Pinay (at the opening session of the *Conseil général de la Loire* the previous January), who stressed the slowing down of industrial activity and the increase of short-time working (ibid., 13 January 1965); the admission by the Prime Minister that this was so, at the New Year reception for journalists (ibid., 14 January 1965); the INSEE monthly enquiry into the situation of industry in September 1964, which reported that the situation was less favourable than at any time since 1960 (quoted in Communiqué of the Council of Ministers, 12 November 1964: ibid., 13 November 1964). *v.* also articles by economic correspondents, in particular by Alain Vernholes and Gilbert Mathieu on the inadequacy of the Government's measures (ibid., 14 November 1964), on the higher rate of increase in

prices in France than in the other Common Market countries, Britain and the USA (ibid., 27 March 1965), on under-investment in France (ibid., 17–18 October 1965), and on the numbers of workers either losing their jobs or working short time (ibid., 17–18 January 1965).

42. Gérard Belorgey, *Le Gouvernement et l'Administration de la France* (Collection U, Armand Colin, 1967), p. 120.

43. Stephen S. Cohen, *Modern Capitalist Planning: The French Model* (Weidenfeld & Nicolson, 1969), pp. 29–30.

44. The first and third Plans had not been submitted to Parliament and the second had been approved by Parliament only after it had been in application for over two years. The fourth was submitted to Parliament before it came into force, but at so late a stage that the choice was merely to take it or leave it.

45. The previous Plan had not been conceived on the basis of the localization of investment, but had allocated sums to the different regions after the Plan had been voted.

46. Quoted in *Année politique*, 1964, p. 96. The Plan was then drafted and debated again in November 1965. Virtually no concessions were made to critics and the scenario in Parliament was largely a repetition of 1964, *v.* ibid., 1965, pp. 152–3.

47. On the 'package-deal' procedure, *v.* Vol. I, p. 90. On the problems of the democratization of planning, *v.* Part VI, Chapters 19–21 of Stephen Cohen's *Modern Capitalist Planning*. He examines the Left's demand for more effective, direct participation at all stages of the planning process, but, while providing statistical evidence of the relative weakness of the Left numerically, maintains that the Left is voluntarily under-represented, many more trade unionists being invited to participate than actually do. He explains the under-representation partly in terms of the trade-union sense of isolation in committees where so many of the participants know each other and have the same social backgrounds, partly in terms of the traditional opposition of trade unionists to capitalism, and therefore their reluctance to co-operate in its working, partly, too, in terms of the divisions within the trade-union movements themselves on the tactics to pursue. He sees the CGT as fundamentally opposed to such participation, the CFTC (now CFDT) as more inclined to be critically co-operative – in favour of what he calls 'contestative participation' – though he would, no doubt, modify this conclusion now that this

body has become so infiltrated by 'Leftists'. Only a very small minority of French trade unionists would share the American trade-union opinion on the acceptability of participation.

48. The desire for decentralization goes back, of course, much farther than the Third Republic. In 1788, the Girondins were in favour of a France that would be a federation of autonomous *communes*. The Jacobins, followed by Napoleon, established the modern centralized State. But there were a number of criticisms of it before the abortive efforts of regionalists under the Third Republic. The extreme Right *Action française* professed attachment to an *ancienne France*, which they saw as made up of largely independent regions under a strong but benevolent Monarchy. There were also regionalist plans during the Fourth Republic.

49. There were originally eight *Igames*, whose function was to advise the Minister on various problems affecting the region, in addition to exercising emergency powers. A decree of 18 March 1958 grouped French *préfectures* in nine regions, in each of which an *Igame* was to be authorized to act on behalf of the Minister in case of disturbances, replacing the Prefects throughout the region. With the setting up of the 1964 regional system, the *Igames* disappeared.

50. The 1968 census gives the number of *communes* as 37,708, of which 16,231 had under 300 inhabitants. These figures indicate the difficulties encountered by successive Governments in their attempts to encourage small *communes* to amalgamate.

51. *v.* Marcel Waline, *Droit administratif* (Sirey, 1959), pp. 264 and 278.

52. Programmes for regional action went back indeed to 1954–5. Under the Fifth Republic, a decree of 7 January 1959 decided on the harmonization of the different administrative regions within those of the regional plans for economic development, and one of 2 June 1960 set up 21 regions formed on the basis of economic affinities, to provide the framework for regional development.

53. *v.* for instance, M. Louis Joxe's emphasis on the need for better organization and co-ordination:

> ... The citizen finds it unreasonable that, in a single *département*, three different services should be concerned with public health and seven with agriculture; nor does it

indicate good organization when a Prefect presides over 120 administrative commissions where 20 would suffice. (*Notre République*, 3 April 1964.)

54. The plan for Paris had been applied earlier. A law of 2 August 1961 decided that the three *départements* making up the Paris region (Seine, Seine-et-Oise and Seine-et-Marne) should form the 'Paris district', whose function would be to stimulate investment and economic development in certain public services in the region as a whole. The head of the organization, the Delegate-general, was appointed by the Council of Ministers on the advice of the Prime Minister and the Minister of the Interior. With the decision that two of the three *départements*, Seine and Seine-et-Oise, should be divided into seven (the city of Paris and six others), the Regional Prefect for the new region, appointed on 10 August 1966, took over the functions of the Delegate-general for the district. The Paris region did have a Regional Administrative Conference, but no CODER. The Paris region came officially into existence only in January 1968.

55. For a description of the system, *v.* decrees of 14 March 1964 (*Journal Officiel*, 20 March 1964, decrees 64-250, 64-251 and 64-252) dealing respectively with the rôles of the Prefect and the Regional Prefect and with the constitution and functions of the advisory organs. *v.* also *Notes et Etudes documentaires*, No. 3212, 22 July 1965 (Documentation française).

56. *v.* article in *Le Monde* (12 February 1964), which states that, over the previous 50 years, during which there had been a great increase of governmental activity in the *départements*, the *services extérieurs* had increasingly escaped the control of the Prefect, with a consequent lack of co-ordination.

57. The authors of *Quelle Réforme? Quelles Regions?* (Editions du Seuil, 1969) quote the following examples of this dependence on Paris:

> Up to two years' delay in obtaining the necessary authorization from the appropriate Ministries to build a school (which usually took from three to six months); a delay of months before the Ministry of Education appointed a mathematics teacher, although the headmaster could easily have found a replacement locally; the closing down of expensive, specialist hospital equipment owing to delays in obtaining the neces-

sary authority from Paris to appoint new nurses; a delay of from five to up to seven to eight years (if there were to be objections) between the decision of a Municipal Council to create an 'urban priority area' and the completion of its first housing units (pp. 17–18).

58. Early criticisms on administrative grounds included:

(i) Divergences on the desirable size of the regions, some critics preferring a smaller number of larger regions, some (including M. Debré) being in favour of a reduction in the number of *départements* to about 50 (*v.* for instance, *Le Monde*, 3 February 1967). M. Debré believed that only such a reduction would make decentralization possible without creating dangers to the authority of the State.

(ii) The fact that some regional boundaries did not correspond with economic realities and the great differences between them in size and importance. For instance, some regions included only two *départements*, others up to seven and eight.

(iii) The strain imposed on the inadequate prefectoral and regional staffs by all the additional paper work required. During the pilot scheme carried out in selected areas before the general plan was applied, the Prefect of Seine Maritime said that, owing to the centralization of all information through the Prefect, he had had to sign 500 letters from the *direction de la conservation* alone within a period of eleven months and 100 from the social-security services within three months, whereas previously he had received no correspondence from these bodies. (*v.* article by André Passeron in *ESOPE*, 28 May 1964, 'La Réforme administrative', summarized in English in French Embassy Document number A/21/10/4, entitled *The French Administrative Reform*).

(iv) The danger of conflict, not only between Prefect and Regional Prefect, but also between the regional and departmental functions of the Regional Prefect, and especially the danger that he might, in working out priorities, favour the *département* of which he was Prefect.

59. On Socialist views, *v.* for instance, *Le Monde*, 3 February 1967, and on Communist views the plan published in *La France nouvelle*, reported in *Le Monde*, 11 September 1964.

60. *v.* for instance, the accusation by Senator Raybaud (GD) that the Government was seeking to protect prefectoral officials from the influence of local elected representatives, and by Senator Héon (GD) that the Government was unwilling to have *real* regional decentralization in the form of regional assemblies constituted by elected representatives of General Councils (*Le Monde*, 4 June 1964). A Congress of Presidents of General Councils held at Pau in September 1964 feared that the planners would seek to 'strangle elected assemblies' (ibid., 11 September 1964). *v.* extracts from speech by M. de Chevigné, president of the General Council of Basses-Pyrénées, quoted in Belorgey, op. cit., pp. 322–3.

61. Quoted by *Le Monde* (31 March 1964) from a study by the Club, *Démocratie nouvelle* (Marseilles). The Club was in favour of the abolition of the General Council and the transference of its functions to the region.

62. *Les Citoyens au Pouvoir. 12 régions, 2000 communes* (Club Jean Moulin, Editions du Seuil, 1968).

63. In practice, of course, in spite of Government encouragements to *communes* to merge, in order to form larger units, the vast majority resisted attempts to change their traditional boundaries. In ten years (1961–71) only 746 *communes* had merged, forming 350 municipalities (*Municipal Organization in France*, French Embassy Document, No. A/86/2/72, p. 3). In 1972, the Government felt it necessary to give reassurances that no *communes* would be forced to merge against their will.

64. *Quelle Réforme? Quelles Régions?*, p. 25.

65. The main exception to this rule was the *Manifeste radical*, produced by Jean-Jacques Servan-Schreiber, and accepted as the official policy of the Radical party. This comes out in favour not only of a United States of Europe, but also of a federal Europe, and of regional executives directly elected and exercising real power. 'After Europe,' he said, 'the region and the *commune* are essential to political activity as we see it.' (*Le Manifeste radical*, Denoël, 1970, p. 157.)

66. *v.* General de Gaulle's references to participation in the 1940s and in the early years of the régime: at Strasbourg, on 7 April 1947, when he spoke of the need to 'share profits and risks'; at St Etienne on 4 January 1948, when he referred to 'a different psychology from that of exploitation'; and in his New Year message for 1961 when he spoke of the need to 'end the

out-dated consequences of the former class struggle, give to those who contribute to the country's development a direct share in it . . .' (31 December 1960). Gaullist supporters were more specific in their references to participation as a means of ending the class struggle. *v.* for instance, the statement by M. Debré on 7 February 1959:

> Our weakness in the past, together with inflation, has perpetuated a sad state of deep social divisions in France. . . . Social unity will not be created by ideologies and slogans . . . but by common effort and a common hope. General de Gaulle has published an ordinance on workers' profit-sharing (*l'intéressement des travailleurs à l'entreprise*) from which, in a few years, much can be hoped for'.

67. A Government Bill on workers' participation in limited companies was actually introduced in 1913 (the *loi Chéron*), but was not voted on, as the war intervened. The subject was, however, debated in the Senate in 1917. There was, indeed, some support on the Left, in the Radical party in particular, for some form of co-ownership or for distribution to workers of some shares in the firm in which they worked, an idea supported by René Viviani, Justin Godard, and Aristide Briand.

68. *La Vie ouvrière* described the plan as '*un marché de dupes*' and a means of exploiting the workers (quoted in *Année politique*, 1959, p. 242. *v.* also some representative opinions quoted on pp. 232 and 249).

69. On the employers' side, only a relatively few idealistic reformists among the *Jeunes Patrons* shared the Government's view that participation could lead to participation in management, and then only if trade unions became better equipped and if there were an improved social climate.

70. *Année politique*, 1959, p. 233.

71. The phrase used was that the Bill should 'lay down the ways of recognizing and guaranteeing the rights of wage-earners to shares ploughed back into concerns'.

72. On this, *v.* Chapter IV, pp. 118 and 399.

73. For a readable account of this development, *v.* John Ardagh, *The New French Revolution* (Secker & Warburg, 1968), Chapters V–IX.

74. Press conference of 9 September 1965 (*Année politique*, 1965, p. 436).

75. For details of the plan, announced on 16 February 1966, *v. Année politique*, 1966, pp. 119–23.
76. The Senate is in many respects representative of local interests and especially of small-town and rural communities. Elections were held for 91 of the 274 seats. The result was that the Gaullist contingent of 30 in the Senate was reduced by two. In the cantonal elections, 977 of the 1562 cantons were concerned. The previous elections in these constituencies had been held in 1958, since General Councillors are elected for six years, a half retiring every three years. Accurate figures are always difficult to obtain because many representatives are not easily classifiable politically. The elections do not create much interest and the poll is generally very low. In 1964, 45 per cent did not vote. Under the Fourth Republic, the abstention rate was, on average, about one-third of the electorate. The results presented a picture of great stability. 77 of the 88 presidents of General Councils were re-elected. The 17 changes appeared to involve a Gaullist loss of one and an MRP gain of seven (*Le Monde*, 20 March 1964).
77. The system of election was by list-voting with two ballots, each list including up to as many candidates as there were seats to be filled. The law of 27 June 1964 introduced three main changes in towns with populations of over 30,000. They were:

   (i) The introduction of *listes bloquées*, that is, the prohibition of '*panachage*' (the selection by voters of names from different lists), and of preferential votes (changing the order of candidates on the list).
   (ii) Prohibition of changes in the composition of lists between the two ballots. This change in effect compelled parties to conclude whatever alliances they intended to conclude before the first, instead of before the second ballot, thus preventing the traditional bargaining period between the two ballots.
   (iii) Lists having failed to obtain 10 per cent of the votes at the first ballot became ineligible at the second (previously the required percentage was 5 per cent).

   In towns with populations of under 30,000, that is, accounting for two-thirds of the electors, these restrictions were not applicable.
78. Quoted in *Année politique*, 1965, p. 16.

79. For a brief account of the press activities relating to 'Monsieur X', *v.* Jacques Chapsal, *La Vie politique en France depuis 1940* (Presses universitaires de France, 1966), pp. 533–5.

80. These included in particular, Professors Georges Vedel and Maurice Duverger, both of whom had long been supporters of a form of presidential government, including the election of the President by universal suffrage. They were not, however, entirely agreed on what should be the relations between President and Parliament, and it was on this point that M. Defferre was both unsure and unconvincing.

81. Speech made at Marseilles on 12 January 1964.

82. Ibid.

83. The Socialist party was due to hold a discussion on institutional problems at its Congress in June 1964. At that time the party leadership seemed to favour a relatively passive rôle for the President of the Republic, and what was called the *contrat de législature*, involving an automatic dissolution of the National Assembly if the Government was defeated. As the campaign for the constitutional reform of 1962 had made clear, the public's response to a candidate who wanted to be President of the Republic in order to do nothing was likely to be: Why vote for him?

84. The seven priorities, as accepted by the Socialist Conference of 1–2 February 1964, were: (i) State education; (ii) democratic planning, including structural reforms through nationalization; (iii) the political and economic integration of Europe; (iv) international détente; (v) collective security, including the abolition of national nuclear forces; (vi) general and controlled disarmament; (vii) an international solidarity treaty to prevent world underdevelopment.

    These options were restated several times, often in slightly different terms. *v. Le Monde*, 6 March 1964 (speech to the Foreign Press Association) and 12 December 1964 (speech at Belfort). The statement included in the resolution voted at the Socialist Congress on 6 June 1965 was substantially the same as that accepted at the Clichy Conference.

85. M. Albert Gazier pointed out that M. Defferre was promising both to apply the Constitution and to amend it (*Le Monde*, 4 July 1964). Indeed, he was proposing to amend not only article 16, but also articles dealing with the referendum and the Constitutional Council (*v.* speech of 12 January 1964 at

Marseilles). His proposal that President and National Assembly should both be elected for five years, but that in the event of disagreement between Government and Parliament there should be a dissolution, raised some questions to which he did not supply very convincing answers. For instance, if a dissolution was accompanied by a presidential election (in order that President and Assembly should be elected for the same term), then this would mean that the country would be without President and Assembly at the same time. If, however, the Assembly was elected only for the remaining period of the presidential term, then different elections might give different results. (*v.* in particular, report of speech at Bordeaux in *Le Monde*, 11 February 1964.)

86. Quoted by Gilles Martinet (PSU) in *Le Monde*, 15 May 1965. The left-wing Gaullists were at the same time reproaching M. Defferre for his fidelity to the Atlantic Alliance. In reality, there was a great deal of difference between Gaullism and Defferrism. Apart from constitutional differences (*v.* note 85), M. Defferre's differences on policy included Atlanticism, Europeanism, disapproval of national nuclear forces, approval of structural reforms (including nationalization), and acceptance of the existing situation on the clerical issue. On some points, his 'Gaullism' was shared by the Left, including the Socialist party – for instance, the belief in 'national independence' in the sense of equality (in principle) between Europe and the United States, the fear of the economic colonization of Europe by the United States, belief in a policy of détente and aid to the 'third world' and approval for the recognition of China.

Where he differed from influential leaders of the Socialist party – and in particular from M. Mollet and his supporters – was in his readiness to avoid alienating Centre parties by insistence on provocative declarations in favour of Socialism and anti-clericalism, which both M. Mollet and his supporters regarded as essential conditions for '*un rassemblement des démocrates*'. *v.* for instance, M. Mollet's five conditions in his speech at Granges-les-Valences on 19 October 1964 (*Le Monde*, 20 October 1964): '*Etre démocrate, révolutionnaire, laïque, patriote et internationnaliste.*' Where M. Defferre differed from the left of his own party was in excluding negotiations with the Communist party except from a position of Socialist strength, when agreement had been reached with parties to the right of the Socialists.

87. The *Convention des Institutions républicaines*, which had already proposed the creation of a federation at its meeting of 24–5 April, approved of M. Defferre's proposed plan on 9 May. The *Comité de Liaison des Démocrates*, which included some members of the *Centre national des Indépendants* as well as Radicals and MRP, approved on 13 May, but the *Indépendants* almost immediately withdrew their support. The MRP Congress of 29 May welcomed it, though conditionally. The Socialist Congress of 3–6 June also supported it, in principle, and on conditions.

88. These had rapidly lost themselves in familiar quarrels. *v.* M. Mollet's statement to the National Council of the party held at Puteaux on 28–9 November 1964, in which he said that he believed that organic unity of the 'Socialist family' was possible, but that Socialists and Democrats of 'the liberal family' could not live together. (*Le Monde*, 1 December 1964.)

89. This phrase was used by M. Mollet both at the Information Conference at Clichy held on 4–5 April 1964 (ibid., 6 April 1964) and in his speech at the party Congress of 3–6 June 1965 (ibid., 6–7 June). He objected to the wording of M. Defferre's proposed Charter, on the ground that the word 'Socialism' was missing. 'The distinctive characteristic of the Socialist party,' he said, 'is that it regards the liberation of man as dependent on the abolition of the capitalist régime and that it is essentially revolutionary.'

90. M. Jules Moch said that he could not support M. Defferre. 'What programme does the MRP propose?' he asked. 'There is no question of Socialism in it any more than there is of secularism [*la laïcité*].' (*Le Monde*, 5 June 1965.)

91. In *Un nouvel Horizon*, M. Defferre had said that 'The only way to shift the Communist party is to set up alongside it a more powerful and more dynamic organization' (quoted in Chapsal, op. cit., p. 545).

92. On the internal quarrels of the PSU, *v.* Vol. I, pp. 253–8.

93. M. Waldeck Rochet at the 17th Congress of the Communist party (*Le Monde*, 15 May 1964).

94. Speech at the 55th Congress of the Socialist party held at Clichy from 3–6 June 1965 (ibid., 5 June 1965).

95. Viansson-Ponté, op. cit., Vol. II, p. 145. The *Centre démocrate* did not want the word 'Socialist' to figure in the title of the proposed federation and also wanted to defer its creation until after the presidential election.

The quarrel about anti-clericalism is a perfect example of the insuperable obstacles to agreement. M. Defferre was in trouble with his own party on account of the following statement made on 3 December 1964 at a meeting at the Ecole des Mines: 'When I am told that all that has been done for denominational education since 1951 – the Barangé and Debré laws – should be abolished by a stroke of the pen, I remain unconvinced.' (*Le Monde*, 10–11 January 1965.)

The following day, *l'Humanité* predicted an alliance between Socialists and MRP and ten days later published an attack on him by M. Waldeck Rochet on the ground that he was 'encouraging opponents of *l'école laïque* to present new conditions'. Various anti-clerical trade-union organizations then took the matter up, and M. Defferre, alleging that he had been badly reported, said: (i) that he believed in 'public funds for public schools and private funds for private schools' – a phrase open to different interpretations, and (ii) that he believed in 'freedom of conscience' 'in the spirit of the separation of Church and State', which begged the question as to whether he was or was not in favour of allowing Catholic education to be given on the premises of State schools by chaplains, a problem much discussed at the time. When the resolution voted at the Socialist Congress on 6 June deliberately included in the conditions of the proposed federation the very words used by M. Defferre and objected to by the MRP, this was regarded as anti-clerical provocation, while the terms of the very cautious approval of the federation in the resolution voted at the MRP Congress had been regarded as no less provocatively anti-Socialist. For texts of the two resolutions, *v. Année politique*, 1965, pp. 432 and 433.

96. *The Economist*, 8 February 1964.

M. Defferre was without M. Mendès France, because the latter refused to be associated with any organization opposed to revision of the article of the Constitution providing for the election of the President of the Republic by universal suffrage. Both M. Defferre and M. Mendès France had voted against General de Gaulle on 1 June 1958. But the former had changed his mind later and finally voted in favour of the Constitution of 1958. M. Mendès France did announce on 27 October 1965 that he would support the candidature of M. Mitterrand. M. Mitterrand, however, was not proposing the revision of this article either.

97. Jean Cau in *Le Monde*, 3 December 1965. Cf. his comment in ibid., of 9 December, just after the first ballot: '. . . a vote for M. Mitterrand is a vote for lies, for an ephemeral, botched-up programme that has neither content nor future'.

98. They were: (i) stability of institutions; (ii) respect for public liberties; (iii) support for the Atlantic Alliance and supra-nationalism; (iv) opposition to France's nuclear deterrent; (v) support for democratic planning; (vi) support of social policies, e.g. raising of the minimum wage, and (vii) support for State education, in which 'public funds should serve public schools'. (*Le Monde*, 23 September 1965, report of M. Mitterrand's press conference of 21 September.) For text of the Charter of 10 September, *v. Année politique*, 1965, p. 442. These principles were reaffirmed in later declarations (*v. Le Monde*, 28 September and 24 November 1965).

M. Mitterrand retained M. Defferre's undertakings to respect the Constitution and to amend it. *v.* for instance, his statement reported in ibid., 24 November 1965: '*J'appliquerai loyalement la Constitution. Le peuple français l'a votée*'.

99. They were: (i) priority to productive expenditure; (ii) social justice; (iii) regional development; (iv) stimulation of private initiative; (v) the construction of Europe (radio programme on 24 November; *v.* ibid., 26 November 1965).

100. General de Gaulle's broadcast of 27 April 1965, widely re-garded as an unofficial opening of his presidential campaign, was almost entirely devoted to foreign policy, and especially to his policy of European independence of the United States, an objective shared by the supporters of a supranational Europe.

101. The four candidates who were eliminated at the first ballot obtained respectively 15·8 per cent (M. Lecanuet); 5·3 per cent (M. Tixier-Vignancour); 1·7 per cent (M. Marcilhacy); and 1·2 per cent (M. Barbu).

102. It is difficult to know exactly how many of M. Lecanuet's votes were shared by the two contenders in the second ballot and how many were wasted. In his study of the election results in

French Politicians and Elections, 1951–1969 (Cambridge, Cambridge U.P., 1960), Philip Williams estimated that, although M. Lecanuet had drawn his main support from much the same areas as General de Gaulle, he had tended to win support among the young rather than the old, men rather than women, and managers rather than shopkeepers. He believed that, in the second ballot, 30–60 per cent (according to regions) of the more conservative electors who had voted for M. Lecanuet transferred their votes to M. Mitterrand, while, over the whole country, somewhat more Lecanuet votes were transferred to General de Gaulle than to M. Mitterrand. But he also noted that: 'The turn-out fell most and the spoiled ballots were commonest in the most right-wing of M. Lecanuet's strongholds' (pp. 198–9).

103. *Le Monde*, 19–20 December 1965. *v.* also letter to *The Economist* (5 March 1966) from a Frenchman who claimed that 'many Frenchmen of all shades of opinion are convinced that their only choice is between "a real government" and "*la pagaie*" (a mess). They reject "*la pagaie*" because it made them feel ashamed for many years before 1958.'

104. *Le Monde*, 21 December 1965, 'Le troisième tour'.

105. The main speculations concerned (i) the extent to which voting had been influenced by the unpopularity of the stabilization plan, and by economic and social preoccupations in general; (ii) the extent to which the popularity of General de Gaulle's foreign policy had increased the Gaullist vote, especially among the working class; (iii) the extent to which traditional Left–Right polarization had been important, and, if it had, whether that would help to explain the relative strength of the Gaullist vote north of the Loire and of the Mitterrandist vote in the traditionally Radical and Socialist regions of the South and South-West; (iv) the effect on the vote of the television campaign, and especially of the admirable performances of General de Gaulle and M. Lecanuet. For detailed electoral studies *v. Projet, Esprit, La revue française de sociologie* and *Preuves* for February 1966.

106. If the pollsters were right in thinking that foreign policy had played a considerable part in influencing votes in the presidential election, then this was an important point. Certainly commentators stressed the absence of interest in foreign affairs in the 1967 elections. *v.* for instance, the following comment

by the leader-writer of *Le Monde* (8 March 1967) immediately
after the first ballot:

> It must be noted that, in general, the important external
> problems have played almost no part in the campaign, in
> contrast to the presidential campaign, when M. Lecanuet's
> European policy helped him against General de Gaulle's
> Common Market policy.
>
> As to France's withdrawal from the Atlantic organization,
> it is a sign of the times that it should have been accepted
> without protest. The Soviet threat has always been regarded
> by certain sectors of the electorate as a myth and, today, the
> great majority no longer take it seriously.

On the question of the boredom of the electorate, *The Guardian*
(26 January 1967) quotes a British commentator who claimed
that six weeks before the election 61 per cent of the voters
were unable to name the candidates in their own constituency.
A possible reason for apathy (apart from the frequency of
elections) was the fact that most of the candidates were old
hands, whereas the electorate was getting younger: according
to Professor Duverger (*v. Le Monde,* 14 December 1966), by
1967 40 per cent were under 40, and half under 45. Another
possible reason was the relatively peaceful economic and social
climate in 1966.

107. *v.* Viansson-Ponté (op. cit., Vol. II, pp. 273–4) on the prevalence of vague verbalism:

> Who is not a democrat, a Republican, in favour of social
> policies, union, progress, liberty? Who would dare to say
> that he was against Europe, even if the word means some-
> thing very different to one man and to his neighbour? Who
> is against stability? Few men on the Left would hesitate to
> call themselves Socialist. The term has lost its virulence and
> most of its revolutionary content, in practice if not in
> theory. . . .

The Federation's programme consisted of 15 points constituting a *contrat de législature.* These were mainly restatements
of previous *options.* The main points were, in foreign policy,
the objective of the disappearance of both the NATO and
Warsaw treaties and the conversion of the *force de frappe* to
peaceful uses; in internal policy, proposals for elected regional

economic assemblies, a three-year plan for agriculture, aiming at making France more competitive in the Common Market, and increased emphasis on social policies, especially housing and education. (*Le Monde*, 28 February 1967.)

108. *v.* for instance, in *Le Monde*, 16 February 1967, the report of a *Centre démocrate* meeting of 6000–7000 to present the candidates of the Paris region, at which there were flags of the Council of Europe, hostesses with green skirts (the 'European' colour), and of meetings of candidates of the UNR, where hostesses wore blue skirts. Pierre Viansson-Ponté reports that the *Centre démocrate* hostesses wore slightly longer skirts!

109. *v.* Viansson-Ponté, op. cit., Vol. II, pp. 285–6. In spite of UNR irritation at M. Giscard d'Estaing's declaration of 10 January 1967 that the attitude of the *Républicains indépendants* to Gaullist policy was one of conditional support (*Oui, mais*), M. Giscard d'Estaing stood out against the constitution of a single majority group in the National Assembly. M. Viansson-Ponté (ibid.) suggests that this was perhaps a tactical error. If so, it was shared by some left-wing Gaullist groups which also resisted being submerged in the monolithic Gaullist parliamentary group.

110. For results *v. Année politique*, 1967, pp. 14–16. Though there was a slight increase in the vote of the majority parties at the first ballot, their percentage of the total vote slightly decreased. The electorate had increased by only about three-quarters of a million since the 1962 elections, but the poll was much higher, so that over four million more votes were cast. Of the 244 'Fifth Republic' Deputies, 43 were *Républicains indépendants*, a gain of nine. The UNR, therefore, lost about 49 seats. (*v. Le Monde*, 15 March 1967.)

111. The Federation also increased its vote, though its percentage of the total vote slightly declined. Second ballot arrangements gave it a net gain of 25 seats, and the Communists a net gain of 32.

112. Viansson-Ponté, op. cit., Vol. II, p. 232.

113. *v. Année politique*, 1966, p. 423, and 1967, p. 400.

CHAPTER IV

1. Pierre Viansson-Ponté, *Histoire de la République Gaullienne* (Fayard, Vol. I, 1970, Vol. II, 1971), Vol. II, p. 119.

2. That this was so was indicated at the opening of the session, when M. Chaban-Delmas was re-elected President of the National Assembly by 261 votes to 214 for M. Gaston Defferre. In spite of the theoretical secrecy of the vote, it was generally known that only one Deputy of the majority had failed to vote for M. Chaban-Delmas (and that was by accident), while only one opposition Deputy had failed (owing to illness) to vote for M. Defferre. Of the nine Deputies belonging to no group, two had voted for the former and seven for the latter. It was, therefore, a matter of simple arithmetic that the remaining votes for M. Chaban-Delmas must have come from the Centre group of 41, which had not wanted a confrontation on this issue. *v.* account of how the voting went in Viansson-Ponté, op. cit., Vol. II, pp. 315–16, which states that 5 of the Centre group spoiled their papers, 4 returned a blank paper, while 16 voted for M. Defferre and 18 for M. Chaban-Delmas. Since 484 Deputies voted, a comparison with the official party-membership figures and the results given in the *Année politique* (p. 19) indicates an error in both. The latter omits the 5 spoilt papers of the Centre, while the former gives 16 Centre votes for M. Defferre, whereas the number cannot have been more than 14. These discrepancies do not, however, invalidate the point M. Viansson-Ponté makes.

3. General de Gaulle approved of the Government's adoption of the special-powers procedure, describing it in his press conference of 16 May 1967 as being 'speedy', justified by 'the uncertain parliamentary situation', and 'entirely regular'. (*Année politique*, 1967, p. 386.)

4. M. Pompidou had not risked defeat on his declaration of general policy, which was not improbable owing to the fact that, during the first month of the session, the votes of the majority were reduced by the appointment of 25 Deputies to the Government. During the following month, though still able to sit, these Deputies were unable to vote owing to the incompatibility rule (*v.* Vol. I, pp. 345–6). M. Pompidou decided, therefore, in accordance with the precedent set by him in April 1966, not to submit the declaration to a vote on 19 April, following the debate.

5. For a brief account of the special-powers procedure, *v.* Vol. I, pp. 85–7. Three censure motions followed Government 'pledges of responsibility' on the Bill, under article 49(iii).

The first, on 19 May, and the second, on 9 June, both received 236 votes; the third, on 16 June, received 237. The fourth, on 10 October, was a censure motion on the initiative of the Deputies (article 49(ii). It received 207 votes. 244 votes were needed to defeat the Government.

6. They were the CGT, FO, CFDT and FEN. The other two, the predominantly Catholic CFTC and the white-collar CGC, associated themselves with the opposition but did not join the strike.

7. Article 38 of the Constitution requires only that the ratifying Bill shall be laid before Parliament before a certain date, not that it shall be voted. It was not, in fact, voted until 23 July 1968. The date chosen by the Government for the tabling of the Bill ensured that Parliament would not be able to discuss it until the opening of the following April session.

8. Up to 30 September, 26 ordinances were made: four on 12 July, dealing with unemployment; three on 17 August and four on 21 August, dealing with workers' profit-sharing; three on 23 September, dealing with social security; one on 22 September, three on 23 September and eight on 28 September dealing with economic matters.

9. The press published a number of examples, showing the kinds of discrepancy that were to be expected. The average sums distributed were likely to amount to no more than 3 per cent of wages (less than was being received in firms under the voluntary scheme of 1959). Upwards of three-quarters of the firms involved might distribute under 1 per cent. Shareholders could, on average, expect to retain between 70 per cent and 100 per cent of the net profits after tax. (*v.* especially articles by Gilbert Mathieu in *Le Monde*, 11 and 25 August 1967.)

10. Calculations were complicated by the need for a weighting system to iron out some of the variations in liability of different firms. The resultant figure was then divided equally between shareholders and workers who qualified for shares (qualifications being based partly on length of service and partly on wage rates).

11. *Année politique*, 1967, p. 124. Another criticism made by M. Loichot was that the system favoured the prosperous firms, since only they would be able to afford to choose the second option. Firms declaring no profits or profits of under 5 per cent would have *no* sums to distribute, of course, and many others just above that limit only very small sums.

(*v.* also article by Marcel Loichot in *Le Monde,* 25 August 1967.)

12. Radio statement of 11 June 1968, reported in *Le Monde,* 21 June 1968, along with a protest against it by the employers' organization. On the Vallon amendment, *v.* Chapter III, p. 97.

13. M. Loichot, whose plan was often described as 'pan-capitalism', proposed a reduction of company tax from 50 per cent to 25 per cent and an allowance of a 3·75 per cent dividend, free of tax. The remaining profits were to be attributed in equal parts as shares to individual shareholders and to the body of workers. The latter half was to be left for 10 years in the firm and to carry an annual dividend. This system would, he thought, provide needed investment and increase both the status and income of workers, who would have a direct interest in the firm's affairs.

M. Pierre Lebrun proposed that workers' shares should be distributed without conditions, but with 'encouragement' to them to invest the sums either in the firm or in some other productive concern – a plan open to criticism on the ground that, since few workers could be expected to follow this advice, it would be highly inflationary. (*v.* brief account of these two plans in *Notre République,* 19 May 1967.)

14. *v.* television broadcast of 24 May 1968, and television interview with Michel Droit on 7 June. In the first, he announced a referendum on participation. In the second, he presented participation as a third solution to the ills of modern, technological society that would avoid the evils of both Communism and capitalism. He claimed that participation would transform conditions by giving all men a common interest in the functioning of the economy:

> Wherever men are engaged on a common economic undertaking, as for instance in an industry, supplying either the necessary capital, managerial or technical capacity or labour, what is needed is that all should form a community in which they have an interest, a direct interest in its production and its efficient working.

He went on to describe in more detail what this meant. This was the most complete and factual statement that he ever made on the subject.

It implies, he said, the attribution to everyone by law of a share in the profits of the firm and in its self-financing out of these profits. It means too, that everyone should be adequately informed about the firm's affairs and should have the right to choose representatives who would be members of it and of its managing bodies, able to express their interests, their points of view and their suggestions.

This, he said, was what he had always believed, and what he had begun to provide for by setting up Works Committees in 1945, and profit-sharing schemes in 1959 and 1967. This was the road along which they must advance. He indicated, however, in a typically cryptic phrase, the limits to participation: 'If', he said, 'deliberation is a collective function, action is a matter for the individual (*si délibérer est le fait de plusieurs, agir est le fait d'un seul*)' (*Année politique*, 1967, p. 384). Cf. statement on 29 June, on the eve of the second ballot:

> Above all, we must achieve the vast social changes that alone can restore social equilibrium and that our youth instinctively demands. In the mechanized society in which they are caught up, men must be assured of their own position, retain their dignity and exercise their own responsibilities. In all our activities, for instance, in universities or factories, everyone must be associated directly with the working, the results and the contribution to society of the concern in which he is involved. In a word, participation must become the rule and the inspiration of a new France. (Ibid., p. 386.)

15. Reply by the confederal secretary of the CGT, M. Henri Krasucki, to a questionnaire on M. Capitant's plan (*Le Monde*, 9 July 1968).

16. Communiqué of the CNPF reported in ibid., 21 June 1968. A similar statement on the need to maintain 'the hierarchy of authority' was made by the *Assemblée générale* of the CNPF (ibid., 10 July 1968).

17. The April number of *Patronat français* had given a most pessimistic report on the economic situation, emphasizing in particular the climate of uncertainty caused by falling production, and by difficulties in the field of foreign trade. The weekly economic supplement of *Le Monde* (16–17 April 1967) was no less pessimistic, and asked whether France was not heading for a general recession: 'Unemployment up, industrial pro-

duction stagnant, a trade deficit, shrinking reserves of foreign currency: ... The situation has not been good since last summer, but the clouds now seem to be massing faster.' The situation was made worse by the fact that all countries in the European Community were also in difficulties. In France, it was exacerbated by the increase in the working population and increasing unemployment.

18. The social-security services (autonomous bodies), which had been in balance in 1963, had a deficit of 156 million francs in 1964, and of 2·278 million in 1966. The estimated 4000-million deficit for 1968 was said to be caused largely by the increasing price of drugs and medicaments and by increased medical charges, as well as by a number of ancillary costs accepted by the services, though not necessarily their responsibility (*Année politique*, 1967, p. 118).

19. On the provisions of the four ordinances of 21 August, *v.* ibid., pp. 292–3, which states that trade-union calls for industrial action had to include also demands for increased wages and pensions, for full employment and for trade-union rights in factories.

20. On the four ordinances of 12 July on unemployment, *v.* ibid., p. 289, and commentaries in *Le Monde*, 5 August and 2 September 1967.

21. Fifteen ordinances were published on 22 September, three the following day and eight on 28 September. For summary of contents, *v. Année politique*, 1967, pp. 114–16.

22. Meetings were held on 11 January between trade-union representatives and employers to study the problem of benefit for partial unemployment. Meetings on wage negotiations in the public sector were held on 16 and 17 January.

At this period, there were violent demonstrations of workers at Redon on 17 January, and outbreaks of violence in Caen on 26 January. About 7000 workers were on strike in support of a wage claim. But they were also seeking guarantees in case a large lorry firm accounting for many of the strikers should go on short time. The Secretary of State for Employment, M. Jacques Chirac, had also expressed anxiety regarding the economic difficulties of Lorraine and the need for from 60,000 to 70,000 extra jobs during the following years. The CGT was also expressing fears that unless rapid action were taken, the unemployment figure would rise considerably by the autumn.

23. *Le Monde*, 20 February 1968: 'Pour une économie de compétition'. *v.* also report on France's under-industrialization by the group set up in 1965 to study the progress of the fifth Plan in the private sector (ibid., 12 March 1968). For a more optimistic interpretation of the facts, *v.* the Prime Minister's television interview of January 1968 (ibid., 13 January 1968).

24. *v.* for instance, M. René Capitant in *Notre République*, 10 November 1967: 'The President of the Republic is not and must not become the head of a super-party. . . . As long as de Gaulle is there we have nothing to fear: He will not allow himself to be imprisoned by any parliamentary majority.'

25. *Demain la République . . .* (Julliard, 1958), p. 43. Disagreements on this point were still at the heart of the Gaullist malaise in 1973.

26. *Le Monde*, 19 August 1967. *v.* the following comment in ibid., 25 August 1967:

> The leader criticizes the Government, but without asking Ministers [i.e. the three *Républicains indépendants* who were Ministers] to resign. The Ministers disavow the party leader, but do not consider resigning from the National Federation of the Independent Republicans.

> *v.* also M. Pompidou's reply, given in an interview to *l'Express*, in which he admitted the existence of a '*malaise*' in the party, but thought M. Giscard d'Estaing's statement 'unfortunate' (*fâcheux*). The fact that he should have considered it important enough to require a reply of this kind indicates that he did not regard it as being unimportant. (*v.* report in *Le Monde*, 5 September 1967.)

27. *Objectif 72* was formed on 9 November 1966. By July 1967, one-fifth of its members were reported to be former members of the MRP.

28. The resolution put forward by the supporters of M. Mollet referred to 1968 as 'the year of fusion', but in reality committed the party only to 'preparation' for fusion. M. Defferre wanted the party to commit itself to 'partial' fusion immediately, but realized that the majority was against this. In reply to a question from the *Nouvel Observateur*, he said:

> If fusion between the Convention, Socialists and Radicals were possible immediately, I should be in favour of it. I am

convinced that it is not possible. And let me say clearly that there are some Socialists who do not want fusion or even partial fusion. (Quoted in *Le Monde*, 25 January 1968)

29. Ibid., 24 February 1968.
30. Speech made on 17 December, at the banquet held during the Congress.
31. *v.* for instance, statement by M. Waldeck Rochet (*Le Monde*, 17 January 1968) that Socialist–Communist unity was 'a long-term task', and the comment of M. Mendès France, who was personally in favour of a joint programme, that 'a host of suspicions, misunderstandings and habits have to be over-come' (ibid., 7 October 1967).

For a brief analysis of the differences between the Federation and the Communists revealed in the joint declaration of 26 February 1968, *v.* Vol. I, pp. 191, 383 and 388.
32. *Le Monde*, 14 November 1967.
33. Ibid.
34. The vote of censure, which was defeated on 24 April (receiv-ing only 236 votes), criticized the Government for lack of ob-jectivity of the State radio and television services, including re-gional radio services (for content, *v. Le Monde*, 19 April 1968).
35. On university extra-territoriality, *v.* Vol. I, p. 409. On the extent to which student and public feeling about the police increased sympathy for the student revolutionaries, *v.* Viansson-Ponté, op. cit., Vol. II, pp. 447–8.
36. *L'Humanité*, 4 May 1968. On public and trade-union opinion at this time *v.* John Gretton, *Students and Workers* (Mac-donald, 1969, pp. 86–8). This is one of many eye-witness accounts, and in some ways the most objective. Most of the eye-witness accounts are suspect, because the authors were either on one side from the start, or got caught up in the movement, often with inadequate knowledge of the political and trade-union backgrounds. Mr Gretton's account is that of a social scientist, acquainted with the background, in sym-pathy with the movement, but aware of the need for accuracy and detachment. *v.* also Viansson-Ponté, op. cit., Vol. II, pp. 448, 471.
37. *L'Humanité*, 3 May 1968. On 24 May, *L'Humanité* attacked Daniel Cohn-Bendit as a 'phoney revolutionary'. who was 'digging the grave of the workers' movement'.

A careful reading of the diary of events published in the pro-revolutionary *Reflections on the Revolution in France, 1968*, edited by Charles Posner (Harmondsworth, Pelican Original, 1970), reveals by its omissions more than by its contents that what trade-union participation there was up to the middle of May was by unofficial elements, and even then mainly in association with action on industrial issues. The only exception was the demonstration of 13 May, and trade-union leaders then made great efforts to limit the contacts between workers and students. *v.* also *Année politique*, 1968, p. 162 on the cautious attitude of the main trade-union confederations.

38. *v. Année politique*, 1968 p. 39 on the unofficial and spontaneous nature of some of the factory strikes, together with the refusal of Renault to allow students demonstrating 'in solidarity' with the workers to enter the factory gates. *v.* also M. Séguy's attack on 17 May on M. Cohn-Bendit as 'playing M. Pompidou's game'. *v.* also Viansson-Ponté, op. cit., Vol. II, pp. 486–9 on trade-union attitudes.

39. *Année politique*, 1968, p. 40.

40. Statement made on the radio, Europe No. 1, on 20 May.

41. Claude Roy, in *Mai* (Geneva, Editions de l'Avenir, 1970), quoted in Viansson-Ponté, op. cit., Vol. II, p. 494.

42. Raymond Barrillon, in *Le Monde*, 23 May 1970.

43. Ibid., 29 May 1968. M. Mitterrand was, of course, as he himself explained later, thinking of a hypothetical situation, in which the proposed referendum had been held and the General had been defeated, or in which the General had resigned for any other reason. As his opponents pointed out, the Constitution provides for such a situation, and it would be for the acting President, in that case, to decide what to do in the interim preceding the holding of elections. M. Mitterrand was, of course, as free as any other citizen to suggest what the acting President should do, and, as President of the Federation 'shadow Cabinet' and recent presidential candidate, he would naturally regard himself as a candidate for the presidency. (For full texts of his press conference and that of M. Mendès France, *v. Année politique*, 1968, pp. 380–1. *v.* also notes 46 and 70.) Viansson-Ponté, op. cit., Vol. II, p. 518, defends M. Mitterrand. The fact remains, however, that, although there was nothing illegal or unconstitutional about his proposal, the timing and the tone constituted political errors.

44. *Année politique*, 1968, p. 42.
45. As shortly became clear, General de Gaulle had, on 29 May, been consulting the Commander of French forces in Germany, General Massu, on the attitude of the army in case of civil disorder. When questioned in the television interview of 7 June, however, he stated that he had at that time seriously contemplated resigning (*v.* ibid., p. 382).

    Viansson-Ponté (op. cit., Vol. II, pp. 524–52) develops an interesting theory that General de Gaulle had deliberately created the climate of anxiety and uncertainty caused by his 'disappearance' on 29 May, in order to ensure the reaction that he in fact obtained the following day from his broadcast dissolving the National Assembly. He argues that the massive Gaullist demonstration had been carefully prepared and was an essential part of the scenario aimed at swinging public opinion over to support for General de Gaulle and for the restoration of law and order. According to this theory, the Prime Minister co-operated by appearing himself not to know what was happening. The theory is worth considering, but is not *in se* really convincing.

46. *Le Monde*, 31 May 1968. On 20 May, the Federation had itself been calling for an election. That M. Mitterrand had by then become temporarily a victim of left-wing 'propaganda by demonstration' is, perhaps, indicated by the tone of his objection to the declaration. It was, he said,

    > ... *la voix du 18 Brumaire, c'est la voix du 2 décembre, c'est la voix du 13 mai. C'est celle qui annonce la marche d'un pouvoir minoritaire et insolent contre le peuple. C'est celle de la dictature. Cette voix-là, le peuple la fera taire. C'est un appel à la guerre civile.*

    The proof as to which of the two men, he or General de Gaulle, had gauged accurately the state of public opinion was indicated by a public-opinion poll published by *France-Soir* only three days later. It gave the following assessment of the reaction of Paris opinion to the President's broadcast:

Approved of dissolution	75%
Approved of the retention of M. Pompidou as Prime Minister	54%
Thought less well of M. Mitterrand than previously	54%

Opposed continual demonstrations   64%
Approved of a return to work on agreed terms   57%
(Quoted in *The Times*, 4 June 1968)

47. The following is a representative selection of studies, with a
few brief descriptive comments.

a. Accounts of the events

In French:

PIERRE VIANSSON-PONTÉ, *Histoire de la République Gaullienne*
(Fayard, 1971), Vol. II, *l'Epreuve* (pp. 388–428) and *La Chute*
(pp. 429–574).
Esprit, June–July 1968.
LUCIEN RIOUX and RENÉ BACKMAN, *L'explosion de mai*
(Laffont, 1968).

In English:

PATRICK SEALE and MAUREEN MCCONVILLE, *French
Revolution 1968* (Harmondsworth, Penguin Special, 1968).
DAVID GOLDEY, 'The Events of May 1968', in *French
Politicians and Elections 1951–1969* (Cambridge, Cambridge
U.P., 1970), pp. 226–81.

b. Analyses and partisan accounts

In French:

JACQUES SAUVAGEOT, ALAIN GEISMAR, D. COHN-BENDIT
and A. DUTEUIL, *Le révolte étudiante* (Editions Le Seuil,
1968). Views of student leaders.
EMILE COPFERMANN (ed.), *Ce n'est qu'un début, continuons le
combat* (Maspéro, 1968). Views of *Mouvement du 22 mars.*
D. AND G. COHN-BENDIT, *Le gauchisme, remède à la maladie
sénile du communisme* (Editions Le Seuil, 1968). *Obsolete Communism: the left-wing alternative* (Deutsch, 1968).
WALDECK ROCHET, *Les enseignements de mai–juin* (Editions
sociales, 1968). Orthodox Communist point of view.
EDGAR MORIN, CLAUDE LEFORT, JEAN-MARIE COUDRAY,
Mai 1968: la brèche; premières réflexions sur les événements
(Fayard, 1968). Academic analysis, pro-student.
RAYMOND ARON, *La révolution introuvable: réflexions sur la
révolution de mai* (Fayard, 1968). Academic, hostile to
revolutionaries.

In English:

CHARLES POSNER (ed.), *Reflections on the Revolution in France* (Harmondsworth, Pelican Original, 1970). A summary of events, and some articles translated from the French. Pro-student.

JOHN GRETTON, *Students and Workers* (Macdonald, 1969). An academic, sympathetic and objective account, together with translated interviews and documents. The best introductory study.

More complete bibliographies are given in both Gretton and Viansson-Ponté.

48. Viansson-Ponté, op. cit., Vol. II, pp. 499, 492 and 493.

49. Charles Posner (ed.), op. cit., p. 53.

> *v.* also p. 14:

> The very ideas that society held to be self-evident, like the need for hierarchical rule, the need for personal initiative, the need for an economic system based on monetary gain, etc., will never be self-evident again to the French population.

50. Interview with Jean-Paul Sartre in *Le Nouvel Observateur*, reported in *Le Monde*, 22 May 1968.

51. Quoted by Edgar Morin in 'La Commune étudiante', ibid., 17–21 May 1968. These four articles are translated in Charles Posner (ed.), op. cit., pp. 111–27.

> *v.* also, in the same work, the following description of what the revolutionaries regarded as 'creative violence' or 'anarchistic creativity':

> It [i.e. the May revolution] demonstrated that a Revolution is not only destructive but also creative. Once and for all it made the violence *implicit* in the consumer society *explicit*. It created, as Glucksmann notes, a new kind of strategy (ibid., p. 51).

André Glucksmann's essay (ibid., pp. 185–98), which is Chapter 5 of his *Stratégie et révolution en France 1968* (Christian Bourgeois, 1968), develops the theory of '*contestation*', which, he argues,

> accompanies every great revolution, undermining the whole social fabric . . .; it makes it easier to bring down society. It accompanied the 1917 upheaval, as it had, well before that,

the 1789 revolution. . . . It is only when the popular classes contest the bourgeois frame of reference in pursuit of a revolutionary perspective that they become *one*. (pp. 186–7)

For complete English version, *v. The New Left Review*, No. 52.

52. André Gorz, 'What are the Lessons of the May event?', in Charles Posner (ed.), op. cit., p. 259.

Cf. the following extract from articles in *Le Monde*, 9–10 June 1968, by Paul Ricœur, Professor of Philosophy in the Faculty of Arts at Nanterre:

The signs are now eloquent. The West has begun its cultural revolution. It is definitely its own revolution, the revolution of advanced industrial societies, even if it echoes or borrows from the Chinese revolution. . . . This revolution attacks capitalism . . . bureaucracy . . . the nihilism of a society that, like cancerous tissue, has no purpose but its own growth.

53. Morin, 'La Commune étudiante' (*Le Monde*, 17–21 May 1968).
54. Posner (ed.), op. cit., p. 126.
55. Etienne Borne in *France-Forum*, October–November 1968.
56. Gretton, op. cit., p. 65, publishes the results of a study on the proportion of working-class families that obtain places in universities, according to which, though agricultural wage-earners and industrial workers constituted respectively 4·3 per cent and 36·7 per cent of the working population, only 0·7 per cent and 1·4 per cent respectively would normally go to a university. Professional and senior managerial staffs, which constituted 4 per cent, and junior managerial staffs, which constituted 7·8 per cent of the working population, would obtain respectively 58·5 per cent and 29·6 per cent of university places. Mr Patrick Gordon Walker gave the following comparative figures for working-class access to universities in Britain and other European countries:

Over a quarter of our university population are the sons and daughters of manual workers. Comparable figures for Sweden are 14 per cent; for France, 8·3 per cent; for West Germany, 5·3 per cent. (*The Times*, 13 May 1968)

57. Gilbert Comte in *Le Monde*, 12 May 1970. Cf. Alfred Grosser in ibid., 1–2 September 1968, who described the May revolu-

tion as 'the rule of madness, whether magnificent or not, of Utopia, of irrationality'.

58. Gretton, op. cit., pp. 118–19.
59. Maurice Duverger, 'Les fruits du printemps' (*Le Monde*, 31 May 1968).
60. Morin, in Posner (ed.), op. cit., p. 119.
61. Ibid., p. 119, where, speaking of the period *after* the occupation of the Sorbonne, Edgar Morin says: 'A great transformation was under way. The leaders of the student revolution began to see themselves as the initiators of the revolutionary movement destined to destroy the bourgeois State.'
62. *v.* for instance, examples of proposals for educational reforms by the *Colloques* at Amiens (*Le Monde*, 19 March 1968) and Pont-à-Mousson (ibid., 27 March 1968). For some of the student proposals, *v.* Gretton, op. cit., pp. 131–4, and Seale and McConville, op. cit., pp. 130–44. *v.* also report in *Le Monde*, 4–5 June 1967, by the Dean of the Paris Science Faculty on the consequences of non-selective entry.

   Some of the students' proposals did more harm than good, particularly during the months following the May events, when they revealed a great deal of disagreement and intransigence on the student side. *v.* for instance, the comment by Frédéric Gaussen in *Le Monde*, 4 July 1968:

   > The audacity of some of what are, judged by former standards, the more moderate plans, makes one wonder whether the May reformists have not adopted the revolutionary slogan: Be realists, ask for the impossible.

63. *v.* examples quoted in Gretton, op. cit.
64. *v. Année politique*, 1968, broadcast of 24 May (p. 379); broadcast of 30 May (p. 381); televised interview of 7 June (p. 383) in which the President appeared to attribute the May events to anarchist '*groupuscules*'; press conference of 9 September (p. 387) when he appeared to attribute it to a mixture of 'university anarchy', politicization of trade unions, and what he called 'a disequilibrium frequently associated in our country with rapid changes'.
65. *Le Monde*, 16 May 1968.
66. Philippe Guilhane in ibid., 13 June 1968.
67. The authorities were in reality facing a very difficult dilemma. If the police were not present at the Sorbonne, there was a

serious risk of violent clashes with the extreme right-wing group, *Occident*. If they were, the result was bound to be hostility both from students and from the public, in view both of the tradition of extra-territoriality of the Sorbonne, and of the traditionally bad relations between police and public. The police themselves resented the Government's apparent concessions to students, and the Government nearly had a police as well as a student problem on its hands.

68. All three had been appointed after the election of March 1967. The Minister of Justice, M. Louis Joxe, who was also acting Prime Minister in the absence of M. Pompidou, was not a politician, but a civil servant, whose previous career was noted for reasonableness and conciliatory talents (in connection with the Franco-Algerian negotiations in particular) rather than for forcefulness.

69. David Goldey, op. cit., p. 228. Cf. the opinion of the editor of *Le Monde*, Jacques Fauvet, in 'Responsabilités' (*Le Monde*, 12–13 May 1968):

> Ill-informed and ill-inspired, it [i.e. the Government] gave the impression of floating with the stream of the student movement, first taking hasty and unfortunate decisions, and then failing to take decisions that might have avoided the worst.

70. *La République nouvelle* (Gallimard, 1962), p. 26. *v.* also in *Pour préparer l'avenir. Propositions pour une action* (Editions Denoël, 1968), his statement that 'For the whole nation to have responded as it did (to the student revolt) could only mean that the organization of society was bad.'

There was never at any moment justification for regarding 'the whole nation' as being on the side of the revolutionaries. *v.* note 46, on the extent to which M. Mitterrand, too, overestimated the significance of the revolutionary demonstrations.

71. The references to past revolutions were frequent. Some have already been mentioned (*v.* for instance, note 51). *v.* also Edgar Morin, 'Une révolution sans visage' (*Le Monde*, 5 June 1968), in which he described the student occupation of the Sorbonne as 'the taking of the University Bastille'. 'All classes', he went on, 'are united in a sort of '89, bringing together students, young workers, *lycées*.' He also describes it as creating 'the Soviet of a new Petrograd', and in an article the following day,

he referred to the *Mouvement du 22 mars* as 'imitating all past revolutions, the Spanish war, the cultural revolution, 17 October, the Paris Commune . . .'. He even added for good measure 'elements of surrealism and Castrism'. *v.* also note 52.

This unity of students and workers, as was pointed out by many writers, and by trade unionists themselves, existed only in the imagination of the revolutionaries. *v.* note 38.

72. *v.* for instance, on the lack of trade-union agreement, the article by the CFDT president, André Jeanson, in Charles Posner (ed.), op. cit. André Jeanson states categorically that

> the CGT would not support the revolutionary process unleashed by the students and workers, because the movement did not develop under its auspices. The movement's proposals about social development, justice and democracy differed sharply from the PCF line. This is why the CGT tried to channel all claims and actions into quantitative issues like higher wages and payment for working days lost through the strike, and tried to stop the movement as soon as minimal satisfaction had been attained. (p. 152)

There was no lack of corroboration on this. *v.* for instance, Girod de l'Ain, 'Le Pari de l'UNEF', in *Le Monde*, 28 May 1968:

> Student trade unionism is not prepared to strike for the reduction of regional wage differentials or increases in SMIG [the national minimum wage], any more than workers' trade-unionism will strike for university refectories.

v. also Maurice Duverger, 'Une Révolution impossible', in ibid., 12 July 1968. Commenting on the lack of a 'will to revolution' in the May events, he stated that

> In so far as the great majority of workers were concerned, except for the young, this was not the result of CGT and Communist party reformism. On the contrary, the reformism of CGT and Communist party reflected it, and this is part of the nature of industrial societies. The mass of the population – including the proletariat – is so far integrated in the existing society that it does not desire its violent overthrow.

73. Viansson-Ponté (op. cit., Vol. II, pp. 556–7) seriously suggests that the restoration of petrol supplies was an important contributory factor to the return of normality.

> The second stroke of genius on this decisive day, the second defeat for the revolution, was the return of petrol. In a country paralysed by strikes, the queues at petrol pumps had soon faded away in face of the ominous notice: 'No more petrol'. . . .
>
> Then, suddenly during the night of 30 to 31 May, to technicians, clerical staff and managers (who had often taken over the wheel of petrol lorries abandoned by their striking drivers) came the Government order to restore the flow of the precious liquid. Just before Whitsuntide, whispers soon swelled into a noise and then into a clamour that spread from one end of the country to the other – petrol is back; the revolution is over; the strikes are going to stop; the weather is fine; the sea the country and the mountains offer us a long weekend. . . .

CHAPTER V

1. *v.* statement of the Radical party on 19 July that the FGDS was bound by no common programme, and the decision on 14 August of the Radical Federation in Basses Pyrénées to suspend all activities in the FGDS (*Année politique*, 1968, pp. 62–3). At the Radical Congress on 23–4 November, an ambiguous resolution was passed, suggesting a 'confederal type of association' with the Socialists and the *Convention* and also expressing hopes of an agreement with the Centre. It was generally interpreted as a departure from the FGDS.

2. For a brief account of these divergences *v.* Pierre Viansson-Ponté, *Histoire de la République Gaullienne* (Fayard, Vol. I, 1970, Vol. II, 1971), Vol. II, pp. 497–9. M. Viansson-Ponté is, however, himself relying on the book by Philippe Alexandre, *Le Duel de Gaulle–Pompidou* (Grasset, 1970), of which *v.* Chapters 13–15. M. Alexandre provides, however, no evidence in support of his case.

3. The exact words of the President's letter to M. Pompidou, as published in *Le Monde*, 12 July 1968, were as follows:

> . . . *Je souhaite enfin que vous vous teniez prêt à accomplir toute*

mission et à assumer tout mandat qui pourraient vous être un jour confiés par la nation.

The words used by the President in the letter acknowledging the resignation of M. Debré in April 1962 were as follows:

> . . . *je pense, comme vous-même le pensez, qu'il est conforme à l'intérêt du service public que vous preniez maintenant du champ afin de vous préparer à entreprendre, le moment venu, et dans des circonstances nouvelles, une autre phase de votre action. (Année politique, 1962, p. 654)*

There is, as was noticed, a significant difference in the wording of the two letters, though what exactly General de Gaulle meant by it was never made clear. But it is a fact that the only office to be '*confié par la nation*' is the presidency of the Republic.

4. According to the account given in Viansson-Ponté (op. cit., Vol. II, pp. 590–3) of the discussions immediately preceding the devaluation, the President consulted the Council of Ministers and there was agreement to support the views of MM. Jeanneney and Faure (the first to be consulted) that there should not be a devaluation, although, up to then, most of the ministers had assumed it to be inevitable. Other accounts merely record a 'majority' in favour of a decision not to devalue.

5. *v. Année politique*, 1968, p. 170.

6. *Le Monde*, 16 January 1969. Interview with M. Paul Huvelin, President of the Employers' Confederation. M. Huvelin admitted, however, that France's foreign-trade situation remained vulnerable.

7. Perhaps the most significant evidence of the benefits obtained by the trade unions was the fact that all three confederations claimed large increases in membership during the second half of 1968. Their demands for the right to form trade-union branches in factories were met to some extent by the law of 19 December which recognized it in factories with more than 50 employees.

8. *v.* Vol. I, pp. 274–5.

9. For details of this agreement, *v. Année politique*, 1969, p. 145.

10. Only 57 of these agreements were directly reached. The rest were negotiated by Works Committees. 167 agreements pro-

vided for acceptance of the second formula for distribution of profit shares, that of the 'blocked account'.

11. There were a number of incidents in both schools and universities in January and February, and in the provinces as well as in Paris. M. Faure made several public statements threatening disciplinary and penal sanctions. The agitation persisted, however, the universities of Nanterre and the Sorbonne being subjected to repeated disturbances, involving a brief occupation of the Sorbonne on 11 February, followed by demonstrations in the streets in protest against the suspension of a number of students, and their being called up for military service.

12. The most important of these were the Trotskyite movements *Jeunesse communiste révolutionnaire* (JCR), *Fédération des Etudiants révolutionnaires* (FER), *Parti communiste internationaliste* (PCI), and *Organisation communiste internationnaliste* (OCI); the Maoist movements, *Voix ouvrière*, *Parti communiste marxiste-léniniste de France* (PCM–LF), *Union des Jeunesses communistes marxistes-léninistes* (UJCM–L); and the anarchist *Mouvement du 22 mars*. For complete list, *v. Le Monde*, 13 June 1968.

13. *Occident* was dissolved on 24 October 1968.

14. One result was the immediate return to France of MM. Bidault and Soustelle. Both later formed political movements, but neither played an active rôle in politics during the next four years.

15. It should perhaps be added that he took the precaution of following up this remark with a number of conditions that would in themselves have alienated the sympathies of many non-revolutionary believers in educational reforms and in participation – the need for the continued authority of the State, the adaptation of university curricula to practical economic requirements, and the enforcement of law and order by university authorities. He added that buildings and time intended to be used for study must not be used for propaganda, '*confrontation*' or politics.

16. *v.* 1791 Constitution (*Titre Premier*, paragraph 8):

> *Il sera créé et organisé une* Instruction publique, *commune à tous les citoyens, gratuite à l'égard des parties d'enseignement indispensables pour tous les hommes.* . . .

17. *v.* the Langevin-Wallon plan of 1947 (*La Réforme de l'Enseigne-*

ment. *Projet soumis à M. le Ministre de l'Education Nationale par la Commission ministérielle d'Etude*, II. *Caractères de l'Enseignement donné au cours des 3 cycles d'études*). Extracts from this report are published in Eric Cahm, *Politics and Society in Contemporary France, 1789–1971* (Harrap, 1972), pp. 562–6. Extracts from the Faure university-reform Bill are also quoted.

18. Selection had already been introduced in the Paris Science Faculty since 1967, and there had already been protests against selection before the Government's announcement in April 1968 that it would become general as from 1969. For instance, on 28 March, a demonstration in the Latin quarter called for the speedier construction of buildings, owing to the overcrowding, while the previous day a demonstration by pupils from 400 *lycées* had demanded that there should be no selection for higher education (*Le Monde*, 29 March 1968).

19. Viansson-Ponté, op. cit., Vol. 11, p. 585.

20. The revolutionaries complained, of course, that education was too much geared to practical requirements. *v*. for instance, Edgar Morin in 'Une révolution sans visage' (*Le Monde*, 5 June 1968), who complained of 'too much adaptation of university studies to the techno-bureaucratic careers of bourgeois society'. But students also complained that university training did not enable them to get jobs. Some of the complaints of restrictive conditions existed well before the May events, in particular, demands for the right to put up notices (*le droit d'afficher*) and have mixed hostels (*la mixité*). Complaints of overcrowding went back many years.

21. The Ministry of Education has always been in process of reform. Since the beginning of the Gaullist régime, there have been three major reforms – the Berthoin reforms in 1959, the Fouchet reforms in 1966, and the Faure Bill (which dealt only with higher education) in 1968. But there have been partial reforms almost every year. For a brief summary, *v*. French Embassy Document No. A/65/1/9 and for a readable account of the system up to the introduction of the 1966 reforms, John Ardagh, *The New French Revolution* (Secker & Warburg, 1968), Chapter X. The only limitation that the Fouchet reforms imposed on the non-selective nature of the French university system in 1966 was the requirement that students with a *baccalauréat* in philosophy could not enrol in a Science Faculty without special permission.

22. *Le Monde*, 17 December 1967.
23. *v.* the following official figures quoted in French Embassy Document No. A/17, *The Problem of Higher Education in France*, p. 9:

> Of 100 students registering for their preparatory year, 72 will never obtain their degree; it is, moreover, this first year that constitutes the essential stumbling block, since 80 per cent of those who pass in the preparatory year will obtain a degree. ... Of 100 children starting their secondary education, 20 will embark upon higher studies and only six will complete them.

v. also Maître Tixier-Vignancour ('Libres Opinions, Contribution à un débat, *Le Monde*, 8 August 1968), who claimed that of every 100 first-year law students, 62 would never reach the second year and only about 20 would ever qualify. He also quoted Professor Zamansky, Dean of the Paris Science Faculty (which did introduce selection from 1967) as estimating that, in general, of about 38,000 students, only some 8000 could expect to qualify.

In a letter to *Le Monde* 22 December 1967), M. Roger Quilliot, a university teacher in Clermont-Ferrand, argued that selection ought to be carried out in the *lycées* at the end of the 'second cycle' (ages 15–17). He believed that 25 per cent should leave school at this stage, 40 per cent should have a technical education and 35 per cent a university education. The result of selection at this stage would be, he thought, a rise in the standard of the *baccalauréat* and consequently of that of the university intake, providing 60 per cent of *baccalauréat* entrants who would go to universities and 40 per cent who would go to institutions preparing for practical careers.

It was no doubt something like this that M. Edgar Faure had in mind in his speech on 24 July on what ought to be the criteria of selection. But he admitted (as M. Roger Quilliot also pointed out) that the alternatives to universities did not exist in sufficient numbers at that time to persuade parents to send their children to them. The question was whether (as M. Quilliot proposed) selection at *baccalauréat* level should be introduced until such time as proper selection in schools could be carried out. In fact, M. Faure, like his predecessors, was unable to withstand the political pressure against selection.

24. Professor Godechot at the *Colloque* held on 26 March 1968 at Pont-à-Mousson (*Le Monde*, 27 March 1968). For a summary of the organization of the educational system, *v.* French Embassy Document No. A/81/3/71, *Education in France*.

25. Quoted by Patrick Seale and Maureen McConville, *French Revolution 1968* (Harmondsworth, Penguin Special, 1968), p. 23.

26. Speech of 24 July in the National Assembly.

27. *v.* articles 35, 36 and 37 of the *Loi d'Orientation de l'Enseignement supérieur* (*Journal Officiel*, 13 November 1968). Political discussion was also to be allowed in *lycées*, in so far as it contributed to the education of future citizens. A brief account of the content of the law is to be found in *Année politique*, 1968, pp. 364–9, and in English in French Embassy Document No. A/81/3/71.

28. There was some objection (especially in the Gaullist party) to freedom of political discussion in universities. One Senator (M. Victor Golvan) described these articles as 'dangerous for the future of the universities'. He believed that the result would be that 'certain Faculties would become bastions of revolution against the will of the majority of students' (Debate of 23–5 October 1968. Quoted in *Année politique*, p. 73).

The difficulties of applying such provisions had in fact been very clearly pointed out by the Minister of Education as far back as 1952, when, in defence of the existing regulations, he said in reply to a written question:

> University teachers are obliged to respect the rule of neutrality which applies to all members of the State teaching profession; however, in view of the intellectual maturity of the students and the special requirements of higher education imposed by the curricula . . . this rule should be applied only in order to prevent the expression of ideas that have ceased to represent objective teaching and belong purely to the field of propaganda.

The problem was not merely that the university authorities had to decide when this situation had been reached, but that they were also responsible for ensuring that the rule as interpreted was enforced. Ample evidence was provided in 1968 that on neither point were the authorities able to act effectively.

Teachers were themselves divided, and they had no effective means of ensuring respect for their decisions without the help of the State, and often not even then.

29. *Le Monde*, 20 September 1968. On this point, *v.* also the evidence of M. Zamansky, who, in the letter to *Le Monde*, of 8–9 September 1968, already quoted, described 'political freedom' as meaning in practice the right of a small group to indoctrinate the rest and to prevent rather than permit real discussion. The *Syndicat autonome de l'Enseignement supérieur* was in favour of the retention of the rule of political neutrality and thought that the experience of Nanterre proved conclusively that 'contestation' led to monopoly and made work impossible. (*v.* statement in ibid., 10 and 11–12 August 1968.)

30. *v.* articles 11–14 (quoted in Cahm, op. cit., pp. 589–90).

31. *v.* articles 26 and 29 (quoted in ibid., p. 592).

32. 'L'Université mal administrée', *Le Monde*, 3 October 1968.

33. There were considerable reservations about the desirability of university autonomy, even among reforming teachers, partly for the reason (already mentioned) that State control was seen in general as a guarantee of academic freedom, and traditionally of freedom from possible Catholic indoctrination. Autonomy was seen by some as possibly creating the danger of new shackles. Maurice Duverger, for instance, asked: 'What sort of freedom could an autonomous university of Clermont-Ferrand expect, dependent as it would be on Michelin, on the local authority and on M. Giscard d'Estaing?' ('La Réforme et son Double', *Le Monde*, 10–11 November 1968). M. Giscard d'Estaing was the local Deputy.

34. 'Une gestion paritaire', *Le Monde*, 11 June 1968.

35. The so-called Charter of Nanterre, produced by a committee of students of universities and a number of other institutions of higher education, was presented to the public in a press conference on 25 June 1968. It also claimed that universities ought to be used as places of asylum for political refugees 'persecuted' by the Government. By 'independence' was meant of course the assumption of all costs by the State, the responsibility for expenditure being handed over to joint staff-student committees or general assemblies.

36. André Gorz, 'The Lessons of the May Events', quoted in Charles Posner (ed.), *Reflections on the Revolution in France* (Harmondsworth, Pelican Original, 1970), p. 259. Frédéric

Gaussen gives the following definition of the student conceptions of '*contestation*' and '*l'université critique*':

> ... the main themes of student '*contestation*' are well-known: denunciation of the university, considered as serving the interests of capitalist society; the class culture that it preaches; criticisms of the consumer society, claims for self-management in factories, the need to intensify the anti-imperialist struggle and solidarity towards the 'third world'. ... These are the main items in the programme of '*l'université critique*'.

37. The CGT refused to be associated with the Grenoble *Université populaire d'été*, and the CFDT said that it was difficult as it was in the holiday period. Grenoble university teachers were conspicuous by their absence and there were few workers. Most of those present were young and mainly interested in politics. The school at the University of Montpellier was slightly more successful, in that there were some working-class participants – though *Le Monde* estimated that they did not exceed 10 per cent, except at meetings at Nîmes and Béziers, where political subjects attractive to non-students had been chosen (*Le Monde*, 20 August 1968).

38. *v.* statement of 17 December (*Année politique*, 1968, p. 92), and of 24 January 1969 (ibid., 1969, p. 11).

39. Ibid., 1968, p. 93. *v.* also M. Faure's statement on Europe No. 1 on incidents at the University of Nanterre: 'If I have proof that a single teacher has any responsibility for these incidents he will be immediately suspended and I shall take disciplinary measures.'

40. Results of poll among students (*The Guardian*, 26 November 1968). The *Journée d'action* called by the activist *Comités lycéens* on 13 November was not very successful, and parents' associations were by then organizing support for the new reforms (*Le Monde*, 14 November 1968).

41. Cf. M. Lecanuet's objection that the measure was intended to stifle the Senate (*étouffer le Sénat*).

42. *Le Monde* (19 March 1969) published full details of the *Conseil d'Etat avis* of 17 March and the accuracy of this account was never challenged. Voted by a large majority, it noted:

   (i) that article 11 of the Constitution was not applicable in the case of reform of the Senate, and that the successful use of this method in 1962 did not constitute a valid precedent;

(ii) that, as a parliamentary assembly, the Senate ought to have both political and legislative power. And a parliamentary assembly ought not to include non-elected members, for nominated members could be regarded as having a '*mandat impératif*', which was contrary to article 27 of the Constitution;

(iii) that the regionalist proposals involved the creation of new local entities, and this provision should be made under article 72, and not by referendum;

(iv) that the new proposals for the amendment of article 89 ought to require a two-thirds and not a three-fifths majority. (This provision was somewhat altered to meet – to some extent only – the objections of the *Conseil d'Etat*.)

43. M. Raymond Bonnefous, a right-wing Senator, produced as evidence on this point the fact that, of 487 Senate amendments to the Companies Act, 400 were made with the agreement of, or at the request of, the Government (*Le Monde*, 13 July 1968.)

44. This view was expressed in the debate of 11–14 December by, among others, M. Giscard d'Estaing.

45. Opposition was expressed in the National Assembly by the following UDR Deputies: MM. Sanguinetti, Baumel, de Grailly and de la Malène. Some *Républicains indépendants* objected to it for precisely the opposite reason, that it would be 'a Senate of corporations and bogus regionalization'. In the Senate debate of 16–18 December, not a single Senator spoke in favour of the proposals.

46. *v.* for instance, speech of 11 March, in which he developed this point (*Année politique*, 1969, p. 395).

47. The most precise and emphatic threat was made in the President's final broadcast before the poll, on 25 April, when he said:

> . . . if I am disavowed by a majority of you, solemnly and on so important a subject, then whatever the number, enthusiasm and devotion of the multitude of those who support me, and who in any case hold the country's future in their hands, my present task as head of the State will

become impossible and I shall cease forthwith to exercise my functions. (*Année politique* 1969, pp. 401–2).

M. Jean-Marcel Jeanneney, the Minister in charge of the measure, had appeared to think that defeat would not involve the President's resignation. In his press conference of 4 March, following the Council of Ministers' agreement on the text of the measure, he said, in reply to a question: 'What is involved is a better organization of political institutions. It is a political matter, not a fundamental requirement of the régime' (ibid., p. 16).

48. Ibid., p. 34.
49. pp. 18–20 (English translation, *Memoirs of Hope*, pp. 306–7.) *v.* also report in *Le Monde* (13 November 1970), immediately after General de Gaulle's death, which quotes a similar statement, said to have been made by General de Gaulle in an interview with André Passeron on 6 May 1966.
50. *Année politique*, 1946, p. 534. English version (extracts only) given in David Thomson, *Democracy in France, since 1870* (Oxford, Oxford U. P., 4th edn 1964), p. 324.
51. *Le Monde*, 29 April 1969; leader entitled 'Roulette russe'.
52. *v.* for instance, the reaction of M. Lecanuet, president of the *Centre démocrate*: 'Since General de Gaulle must in any case retire, it would be better to make this inevitable change now, while France is calm, than later in the midst of a national crisis' (quoted in *Année politique*, 1969, p. 33).
53. 'The Political Principles of General de Gaulle,' *International Affairs*, October 1965, p. 661.
54. André Malraux, in his book *Les chênes qu'on abat* (Gallimard, 1971), quotes General de Gaulle as saying: '*En mai tout m'échappait. Je n'avais plus de prise sur mon propre gouvernement.*'
55. Quoted by André Malraux in a television interview on his book, reported in *Le Monde*, 17 March 1971. The actual phrase is as follows:

Je me suis trouvé en face de l'ennemi vrai que j'ai eu toute ma vie, qui n'est ni à droite ni à gauche, et qui est l'argent. Le référendum vrai n'était pas sur les régions ni sur le Sénat. Il était sur la participation .

56. According to the report of an interview with André Passeron on 6 May 1966, quoted in ibid., 13 November 1971, General

de Gaulle issued the following specific warning against attaching importance to such remarks.

> I reflect at length on things that I want to make known and that I regard as important. I write them down and repeat them because I want people to know them. That is important. In my view, these are the only things of importance.

On his casual remarks, he is reported as saying:

> Then there are the others, the things that I say without having prepared them, thought about them or learnt them, and that I might say to anyone . . . these in my view do not count, they have no importance. But you report them as well. And they are not of any interest.

57. Quoted by Pierre Viansson-Ponté in *Les Gaullistes* (Edition du Seuil, 1963), p. 45.
58. Statement first made in Rome on 17 January 1969 (*v. Année politique*, 1969, p. 6), and repeated in a more indirect way in a Swiss television programme on 13 February, when he said '*J'aurai peut-être, si Dieu le veut, un destin national*'.
59. Robert Buron, *Travailler avec de Gaulle* (Hebdo-TC, 19 November 1970), p. 18.
60. 'Un homme' (*Le Monde*, 13 November 1970).
61. According to Gilbert Mathieu, the phrase was attributed to him by Paul Ramadier, ibid., 12 November 1970. Its accuracy was denied by General de Gaulle in a television interview on 13 December 1965, when he said: '*Ce sont des blagues pour les journaux*'.
62. French edition, pp. 283–314 (English translation, pp. 270–301).
63. 'De la démocratie directe à l'action directe' (*Le Monde*, 25 February 1964).

CHAPTER VI

1. *Année politique*, 1969, p. 44.
2. Ten of the sixteen Presidents of the Third and Fourth Republics had been President of one or other of the two parliamentary assemblies.
3. His actual words, in an interview given on Europe No. 1 on

3 May 1969, were: *'je ne suis pas investi par le peuple français, je ne suis qu'un intérimaire; il faut être modeste et décent'*.

4. *Année politique*, 1969, p. 43.

5. Statement broadcast by *France-Inter* on 21 May 1969 (quoted in *Le Monde*, 23 May 1969).

6. *Année politique*, 1969, p. 44.

7. These elements included M. Mitterrand's *Convention des Institutions républicaines* (CIR), the *Union des Clubs pour le Renouveau de la Gauche* (UCRG), led by M. Alain Savary, the *Union des Groupes et Clubs socialistes* (UGCS) of M. Poperen, and the *Centre d'Etudes, de Recherches et d'Education socialistes* (CERES), all of which held the view – later accepted by the reorganized party – that Socialists should try to reach an agreement with the Communist party. Both M. Savary and M. Mitterrand wanted a single left-wing candidate as there had been in 1965. There was also some opposition to M. Defferre himself, owing to his efforts between 1963 and 1965 to achieve an understanding with Centrists (*v.* Chapter III, pp. 104–8).

8. On M. Mendès France's statement on 29 May 1968, *v.* Chapter IV, pp. 130, 143. On his attitude to the 1958 Constitution, *v. La République moderne* (Gallimard, 1962), Chapter III.

On criticisms of the procedure, *v.* the following comments:
(i) by M. Raymond Barrillon in *Le Monde*, 18–19 May 1969:

> If a would-be President of the Republic and his intended Prime Minister present themselves together to the electorate, then (if successful) are not both of them chosen by the electors and so of equal personal standing?

(ii) by M. Pierre Viansson-Ponté in ibid., 22 May 1969:

> The appearance of M. Pierre Mendès France beside M. Gaston Defferre constitutes a fundamental change in the working of the Constitution. For the first time a presidential candidate and his future Prime Minister have presented themselves as a team before the election, one of them laying down general principles (*les grandes options*), the other precise details of his policies. This constitutes a transference of the seat of power from the head of the State to the head of the Government. According to the Constitution, the head of State is the guardian of the Constitution, the judge of the regular

functioning of the State (*les pouvoirs publics*), and the guarantor of national independence, while the Government decides and directs the policy of the nation.

9. 'Reconversion de la Gauche', in *Le Monde*, 21 June 1969.
10. Maurice Duverger in ibid., 21 May 1969.
11. Alfred Grosser in ibid., 22 May 1969.
12. In ibid., 18–19 May 1969.
13. For M. Poher's main policy declarations, *v.* his statement of 21 May (ibid., 22 May 1969), his 12 '*options*' of 27 May – six of which would have ensured the combined opposition of Gaullists and Communists (ibid., 28 May 1969) – and that of 22 May (ibid., 25 May 1969), mainly on foreign policy. M. Poher also contradicted himself at times, for instance, stating at first that he did not think it desirable for an acting President to be a candidate and then giving somewhat unconvincing reasons for his decisions to stand after all. (*v.* ibid., 15 May 1969, and his declaration at Charenton on 22 April that he did not think it right to stand.)

M. Poher's replies to questions as to what he would do in case of a deadlock between President and National Assembly were not very convincing either. He stated that he would not dissolve the Assembly automatically – whereas M. Defferre explicitly undertook to dissolve in that situation – but that he would do so 'as a last resort' (ibid., 15 May 1969). The objections to his position were summed up clearly by Raymond Barrillon (ibid., 15 May 1969):

> If M. Poher is elected, how will he find a Prime Minister who can obtain the consent of the powerful Gaullist majority that has existed in the National Assembly since last summer to carry out the policy approved by the nation? If he dissolves the National Assembly, will those who now support him carry on the fight for his policy with the same ardour? ... In a word, where is the Centrist majority for a Centrist Prime Minister and a Centrist President?

Nor could a dissolution be guaranteed to provide a way out of the deadlock. The electorate could return a majority identical to the outgoing one, but the President would then have exhausted his resources for a year (*v.* Constitution, article 12). Maurice Duverger's argument that an election for President and Assembly at the same time (as happens every four years in the United States) would be likely to produce a similar majority for both is not very convincing either. The referendum and general election of 1962 produced somewhat dissimilar results and the election of 1968, which produced a massive Gaullist majority, was followed less than a year later by the defeat of the President in the referendum of 1969. In fact, as M. Chaban-Delmas himself recognized, the 1958 Constitution offers no way out of such a situation. The possibility of its arising remains, in his words, the 'Achilles heel' of the régime (statement of January 1970 to the *Cercle de l'Opinion*, quoted in *Le Monde*, 29 January 1970).

14. *v.* for instance, the article by M. René Capitant, 'L'Enterrement des réformes', in ibid.; 18 May 1969. For M. Capitant, 'change' was a betrayal, in the interests of orthodox conservatism.

15. The general model was described in *The Guardian* (19 May 1969) as follows:

> First a eulogy of General de Gaulle which Mark Antony at another Caesar's tomb would not be ashamed to acknowledge, a modest acknowledgement of M. Pompidou's own lesser stature, but all the same, the detailing of the long and diverse apprenticeship which has fitted him for office. . . .

16. Interview in *Paris-Match*, quoted in *The Times*, 13 May 1969.

17. *v.* the following description by Pierre Viansson-Ponté of M. Debré's conception of his mission:

> For him, the only reply to everything, everywhere and always is Gaullism and nothing but Gaullism. His faith would move mountains, but only the faithful to whom his 'Letter' is addressed share the ardour of his exaltation of the General's greatness, the eternal qualities of Gaullism, and the glory of France – three notions that are for him indissolubly linked, yesterday, today and for ever.

Extract from a review of M. Debré's *Lettre à des militants sur la continuité, l'ouverture, et la fidélité* (Plon, Collection Tribune libre, 1970, published in *Le Monde*, 14 August 1970).

In a debate at the UDR National Council meeting (28–9 November 1969), M. Alexandre Sanguinetti, a prominent Gaullist Deputy who supported the Pompidolist position, had argued that the Constitution ought not to be considered as if it had been 'handed down by God the Father', to which M. André Fanton had replied: 'It is precisely because General de Gaulle is no longer here that we ought to consider the Constitution as unalterable.' This would seem to be tantamount to claiming that de Gaulle *was* God the Father!

18. Statement by M. Pierre Messmer on Radio Luxembourg, announcing the reconstitution of the movement, *Présence du Gaullisme* (*Le Monde*, 14 April 1970).

19. Although neither the *Amicale* nor the extra-parliamentary movement was intended to be more than a 'ginger group' on behalf of Gaullist 'purity' within the UDR, M. Joël le Tac resigned from the *Amicale* in June on the ground that it was *'une petite machine de guerre au sein de la majorité'* (ibid., 5 June 1970).

20. This led to his expulsion from the *bureau politique* of the party on 26 October 1969 and from the party the following month. *v.* also his statements (quoted in ibid., 1–2 March 1970) regretting that the General had not continued in power, which he thought would have been possible for some time if it had not been for 'French stupidity'.

21. Ibid., 28 April 1970. M. Capitant described his reluctant decision in 1968 to join M. Pompidou's Government, when reshuffled on 31 May, as consenting to 'swallow the insult' (*avaler la couleuvre*) of having to serve under M. Pompidou.

22. Ibid., 11 August 1970.

23. Ibid., 24 March 1970.
    v. also the article by David Rousset entitled 'L'Inertie de l'UDR' in ibid., 24 June 1970, in which he criticized the party for its conservatism as well as for its inertia, accusing it of having no adequate financial or social policy, and of having no intention either of carrying out the policy described by the Prime Minister as *concertation* – the negotiation of collective contracts intended to preserve industrial peace – or of introducing any real measure of profit-sharing in industry.

24. The following picture of the situation in the UDR was given by Pierre Viansson-Ponté in ibid., 25 June 1970:

> . . . underlying, sullen conflict between the Elysée and Matignon (separated by an abyss), frequent altercations between the UDR, *Centre Démocratie et Progrès* and *Républi-*

cains indépendants, quarrels between technocrats, orthodox Gaullists in the parliamentary group and the Faurists, controversy between supporters and opponents of the wider-based Government coalition – all these differences, clans, visions of the past and hopes for the future are to some extent present. . . .

25. Ibid., 28–9 June 1970.
26. Statement to a meeting of the Gaullist parliamentary group on 6 April 1971 (ibid., 8 April 1971).
27. Among complaints reported as being made by the parliamentary group were suggestions that M. Chaban-Delmas was more 'remote' than M. Pompidou had been as Prime Minister (Raymond Barrillon in ibid., 24 April 1970), that university problems were not being tackled and that nothing was being done about the 'new society' (ibid., 26 June 1970). The defensive tone of M. Chaban-Delmas' speech at Versailles in June was also indicative of his realization of the existence of dissatisfaction in the party. He then outlined more than half-a-dozen measures that had to be taken, dealing with social security, education, the introduction of monthly wage-payments, housing, help to small tradesmen and shopkeepers and steps to apply his policy of *concertation* (*v.* ibid., 28–9 June 1970). There were also criticisms that the *ouverture* had not been preceded by any consultation of the party, and that this was a return to the habits of the Fourth Republic (*v.* for instance MM. Christian Fouchet and Robert Grossmann at Versailles, ibid., 28–9 June 1970).
28. Statement on television just before the second ballot (ibid., 8–9 June 1969).
29. *v.* for instance, the tone of his first New Year message with its emphasis on sympathy for the sick, the bereaved and the poor, and on the need for increased welfare, justice and fraternity. General de Gaulle had tended to stress economic progress and the greatness of France (*Année politique*, 1969, p. 416). *v.* also his hopes for the creation of 'a kind of dialogue' in his press conferences (first press conference, 7 July 1969, ibid., p. 403).
30. For instance, at his second press conference on 22 September 1969, he was asked what he thought about participation, why he had moved M. Faure from the Ministry of Education, and his views on the suicide of a young teacher in Marseilles who

had been convicted of debauching a minor (*détournement de mineur*) – the Russier case.

31. Pierre Viansson-Ponté in *Le Monde*, 4 October 1969.

32. At the first press conference, only about 100 journalists were present instead of the traditional 400–500, and instead of serried ranks of Ministers, seated in strict order of precedence, only one Minister (the Government spokesman, M. Léo Hamon) was present in addition to the Prime Minister.

33. For instance, the deliberate dramatization of the two vetoes on British membership of the Common Market (14 January and 27 November 1967), the results of which would have been obtained anyway by the unspectacular efforts of M. Couve de Murville, the advance announcement in the press conference of 21 February 1966 of the withdrawal from NATO, the maintenance of tension regarding his candidature in 1965 until a few weeks before the opening of the election campaign, and the provocative statement on Canadian separatism in 1967.

34. There were certainly rumours of disagreements between General de Gaulle and M. Pompidou regarding tactics at the time of the May events (*v.* Chapter V, note 2). But these were exceptional circumstances.

Rumours of disagreements were stated to be 'common knowledge' (*Le Nouvel Observateur*, quoted in *Le Monde*, 5–6 October 1969); they were taken for granted by mid-1970 (*v.* quotation from Viansson-Ponté, note 24), and the situation was even described in one paper as one of 'cold war' ('Minute', quoted in *Année politique*, 1970, p. 19). There were comments on the President's omission of any mention of the Prime Minister in his broadcast of 11 March 1970, or of the 'new society'. (*v.* other press comments in ibid., 1970, p. 19.)
For statements by M. Chaban-Delmas on the relations between President and Prime Minister, *v.* in particular, the following:

(i) Statement to the '*Cercle de l'Opinion*' on 29 January 1970, which is by far the most complete. After referring to the 'Achilles heel' of the Constitution and the need for 'close, almost intimate, relations' between the President and the Prime Minister, he added:

> There is no room in the mind of the Prime Minister for the slightest envy or rivalry. On the other hand, there must not be rigorous or rigid subordination. The Prime

Minister must express his feelings freely, even if he does not agree with the President on a specific problem.

In a word, problems must be studied together, it being understood that the head of State has the last word, and once his decision has been made, it is for the Prime Minister to act without hesitation. (*En définitive, il faut que la recherche puisse se faire en commun, étant entendu que l'orientation finale revient au chef de l'Etat et que celle-ci une fois prise il incombe au Premier Ministre d'agir carrément.*) (*Le Monde*, 31 January 1970)

(ii) Reply to question by M. François Mitterrand on what would happen if the President asked the Prime Minister to resign and he refused:

. . . according to article 12 of the Constitution the President of the Republic has the power to dissolve the Assembly. On the other hand, it [i.e. the question] is shocking, for it would mean that the Prime Minister was hanging on to power. (Ibid., 17 October 1970)

(iii) Interview to *Sud-Ouest* on 3 September 1970:

The Prime Minister is not on the same footing as the President of the Republic, if only because he has not been chosen by the people but is nominated by the head of State. (Ibid., 4 September 1970)

35. *Immuable et changeante* (Calmann-Lévy, 1959), p. 41: '*Le chef de l'Etat préside à nos querelles plutôt qu'il ne les résout.*'
36. Sirius in *Le Monde*, 29 April 1969: '*Charles de Gaulle s'en va, aucun problème ne se trouve pour autant résolu.*'
37. *v.* for instance, the OECD annual report of 1969 on the economic situation in France.
38. *Le Monde*, 27 November 1969.
39. The phrase '*la société bloquée*' was originally that of the French sociologist, Michel Crozier. It was taken up by M. Chaban-Delmas in his declaration of general policy.
40. M. Séguy was claiming that purchasing power had fallen by 8 per cent since May 1968. An INSEE report admitted a fall of purchasing power greater in the public than in the private sector, and explained this in part by the fact that, whereas more hours were being worked in the private sector, in the

public sector hours had been reduced. M. Séguy was not, however, at this point of time anxious for militant action, for one thing because he was still trying to get rid of wild-cat strikes in his own organization, and for another because he could not count on co-operation from the CFDT, which was then in favour of independent strike action.

41. M. Chaban-Delmas described the inadequacies of the 'stagnant society' as being mainly the inefficiency of the centralized State, the out-of-dateness of social structures, and the persistent fragility of the economy. His programme, by which he presumably hoped to create a 'new society', included a reformed radio and television service, more independence for nationalized railways, electricity and gas services, more vocational training, a shorter period of military service, improved communications, modernized industrial and agricultural development, improved working and social conditions, shorter hours of work, development of the social services, increased minimum wages and old-age pensions. In fact, something for everybody, but nothing very new, or that would help to give the programme more credibility than similar programmes of his predecessors had had. (For text of speech, *v. Le Monde*, 18 September 1969.)

42. Quoted in *Année politique*, 1969, p. 72.

43. The new system, SMIC (*salaire minimum interprofessionnel de croissance*), introduced in January 1970, provided the lowest-paid workers with an increase of between 10 and 11 per cent between June 1969 and 1970. The *'actionnariat Renault'*, voted on 2 January 1970, was an attempt to extend the profit-sharing scheme (*v.* Chapter III, pp. 96–8) to the public sector. Initially, it provided shares for some 5 per cent of the labour force (those with five years' service). The scheme was intended ultimately to be extended to permit up to 25 per cent of the notional capital of Renault to be owned by workers. The shares were (like those in private industry) to be subject to restrictions on the right to sell them within a certain period. It was hoped that the scheme would improve labour relations, but this was by no means certain, as there was a good deal of suspicion among workers of anything that sought to blur the lines between workers and bosses.

Monthly payments (*la mensualisation*) had been wanted by the trade unions for some time. They extended to workers formerly paid at hourly rates certain advantages possessed by those on monthly salaries, such as sick pay for longer periods and a lump sum on dismissal or retirement. Agreements affecting some 40 per cent of workers were to be concluded by 1974.

44. *Le Monde*, 17 October 1970.
45. Speech of 4 December delivered to the Senate.
46. M. Pompidou mentioned regionalization during his tours of the Cantal and Alsace (in May and June 1970) and made a statement at Lyons on 30 October 1970, in which he reaffirmed that Government policy was to retain the existing structure of *communes* and *départements* and to create no new 'regional' local area. The body that would replace the CODER was not to be directly elected and the regional Prefect would continue to be chosen by the Government. The Prime Minister, when interviewed on 3 September 1970 by the paper *Sud-Ouest*, gave a number of reasons for putting off regionalization (*v. Le Monde*, 4 September 1970), and, in a speech the following December to members of the *Mouvement national des Elus locaux*, held out only distant hopes of an elected regional assembly, when both *communes* and *départements* had been modernized, a task that he thought could take years (*v.* ibid., 12 December 1970). The speech of 15 October 1970 was followed by the introduction of a Bill mainly concerned with giving slightly more freedom of action to *communes*, and promising further measures in 1971.
47. M. André Passeron in ibid., 5 November 1970.
48. *v.* ibid., 2 September 1971.
49. *v. Le Manifeste radical* (Denoël, 1970), pp. 155–66. On the Europeanization of regionalism, *v.* the following passage:

> Whether the number of regions in France should be ten or twelve is a matter for argument; but it is a secondary matter. What is essential is that the regions should be in tune with Europe (*à la dimension de l'Europe*). (p. 157)

He goes on to argue that the responsibility of the State for regional services must be ended and that some civil servants now carrying out these functions must be sent to regions, *départements* and *communes* where they would be 'responsible exclusively' to elected local representatives. (p. 160)

> Thus, power, the sovereignty of the people, would be exercised in a series of new centres of decision, from Europe

to the village and the town district (*depuis l'Europe jusqu'au village et au quartier*). (p. 164)

50. On this *v.* for instance, the articles by Jacques Fauvet and Maurice Duverger following the Lyons speech by the President and the interview by the Prime Minister quoted above. M. Fauvet ('La région des Notables', *Le Monde*, 1–2 November 1970) argues in favour of real decentralization, while Maurice Duverger in 'Mythes et Réalités de la décentralisation' (ibid., 16 December 1970) points out the political obstacles that have always militated against any fundamental change in the French system.

51. *v.* ibid., 1 April 1970, which reports on 'a year of co-management' in three universities, and gives details of student abstention in different UER. Some UER, it was reported, had no elected student representatives at all.

52. Some were old problems, such as the stage at which Latin should be taught in secondary schools, and the desirability of comprehensive teacher-training colleges (favoured by the Left as being 'anti-élitist').

53. Technical questions concerned, for instance, the rules governing examinations, now that the system of 'continuous assessment' was admitted, and also M. Faure's decision to recognize (in the exceptional conditions of 1968) the equivalence of Catholic and State diplomas, which was, of course, highly unpopular with the Left. The Minister's decision to restrict the numbers of medical students in the second year, in view of the shortage of hospital training facilities, was also criticized and led to a student strike.

54. On the UER, *v.* for instance, André Latreille (*Le Monde*, 18–19 October 1970), who discusses their heterogeneity and illogicality, and Maurice Duverger (ibid., 15–16 November 1970), who describes different types of UER and concludes that, if Faculties could be considered as 'a small number of large castles protected by ramparts', UER were 'a large number of small castles, equally separate one from another'.

55. Figures given by Maurice Duverger in ibid., 12 July 1969, and 15–16 November 1970. There were then 65 universities. By 1971 the number had increased to 67.

56. The three chief objections expressed were (i) the restricted area of independence. Paris continued, not only to control

finance, the national diplomas that constituted qualifications for so many jobs, and the appointment of teachers, but also to take a great many petty decisions (concerning, for example, things like the engagement of secretaries, or supplies of equipment) which meant frustrating delays. (ii) There could be no real equality or competition between universities while students (outside the centre of Paris) were obliged to attend the university in the area in which they were domiciled. The attraction of Paris was such that, with the tremendous expansion of Paris universities (which took in a quarter of the total student population), provincial universities were losing staff to Paris. (ii) The number and range of the various UER varied enormously and the distribution was haphazard, so that some related subjects were often geographically separated. Some universities existed only on paper, in the sense that a great many of the UER that were needed to provide complete courses had not been formed. Some universities shared premises. Some were housed in a number of separate buildings. On the other hand, some provincial universities and some Paris Faculties (Law and Medicine) continued to exist in practice as they had been, and merely divided themselves into subdepartments called UER. For instance Paris VI was predominantly the old Faculty of Science; Censier provided mainly language courses.

57. Frédéric Gaussen, *Le Monde*, 17 February 1970.
58. Ibid., 31 January 1970.
59. In April 1970, the Minister of Education announced that he was putting at the disposal of the *Recteur* of Paris some 300 persons (unarmed) whom Deans could call in to preserve order. Nanterre had tried this system in 1969 and had had to give it up owing to the opposition that it aroused among students (*v.* ibid., 16 April 1970). Nevertheless, Maurice Duverger maintained that some universities relied permanently on the protection either of these strong-arm men (*vigiles*) or of police, in order to function at all (ibid., 2 December 1970).
60. Ibid., 25 June 1970.
61. Ibid., 17–18 July 1969. Article by Frédéric Gaussen on the situation at the University of Vincennes.
62. M. Pierre Grappin, Dean of the Faculty of Arts of Nanterre, resigned in 1968. His successor, M. Paul Ricœur, resigned in March 1970 (he had sympathized with the revolutionaries).

After twice declining, M. René Rémond agreed to replace him. The Dean of the Faculty of Law, M. Jean-Maurice Verdier, resigned in April 1970. M. Edgar Faure refused to replace him, giving as his reason the incompatibility of the office with that of Deputy. The Director of the *Ecole normale supérieure*, M. Flaxelière, had resigned before the Maoist incident involving arson, because he could no longer guarantee the safety of either persons or property. The School had, he said, become a 'Red base' and was run *de facto* by extremists.

63. For a brief account of this incident, *v.* Vol. I, pp. 251–2 and p. 400.

64. *v.* The President of the Republic in an interview on 12 March (*Année politique*, 1970, p. 420), and at Albi on 5 April (ibid., p. 24); *v.* also the Minister of Education to the UDR group of the National Assembly in January 1970, and the Minister of the Interior on 22 January to the Association of *Maires* at Rodez; *v.* also the Government spokesman, M. Léo Hamon, on 1 April, on the Government's determination to deal firmly with violence.

65. In a message to a Maoist meeting of 8 June 1970, at the *Mutualité* in Paris. He announced: '*un été chaud qui portera l'insécurité chez les bourgeois*' (quoted in *Année politique*, 1970, p. 44).

66. From a statement by the Prime Minister in a television interview on 7 April 1970: '*Il est nécessaire que les casseurs soient les payeurs.*'

67. Introduced in April, the Bill was finally voted on 4 June 1970. Judges were made responsible for deciding when provocation constituted a valid defence. The law provided severe penalties, including up to five years' imprisonment and also damages. These were not limited to damage for which defendants were responsible, but included damage provoked by their actions. For content of the Bill, *v. Le Monde*, 6 June 1970, and for a discussion of its shortcomings, Maurice Duverger in ibid., 22 May 1970.

68. Ibid., 23 January 1971. In fact, the confidence and personal authority of the President had been commented on when he made his 'report' on 15 December 1969. *The Times* (17 December 1969) regarded the opening words of the broadcast as a striking example of the use of 'the Presidential *je*', while M. Fauvet himself (*Le Monde*, 17 December 1969) noted that the speech revealed that 'the President remains head of the executive, the Prime Minister has not become its head'.

69. Made on 18 November 1969 to the UDR parliamentary group. The Prime Minister insisted on the increased need, now that de Gaulle was no longer there, for the party to remain united, and condemned the indiscipline of Gaullist movements.

70. To the group *Jeunesse et Progrès* on 30 September 1971 (*Le Monde*, 2 October 1971). Cf. his warning at the UDR National Council meeting the previous 25–7 June: 'We are not doing what General de Gaulle hoped that we should do. We are stopping on the banks of great rivers to have a bathe and others are stealing our clothes.'

71. *Le Monde*, 14–15 November 1971.

72. M. Gabriel Vancalster, UDR Deputy for the Nord, resigned in December 1970, MM. Vendroux and Fouchet in February 1971, M. David Rousset, a left-wing Gaullist Deputy, left the Gaullist parliamentary group in November 1971, giving as his main reasons the Government's inadequate economic and monetary policies. 'I have rejoined de Gaulle in spirit', he said (ibid., 14–15 November 1971). M. Jeanneney left in November 1971 (*v.* his criticisms of the UDR in ibid., 5 June 1971, and to *l'Express*, 6–12 November 1972, after the announcement that he had joined the Centrist *Mouvement réformateur*).

73. For a brief account of the different left-wing Gaullist movements, *v.* Vol. I, pp. 225–31.

74. *Le Monde*, 19 May 1971, 'Les Prosaïques'.

75. 7 December 1972, Pierre Mathias in ibid.

76. *v.* account in ibid., 14 July 1971.

77. M. Sanguinetti made his proposal on 10 October 1971. The Prime Minister's reply was made to the Central Committee of the UDR on 21 November (ibid., 23 November 1971).

78. M. Poniatowski's proposals for multiple candidatures were made on 3 and 10 May, and for a '*grande fédération*' in an interview in the right-wing paper, *Les Informations* (16–23 August 1971).

79. *Le Monde*, 22 October 1971.

80. The affair of the *Garantie foncière* reached the headlines in July 1971, but the final verdict of the appeal court, after which M. Rives-Henrÿs resigned his seat, came only on 2 May 1972. The affair was, therefore, intermittently in the headlines for some ten months.

81. For statements by M. Chaban-Delmas, *v. Le Monde*, 17 and 19 February 1972.

82. The system (*l'avoir fiscal*) provided for a rebate of 50 per cent of the tax on dividends deducted at source. The method of application was extremely complex, and the press devoted columns to explanations and illustrations of how it worked. The main purpose of the complications was to restrict the benefits of the concession to French taxpayers. What was politically damaging about the figures was the demonstration that, thanks to the concessions, the Prime Minister appeared not to have paid a centime in direct taxation over a period of four years, an achievement undreamed of by other taxpayers (Pierre Viansson-Ponté, 'Les Malheurs d'un homme heureux', in *Le Monde*, 3 February 1972). As M. Chaban-Delmas explained, this 'achievement' was partly due to special factors and partly to the high level of tax allowance that he had enjoyed as President of the National Assembly. The effects of the concession were certainly, as commentators pointed out, very regressive. *v.* for instance, the figures quoted by Maurice Duverger, 'Petits et grands scandales' (ibid., 9 February 1972), who claimed that legal and illegal methods of avoiding tax were available to only 3 per cent of workers, while 47 per cent of middle-class taxpayers and 78 per cent of farmers had greater or lesser opportunities. It should be noted that the various figures quoted on this point varied greatly. The point was frankly propagandist and in no way reflected on M. Chaban-Delmas.

83. M. Giscard d'Estaing announced in October 1971 that he would make no electoral declaration until 1 October 1972. But since his secretary-general was free to discuss electoral tactics, and did so, this allowed him in practice to take soundings without committing the party.

84. Other Gaullists involved in some way in these or other affairs were Me Rochenoir, legal adviser to the *Garantie foncière*, M. Roulland, a former Gaullist Deputy, three Gaullist Deputies who resigned (MM. Edouard Charret – 8 September 1972, Gérard Sibeud – 27 September, Henry Modiano – 8 October), and a Minister who belonged to the left-wing Gaullists, M. Phillippe Dechartre, who resigned in May 1972, following a court verdict which, the Prime Minister stated, in no way impugned his honour (statement in the National Assembly of 10 May 1972).

85. On M. Pleven's explanation of his decision, *v.* in particular,

Le Monde, 10–11 October 1971. For the arguments for and against it, *v.* M. Tixier-Vignancour and R-G. Schwarzenberg in ibid., 15 October 1971.

86. For an account of the differences between the two texts, *v.* ibid., 26 January 1972. For the text of the Constitutional Council's decision, *v. Journal Officiel*, 25 January 1972.

87. Among these were interpretations of some ambiguities in the rules governing the use of 'continuous-assessment' methods of controlling the standard of university degrees and of degrees awarded by non-State (i.e. Catholic) universities.

88. The Constitutional Council's decision of 16 July 1971 eliminated the vital article of the Bill (article 3) on the ground that to give an official the power to defer giving an association the 'receipt' that conferred legal status on it until a court had pronounced on its conformity with the law was a requirement of 'preliminary authorization' (*autorisation préalable*). This was held to be contrary to the preamble of the Constitution, which accorded a fundamental right of association.

89. In the session 1971–2, 27·4 per cent voted, as against 37 per cent in 1970–1, and 52 per cent in 1969–70. Most of those elected were members of the Communist student union (*Le Monde*, 28 June 1972).

90. Ibid., 23 March 1972.

91. Alain Krivine in ibid., 11 March 1972.

92. On the terms of this law, *v.* Chapter II, pp. 57–9.

93. The Bill was voted on 27 April 1971 by 376 votes to 92, that is, with only Socialists and Communists voting against. The campaign against the original Bill in 1959 had attracted 10,000 signatures and a demonstration of 100,000 people. *v.* article by Frédéric Gaussen in *Le Monde*, 29 April 1971.

94. The first, on 20 April 1971, was a progress report on the first thirteen months of his policy for a 'new society', in which he noted as continuing problems those of inflation and a too low level of exports, the need for technical training, housing, better transport. The second, on 23 May 1972, included a long list of proposals to help the old, the young unemployed, the lower paid, and to improve investment, the telephone service, motorways ... etc. The economic commentator of *Le Monde* described it as consisting of confirmation of earlier promises, decisions that would be followed by no immediate effects, and long-range important measures such as those concerning

widows' pensions, motorways and the modernization of old houses. He described the programme as modest and unimaginative in comparison with the intentions of four years earlier, when the plan for a 'new society' was launched – a kind of 'ritual gesture' (*Le Monde*, 25 May 1972). Gaullists criticized it as being disappointing and lacking in dynamism. The loyalists such as MM. Debré, Germain, etc. had never had much enthusiasm for the new society.

95. The CGT called for a day's 'national strike' in support of this claim on 7 June, but the other confederations did not support it, describing it as 'political' and as 'electoralism'. In reality, it was intended mainly as a demonstration of the strength of the CGT.

96. Raymond Barrillon in *Le Monde*, 2 August 1972.

97. Jean-François Revel in *l'Express* (quoted in *Le Monde*'s review of the weekly press, 19 July 1972).

98. For text of the agreement, *v. Le Monde*, 29 June 1972. This was their first agreement on a Government programme since 1936.

99. Jean-François Revel, *l'Express*, 26 June to 2 July 1972.

100. Statement made at an international meeting of Socialist leaders on 28 June 1972 (*Le Monde*, 30 June 1972).

Cf. the statement made by M. Charles Hernu, a member of the *comité directeur*, on 5 November 1972 at Châteauroux:

> Every day that passes shows that the common programme of the Left will not be achievable unless Socialists and the Radical Left guarantee democratic freedoms. For that, it is necessary that forces should be more equally balanced. The democratic and Socialist Left must be the larger and more active partner. That will enable us to compete within the framework of the common programme, and to pretend that that is not so is nothing but hypocrisy.

101. A decision taken by the Socialist *comité directeur* at a meeting on 14 October 1972. The left-wing section of the party led by M. Jean Poperen had wanted to hold joint meetings in the *départements*. This proposal was defeated (*Le Monde*, 17 October 1972).

102. Ibid.

103. In the original French, the two sentences appeared as follows:

Si la confiance du pays était refusée aux partis majoritaires, ceux-ci renonceraient au pouvoir pour reprendre la lutte dans l'opposition. Mais le pouvoir démocratique, dont l'existence implique le soutien d'une majorité populaire, aura pour tâche principale la satis-faction des masses laborieuses et sera donc fort de la confiance sans cesse plus active qu'elles lui apporteront. (v. Programme commun de gouvernement, Editions sociales, 1972, p. 149)

The Socialist party programme included the commitment con-tained in the first sentence, though it did not use the precise phrase. *v. Changer la vie*, Flammarion, 1972, pp. 24, 100, and 113. The Communist party programme of October 1971 stated that Communists would respect the verdict of the people, and that the Government would resign if defeated on a vote of confidence or censure. *v. Programme pour un Gouverne-ment d'union populaire*, Editions sociales, 1972, pp. 128 and 136.

104. *v.* article by M. Pierre Joxe, 'La droite et l'alternance', *Le Monde*, 28 October 1972.

105. Raymond Barrillon, 'La Gauche et ses petites phrases', ibid., 4 October 1972.

106. André Wurmser in *Humanité*, 16 September 1972. M. Wurmser contributed another *'petite phrase'* that raised some queries: 'The Government will not be irremoveable, but the régime will.'

107. M. Peyrefitte expressed his views on *'l'alternance au pouvoir'* in a press conference on 6 October and on 22 October at Nantes, without apparently being called to order or disavowed in any way by the Prime Minister or the President. The two state-ments certainly seemed to amount to a Gaullist claim (i) that in practice the existence of a powerful Communist party ruled out *'l'alternance'* because Communists were cheats (*des tricheurs*), and (ii) that the impossibility of *alternance* implied the maintenance of the UDR as a dominant party within the majority. (*v.* reports of his speeches in *Le Monde*, 8–9 and 24 October 1972.)

v. also statements by M. Robert Boulin on 5 November 1972 to the UDR *assises départementales* of the Orne: '. . . *l'alternance politique, du fait de la coalition socialo-communiste n'est plus pos-sible*', and on 22 October: '*L'alternance ne peut se faire qu'au sein de la majorité*' (ibid., 24 October 1972). The Prime Minister said that he did not believe in Communist sincerity and that the Socialists would be hostages of the Communist party (ibid., 30 June 1972).

108. 'Une majorité sans alternance', *Le Monde*, 29 December 1972.
109. Press conferences of 21 September 1972 (ibid., 23 September 1972), and 9 January 1973 (ibid., 11 January 1973).
110. On Gaullist arguments on what the President ought to do, *v.* for instance, the article by five 'Faurist' Deputies in ibid., 5 January 1973. *v.* also M. Mitterrand's view quoted in *Les Informations* on 2 October 1972. MM. Mitterrand and Marchais both expressed themselves as satisfied with the President's reply on this point on 9 January, and announced that they were dropping the matter. It is difficult to see in what way this presidential statement differed from earlier ones. *v. Le Monde*, 13 January 1973.
111. Ibid., 14 October 1972. On politico-Constitutional disputes *v.* also pp. 71–4, 192–4, 346–8 and Vol. I, pp. 112–31.
112. *Le Projet réformateur* (Robert Laffont, 1973). The programme included a number of progressive social reforms, including acceptance of the CGT's claim for a minimum wage of 1000 francs per month, increased family allowances and old-age pensions. It also stressed the need for increased public investment and greater social equality. Its economic and social proposals were very similar to those of the common programme. Its emphasis was, however, more regionalist and Atlanticist, and it also expressed support for supranational European institutions.
113. M. Defferre's calculation was that, if Centrist candidates stood down at the second ballot, without specific recommendations to their supporters, two-thirds of them would vote for the Gaullists and their allies (*Le Monde*, 22 June 1972). In 1968, 100 UDR seats were won by majorities of under 1500. A swing of 3 to 4 per cent could therefore threaten the majority (ibid., 27 July 1972).
114. 'La Fonction centriste', ibid., 14 October 1972.
115. Quoted in ibid., 14 October 1972.
116. Declaration of general policy of 3 October 1972 (ibid., 5 October 1972).
117. Ibid., 11 November 1972.
118. Letter to ibid., 19–20 November 1972. On other Socialists who expressed doubts, *v.* ibid., 10 November 1972.
119. *l'Express*, 27 November–3 December 1972.
120. Statement made in September 1970 at the UDR *Journées d'études* at Chamonix from 16–18 September.

121. It was noted by commentators that M. Pompidou's statements sometimes sounded more prime-ministerial than presidential. *v.* for instance, the comment made by Sirius, after the Prime Minister's first declaration of general policy: 'The Prime Minister having made a presidential speech to the National Assembly last week, the President was obliged to make a prime-ministerial declaration' (*Le Monde*, 24 September 1969).

   How far General de Gaulle's portrait of M. Pompidou in *L'Effort* represented his real views is, of course, a matter of speculation. But the picture that does emerge (*v.* pp. 112–15) is certainly one that fits a head of Government more than a head of State, although, when *L'Effort* was written, M. Pompidou had been President for some time.

122. According to a SOFRES opinion poll, published in *Le Figaro*, 15–16 July 1972, 61 per cent of those questioned thought that of six persons listed, he had the best chance of a political future (M. Messmer was not one of the six). The results of an opinion poll published in *l'Aurore*, 6 July 1972, showed that 44 per cent of those questioned thought that he was the best of the Ministers. A year earlier, he had come only eighth on the list (André Fontaine, 'Les batailles à l'ombre de la bataille', *Le Monde*, 28 July 1972).

123. 'Le temps de la perplexité', ibid., 19–20 January 1972.

124. 'L'Ordre dans le désordre', ibid., 4 April 1972.

125. 'Remaniement et Démission. La seule ouverture', ibid., 17 May 1972.

126. *v.* pp. 348–52.

127. Both this appeal, made on the eve of the second ballot, and the President's television interview of 8 February, just before the campaign opened officially, were criticized. On the latter Jacques Fauvet wrote:

   > It is he who is the head of the executive, he who is the initiator of policy, he who is the sword and buckler of the Government majority. . . . General de Gaulle intervened in politics both more and less; he was careful never to mention names, whether of men, parties or groups within parties, and he restricted himself to the level of history and principle. (*Le Monde*, 10 February 1973.)

128. The figure was, in fact, considerably better than that reported to have been predicted by President Pompidou. According

to *l'Express* (26 February–4 March 1973), he said: 'The Government parties will have 260 Deputies, if I understand anything about politics.'

The figures as reported immediately after the election were:

Gaullists	184
Républicans indépendants	54
CDP	23

These 261 Deputies could normally count on the votes of 14 Deputies not included in the Government coalition. At this stage, the results were still unknown for Réunion (2nd constituency), Polynesia, and Corsica (2nd constituency). The sitting members in two of these were Gaullists.

129. According to the Ministry of the Interior's figures published in *Le Monde*, 7 March 1973, the Gaullist URP coalition polled 8,364,904 votes at the first ballot, i.e. 34·48 per cent of the valid votes cast. In 1967, the UDV[e] coalition had polled 8,453,512, i.e. 37·75 per cent. These figures do not include the results for the three constituencies mentioned in the note above, and the 1967 statistics quoted do not include the results for French Somaliland and Polynesia, and so are roughly comparable. There are always some discrepancies between figures quoted by different sources, but they are not usually sufficient to invalidate the comparisons. *v.* for instance, *Le Monde*, 7 March 1973, which gives the 1967 Gaullist coalition vote as 8,448,982 (37·73 per cent). It was estimated that, of the 1973 total, over 900,000 could be attributed to the CDP, which did not join the Government coalition until 1969. If this is so, then the combined Gaullist–*Républicain indépendant* vote of 1973, 7,463,768, shows a considerable drop in the Government coalition's vote, as compared with 1967, in spite of an increase of the electorate by over two million and a very high poll.

130. The percentage of voters in the first ballot in 1973 was given in the early results as 80·88 and the percentage of valid votes cast was 79·08. In 1968, 79·95 per cent voted in the first ballot (75·58 per cent of valid votes); in 1967, 80·92 per cent (79·11 per cent of valid votes); in 1962, the figures were 68·72 per cent (66·60 per cent of valid votes) (*Le Monde*, 7 March 1973 and *Année politique*, 1967, p. 14).

131. In the first ballot in 1973, the Communist party polled 5,156,619 votes (21·25 per cent); in 1967, 5,039,032 (22·51 per cent); in 1962, when the poll was unusually low, 4,003,553 (21·84 per cent). The comparable figures for the Socialist–Radical UGSD in 1973 and the Socialist-Radical-Convention FGDS in 1967 are:

UGSD 4,939,603 (20·36 per cent)
FGDS 4,224,110 (18·96 per cent)

132. It is not possible to obtain a clear picture of the evolution of the Centre on the basis of the published statistics, since the 1967 *Centre démocrate* included those Centrists who, in 1969, formed the pro-Government CDP, while the 1973 *Mouvement réformateur* included, along with Centrists, the section of the Radical party led by M. Jean-Jacques Servan-Schreiber.

133. Of the 30 Ministers, all of whom were candidates, 13 were returned at the first ballot and all but two of the remaining 17 at the second. MM. Pleven and Schumann were defeated.

PART II

CHAPTER VII

1. Quoted by Jean-Baptiste Duroselle in 'Changes in French Foreign Policy since 1945' (*France: Change and Tradition*, Gollancz, 1963), p. 307.

2. J. Caillaux, *Mémoires*, Vol. I (Plon, 1942), quoted by Alfred Grosser, *La IVe République et sa politique extérieure* (Armand Colin, 1961), p. 40n. For examples of French lack of interest in foreign policy in election campaigns, *v.* also pp. 34–5.
Cf. also Charles Seignobos, *La signification historique des élections françaises de 1928*:

It can be said without exaggeration that, up to 1914, foreign relations were dealt with by a small number of professional diplomats, together with the President of the Republic, the Minister of Foreign Affairs and, at times, the Prime Minister. Neither electors nor Deputies sought to intervene. . . .

3. Delcassé, for instance, carried out an essentially personal policy between 1898 and 1905. In 1950, the Schuman plan for a Coal

and Steel Community was presented to Parliament as a *fait accompli* in December 1951. M. Pompidou stated that only three members of the Cabinet had advance knowledge of the decision to withdraw from NATO.

It should be added that Foreign Ministers were themselves sometimes presented by *faits accomplis*. For instance, the deposition of the Sultan of Morocco in 1953, the arrest of the five Algerian nationalist leaders in October 1956 and the Sakhiet-Sidi-Yussef incident were all carried out by representatives on the spot, and responsibility accepted *a posteriori* by the Government. On the difficulties of Foreign Ministers in this connection, *v.* the article by M. Robert Schuman in *La Nef*, March 1953. An extract from it is quoted in Grosser, op. cit., p. 52.

4. *Mémoires de Guerre*, Vol. III, *Le Salut*, (*Le Rang*) (Plon, 1959), p. 90.

5. Quoted in *Troubled Neighbours*, ed. Neville Waites (Weidenfeld & Nicolson, 1971), p. 14.

6. *v.* for instance, the following extract from Thierry Maulnier's 'Lettre aux Américains', published in *Le Figaro*, 9 January 1957, apropos of the Suez affair:

> *Sous les regards de trois cents millions d'Arabes, vous nous avez humiliés devant un Nasser. . . . C'est aussi le vide devant les Russes qu'en prenant parti contre nous en Algérie vous ferez en Afrique du Nord. . . . Or on ne prive pas un vieux peuple encore orgueilleux de ce qui constitue le seul avenir digne de son passé sans risquer de l'entraîner, contre son propre intérêt, à des mouvements passionnels imprévisibles.*
>
> *La France défend en Afrique du Nord* SA DERNIERE CHANCE. *Entre sa vocation africaine et l'amitié américaine, ne la forcez pas à choisir.* (Quoted in Grosser, op. cit., p. 391.)

7. *Mémoires de Guerre*, Vol. I, opening paragraph.

8. *v.* the statement in *Réflexions sur l'Alliance atlantique*, quoted on p. 273.

9. Press conference of 11 April 1961 (*Année politique*, 1961, p. 649).

10. *La Diplomatie française* (Collection *Que sais-je?*, Presses universitaires de France, 1946), p. 121.

11. Quoted by Raoul Girardet, 'L'Influence de la tradition sur la politique étrangère de la France' in *La politique étrangère et*

ses fondements, ed. Jean-Baptiste Duroselle (Armand Colin, 1954), pp. 157–8.

12. *France: Change and Tradition,* p. 311; *v.* pp. 308–12 for examples of this attitude.

13. Speech of 15 September 1919 (quoted by Girardet, op. cit., pp. 158–9).

14. Speech at Compiègne on 7 March 1948 (quoted in Roger Massip, *De Gaulle et l'Europe,* Flammarion, 1963, p. 150, and *Mémoires de Guerre,* Vol. III, cit. *infra,* p. 457 n.7.

15. The Brazzaville Conference was attended by eighteen colonial Governors, but not by one native representative, and the Declaration specifically ruled out independence: 'the formation of independent Governments, however far off, cannot be contemplated'. What the Conference visualized was gradual progress towards partial self-government through colonial assemblies. The Minister for the Colonies in General de Gaulle's *Comité français de Libération nationale,* M. Pleven, stated at the Brazzaville Conference that France had: 'neither peoples to be freed nor racial discrimination to abolish. . . . There are populations that we intend to lead step by step to a more complete personality, and to a political freedom that will know no other independence than France's independence.'

16. For a brief account of the institutions of the Community, *v.* the author's *Fifth French Republic* (Methuen, 1965 edition), Chapter 9.

17. Speech at Brest on 21 July 1945 (quoted in Roger Massip, op. cit., p. 187).

18. G. Goodwin, *European Unity – A return to realities?* (The thirtieth Montague Burton lecture on international relations, Leeds, Leeds U.P., 1972), p. 8. For a detailed study of Franco-British disagreements, *v.* Waites (ed.), op. cit.

19. *Mémoires de Guerre,* Vol. III (*Le Saint*), Documents: Report of conversation with Marshal Stalin of 8 December 1944. It must be remembered that General de Gaulle was at that moment negotiating a treaty of alliance with the Soviet Union.

20. James Joll, *Europe – A Historian's View* (Twenty-seventh Montague Burton lecture on international relations, Leeds, Leeds U.P., 1969, p. 10).

21. *The Sunday Times,* 4 January 1959.

22. *Mémoires de Guerre,* Vol. II (*L'Unité*), p. 224.

23. *v.* pp. 314–17.
24. *v.* pp. 293–7.
25. *v.* pp. 251–2.
26. Goodwin, op. cit., p. 7.
27. *Immuable et changeante* (Calmann-Lévy, 1959), p. 225.
28. *v.* for instance, Jean Lacouture, *De Gaulle* (Hutchinson, 1971), p. 2: 'Of all contemporary statesmen Charles de Gaulle is the one whose political destiny will be seen to have depended most constantly on words.'

    v. also Pierre Mendès France, article in *Le nouvel Observateur*, quoted on p. 313.

CHAPTER VIII

1. Press conference of 1 October 1948. The actual phrase used was in reply to a question as to whether General de Gaulle, if in power, would change French foreign policy. His reply was:

   > I should not have to change France's foreign policy, because at present France has no foreign policy. Her political system makes it impossible for her to have one, just as it makes it impossible for her to have any economic policy that deserves to be called one, or any social or financial policy, etc. . . . The truth is that there is no policy at all. I shall, therefore, not change this non-existent policy. But my policy will be that of France. (*Le Rassemblement*, 9 October 1948)

2. *La Nef*, December 1952, pp. 145 and 147.
3. Robert Schuman's statement was made at Bruges in 1953. Edouard Herriot's in *La Nef*, December 1952, p. 11, and General de Gaulle's press conference of 29 March 1949 is quoted in René Courtin's *l'Europe de l'Atlantique à l'Oural* (Editions l'Esprit nouveau, 1963), p. 119.
4. Jacques Fauvet, *La quatrième République* (Arthème Fayard, 1958) p. 251.
5. Broadcast of 13 June 1958 (*Année politique*, 1958), pp. 544–5.
6. Speech to Congress of 25 April 1960 (ibid., 1960, p. 644.)
7. Carlo Laroche, *La Diplomatie française* (Presses universitaires de France, 1946), pp. 115 and 121.
8. Speech at Marseilles on 17 April 1948. *v.* also speech at Compiègne, 7 March 1948, in which he said that France's 'dignity'

and 'duty' both required her to be 'the centre and the key' of a group of nations 'having as its arteries the North Sea, the Rhine and the Mediterranean'. (Both speeches are quoted in Roger Massip, *De Gaulle et l'Europe*, Flammarion, 1963, p. 150.)

9. Speech at Strasbourg, 22 November 1959, quoted in Courtin, op cit., p. 124.

10. Speech at Limoges, 20 May 1962, quoted in Massip, op. cit., p. 153.

11. Pierre Lefranc, *Président du Comité de Soutien du Général de Gaulle*, in 'Libres Opinions, L'indépendance nationale', *Le Monde*, 20 February 1970.

12. André Philip, in ibid., 31 January 1963.

13. For details of the Fouchet Plans, *v. Towards Political Union*, documents published by the general directorate of parliamentary documentation and information of the Political Committee of the European Parliament, January 1964.

14. Speech to the Foreign Affairs Committee of the National Assembly, 7 February 1963.

15. For a detailed account of this controversy, *v.* John Lambert, 'The Constitutional Crisis 1965–66', in the *Journal of Common Market Studies* of May 1966. For a briefer account, *v.* the author's *The Uneasy Entente* (Chatham House Essays, Oxford, Oxford U.P., 1966), pp. 56–63.

16. In his speech at Strasbourg, 22 November 1964, General de Gaulle defined 'European Europe' as meaning 'independent, powerful and influential, at the heart of the free world' (*Année politique*, 1964, p. 439). In his previous press conference on 23 July, he had defined it as follows: 'A European Europe means that Europe exists by herself and for herself, or in other words, that in the midst of this world she has her own policy.'

17. Statement of 5 November 1964 in the National Assembly (*Année politique*, 1964, p. 302). *v.* also General de Gaulle's press conference of 28 October 1966 (ibid., 1966, p. 418).

18. 'Contre la force multilatérale', *Notre République*, 1 January 1965.

19. *v.* in particular, General de Gaulle's press conference of 4 February 1965, in which he stated that the problem of German reunification could be settled only in a European framework, and appeared to be relegating any serious consideration of the possibility to the distant future when 'Europe

from the Atlantic to the Urals' would exist or be in process of creation.

20. Figures given in *Le Monde*, 21–2 January 1968, showed a total of one and a half million student exchanges. At the beginning of the year there were 3000 German students in France and only 750 French students in Germany, and even this represented an increase in the proportion of French students as compared with the years 1964–7. Over 50 per cent of Germans were studying French at school. 18 per cent of French children were choosing German as their first and 33 per cent as their second foreign language.

21. Jean Lecanuet, leader of the *Centre démocrate* (quoted in *Le Monde*, 24 November 1964).

22. Maurice Duverger in ibid., 12 June 1964.

23. Quoted by Maurice Duverger in ibid., 24 February 1968.

24. Ibid.

25. Interview in ibid., 31 January 1970.

26. Speech in the National Assembly on 18 June 1965.

27. Press conference of 16 May 1967 (*Année politique*, 1967, p. 388). Cf. press conference of 27 November (ibid., pp. 398–9).

28. Jacques Baumel at the Council of Europe on 24 April 1964.

29. Press conference of 16 May 1967 (*Année politique*, 1967, p. 388).

30. *v.* in particular, the press conferences of 29 July 1963, 31 January 1964, 9 September 1965, 28 October 1966, 16 May 1967) in ibid., 1963 (p. 419), 1964 (p. 424), 1965 (p. 437), 1966 (p. 418), 1967 (p. 388).

31. *Le Monde*, 30 January 1963: 'Les Polaris, l'Angleterre et le Marché commun'.

M. Fontaine assumed, however, that the *tone* of the President's press conference the following month was affected by the *speed* with which Mr Macmillan accepted US *conditions* at Nassau, a view borne out by the following unofficial comment said to have been made by the President at a reception given to Deputies early in 1963:

> Mr Macmillan came to tell me that we were right to have our strike force. 'We, too, have our own,' he said. 'We ought to combine them in a European framework independent of the United States.' Whereupon, he left me to go to the Bahamas. Naturally, what happened there made me change the tone of my press conference of 14 January.

Since there are a number of such 'unofficial' presidential pronouncements made on similar occasions, some of which were formally repudiated later, others merely ignored, it would be advisable to treat this source with some caution. M. Fontaine's own conclusion was that, at that time, the President thought that Britain was going downhill economically and would eventually be obliged to apply for entry on terms that would be more satisfactory to the Six, and that, in the interim, 'Europe' would have become independent of the US.

A recent American account of the Nassau meeting described as a 'favorite Gaullist myth' the theory that President Kennedy and Mr Macmillan had agreed before the Rambouillet meeting that Britain should acquire Polaris and that Mr Macmillan misled General de Gaulle and was thus guilty of duplicity. The truth, he claims, is that the Nassau Agreement was the result of 'hasty improvisation and high-level imprecision, of decisions taken by the President in Nassau before he was ready to take them in Washington', and that it was only at Nassau that Mr Macmillan disclosed to President Kennedy his ambition to acquire Polaris. Mr Macmillan, according to this account, could perhaps be accused of duplicity in that he did not reveal at Nassau how badly the interview with General de Gaulle had gone (*v.* John Newhouse, *De Gaulle and the Anglo-Saxons*, André Deutsch, 1970, pp. 213–18). The author does not, in fact, accuse Mr Macmillan of duplicity, but merely suggests that he was technically 'disingenuous'.

32. *v.* interview of 8 February 1963 by M. Edgard Pisani, then Minister of Agriculture (*Le Monde*, 10–11 February 1961). M. Couve de Murville and M. Debré were still maintaining this point of view in 1966 and 1967 (*v.* the former's speech to the National Assembly Foreign Affairs Committee, reported in ibid., 18–19 June 1966, and the latter's speech at the *dîner-débat* of *Les Echos*, reported in ibid., 11 October 1967). A leader in ibid., 13 October 1967, suggested that France feared German and British collaboration in an attempt to change the agricultural policy. During the 1969 Presidential campaign, M. Poher and the Defferre–Mendès France tandem both reaffirmed that agriculture was the main cause of Britain's exclusion. (*v.* however, Uwe Kitzinger, *Diplomacy and Persuasion* (Thames & Hudson, 1973, Chapter 1), who believes that sterling was also a stumbling block during de Gaulle's presidency.)

33. *Le Monde*, 11 July 1969.
34. At a meeting of the Council of Ministers on 10 July (*v. Année politique*, 1967, p. 212).
35. Guy de Carmoy, *The Foreign Policies of France* (Chicago, Ill., U. of Chicago Press, 1968), p. 441.
36. *v. Mémoires d'Espoir: Le Renouveau 1958–1962* (Plon, 1970), pp. 167, 188, 190, 199 (*Memoirs of Hope: Renewal 1958–1962, Endeavour 1962*, Weidenfeld & Nicolson, 1971, pp. 159, 178, 179–180, 188).
37. *v.* for example, the French Government statement that '. . .

> WEU was created in 1954 in response to military consider-ations at that time. But what we have been seeing since the end of last year is an offensive whose object is to establish regular discussions between the Seven of questions concern-ing politics, defence, technology and currency; the obvious intention is to encroach on Common Market territory' (*Année politique*, 1969, p. 225).

38. The French text of article VIII of the WEU Treaty (as revised in 1954) is to be found in ibid., 1954, p. 666. The English text is as follows:

> (1) For the purposes of strengthening peace and security and of promoting unity and of encouraging the progressive integration of Europe and closer co-operation between Them and with other European organizations, the High Contracting Parties of the Brussels Treaty shall create a Council to consider matters concerning the execution of the Treaty and its Protocols and their annexes.
>
> (2) This Council shall be known as the 'Council of Western European Union', and it shall be so organized as to be able to function continuously; it shall set up such subsidiary bodies as may be considered necessary; in particular it shall establish immediately an Agency for the Control of Armaments whose functions are determined in Protocol No. IV.
>
> (3) At the request of any of the High Contracting Parties the Council shall immediately be convened in order to permit Them to consult with regard to any situation which may constitute a threat to peace, in whatever area this threat may arise, or a danger to economic stability.

(4) The Council shall decide by unanimous vote questions for which no other voting procedure has been or may be agreed. In the cases provided for in Protocols II, III and IV it will follow the various voting procedures, unanimity, two-thirds majority, simple majority, laid down therein. It will decide by simple majority questions submitted to it by the Agency for the Control of Armaments.

39. *v. The Times* and *The Guardian*, 26 February 1969, also *The Times*, 2 March 1969 and *Année politique*, 1969, p. 227.

40. *v.* for instance, André Fontaine's article in *Le Monde*, 11 March 1969, 'Comment avorta le dialogue franco-britannique'. He suggests that though there were still reasons for believing that Great Britain might want to break up Europe, there was no reason for the British to suspect any kind of 'trap'. The latter suggestion certainly makes sense. As pointed out by M. Debré, there was nothing new in the President's proposal (*v.* his version given to the Community Ambassadors on 24 February). The President had, indeed, explicitly suggested in his press conference of 27 November 1967 that he would consider any change in the organization of the Community that might become necessary and had invited proposals from the other members. He had also perpetually said in press conferences that, if the Fouchet proposals for political co-operation were still unacceptable, he would be prepared to listen to any other proposals that might be put forward.

   Nor was there anything 'sinister' in the suggestion for bilateral conversations. Only a few months later, Dr Luns and Chancellor Brandt had bilateral talks. It is possible that the President was considering raising again his previous suggestions that Great Britain might accept some form of 'association' short of actual membership of the Community. It is even possible that he was merely seeking to improve the Franco-British climate.

41. On 24 February, M. Debré called a meeting of the Ambassadors of France's five partners, at which he endeavoured to allay any fears regarding the proposed 'Council of Four', referring to its proposed rôle as essentially one of military co-operation. According to the *Année politique* report, he failed to convince them (*Année politique*, 1969, p. 227).

42. Made during a visit to Paris in July (*Le Monde*, 22 July 1969).

43. For the most important French statements of the conditions
    defined in the 'triptych', *v.*:

    (i) the Foreign Minister's statement at the Council of Foreign
        Ministers in Brussels on 15 September 1969 (*Année poli-
        tique*, p. 294); that of the following month, which empha-
        sized the priority to be given to the achievement of the
        agricultural financial agreement (ibid., p. 305); the policy
        declaration by the Foreign Minister of 28 April 1970 (*Le
        Monde*, 29 April 1970), in which he emphasized the impor-
        tance of the third condition, namely, agreement by the
        Six on a preliminary negotiating position.

    (ii) the presidential press conference of 10 July 1969; the
        statement at the Bonn meeting of 8 September in which
        the phrase '*achèvement, approfondissement, élargissement*' was
        again put forward; the presidential statement at the Hague
        summit in December 1969 (*Année politique*, p. 317).

    (iii) the Prime Minister's statement to the National Assembly
        of 26 June 1969.

Statements such as that in the presidential press conference
of 10 July 1969, that France had no objection 'in principle' to
British membership, or by M. Schumann to the Franco-British
Society in London in January 1970, affirming that, in the long
term, Britain's presence would be essential to Europe, were
invariably seized on by the British press as affording grounds
for optimism, but were usually accompanied in the French
press by explicit reminders that a change of tone implied no
essential modification of the French position (*v.* for instance,
the comment in *Le Monde*, 24 January 1970, on M. Schumann's
statement in London). For the French, it was the conditions
that mattered, but, ever since the 'veto' of 1967, French
Government circles had consistently sought not to *appear* to
be imposing a veto. In reality, adherence to the conditions,
as interpreted by France, would have made a veto unnecessary,
and it was only when one of them was, in effect, abandoned
that negotiations really got under way. M. Schumann himself
pointed out that interpretations of his remarks relating to the
transitional period had been over-optimistic (*The Guardian*,
24 January 1970). On 29 January, when the European Parliament accepted, by a large majority, a resolution supporting
the communiqué issued after the Hague meeting (which in
reality committed nobody to anything), the Gaullist delegation

abstained, insisting on the need for close consultations between the Six before the opening of negotiations.

44. Ratification was approved by 420 to 34 votes, that is, with only the Communists opposing (*Année politique*, 1970, p. 281).

45. Roger Berthoud in *The Times*, 10 May 1971.

46. For details, *v. Année politique*, 1970, pp. 299–300.

47. The Commission's 'Barre Plan' on monetary and economic co-operation was approved in principle in January 1970, but there were divergences between Germany and Holland on the one hand, and France and Belgium on the other, regarding the immediate steps to be taken to apply it. The 'Werner Committee' submitted a report in October which sought to reconcile the differing points of view. Basically, the divergency concerned the problem of priorities, France and Belgium giving priority to monetary unification, Germany and Holland to that of economic union.

48. Press conference of 21 January (*Le Monde*, 23 January 1971).

49. *v.* report in ibid., 19 May 1971. His precise words were: 'I am aware of the relations between Great Britain and New Zealand, and I believe them to be sentimental rather than commercial, even though they are concerned in the end with tons of butter and cheese. . . . As we ourselves produce butter and cheese, we have our own points of view in this matter and they are not wholly sentimental.'

50. Speech made on 26 June 1971 (*Le Monde*, 29 June 1971). *Le Monde*'s report does not include this remark which was reported in *The Times* of 28 June. Mr. Rippon (*The Times*, 29 June) commented that it was a speech intended for domestic consumption and that politicians were obliged to make such speeches in their own countries.

51. By then four major problems remained unsettled. These were the question of New Zealand dairy produce, the size of the British contribution to Community funds and the length of the period of transition during which there would be progressively increasing contributions, the future of Commonwealth sugar, governed up to 1974 by the Commonwealth sugar agreement, and the question as to whether Britain should accept Community preference immediately or be granted a period of transition. France wanted immediate British acceptance of Community preference, the phasing out of preferences for New Zealand butter and cheese by 1977, the replacement of Commonwealth

sugar suppliers by French beet sugar producers, and much larger British contributions to the Community funds during the transition period than the figure proposed by the British delegation. The last three were settled by compromises substantially nearer to the French than to the British demands, and Britain agreed to the French demand on Community preference.

52. On this, *v.* Kitzinger, op. cit., Chapters 2–5. Mr Kitzinger gives a fascinating blow-by-blow account of the negotiations. Though himself an enthusiastic supporter of Britain's membership of the Community, his account demonstrates convincingly that France succeeded in getting most of her way all along the line, and that her negotiating team was organized with great efficiency in order to do this.

53. It may or may not be significant that, in reflecting on the consequences of the monetary crisis caused by the United States measures of August 1971, M. Jean-François Deniau, whose views were generally close to those of the French Government, should have suggested amendment of the MacMahon Act, which, from 1946 onward, had prevented Britain from sharing nuclear secrets with France.

54. *The Times*, 26 May 1971.

55. Kitzinger, op. cit., p. 71.

56. *Deuxième Rapport général sur l'activité des Communautés, 1968* (Brussels–Luxembourg, February 1969), p. 14.

57. Jean Schwoebel in *Le Monde*, 30 November–1 December 1969.

58. Pierre Drouin, ibid., 29 October 1969.

59. *v.* for instance, the following statement by a dedicated and well-informed British supporter of the Community and of British membership of it:

> . . . the Spring of 1968 sees the Community losing the last of its momentum, not least as a result of reactions to the veto, and unlikely to develop beyond its present stage, even to become an effective union. National interests are increasingly resuming their priority over Community affairs or obligations. The generation in power throughout the Community and beyond no longer has a vision of a united Europe, and to the dissatisfied younger generation the European idea seems no more than a dream that has failed. (John Lambert, *Britain in a Federal Europe*, Chatto & Windus, 1968, p. 203)

60. Pierre Drouin, *Le Monde*, 29 October 1969.
61. Jacques Bouchacourt, Deputy for the Nièvre, Secretary of the *Groupe parlementaire pan-européen*, in *Le Monde*, 'Libres Opinions, Mythes et Réalités', 19 January 1971.
62. Ibid., 12 October 1971. Cf. statement by a member of the European Parliament in October 1971 that the Common Market was facing 'the worst economic situation since its inception' and the European Commission's quarterly report for October, which emphasized the general slowing down of the Community's activity and the rising unemployment figures. Its continuing internal conflicts were evident in the Brandt–Pompidou and Heath–Pompidou meetings of January and May 1973.
63. 'Nécessités américaines, vertus européennes', II: 'Du bon usage d'une crise', *Le Monde*, 20 October 1971.
64. The British concession was to agree to an initial contribution in 1973 of 8·64 per cent of the Community Budget, rising to 18·92 per cent by 1977 (£150 million to £350 million). The British had wanted 2·6 to 3 per cent and the French 20 per cent. The French concession to British desires for guaranteed outlets for Commonwealth sugar was to undertake – when the general convention of association applying to her own former overseas possessions came up for renewal in 1974, along with the Commonwealth sugar agreement – 'to take into account' the interests of producers of primary products, including sugar. The exact phrase used was '*aura à cœur de sauvegarder les intérêts* ...', which appeared in the English version as 'will have as its firm purpose' (*v.* Protocol 22 of the Treaty of Accession). In fact, the French phrase means nothing so precise. In the expressive phrase of Lord Campbell, the French expression was 'what his carpenter ... said when he meant that he would not in fact have time to do the job, but would feel slightly guilty about it'. (*v.* Kitzinger, op. cit., p. 134–8.)
65. Ibid., p. 71.
66. M. Gaston Defferre, in a speech to the Socialist Congress on 2 February 1964.
67. *v.* his broadcast of 14 December during the presidental election campaign of 1965, in which he dismissed 'Europeans' as being content, to 'jump up and down in their seats, shouting Europe, Europe, Europe'.
68. *v.* statement by M. Waldeck Rochet, secretary-general of the

French Communist party, on 10 January 1968 (*Le Monde*, 12 January 1968).

69. *v.* statement by M. Waldeck Rochet opposing supranationalism in the EEC and calling for the democratization of its 'technocratic' structure (*Le Monde*, 5 January 1968). On what was implied by democratization, *v. Programme commun de gouvernement* (Editions sociales, 1972), pp. 177–81. Most of the specific reforms advocated were to be 'asked for' by a Socialist–Communist Government, which, of course, offered no guarantee that they would be accepted by France's partners.

70. In the *Bundestag* debate of 12 March 1957 (quoted in W. Pickles, *Not with Europe: The Political Case for Staying Out* (Fabian Tract 336, 1962).

71. According to an estimate by the head of the International Federation of General and Chemical Workers, 65 per cent of all mergers in EEC countries in 1968 and 1969 were with non-EEC countries (*The Guardian*, 30 March 1970).

72. *Basic Statistics of the Community*, 1970, pp. 83 and 87. By 1971, German exports to other members of the Community had increased by 288 per cent in ten years, and French exports to other members by 400 per cent. But French exports to Germany had increased by 500 per cent (Pierre Drouin in *Le Monde*, 21 January 1971).

73. Ibid., 15 August 1971.

74. *v.* article of 20 October 1971, quoted above, note 63.

75. In his reply to a question on this point, the President said that he thought a Minister for European Affairs was still a long way off, and that Europe was still *'une réalité suffisamment forte pour être traitée indépendamment des affaires étrangères'* (*Le Monde*, 18 March 1972).

76. There had been hints by the Foreign Minister, M. Maurice Schumann, at the Bonn meeting of the Atlantic Council on 31 May, that the summit meeting was not yet a certainty, and by M. Pompidou on 2 June.

77. Message to Parliament of 5 April 1972 (*Le Monde*, 7 April 1972).

78. *v.* the statement by M. Jacques Vendroux, General de Gaulle's brother-in-law, that the Europe to which France was being committed was not that desired by General de Gaulle (*Le Monde*, 18 April 1972), and Etienne Borne (Christian Democrat) in ibid., 8 April 1972, on the President's use of 'a typically Gaullist procedure in order to obtain the approval of the

French people for a policy completely contrary to the consistent ideas of General de Gaulle'.

79. *v.* the President's first television statement on 11 April 1972, and his final television broadcast on the eve of the referendum on 21 April 1972 (ibid., 13 and 22 April 1972).

80. *v.* results in ibid., 30 April–2 May 1972, and comment by André Fontaine in ibid., 7–8 May 1972.

81. While Queen Juliana of the Netherlands made a very integrationist speech at the dinner given for her at Versailles in June 1972, the President made a very anti-integrationist speech (ibid., 21 June 1972).

CHAPTER IX

1. *La IVe République et sa Politique extérieure* (Armand Colin, 1961), p. 402.

2. *v.* p. 288.

3. 'Réflexions sur l'alliance atlantique', in *13 mai 1958–13 mai 1962* (Plon, 1962), p. 45.

4. *Combat*, 4 July 1958 (quoted in John Newhouse, *De Gaulle and the Anglo-Saxons*, André Deutsch, 1970, pp. 57–8).

5. Alfred Grosser, 'General de Gaulle and the Foreign Policy of the Fifth Republic', in *International Affairs*, April 1963, p. 211.

6. *v.* opening paragraph of Volume I of General de Gaulle's *Mémoires de Guerre*, *L'Appel* (Plon, 1954), p. 1. According to Jean-Raymond Tournoux, this paragraph is all we need to know in order to understand General de Gaulle's policies. All the rest, he says, is interpretation.

7. *v. Mémoires de Guerre*, Vol. III, *Le Salut*, 'Discordances' (pp. 179–80). This passage summarizes the essentials of what General de Gaulle describes as the 'vast plan' that he had for France at the time of the Liberation. As this volume was not completed until much later and published only in 1959, after his return to power, it may owe something to hindsight. The following is the complete paragraph:

> To guarantee her security in Eastern Europe, by preventing a new Reich from threatening her again. To collaborate with both the West and the East, and, if necessary, to ally with one side or the other, without agreeing to any kind of dependence. To achieve the progressive transformation

of the French Union into a free association and so prevent the as yet undefined risk of its breaking up. To bring about the political, economic and strategic association of the States bordering on the Rhine, the Alps and the Pyrenees. To make this organization one of the three great world powers and one day, if necessary, the arbiter between the Soviet and the Anglo-Saxon camps. All that I have said and done since 1940 has been with these possibilities in mind. Now that France is herself again, I shall try to attain these objectives.

8. Speech at Mézières on 22 April 1963. The phrase occurs in the following context:

> We have also an international task . . . it is, in the first place, to help in the building of a united Europe. Economic Europe first, then political Europe, then the Europe of the Europeans, fraternal Europe at last, which is something that we have never seen. . . .

9. The problem of the army and the régime was, of course, the essential problem, but the restoration of discipline was not enough. The modernization and especially the nuclearization of the army were also problems that were causing stresses within the army. *v.* the special number of *La Nef*, '*L'Armée française*' (Julliard, July–September 1961).

10. *v. Mémoires d'Espoir, L'Effort,* pp. 20–9 (English translation, pp. 307–9).

11. For a summary of the terms, *v.* Newhouse, op. cit., pp. 70–1, *Le Monde*, 11–13 November 1958, and 28 October 1960, and Guy de Carmoy, *The Foreign Policies of France* (Chicago, Ill., U. of Chicago Press, 1968), p. 275. For General de Gaulle's own much later explanation of his intentions, *v. Mémoires d'Espoir, Le Renouveau*, pp. 212–15 (English translation, pp. 200–3).

12. Mr Newhouse, op. cit., quotes the proposal as referring specifically to 'the Arctic, the Atlantic, the Pacific and the Indian Ocean' (p. 70), but cf. press conference of General de Gaulle, 5 September 1960 (*Année politique*, 1960, p. 658), where he refers to Europe, the Middle East and Africa only.

13. *v. Mémoires d'Espoir, Le Renouveau*, p. 215 (English translation, p. 203). Newhouse, op. cit., p. 64. For the development of

the argument that the memorandum was merely 'a tactical manœuvre', *v.* Newhouse, pp. 71–80.

14. *v.* statement to the National Assembly during the debate of 13 October: 'Participation in atomic strategy, participation in the supreme decision, that is our aim', and statement on 25 October that General de Gaulle was merely seeking a measure of three-power consultation and co-operation. *v.* also de Carmoy (op. cit., p. 279), who quotes the secret correspondence between General de Gaulle and President Eisenhower, in which the General was expressing hopes for 'an equal share in joint decisions on the use of nuclear arms'. Both Mr Newhouse (op. cit., pp. 78–9) and M. de Carmoy appear to rely a good deal on American journalistic or diplomatic sources.

15. *Année politique*, 1960, p. 658.

16. *v.* Newhouse, op. cit., pp. 71–3. The argument that General de Gaulle deliberately leaked the terms of his memorandum in order to promote resistance to his own initiative (p. 78) perhaps underestimates the ease with which confidential documents are regularly leaked in Paris! Perhaps, too, it underestimates the extent to which General de Gaulle liked to throw out suggestions, like pebbles into a pool, in order to watch the ripples, but without necessarily having any precise long-term purpose. The fact that he provided no incontrovertible evidence as to what his real purposes were was also an essential part of this strategy, for it achieved at least one of his permanent objectives, namely to ensure that his words and acts were perpetual talking points. On the other hand, it must be admitted that the Italians specifically stated that the terms had been communicated to them by France, and the reactions in the German and Italian press were along predictable lines. (*v.* account in *Année politique*, 1958, pp. 451–3.) *v.* note 56.

17. Speaking in the National Assembly on 24 October 1960, the Prime Minister actually referred to the memorandum as having been published, so well known were the generally accepted reports of its contents. This slip of the tongue was corrected in the report of his speech published in the *Journal Officiel* (*Année politique*, 1960, p. 562).

18. In his press conference of 25 March, the President claimed, apparently in defence of this decision, that France might be called on to defend regions south of the Mediterranean. Of

course, nothing prevented her from using her naval forces in the Mediterranean in time of peace, for they were then under national command. It is difficult to justify the decision to withdraw these units in time of war, when, as Guy de Carmoy points out (op. cit., p. 276), a unified command would be essential. The real reason was undoubtedly political. The President resented the fact that considerable parts of the American and British fleets were not under NATO control. France also resented the distribution of Commands in NATO. The Deputy-Supreme Commander at SHAPE was British, whereas the French Naval Deputy was regarded by the French as being merely an adviser without any real powers. Of the four main European Commands, Britain held two (North Europe and the Mediterranean), whereas France held only one (Central Europe). Of the sector Commands, France held only one (West Mediterranean), whereas Britain held four (North Europe, Naval forces, Central Europe, Air forces, Mediterranean–Gibraltar, and south-east Mediterranean). In the Atlantic sector, the French held only two sub-sectors, and in the Channel Committee the British held more sector Commands than the French. France objected, too, to the progressive displacement of the French by the English language.

19. *v.* press conference of 5 September 1960 (*Année politique*, 1960, p. 658). On General de Gaulle's differences with NATO during this period, *v.* de Carmoy, op. cit., pp. 277–8.

20. *Année politique*, 1959, pp. 631–2.

21. Statement in the National Assembly on 29 October 1963.

22. The description of it given by the then secretary-general of the Gaullist party was: 'militarily worthless, technically absurd and politically dangerous'. *Le Monde*, 17 December 1964.

23. Georges Broussine in *Notre République*, 4 June 1965.

24. A significant exception was the press conference of 23 July 1964, where the President did outline the theory of 'relative deterrence'. M. Pompidou also appeared to subscribe to it, to judge by the few words devoted to it in his speech to the National Assembly on 2 December 1964.

25. For text of the press conference of 14 January 1963, *v. Année politique*, 1963, p. 402.

26. 'The Raison d'être of French defence policy', *International Affairs*, October 1963, p. 502.

Among Gaullists who have discussed the theory in language

comprehensible to the layman, *v.* also the same author's *Stratégie de l'âge nucléaire* (Calmann-Lévy, 1960; (English translation, *The Balance of Terror*, Boston, 1961); Alexandre Sanguinetti, *La France et l'arme atomique* (Julliard, 1964), and his article, 'Etude de la dissuasion', in *Stratégie* (Centre d'Etudes de politique étrangère, Institut français d'études stratégiques, July–September and October–December 1964). For a more technical account, *v.* General André Beaufre, *Introduction à la stratégie* (Armand Colin, 1963; English translation, *Introduction to Strategy*, Faber & Faber, 1965). For an analysis and refutation of Gaullist theories, *v.* Raymond Aron, *Le Grand Débat* (Calmann-Lévy, 1963; English translation, *The Great Debate*, New York, Doubleday, 1963). For a good British account of French nuclear policy in relation to defence policy, *v.* Wolf Mendl, *Deterrence and Persuasion* (Faber & Faber, 1970).

27. Louis Vallon, *Le grand Dessein national* (Calman-Lévy, 1964), pp. 185–6. *v.* also General de Gaulle's own account of his reply to President Eisenhower, when the latter expressed doubts regarding the effectiveness of the French deterrent: '. . . It is enough to be able to kill the enemy once, even if he possesses the means to kill us ten times over' (*Mémoires d'Espoir, Le Renouveau*, p. 227. English translation, p. 215).

28. *Le Grand Débat*, pp. 121–2.

29. Jules Moch, *Recontres avec . . . Charles de Gaulle* (Plon, 1971), pp. 343–4.

30. For a much more detailed criticism, *v.* Raymond Aron, op. cit., Chapter IV.

31. *v.* for instance, the following statement by General Gallois: 'Only a real interdependence which is based on a genuine exchange [i.e. on the planning and technology of modern armaments programmes] will enable the rest to avoid submitting to the interests of the strongest' ('The raison d'être of French defence policy', *International Affairs*, October 1963, p. 510). *v.* also André Beaufre, 'The sharing of nuclear responsibilities', (ibid., July 1965, p. 412) on the French demand for a 'share in the formulation of plans and in the decisions on the use of those [i.e. tactical nuclear] weapons'. In his view, there could be no collective control of deterrent strategy in peacetime. It would be necessary, therefore, to reorganize NATO in order to replace an integrated strategy by 'the organization of an effective co-ordination of national deterrent strategies' (p. 417).

32. Quoted in *Le Monde*, 4 December 1964.
33. Speech in National Assembly on 14 May 1963.
34. *v. Changer la vie, programme de gouvernement du parti socialiste* (Flammarion, 1972), p. 206. This is a careful statement that a Government of the Left will 'decide on the cessation' of nuclear production and of nuclear tests, but take due account of the international situation and the time needed in order to carry out the decision. *v.* also Common programme, pp. 171–2, which takes similar precautions.
35. *Encounter*, March 1963.
36. On this argument, put forward by Stanley Hoffman, *v.* Aron, op. cit., p. 155 (note) and also Stanley Hoffman, 'Les conflits internationaux', in *Revue française de Science politique*, April 1964, p. 319. According to John Newhouse, op. cit., p. 186 note), a senior member of the Kennedy administration informed the French Government in the bluntest language that French nuclear weapons would never trigger off action by the American strike force.
37. Press conference of 9 September. *v. Année politique*, 1965, p. 439. M. Couve de Murville was reported as having said in 1967 that he had known since 1958 that General de Gaulle intended to take France out of NATO (*v. Le Monde*, 2 March 1967).
38. *v.* the following passage from the press conference of 21 February 1966:

> Between now and 4 April 1969, at which date the period of her obligations under the treaty comes to an end, France will (without ceasing to be a member of the alliance) continue to modify the application of the provisions of the treaty as they concern her. . . . She will restore the normal conditions of sovereignty, under which all that is French – including all forces on the ground, in the air and on the sea, and all foreign forces in France – will be under the sole control of French authorities. (*Année politique*, 1966, p. 411)

39. For texts of these letters, together with the *aide-mémoire* to the NATO allies, *v.* ibid., pp. 413–15.
40. Ibid., p. 414.
41. de Carmoy, op. cit., p. 316.
42. *Le Monde*, 18 June 1966. Among other typical Gaullist statements, *v.* Jacques Vernant in *Revue de Défense nationale* (August-

September 1962); Jacques Debû-Bridel in *Notre République* (1 July 1966), who affirmed the concordance of Gaullist and Communist policies regarding Germany and the Vietnam war, and described General de Gaulle's visit to Moscow of that year as 'completing the withdrawal of France from NATO'; François Mauriac in *Le Monde* (6–7 November 1966), who wrote that 'what has most fascinated our people, whose prestige has been diminished by a shameful defeat and four years of enemy occupation, and whose empire has been amputated, is the demonstration that American hegemony is not inevitable in Europe – that it is not even inevitable for the small country of France, which in 1966 is freer and more independent than when she was a great nation'.

43. Speech in the National Assembly debate of 14 April 1966.
44. Speech in the censure debate of 19 April 1966.
45. *Témoignage chrétien*, 24 March 1966.
46. Speech in the National Assembly debate on 19 April 1966.
47. Speech in the National Assembly debate on 14 April 1966.
48. Speech in the censure debate of 19 April 1966.
49. The wording of the motion, and in particular, the decision whether or not to restrict it to censuring the Government's foreign policy, had given rise to a great deal of controversy within the opposition parties. The Socialists were anxious that the Communists as well as the Centre 'Europeans' should support it, but the former refused to vote against the Government's withdrawal from NATO. In the event, the motion was worded so as to include criticisms of certain aspects of economic and social policy as well as foreign policy. It was, however, signed only by 40 Socialist and 9 Radical Deputies.
50. *Le Monde*, 31 March 1966. *v.* also his article of 20 April 1966 on the need for the gradual evolution of Europe towards independence of the United States, together with that of Alfred Grosser on the same date, expressing the French conviction that the United States could not afford *not* to defend France. *v.* also leader in *Le Monde* of 14 April 1966, which argued that the real problem was political, and resulted not from the French desire for independence of the United States, but also from the fact that the latter

though prepared for solidarity with their allies against a threat of aggression in Europe, which most Europeans regard as less and less likely, are not conscious of the need for solidarity outside Europe regarding the solution of the great problems on which the maintenance or the restoration of peace really depends: the place of China in the world, the Vietnam war, the sharing of nuclear responsibilities . . . etc.

51. *Le Monde*, 16 April 1966.
52. Ibid., 7 June 1966.
53. *v.* Socialist programme, pp. 198–200, and Socialist–Communist 'Common Government programme', pp. 174–5.
54. *Le Monde*, 10 March 1966.
55. For the official Government case, in particular on these points, *v.* speeches made in the National Assembly on 13 April by the Prime Minister, M. Pompidou, and on the following day by the Foreign Minister, M. Couve de Murville.

The following are the relevant passages on the problem of the reform of the structure of NATO:

> . . . after expressing our opinions on various occasions both to representatives of the United States and to the Secretary-general of NATO, after the President of the Republic had clearly defined our intentions many times and in particular at his press conference last February, we took the decision, failing any better alternative, to act on our own account. . . .
> (M. Pompidou)

> It is easy today to say to all and sundry that we did not want negotiations. After talking for eight years to people who turned a deaf ear we could come only to one of the two following conclusions: either to give up all idea of change and make the best of a system which, as time went by, seemed more and more outdated and more contrary to our interests as well as to our policy, or else to take for ourselves, as far as France was concerned, the decisions that were needed. The Government waited a long time, but was obliged in the end to come to the second conclusion.
> (M. Couve de Murville)

56. This statement was first made in an informal interview given to *Paris-Match* and was officially made public by the State Department on 12 April 1966. It was repeated on 30 May 1966. In an interview to the Brussels paper, *Le Soir*, on 9 May, M. Paul-Henri Spaak said that there had been no discussion in

NATO of any French proposals for reform because 'France dared not risk such a discussion, knowing that the extreme case that she was putting would not have stood up to the wisdom of the arguments against' (quoted in *Le Monde*, 12 May 1966). In his book, *De Gaulle and the Anglo-Saxons*, John Newhouse affirms, though without giving any source, that the Americans had persistently urged General de Gaulle to put forward suggestions on NATO reform, but that, in January 1966, the French President had informed the Secretary-general of NATO, Signor Manlio Brosio, that 'France would *not* put forward proposals aimed at making NATO a more desirable instrument from France's point of view', because he thought that they 'would not receive proper consideration, for the Americans were, after all, fighting a war in Vietnam and would be unable to focus seriously on NATO reform' (p. 285).

According to Newhouse (op. cit., p. 79), Washington released documents on the 1958 de Gaulle Memorandum and the various proposals for talks on Western defence in August 1966 (Congressional hearings), having leaked them to C. L. Sulzberger in 1963 (*v.* summary in *Le Monde*, 16 August 1966). De Carmoy (op. cit., pp. 274–6) gives a brief summary of the 1958 Memorandum, based on the account given by Schoenbrunn (*The Three Lives of Charles de Gaulle*, New York, and Hamish Hamilton, 1966), supposedly inspired by Washington. The somewhat involved account in Newhouse (pp. 69–84) of the exchanges in 1958 includes the suggestion that de Gaulle never intended the proposal seriously, but was merely trying to create reactions favourable to his anti-NATO policy. (*v.* also p. 279 and p. 459, note 16.)

57. *Année politique*, 1966, p. 411. *v.* also *Mèmoires d'Espoir, Le Renouveau*, p. 227 (English translation, p. 214).

58. Speech in the National Assembly in the debate of 13 April 1966.

59. Aron, op. cit., p. 187.

60. *Le Renouveau*, p. 214 (English translation, p. 202).

61. The President did lay down a time limit of one year for the completion of the withdrawal of foreign forces from France, which perhaps, in his mind, constituted the required notice of one year. Or it may be that France regarded this requirement as being applicable only in the case of withdrawal from the Alliance, which is what article 13 of the treaty is concerned

with. M. Couve de Murville admitted that the distinction made by France between membership of the Alliance and membership of the NATO organizations was not generally made and that the term NATO was normally used to refer both to the Alliance and the organizations, but he maintained that 'the one is by no means the condition of the other' and that they were 'not necessarily linked' (*v.* speech in the National Assembly on 14 April 1966).

62. Speech of 20 October 1965 in the National Assembly debate.

63. This accusation was, indeed, made in the debate on the withdrawal from NATO. M. Pleven, in the speech of 14 April, already quoted, also said: 'If we are to believe the Government, negotiation is impossible. But where and when has any attempt been made to negotiate that would justify the affirmation? Your haste proves your desire to create an irreversible and, in our view, irreparable situation.'

64. Broadcast of 27 April 1965, *Année politique*, 1965, p. 432.

65. *v.* article in *Le Monde* of 13 February 1970. General Jousse also estimated that France's nuclear potential was only one fifteen-thousandth of that of the USSR. In 'The Sharing of Nuclear Responsibilities' (*International Affairs*, July 1965, p. 411), General Beaufre admitted that the United States controlled 98 per cent of the nuclear capacity of the Atlantic Alliance.

66. Debate in the National Assembly of 14 April 1966.

67. *v.* for instance, Louis Vallon in *Notre République*, 15 September 1967, who advocated French withdrawal from the Alliance by August 1968, adding: 'We must resist American hegemony by extending Europe to the East, or we shall become part of a small, integrated Europe, subordinate to the United States.'

68. *v.* press conference of 9 September 1968, in which the President said that the events in Czechoslovakia were to be condemned 'especially because they are absurd in the context of European détente'. He added, however, that the repercussions of these events showed that 'though our policy may appear to have suffered a temporary setback, it is nevertheless right, because it is in harmony with the fundamental realities of Europe'.

69. *Année politique*, 1968, pp. 302–3.

70. He added, however, that France continued to reject integration.

71. On 10 June 1970, M. Pompidou said: 'It is in the spirit of independence that we intend to continue our alliance, and

especially that with the United States of America, our friends and permanent allies.'

72. *v.* article by General Ailleret in *Revue de Défense nationale*, December 1967.

73. Quoted *in Le Monde*, 30 January 1968.

74. *v.* article in *Revue de Défense nationale*, May 1969.

75. In his press conference of 4 March 1969, Mr Nixon said that he would 'hold out some hope that as our conversations continue, we can find a number of areas for mutual co-operation and consultation on the military side as well as in other respects'. He was careful, however, not to hold out any hopes of France's return to NATO.

76. *v.* press conference on 7 October 1970 in Moscow, quoted Chapter X, note 69.

77. *v.* General Georges-Picot in *Le Monde*, 31 July 1971, and Jacques Dauer (a left-wing Gaullist) in ibid., 24 July 1971.

78. M. Alexandre Sanguinetti in ibid., 26 January 1972.

79. Speech by the Minister of Defence, M. Michel Debré, to the General Assembly of Western European Union, on 6 December, 1972.

80. The delivery of the first nine missiles was in June 1971, immediately following President Pompidou's first visit to the missile base, *v. Le Monde*, 22 June 1971.

81. *v.* ibid., 26 January 1972.

82. The Minister of the Armed Forces, M. Messmer, had already stated before the 1968 financial difficulties that there would be no Polaris missiles before 1973 and ICBMs only in the 1980s. *v. Revue de Défense nationale*, March 1968. On the general programmes of French nuclear weapons, *v.* Wolf Mendl, op. cit., pp. 85–117.

83. The British had already withdrawn from ELDO in 1968. The French withdrew from the joint project for a swing-wing aircraft, and there were increasing doubts (in Britain more than in France) regarding the prospects for Concorde in view of its perpetually escalating costs. There were disagreements between France on the one hand and Germany, Britain and Holland on the other regarding the process to be adopted for the planned isotope-separation plant. In October 1969, a working party had submitted 47 plans for European technological co-operation to nine European countries, yet at the Hague summit in December 1969, no mention was made of

any. There were merely references to a research project on atomic energy to make better use of Euratom and to the possibility of a European university. *v. Année politique*, 1969, p. 321.

CHAPTER X

1. Speech by Michel Debré of 26 June, quoted in *Le Monde*, 3 July 1970.
2. Speech by General de Gaulle at Langres, quoted in René Courtin, *l'Europe de l'Atlantique à l'Oural* (Editions l'Esprit nouveau, 1963), pp. 138–9.
3. The passage in Hamlet is:

> . . . Rightly to be great,
> Is not to stir without great argument,
> But greatly to find quarrel in a straw
> When honour's at the stake.
> (Act IV, Scene IV)

4. Television interview of 14 December 1965, *Le Monde*, 16 December 1965.
5. Press conference of 2 July 1970, *ibid.*, 4 July 1970.
6. Declaration to the press of 17 August 1950, quoted in Roger Massip, *De Gaulle et l'Europe* (Flammarion, 1963), p. 151.
7. Between 1962 and 1965, France contributed on average around 2 per cent per annum of her national income in aid to countries of the third world, as against 1 per cent each contributed by the United States, Britain and Germany. Of this total, 86 per cent went to countries in the franc area. (Figures given in OECD reports, quoted by Guy de Carmoy, *The Foreign Policies of France* (Chicago, Ill., U. of Chicago Press, 1968), pp. 238–9.)
8. J. Gagliardi and P. Rossillon, *Survivre à de Gaulle* (Plon, 1959), p. 109. The two authors belonged to a Gaullist movement, *Patrie et Progrès*, which included a number of young civil servants. M. Rossillon was a French official responsible for organizing cultural co-operation in Canada at the time of General de Gaulle's visit in 1967.
9. From 1967 onwards, even President Sekou Touré of Guinea proclaimed his desire to restore contacts with France, having experimented with the alternative of relying on aid from countries behind the iron curtain.

10. *Le Monde*, 26 November 1965. *v.* also articles in *Le Monde* on 30 June and 6 July 1966, on discussions in the organization of the African States regarding the formation of such a Community.

11. *Année politique*, 1964, p. 423.

12. Ibid., 1967, p. 396. In 1968, there was a flare-up of Canadian resentment, apropos of alleged separatist activities by M. Rossillon.

13. *Le Monde*, 14–15 June 1970.

14. *v. La Politique extérieure de la Ve République* (Collection Jean Moulin–Le Seuil, 1965), pp. 167–8. (English translation, *French Foreign Policy under de Gaulle*, Boston and Toronto, Little, Brown, 1967, pp. 139–40.) also p. 79 (English, p. 61).

15. He did, however, in several places refer to France's interest in the creation of *'un vaste ensemble'*, including South America, which could counterbalance the influence of Washington and Moscow, and he also stressed the right of national self-determination. (*v.* accounts in *Le Monde*, 10–13 October 1964.)

16. Article in *Le nouvel Observateur*, published in *The Guardian*, 4 January 1968.

17. *Le Monde*, 26 September 1964. This was in a speech in Ecuador, on 24 September.

18. Comment by Guy Mollet in *Démocratie 64*, October 1964.

19. *v.* for example, the phrase in the broadcast of 27 April 1965 – widely regarded as the *de facto* opening of the presidential election campaign – 'never has so much attention been paid to us' (*il n'y eut jamais plus d'empressement autour de nous*), and his statement in the press conference the following September that France's national recovery was shown in her population curve, her production, foreign trade, standard of living, monetary reserves, and in 'the spread of our language and our culture, the power of our arms and our sporting results'.

20. *Le Monde*, 30 July 1968.

21. The first phrase occurred in the press conference of 5 September 1961, the second in that of 11 April 1961. The often-quoted description of the UN as *'le machin'* (thingummybob) was made in a speech in October 1963 during a tour of the French provinces.

22. *Année politique*, 1961, p. 648.

23. *v.* the opening paragraph of the Note of 17 August 1961, published by the French Ministry of Foreign Affairs: 'A

communiqué of 28 July made the Government's position regarding Bizerta clear. It stated that the only hope of a solution lay in direct negotiations between France and Tunisia.' (Published in *Année politique*, 1961, p. 663.)

24. At the meeting of the Security Council on 4 March 1964, France abstained on the issue of an international force for Cyprus. In this case, the method of financing it was not in dispute.

25. France alone abstained on the Security Council's motion (12 November 1965) condemning UDI. France had condemned the action, but considered that Rhodesia was a domestic affair and concerned only Great Britain (statement in the General Assembly of 12 October).

26. On 22 May 1965.

27. *Année politique*, 1965, p. 428.

28. *v.* for instance, M. Couve de Murville's speech of 29 September to the General Assembly of the United Nations: 'The General Assembly is the expression of international public opinion, and it should consequently be the highest world political forum.'

29. *v.* press conference of 15 May 1962, replying to question on France's attitude to NATO (*Année politique*, annexe, p. 664). *v.* also press conference of 4 February 1965, in which General de Gaulle proposed a five-power agreement, preferably at Geneva, to go back to the position at the time at which the United Nations was set up (ibid., p. 429).

30. Press conference of 5 September 1961 (ibid., 1961, p. 666).

31. Press conference of 29 July 1963 (ibid., 1963, p. 416).

32. In 1966, for instance, after a considerable increase in the amount of trade between France and the Eastern bloc, it still accounted for only about 5 per cent of France's total trade, as against over 50 per cent with Western Europe (of which 41 per cent was with EEC countries) and 9 per cent with the USA. (*v. Le Monde*, 15 September 1967.)

33. *v.* statement by M. Debré on 8 January 1969, at the third session of the *Grande Commission Franco-Soviétique* (*Le Monde*, 10 January). Apart from the agreement (of doubtful value) by the USSR to use the French colour-television system, the pattern of trade, though it showed a noticeable percentage increase, was still unimpressive, as compared with French trade in other areas, and showed a persistent tendency for imports from the Eastern bloc to exceed exports to it.

34. *v.* for instance, the following comment of a French journalist on the status of France in the United Nations: 'In the present atmosphere, the explosion of French bombs makes less noise in the General Assembly than do the bombs exploding in Vietnam.' He described France as *'la première puissance neutraliste'*, attributing her prestige to decolonization, anti-Americanism, her relations with the Soviet Union and her opposition to the war in Vietnam. He noted, however, some objections among the Afro-Asians to her attitude to the United Nations (*v.* article by Camille Fondère in *Le Monde*, 28–9 August 1966).

35. *Année politique*, 1964, p. 426.

36. It was not until July 1970 that the first official visit to China by a French Minister took place. (M. Malraux did visit China in 1965, but this was an unofficial visit, and M. Malraux himself was not an influential Minister.)

37. Statement by the Prime Minister, M. Pompidou, in April 1968, at a dinner for the Prime Minister of Syria (*Le Monde*, 4 April 1968).

38. Ibid., 26 September 1969.

39. *v.* press conference of 5 September 1960 (*Année politique*, annexe, p. 658).

40. A report by a Gaullist parliamentary delegation in 1964, following a visit to Vietnam, made it quite clear that, in their view, the result of unification would be a Communist take-over. In that respect, the situation remained the same in 1966 and 1967.

41. Alfred Fabre-Luce, *L'Or et la bombe* (Calmann-Lévy, 1968), Chapter IV. The comment is not unfair in the light of General de Gaulle's phraseology, both in the Pnom Penh speech and in his press conference of 28 October 1966 (*v. Année politique*, annexe, p. 417).

42. It is doubtful whether General de Gaulle himself really believed that he carried any weight with the Soviet Union. He was reported as having commented on his 1966 visit: 'They played their record; I played mine.' (Quoted in *Le Monde*, 28 June 1966.)

43. *v. Le Salut* (Plon, 1959), pp. 198–9.

44. Pro-Israeli feeling was also part of the anti-Germanism of the French Left and was no doubt intensified by the Socialistic policies of Israeli Governments. Israel was also the only ally of

France in the Middle East area during the Algerian war and voted consistently in favour of France in the United Nations.

45. A number of protests were made – for instance, by the *Comité de solidarité française avec Israël*, the *Comité de co-ordination des organisations juives en France*, *La Ligue contre le racisme*, the *Ligue des droits de l'Homme*, the *Association France–Israël* . . . etc. The French Socialist party described the French policy of embargo as 'hypocritical' and its so-called neutrality as a pretence (*v. Le Monde*, 11–12 January 1970). *Le Monde*'s leader on 23 January 1970 was no less outspoken: 'What is really objectionable about the Government's behaviour is the obstinacy with which it tries to make us believe that the delivery of arms to Libya does not affect its impartiality in the Middle-East conflict.'

46. For a comprehensive statement of the Government's justification, *v.* M. Debré's speech to the National Assembly's National Defence Commission on 21 January 1970 (*Le Monde*, 23 January 1970).

47. Ibid., 24 January 1970.

48. The Tlemçen agreement signed on 27 May 1970. *v.* ibid., 3 and 10 February, 5–6 and 15 April 1970, which show the increasing Moroccan desire to improve relations with France.

49. The agreement was initialled during a visit of the Algerian Foreign Minister to Tunisia at the beginning of January. A treaty of 'fraternity, neighbourliness and co-operation' between Algeria and Tunisia was signed on 8 January 1970.

50. The French Foreign Secretary had already paid an official visit to Algeria the previous 2–3 October. President Boumedienne's statement was made early in January (*v. Le Monde*, 6 January 1970).

51. Ibid., 23 June 1970.

52. In the *Journal du Jura*, quoted in ibid., 29 January 1970.

53. Ibid., 23 June 1970.

54. Speech of 21 January 1970, made to the UDR group in the National Assembly.

55. 'Une Politique méditerranéenne?', *Le Monde*, 24 January 1970.

56. *Memoirs of Hope, Renewal*, p. 211 (*Le Renouveau*, p. 223).

57. Ibid., p. 214 (*Le Renouveau*, p. 254).

58. Ibid., p. 256 (*Le Renouveau*, p. 256).

59. Press conference of 28 October 1966 (*Année politique*, 1966, p. 417).

60. French parliamentary parties were, at that time, so preoccupied with party tactics in view of the forthcoming elections, the budget debates and the Ben Barka affair that it is doubtful whether many noticed, let alone deplored, the consequent worsening of Franco-American relations as a result of these declarations of General de Gaulle. In a television interview shortly after the Pnom Penh speech, the *Centre démocrate* leader, M. Lecanuet, merely contributed a proposal that Americans should 'get out of Vietnam following an agreement', without indicating how any agreement could be reached. *Le Monde*, 14 September 1966.

61. Ibid., 9–10 May 1965.

62. de Carmoy, op. cit., p. 478.

63. John Newhouse, *De Gaulle and the Anglo-Saxons* (André Deutsch, 1970), p. 306.

64. Ibid., pp. 351–2.

65. *Memoirs of Hope, Renewal*, pp. 168–9 (*Le Renouveau*, p. 179).

66. Ibid., p. 11 (*Le Renouveau*, p. 15).

67. Ibid., p. 200 (*Le Renouveau*, p. 212).

68. General de Gaulle's prompt announcement of French support for the United States at the time of the Cuba crisis was held by some to have been dictated by the view that Cuba was in the United States sphere of influence and that the Soviet action was thus a threat to the territory of the United States. It could, therefore, provide a useful precedent, should General de Gaulle want at some time to invoke United States support in the presence of what he regarded as a threat to French territory or to the territory of a country that France claimed to be in her own sphere of influence.

69. Ibid., p. 208 (*Le Renouveau*, p. 221). *v.* also President Pompidou's commitment in his broadcast of 10 June 1969, and his statement in his press conference in Moscow on 7 October 1970:

    We have left the military integrated organization and we have no intention of returning to it. But we are members of the Atlantic Alliance and we have no intention of leaving it. (*Le Monde*, 9 October 1970)

70. *Memoirs of Hope, Renewal*, p. 215 (*Le Renouveau*, p. 227).

71. Newhouse, op. cit., p. 36.

72. Speech to the Consultative Assembly on 23 November 1944. *v. Année politique*, 1944–5, p. 490.

73. *Memoirs of Hope, Renewal*, p. 212 (*Le Renouveau*, p. 225).
74. *Carrefour*, 23 April 1958.
75. Philip de Saint-Robert in *Notre République*, quoted by Fabre-Luce, op. cit., Chapter IV.
76. *La Politique étrangère du Gaullisme* (Julliard, 1964), p. 135.
77. *Le Monde*, 24 February 1970.
78. Ibid., 14 March 1970.

PART III

CHAPTER XI

1. *v.* for instance, Philip Williams and Martin Harrison, *De Gaulle's Republic* (London, Longman, 1960) and *Politics and Society in de Gaulle's Republic* (London, Longman, 1971); Roy Macridis and Bernard Brown, *The De Gaulle Republic* (Dorsey Press Inc., Homewood, Illinois, 1960); Léo Hamon, *De Gaulle dans la République* (Plon, 1958); and Pierre Viansson-Ponté, *Histoire de la République Gaullienne* (Fayard, 1970 and 1971).
2. Statement to the Central Committee of the Gaullist party in April 1971. M. Peyrefitte, his successor, also made similar statements, rejecting a Gaullism that was merely the cult of 'a dead God' (meeting of Gaullist constituency and departmental secretaries in October 1972). Nor were such statements limited to officials of the party, who might consider themselves in duty bound to make them. Deputies such as M. Charles Pasqua, a member of the *Amicale*, admitted that M. Pompidou was best fitted to conserve the Gaullist heritage (*Le Monde*, 15 November 1972). And even M. Malraux is reported to have said that the Fifth Republic would be '*la République pompidolienne*' (quoted by Viansson-Ponté, in ibid., 23 March 1972).
    In addition to statements already quoted by fundamentalist Gaullists, *v.* Dominique Gallet, leader of the left-wing Gaullist *Front des jeunes Progressistes*, for whom the nation was 'foundering in the evil-smelling marshes of Pompidolisme' (*Le Monde*, 9 March 1972).
3. Ibid., 23 October 1971. Cf. Pierre Viansson-Ponté in 'La Dégradation des Politiques' (ibid., 27 May 1972): '. . . the transition is over, but the future is not yet born'.
4. *v.* pp. 268–9.

5. At a press conference following New Year greetings to the President from French and foreign press associations on 2 January (*The Times*, 3 January 1973).

6. In the Socialist weekly *Unité*, quoted in *Le Monde*, 14 October 1972.

7. 'Modèle 1900', in ibid., 12–13 November 1972.

8. *v.* General de Gaulle's description in the Bayeux speech in June 1946: *'notre perpétuelle effervescence politique'*.

9. Georgette Elgey, *La République des illusions* (Fayard, 1965).

10. In addition to the open disagreements between the two party programmes, supposed to have been resolved by the compromises achieved in the 'common programme', the joint declaration of the Communist party and the Democratic and Socialist Left in February 1968 had contained important differences (*v.* Vol. I, pp. 191–2 and 387–8, note 81) and the balance-sheet of Socialist–Communist talks, published in December 1970, had revealed irreconcilable differences. There were also disagreements on the conduct of the campaign and criticisms by a number of Socialist Deputies (in addition to those made by MM. Charles Hernu and Arthur Notebart, *v.* pp. 204 and 438, n.100. A right-wing Socialist Deputy, M. Max Lejeune, was expelled from the party and some local Socialist parties in his constituency dissolved. At least one member of the Socialist Directing Committee, M. Eric Hintermann, announced that he and his friends who were opposed to the common programme intended to reopen the question of Socialist strategy 'after the election' – i.e. they openly admitted that the whole operation was really governed by electoral considerations. During the campaign, each party tried to present the common programme as being essentially its own, implying that compromises had been made by the other.

11. At the twentieth Congress of the Communist party in December 1972, the average age of delegates was 33. Membership figures were announced at a meeting of federation secretaries on 11 December 1972 as being 400,000, which was the figure quoted in December 1970. This figure showed a steady decline from 1954 onwards, when it had been over the half-million mark. Yet over 40,000 new members were announced in 1972. Indeed, membership figures were usually accompanied by the announcement of some 30,000 to 40,000 new members. Of the 1326 delegates at the 1972 Congress, 72 per cent were

said to have joined the party since 1958 and 39 per cent since 1968. (Figures quoted in *Le Monde*, 12 and 19 December 1972.)

12. *v.* references to this problem in presidential press conferences of 21 September 1972 and 9 January 1973. In January, he merely reiterated what he had previously said, but more briefly, namely, that he would have to ensure that a Government had the support of the National Assembly, and that he had the power to dissolve the Assembly if he considered it necessary (*v.* text of press conferences in *Le Monde*, 23 September 1972 and 11 January 1973). On 8 February, however, in a broadcast just before the official opening of the election campaign, he said that the Left's accession to power would 'completely upset the institutions' of the Fifth Republic. 'Let no one count on me [he went on] to deny all that I believe in, and that the French people have solemnly approved.' (Ibid., 10 February 1973.)

13. *v.* Vol. I, pp. 64–8.

14. Statement at the UDR *Journées d'études parlementaires*, 15–17 September 1971. *v.* also statement immediately afterwards to a meeting of the Toulouse UDR federation (*Le Monde*, 17 and 21 September 1971).

15. *v. Le Phénomène gaulliste* (Fayard, 1970), pp. 64–5. English translation *The Gaullist Phenomenon* (George Allen & Unwin, 1971).

16. Two articles in *Le Monde*, 31 October and 1 November 1972.

17. Pierre Dabezies, 'Le Déclin du Parlement' (*Projet*, June 1971).

18. Forecast given in the weekly periodical *Le Point* at the beginning of January 1973 by Mr Edmond Stillman, director of a survey carried out on behalf of the French Government by the European division of the Hudson Institute of New York. The report was published later under the title *L'Essor de la France*.

19. Pierre Viansson-Ponté, 'Les Mots et les Choses' (*Le Monde*, 20 April 1972).

Bibliography

The sources quoted below include only the more recently published general material in book form, together with a small selection of documents published by the French Embassy and *Documentation française* on economic and social policy, and on French overseas aid. Articles in periodicals, and material dealing with special topics, are indicated in the notes. English translations have been noted where known.

Internal Politics

(a) GENERAL

ARON, RAYMOND, *Immuable et changeante*, Paris, Calmann-Lévy, 1959.

CAHM, ERIC, *Politics and Society in Contemporary France (1789–1971) A documentary history*, London, Harrap, 1972.

CHAPSAL, JACQUES, *La vie politique en France depuis 1940*, Paris, Presses universitaires de France, 1966. New edition 1969, by Alain Lancelot.

GOGUEL, FRANÇOIS, *Modernisation économique et comportement politique*, Paris, Armand Colin, 1969.

VIANSSON-PONTÉ, PIERRE, *Histoire de la République Gaullienne*, 2 Vols. Paris, Fayard, 1970 and 1971.

WILLIAMS, PHILIP and HARRISON, MARTIN, *Politics and Society in de Gaulle's Republic*, London, Longman, 1971.

(b) DE GAULLE, GAULLISM, GAULLIST AND ALLIED POLITICS

ALEXANDRE, PHILIPPE, *Le Duel de Gaulle-Pompidou*, Paris, Fayard, 1970.

CHARLOT, JEAN, *Le Phénomène Gaulliste*, Paris, Fayard, 1970 (*The Gaullist Phenomenon*, London, Allen & Unwin, 1971).

CONTE, ARTHUR, *La Succession*, Paris, Julliard, 1963.

— *Sans de Gaulle*, Paris, Plon, 1970.

CRAWLEY, AIDAN, *De Gaulle*, London, Collins, 1969.

DEBRÉ, MICHEL, *Au service de la nation*, Paris, Stock, 1963.

— *Lettre à des militants sur la continuité, l'ouverture et la fidélité*, Paris, Plon, 1970.

FABRE-LUCE, ALFRED, *Le plus illustre des Français*, Paris, Julliard, 1962.

— *Le Couronnement du Prince*, Paris, La Table ronde, 1964.

FOUCHET, CHRISTIAN, *Au service du général de Gaulle*, Paris, Plon, 1971.

GAULLE, CHARLES DE, *Mémoires de Guerre, L'Appel, 1940–1942*, Paris, Plon, 1954; *L'Unité 1942–1944*, Paris, Plon, 1956; *Le Salut 1944–1946*, Paris, Plon, 1959 (*The Call to Honour*, London, Collins, 1955; *Unity*, London, Weidenfeld & Nicolson, 1959; *Salvation*, London, Weidenfeld & Nicolson, 1960).

— *Mémoires d'Espoir, Le Renouveau 1958–1962*, Paris, Plon, 1970; *L'Effort, 1962–*, Paris, Plon, 1971 (*Memoirs of Hope, Renewal 1958–1926, Effort 1926–*, London, Weidenfeld & Nicolson, 1971).

— *Discours et Messages*, 5 Vols. Paris, Plon.

HARTLEY, ANTHONY, *Gaullism, the Rise and Fall of a Political Movement*, Routledge & Kegan Paul, 1972.

LA GORCE, PAUL-MARIE, *De Gaulle entre deux mondes*, Paris, Fayard, 1964.

LACOUTURE, CHARLES, *Charles de Gaulle*, Paris, Editions du Seuil, 1965 (*De Gaulle*, London, Hutchinson, 1970).

MALRAUX, ANDRÉ, *Les Chênes qu'on abat*, Paris, Gallimard, 1971.

MAURIAC, CLAUDE, *Un autre de Gaulle*, Paris, Hachette, 1970.

MAURIAC, FRANÇOIS, *De Gaulle*, Grasset, 1964 (*De Gaulle*, London, The Bodley Head, 1966.)

MOCH, JULES, *Rencontres avec . . . de Gaulle*, Paris, Plon, 1971.

MORAZÉ, CHARLES, *Charles de Gaulle*, Paris, Editions du Seuil, 1965.

NUNGESSER ROLAND, *Pour une société nouvelle. La Révolution qu'il faut faire*, Paris, Plon, 1970.

Party programmes, 1973, of *Union des républicains de progrès* (Gaullists and allies)

Speech by Prime Minister, M. Pierre Messmer, at Provins on 7 January 1973. 'Bilan et perspectives' (*Le Monde*, 9 January 1973).

Un sens à la vie. (*Républicains indépendants*).

ROUANET, PIERRE, *Georges Pompidou*, Paris, Grasset, 1969.

SOUSTELLE, JACQUES, *Vingt-huit années de gaullisme*, Paris, La Table ronde, 1968.

VALLON, LOUIS, *Le grand dessein national*, Paris, Calmann-Lévy, 1964.

— *L'Anti-de Gaulle*, Paris, La Table ronde, 1969.

VIANSSON-PONTÉ, PIERRE, *Les Gaullistes*, Paris, Editions du Seuil, 1964.

WILLIS, F. ROY, *De Gaulle, Anachronism, Realist or Prophet*, New York, Holt, Rinehart and Winston, 1967.

(c) POLITICS OF THE LEFT AND CENTRE PARTIES

BARRILLON, RAYMOND, *La gauche française en mouvement*, Paris, Plon, 1967.

DEFFERRE, GASTON, *Un nouvel horizon*, Paris, Gallimard, 1965.

GUILLE, GEORGES, *La gauche la plus bête*, Paris, Table ronde, 1970.

MITTERRAND, FRANÇOIS, *Ma part de vérité*, Paris, Fayard, 1969.

MOLLET, GUY, *13 mai 1958–13 mai 1962*, Paris, Plon, 1962.

— *Les chances du socialisme*, Paris, Fayard, 1968.

Party programmes, 1973, of Left and Centre parties

Changer de cap. Programme pour un gouvernement démocratique dunion populaire, Paris, Editions sociales, 1972 (Communist).

Changer la vie. Programme de gouvernement du parti socialiste, Paris, Flammarion, 1972.

Programme commun de gouvernement du parti communiste et du parti socialiste, Paris, Editions sociales, 1972.

Le Projet réformateur, programme de gouvernement, Paris, Robert Laffont, 1972 (Jean Lecanuet and Jean-Jacques Servan-Schreiber).

PSU, *Manifeste de 8e Congrès*, TEMA-Action, 1972.

Ce que veut la ligue communiste, Paris, Editions Maspéro, 1972.

PHILIP, ANDRÉ. *La Gauche, Mythes et Réalités*, Paris, Aubier, 1962.

SERVAN-SCHREIBER, JEAN-JACQUES, *Le Manifeste radical*, Paris, Denoël, 1970.

SUFFERT, GEORGES, *De Defferre à Mitterrand*, Paris, Editions du Seuil, 1966.

WILLIAMS, PHILIP M., *French Politicians and Elections, 1951-69*, Cambridge, University Press, 1970.
— *Wars, Plots and Scandals in post-war France*, Cambridge, University Press, 1970.

(d) ECONOMIC AND SOCIAL POLICIES

ARDAGH, JOHN, *The New French Revolution*, London, Secker & Warburg, 1968.
CLUB JEAN MOULIN, *Quelle Réforme? Quelles Régions?*, Paris, Editions du Seuil, 1969.
COHEN, STEPHEN S., *Modern Capitalist Planning: The French Model*, London, Weidenfeld & Nicolson, 1969.
FOURASTIÉ, JEAN and COURTHÉOUX, J-P., *La Planification économique en France*, Paris, Presses universitaires de France, 1963.
HANSEN, NILES, *French Regional Planning*, Edinburgh, University Press, 1968.
LYNES, TONY, *French Pensions*, London, G. Bell & Sons, 1967.
PAVIE, PHILIPPE FOULQUES, *Prononcez-vous sur la participation*, Paris, Collection Données du problème, EMCERI Editions, 1969.
P.E.P. *French planning: Some Lessons for Britain*, Vol. XXIX, No. 475, 1963.
PERROUX, FRANÇOIS, *Le IVᵉ Plan français*, Paris, 'Que sais-je?', Presses universitaires de France, 1962 (*The IVth French Plan*, London, National Institute of Economic and Social Research, 1965).
PISANI, EDGARD, *La Région, pourquoi faire?*, Paris, Calmann-Lévy, 1969.
SHONFIELD, ANDREW, *Modern Capitalism*, Oxford, R.I.I.A., 1965.

(e) DOCUMENTS ON ECONOMIC AND SOCIAL POLICY
PUBLISHED BY FRENCH EMBASSY AND *Documentation française* SERVICES

French Embassy, Press and Information Service

The Fifth French Economic and Social Development Plan, 1966-70 (A/44/12/6).

The Sixth Plan (1971-5) (A/85/1/72).
Planning and Development of the Paris region (A/47/9/9).

France: a Blueprint for 1985 (A/24/1/5).
French Industrial Production: Facts and Figures (A/70/9/9).
Agriculture in France (A/83/7/71).
Twenty-five Years of Social Security (B/61/2/7).

Notes et Etudes documentaires (Documentation française)

Rapport de M. Toutée, No. 3069, 2 March 1964.
L'organisation régionale de la France, No. 3212, 22 July 1965.

Foreign Policy

(a) GENERAL

ARON, RAYMOND and LERNER, DANIEL (directeurs), *La Querelle de la C.E.D.*, Paris, Armand Colin, 1956.

CARMOY, GUY DE, *Les politiques étrangères de la France 1944–1966*, Paris, La Table ronde, 1967 (*The Foreign Policies of France 1944–1968*, Chicago, Ill., University of Chicago Press, 1970).

COUVE DE MURVILLE, MAURICE, *Une politique étrangère 1958–1969*, Plon, 1971.

DUROSELLE, J-B. (ed.), *La politique étrangère et ses fondements*, Paris, Armand Colin, 1954.

— Changes in French policy since 1945, in *France: Change and Tradition*, London, Gollancz, 1963 (*In Search of France*, Cambridge, Mass., Harvard University Press, 1963).

GROSSER, ALFRED, *La IVe République et sa politique extérieure*, Paris, Armand Colin, 1961.

— *La politique extérieure de la Ve République*, Paris, Jean Moulin/Le Seuil, 1965 (*Foreign Policy under de Gaulle*, Boston and Toronto, Little, Brown, 1967. With additional chapter).

KULSKI, W. W., *De Gaulle and the World. The Foreign Policy of the Fifth French Republic*, New York, Syracuse University Press, 1966.

MARCUS, JOHN T., *Neutralism and Nationalism in France*, New York, Bookman Associates, 1958.

REYNAUD, PAUL, *La politique étrangère du Gaullisme*, Paris, Julliard, 1964.

(b) FRANCE AND EUROPE

ARMAND, LOUIS and DRANCOURT, MICHEL, *Le pari européen*, Paris, Fayard, 1968.

BRUCLAIN, CLAUDE, *Le Socialisme et l'Europe*, Paris, Jean Moulin/ Le Seuil, 1965.

CAMPS, MIRIAM, *European Unification in the Sixties*, Oxford University Press, 1967.

COURTIN, RENÉ, *L'Europe de L'Atlantique à L'Oural*, Paris, L'Esprit nouveau, 1963.

GLADWYN, LORD, *De Gaulle's Europe, or why the General says No*, London, Secker & Warburg, 1969.

KITZINGER, UWE, *Diplomacy and Persuasion*, London, Thames & Hudson, 1973.

MASSIP, ROGER, *De Gaulle et L'Europe*, Paris, Flammarion, 1963.

PICKLES, DOROTHY, *The uneasy entente*, Oxford R.I.I.A., Chatham House Essays, 1966.

SERFATY, SIMON, *France, De Gaulle and Europe*, Baltimore, Johns Hopkins Press, 1968.

WAITES, NEVILLE (ed.), *Troubled Neighbours*, London, Weidenfeld & Nicholson, 1971.

WILLIS, F. ROY, *France, Germany and the New Europe 1945–1963*, Stanford, Calif., Stanford University Press, 1965.

(c) FRANCE, THE ATLANTIC AND DEFENCE

ARON, RAYMOND, *Le Grand Débat*, Paris, Calmann-Lévy, 1963 (*The Great Debate*, New York, Doubleday, 1965).

BEAUFRE, GENERAL, *L'O.T.A.N. et L'Europe*, Paris, Calmann-Lévy, 1966 (*Nato and Europe*, New York, Alfred A. Knopf, 1967).

CLUB JEAN MOULIN, *La force de frappe et le citoyen*, Paris, Editions Le Seuil, 1963.

DOCUMENTATION FRANÇAISE, *La politique militaire française et ses réalisations*, Paris, Notes et Etudes documentaires, No. 3343, 1966.

FABRE-LUCE, ALFRED, *L'or et la bombe*, Paris, Calmann-Lévy, 1968.

FONTAINE, ANDRÉ, *L'alliance atlantique à l'heure du dégel*, Paris, Calmann-Lévy, 1959.

GALLOIS, GENERAL, *Stratégie de l'âge nucléaire*, Paris, Calmann-Lévy, 1960 (*The Balance of Terror*, Boston, Mass., Houghton Mifflin, 1961).

HUNT, KENNETH, *NATO without France*, London, Institute for Strategic Studies, Adelphi Papers, No. 32, December 1966.

MOCH, JULES, *Non à la force de frappe*, Paris, Robert Laffont, 1963.

NEWHOUSE, JOHN, *De Gaulle and the Anglo-Saxons*, London, André Deutsch, 1970.

PLANCHAIS, JEAN, *Le malaise de l'armée*, Paris, Plon, 1958.

— (*et al.*), *L'Armée française*, La Nef, Cahier 7, July–September 1961, Paris, Julliard, 1961.

SANGUINETTI, ALEXANDRE, *La France et l'Arme atomique*, Paris, Julliard, 1964.

WOLF, MENDL, *Deterrence and Persuasion*, London, Faber & Faber, 1970.

(d) FOREIGN POLICY OUTSIDE THE EUROPEAN AND ATLANTIC SPHERES

ARON, RAYMOND, *De Gaulle, Israël et les Juifs*, Paris, Plon, 1968.

— *La tragédie algérienne*, Paris, Plon, 1957.

— *L'Algérie et la République*, Paris, Plon, 1958.

HAYTER, TERESA, *French Aid*, London, Overseas Development Institute, 1966.

JEANNENEY, JEAN-MARCEL, *French Aid*. Report of Commission on French Aid. London, Overseas Development Institute, 1964.

PICKLES, DOROTHY, *Algeria and France*, London, Methuen, 1963.

SOUSTELLE, JACQUES, *Aimée et souffrante Algérie*, Paris, Plon, 1956.

—— *Le drame algérien et la décadence française, réponse à Raymond Aron*, Paris, Plon, 1957.

WILLIAMS, ANN, *Britain and France in the Middle East*, London, Macmillan, 1968.

(e) DOCUMENTS ON FRENCH OVERSEAS AID PUBLISHED BY FRENCH EMBASSY PRESS AND INFORMATION SERVICE

France's Relations with her Overseas Dependencies (1939–1968) (A/62/10/8).

A Survey of French Aid to Developing Countries (A/34/1/6).

Index